High Lonesome

▼ ▼

The University of North Carolina Press   *Chapel Hill & London*

The American Culture of Country Music

High Lonesome

▼ ▼ ▼ ▼ ▼ ▼ ▼ ▼ ▼ ▼ ▼ ▼ ▼ ▼ ▼ ▼ ▼

CECELIA TICHI

© 1994 Cecelia Tichi

Manufactured in the United States of America

The paper in this book meets the guidelines for permanence
and durability of the Committee on Production Guidelines for
Book Longevity of the Council on Library Resources.

Library of Congress Cataloging-in-Publication Data

Tichi, Cecelia, 1942–

High lonesome : the American culture of country music /
Cecelia Tichi.

p.   cm.

Discography: p.

Includes bibliographical references (p.   ) and index.

ISBN 0-8078-2134-9 (cloth: alk. paper)

1. Country music—History and criticism.   I. Title.

ML3524.T5   1994

781.642'0973—dc20   93-36130

CIP

MN

98   97   96   95   94   5   4   3   2   1

FOR BILL, CLAIRE, JULIA

Contents

▼ ▼ ▼ ▼ ▼ ▼ ▼ ▼ ▼ ▼ ▼ ▼ ▼ ▼ ▼ ▼ ▼ ▼ ▼ ▼

A section of color illustrations follows page 144.

Preface and Thanks

▼ ▼ ▼ ▼ ▼ ▼ ▼ ▼ ▼ ▼ ▼ ▼ ▼ ▼ ▼ ▼ ▼ ▼

In the car—that's where this book began. That's where country music often starts. The dashboard radio is the invitation, the introduction, sometimes *the* venue for listeners of this music. It was for me. A newcomer to Nashville in 1987, I began listening to top-40 country radio (WSM and WSIX) while driving to and from work at Vanderbilt University. To some extent, the music was familiar. (Just to be alive in the United States in the twentieth century is surely to know the sound of the slide guitar and the nasal vocal style that is country music's trademark. Hasn't everybody belted out a parody version of Tammy Wynette's "Stand By Your Man" or "D-I-V-O-R-C-E"? Doesn't everyone know the name, if not the music, of Hank Williams?)

In many ways, however, country music was unfamiliar. I did not know, for instance, that in the mid-1980s country was undergoing a renaissance, with artists like Steve Earle, Nanci Griffith, Lyle Lovett, and the O'Kanes (Kieran Kane and Jamie O'Hara) invigorating this music as new traditionalists like Gram Parsons and Emmylou Harris had in the seventies. Harris herself was just then (ca. 1987) moving from the electric to the acoustic sound. I did not know that, before the TV and movie phenomenon *Dolly!*, there was a Miss Dolly Parton singing and recording duets with *Grand Ole Opry* star Porter Wagoner. (For that matter, I did not know that country duets were themselves an important tradition, including the Louvin Brothers, Wilma Lee and Stoney Cooper, and the Everly Brothers whom I had associated solely with the lineage of rock 'n' roll.) I knew virtually nothing of bluegrass music, sometimes dubbed country jazz or white jazz, and had never listened to the *Grand Ole Opry* on the radio or ventured, as yet, to a weekend live performance at the Opry House. Having lived in the Boston-Cambridge area for some twenty years, I did not listen to the weekly *Hillbilly at Harvard* student radio program and was largely unaware that Rounder Records, a major country music record label, was growing by leaps and bounds practically on my doorstep.

My ignorance, in short, was oceanic. Two country music memories served, and two only: a 1950s Saturday night date at the Wheeling, West Virginia, WWVA *Jamboree* where, as a high schooler, I was half entranced and half embarrassed by this hillbilly cornball music whose very allure was somehow threatening (as if hillbilly-ness might be contagious); and a riveting Merle Haggard concert in Key West, Florida, in 1967, a concert attended because, frankly, in Key West there was not all that much to do. A marital "dowry" of merged record collections had brought Chet Atkins, Johnny Cash, Buck Owens, and Linda Ronstadt recordings into my habitat but not into my life.

The *Trio* album, gift of a Boston friend, proved to be the pivot. The 1987 Grammy-winning, platinum collaboration between Emmylou Harris, Dolly Parton, and Linda Ronstadt was my open door into the wider world of country, a world beyond the market-driven narrow band of commercial country radio. Country music, I was warned by a knowledgeable friend, is an Alice-in-Wonderland experience. Once down the rabbit hole, an entire world awaits, vast and thickly populated with a wide range of diverse singers, instrumentalists, bands, songs numbering in the thousands, and numerous books and articles. Top-40 radio is only the iceberg tip.

Chipping away at the 'berg became an imperative, first, because of my discovery of the music itself. This has been a time of special, personal openness to its richness and variety, its sounds, its moods, voices, instrumental colors. To have this music in one's life is to have an important source of solace and nourishment. Increasingly, CDs, tapes, and old LPs of country artists extending decades back became my "Continuing Ed.," as did the music clubs in Nashville—especially the Station Inn and the Bluebird Cafe, where superb musicians play almost every night of the week. Country music concerts throughout the year, quite a few of them benefits, and even TV tapings have proved sustaining in ways far beyond the term *entertainment*.

A labor of love is a rare privilege. For one who works with words, it is a gift to be able to write a book on a subject surpassing intellectual interest to reach the realm of the heart. This book arose from the discovery that my newfound music interest was linked in profound ways to my area of professional knowledge, American literature. Country music, I realized, is really about the *country*—the U.S.A.—as the nation has been represented in its literature and its visual arts. Perhaps only a scholar/teacher of American literature would see the connections. Perhaps it takes someone steeped in the standard or canonical American texts year in and year out, then transported to Nashville (Music City U.S.A.) and immersed for five years in its musical traditions, to see the connections developed here in *High Lonesome*. Between the car radio and the classroom, I began to understand, my workday was not disjointed, but connected. When I left the car and entered the classroom, the issues I was teaching were often the same issues to be heard in country songs. Engaged in classroom readings of Ralph Waldo Emerson, Herman Melville, Harriet Beecher Stowe, or Nathaniel Hawthorne, I was helping students

L·I·V·E BLUEGRASS MUSIC THE STATION INN
402 12th Ave. So.
Nashville, TN

grapple with issues rife in country music. Back in the car, sliding in a country music tape, I was experiencing the same cultural concerns expressed in the day's readings. To borrow a term from a classic country song, the circle was unbroken.

Enjoying country music is one thing, writing about it quite another. School lessons in brass instruments eons ago would be laughable preparation for writing on music. This project needed the help of a musician. Call it happenstance, luck, or providence—something led me to Holly Tashian of the duet team Barry and Holly Tashian, recording artists, songwriters, and performers at music clubs, bluegrass festivals, and the *Grand Ole Opry*. Holly agreed to help me: for instance, to explain the structure of the country song, the chord patterns, the reasons why a certain song might follow or deviate from a certain norm. Holly would listen to a song, pick up her Martin guitar, and figure it out. She not only explained the hows and whys of songs but patiently abided until this book found its true focus and its form. Along the way, she provided the subtlest guidance, alerting me to artists and styles and songs I otherwise would have missed and saving me from stupid mistakes. Holly agreed to become a consultant and stayed on to become a friend, as did Barry Tashian, who also took an active interest in this project and supported and contributed to it.

It is important to know that throughout this book, musical intervals are most often discussed according to what is called the Nashville number system. Widely used in country music, it is "a method of transcribing music to paper so that a song can be understood on the basis of chord relationships rather than notations in a fixed key." As one guide to music in Nashville says, "Numbers assigned to each note of the major scale represent chords as well as single notes. In the key of A, we have the major scale, A, B, C#, D, E, F# and G#. These become chords 1 through 7 in the key of A. It may seem too simple, but this is the method of assigning numbers to chords, which is the basis of the Nashville Number System. In the key of B, B becomes 1, etc. In the key of C, C is 1. And so on for the other keys." There is also a shorthand notation for minors, majors, notes diminished and augmented, dynamics, modulation, and so forth.

This project has benefited from the suggestions, support, and scrutiny of many individuals. The University of North Carolina Press ventured boldly into a multimedia project of untold complexity, and I thank editor-in-chief Barbara Hanrahan for piloting it, as well as guiding revisions based on her critical reading. Pam Upton's editing has been a real safety net, and any author is blessed to be in the hands of designer Rich Hendel. William L. Andrews of the University of Kansas and Amy Schrager Lang of Emory University provided encouragement and guidance as reviewers for the Press. Long before they saw the manuscript, Barbara Bennett read early chapter drafts and responded enthusiastically over the lunch table. I also thank her for keeping an eye on the legal issues involved in the project. Teresa Goddu took time from a full schedule to read this entire book in typescript and to make a number of excellent suggestions. David Sanjek sent me publications and interview tapes in the spirit of collegial generosity. I thank Wendy Martin and the Claremont Graduate School for sponsoring a talk based upon this work. The question-and-answer sessions afterward, as anyone at work on a book knows, are vitally important for clarifying all sorts of issues. A number of individuals have helped this project by suggesting songs or other texts that proved to be significant and by helping me in various ways: Lance Bacon, Clay Bailey, Paul Elledge, William Ferris, Jane High, Teresa Hughes, Donna Noland, Donnie Noland, Pallas Pidgeon, Richard ("Pete") Peterson, Riqué, Vicki Ruiz, Alan Thomas, and Valerie Traub. The complicated process of securing permissions and licenses was helped greatly by Rachel Brenner, René McCarthy, Virginia Schaefer, and Sian Hunter White, and I am most grateful to all of them. I thank The Great Escape, a Nashville retail store specializing in secondhand and rare albums, for permitting me to borrow numerous albums for photographing. Once again in a book project, Jamie Adams of Vanderbilt's Learning Resource Center has done a great deal of (and a great job with) the photography.

Any student of American country music recognizes the vital importance of the Country Music Foundation's library and archive, whose reading room is such a pleasant and rewarding place to work. The librarian, Ronnie Pugh, has been most helpful at crucial points in my research, and I thank him and also the foundation's photographic archivist, Chris Skinker, who helped me locate several illustrations appearing throughout this book.

Vanderbilt University has most generously supported this project. At a time of tight budgets in academe as elsewhere, I am very grateful to the Graduate School and the College of Arts and Sciences for funds that enabled this work to proceed at a pace and in a form otherwise not possible. Sabbatical leave during the fall of 1992 gave me an opportunity to move ahead in drafting and revising. Vanderbilt's backing enabled this project to be completed in a timely fashion with benefit of music and art images.

A word of caution is in order for any scholar/critic drawn to a cultural studies project of this kind involving legally secured intellectual property. Be advised that free speech can cost much money, time, and trouble. Some of the song lyrics discussed in this book, for instance, are paraphrased because permission to quote them is too expensive (hundreds of dollars for a short phrase). Permission to quote words or reproduce images even in an educational book can be a lengthy, costly, frustrating, and time-consuming process. The worlds of scholarly inquiry and of commercial ventures do not speak the same language, and the critic who fails to understand this is in for a bruising initiation. The thanks offered in the paragraphs above acknowledge those who helped me negotiate with law firms, music publishing companies, recording companies, and individuals. Many months of steady work have been required.

At home, meanwhile, my family has supported this project (and at times endured it) as I monopolized the car tape deck on short hops and long hauls. Bill Tichi, long appreciative of country music, has been bemused by the fervor of this recent convert. Attending concerts and performances with me, he also discussed the music and read drafts of chapters, making suggestions along the way. Claire and Julia came from Boston with the stereotypical bias against "hick" music and then changed their minds, less from top-40 radio than from their mother's tapes, CDs, and LPs and from live country and bluegrass music in Nashville. Their musical life is richer for the work of artists featured in this book, and they know it.

To make it easier for others to have access to the music discussed here, a list of independent recording companies follows. Much of the music discussed in this book is available from these "indie" labels. All will furnish catalogs on request. All are waiting to ease the curious listener down that rabbit hole.

RECORDING COMPANIES

Flying Fish Records
1304 W. Schubert
Chicago, IL 60614
Fax 312-528-8262

Rounder Records
Post Office Box 154
North Cambridge, MA 02140-0900
Fax 617-868-8769

Rebel Records
Post Office Box 3057
Roanoke, VA 24015

Sugar Hill Records
Post Office Box 4040
Duke Station
Durham, NC 27706

High Lonesome

Country music is our heritage.

They oughta teach it in the schools.

— Chet Atkins, interview

The pathos, the miseries,
the happiness, life itself...
—Jack Stapp,
    music publishing
    executive, on
    country music

It's wonderful people
aren't apologizing for
country music anymore.
I've always believed in
country music, and I have
always done country
music, since the beginning
of my recording career.
And I always heard the
line, "It's too country."
To which I'd say, that's
what I do: country.
—Emmylou Harris,
    newspaper interview

▼ ▼ ▼ ▼ ▼ ▼ ▼ ▼ ▼ ▼ ▼ ▼ ▼ ▼ ▼ ▼ ▼ ▼ ▼

Pathos, Miseries, Happiness, Life Itself
An Introduction

This book does country—does it with a head-on recognition that *country* is synonymous with *nation*. When TV and newspaper reporters speak or write of "the country," they usually mean the United States of America. "Country" is their shorthand term both for rural areas and for cities and suburbs too. We understand and accept the all-embracing reference immediately. Country means nation—just as in this book, country music is emphatically national music. It belongs not solely to the locales to which folklorists and historians of music have assigned it, like the Texas honky-tonk, the Louisiana bayou, or the Appalachian hollow, but more broadly to the centuries-long cultural identity of this country—this nation—even in this era of keen interest in multiculturalism.

This book asks, How does country music fit the country? How does a vibrant, enduring, indigenous American musical tradition fit into the mainstream culture of this nation?

The very question may seem odd. Or already answered, not only by music historians but the record-buying public. When *Time* puts country superstar Garth Brooks on its cover (March 30, 1992) and proclaims that country has captured music's mainstream, when writers and performers agree that country in the 1990s has gone suburban to become the new pop music with mass appeal, when albums like Brooks's go multiplatinum and radio stations across the United States scramble to move into a country format (residents of the midsized city of Hartford, Connecticut, to use just one example, have *four* country stations within listening range), then it seems silly to ask about country music's place in the nation. Surely it's enough to know that this music is phenomenally successful by having it both ways, enjoyed all across the United States on the basis of its distinctly country flavor. Why insist that country music serve some version of "the national interest?"

Let's approach this with a scenario. Suppose you and your family or friends decide to drive cross-country for a summer vacation. You head west from your home in, say, Philadelphia one hot July right after the picnics and fireworks of the Fourth. You plan to cross the United States, the Plains and the Divide, and along the way you listen to a succession of country music stations playing older favorites and current hits at the top of the country charts: songs by Garth Brooks, Alan Jackson, George Jones, Hal Ketchum, Dolly Parton, Reba McEntire, Willie Nelson, Rodney Crowell, the Oak Ridge Boys, Shenandoah, Alabama, Clint Black, Lorrie Morgan, Marty Stuart, k. d. lang, Vern Gosdin, Vince Gill, Tammy Wynette, Dwight Yoakam, K. T. Oslin, Johnny Cash, Randy Travis, Travis Tritt, Emmylou Harris.

Opting for a southerly route down Interstate 81, you cross through southeastern Virginia into Tennessee, perhaps unaware that the beautiful surrounding green mountain ridges and valleys are the cradle of American country music, which "evolved primarily out of the reservoir of folksongs, ballads, dances, and instrumental pieces brought to North America by Anglo-Celtic immigrants" who settled in these Appalachian hills and hollows. Passing through this part of Tennessee and Virginia (with Kentucky in hailing distance), your group tunes in to a radio station playing bluegrass, the "high lonesome sound" manifestly expressing this old ballad tradition. Setting the cruise control, you listen to Bill Monroe and his Blue Grass Boys, to the Stanley Brothers or Flatt and Scruggs, and to several bluegrass bands with names like Northern Lights, the Doug Dillard Band, Live-wire, Lonesome Standard Time, Alison Krauss and Union Station. At 60 mph, you are speeding through country music's point of origin as you listen to the Nashville Bluegrass Band play and sing the lines, "Sometimes it feels like the highway's my home / The interstate's the street where I live." An apt traveler's tune, you think, noting the title, "When I Get Where I'm Goin'" (*Waiting for the Hard Times to Go*, 1993). It's as if the deejay picked the song just for you.

High on the Cumberland Plateau, heading toward Nashville, by now on I-40, you joke about stopping in Nashville to look up Garth Brooks. Certainly you plan to visit Memphis to see Elvis's Graceland, which you associate solely—and wrongly—with rock 'n' roll, not country. Along Routes 40, 76, and 81, you listen to rock and to rhythm-and-blues, then to National Public Radio's classical programs (Mozart across Missouri) and, late each afternoon, *All Things Considered.*

The odometer clocks miles by the hundreds, then thousands, and you and your group, seeing styles change to Western boots and wide-brimmed hats, increasingly think of yourselves as romantic pioneers of a sort, especially approaching the Rockies, for the mountain ranges look much like pictures of Western landscapes seen all your lives, even down to mountain valleys suggesting the path or roadway leading toward the setting sun. And the cinematic quality is not lost on you, because you've seen numerous "road" movies, including *Thelma and Louise* (1991). Now in the West, you begin thinking of yourselves as a kind of "road" movie, though you might feel a bit embarrassed to say so. It occurs to you that your American vacation is happening right on the road, that your destination is maybe less important than the drive itself—the movement across vast spaces, plains and valleys, hills and mountains. You feel somehow certified or validated by the road trip, which feels quintessentially American. Across Colorado, you sing along with a country song coming over the radio. You try to remember the words to "Rocky Mountain High."

This scenario could end at Denver, but let's push it a bit farther to open up some possibilities. Say two days later you have crossed into California and are visiting San Francisco's North Beach section. You learn from a local resident that the area is famous as a onetime center for the rebellious Beat-generation writers of the 1950s, and that the best-known statement of the Beats relates to your own road travel. Jack Kerouac's *On the Road* (1957) is a picaresque automobile-age adventure. You remember that a 1960s, then 1993, TV series, *Route 66*, was based on a famous American highway and dubbed a "Kerouac-style adventure." If you know country artist Steve Earle's "The Other Kind," you could recall a reference to Kerouac. Neat coincidence, TV and the Beat writer hooked up with the country singer/songwriter and with your group, too—but you don't dwell on it.

Instead, elated to have driven coast to coast, you are claiming a certain fellowship of the road with the postwar Kerouac. One lasagna lunch later, you stop into the North Beach's City Lights Bookstore, shrine of the Beats. Surrounded by books, mindful of classroom days, you notice paperbacks of other American "road" writers like Walt Whitman, who imagined his "right hand pointing to . . . the public road" and whose "Song of the Open Road" (1867) celebrated "the long brown path before me leading wherever I choose."

Back in the car, en route to the motel, you turn once again to a country radio station—the kind of music you have listened to all across the continent—and note that Hank Snow's "I'm Movin' On," Rodney Crowell and Donivan Cowart's "Leaving Louisiana in the Broad Daylight," Ricky Van Shelton singing "Backroads," Willie Nelson's "On the Road Again," and Emmylou Harris singing John C. Fogerty's "Lodi" all have something in common. All are about life on the American road.

At this point, you have a unique opportunity to grasp the extent to which, in this historically mobile nation, country music is virtually a missing puzzle piece in the many representations of the American road. If literature, film, and the visual arts all celebrate the American road as a long-term, important, and prominent part of the national culture, so does country music, contributing extensively to the meanings we attach to the road. They are meanings you vacationers attach to yourselves on this trip: escape, freedom, adventure, self-discovery, initiation, success, knowledge. Your group, in fact, has been taking part in an American national experience imprinted repeatedly in numerous imaginative forms—and very much present in country music. As a traveler, you find yourself at the center of the music and of the poems and novels and paintings of the road. Most important for this book, your trip suggests the extent to which country music is a crucial and vital part of the American identity. The country songs show a profound understanding of the power of the road—the "open road," as Whitman called it—as form and symbol in the formation of an American self-concept over centuries. As you have discovered, the road is much more than a pass-through, a transportation device, a means from *here* to *there*. Surpassing all these, it is a place in and of itself, a fundamental defining part of an American experience.

So far, this road venture seems mainly jubilant, a celebration of self and space. But there are somber sides to country music, as to American cultural life. Perhaps the national ideology of "the pursuit of happiness" has simply proved too burdensome over the centuries. Once again, your vacation is helpful here. You are traveling, remember, in the month of July, setting off just after the July 4th commemoration of the 1776 signing of the Declaration of Independence. But when Thomas Jefferson wrote that phrase, "the pursuit of happiness," into the Declara-

tion, he could not have imagined the strain it would ultimately impose on the citizenry. A national founding document authorizing not just life and liberty but *the pursuit of happiness* has become especially burdensome in a twentieth-century consumer and media culture, in which images and objects promising "happiness" can only tantalize, and when human relationships so often prove difficult, painful, or impossible.

Emotional life in America, according to our artists and analysts, is much less a storybook conclusion to "the pursuit of happiness" than it is, all too often, a face-to-face encounter with loneliness. The artists of country music have confronted this issue directly and in a wide range of styles over decades, most memorably in Hank Williams's classic "I'm So Lonesome I Could Cry." But other artists and writers have also acknowledged this reality up front. Heading back east and approaching the Mississippi, you might slip in a books-on-tape cassette and listen to Mark Twain's *Adventures of Huckleberry Finn*, hearing that young Huck, rafting on the river "roadway" of the Mississippi, watches "the lonesomeness of the river . . . just solid lonesomeness." Stopping in Chicago for a day or so, you might decide to stroll Michigan Avenue and visit the Art Institute, where you stand face-to-face with Edward Hopper's *Nighthawks* (1942), the famous and much-reproduced twentieth-century painting of figures in a diner at night. Seen through the plate-glass windows of the diner, they look like loneliness itself. Back on the interstate, you complete the theme by playing some more country tapes: Roy Orbison   5 singing the up-tempo "Only the Lonely" or Patsy Cline, Tammy Wynette, or Emmylou Harris singing the haunting slow ballad "Lonely Street." Together, these texts become a sensory surround of a prominent American trait, loneliness — a part of the national experience so deeply embedded in the culture that it continues over centuries to insist on its own message in our literature, social commentary, and art, prominent among these the art of country music.

What, finally, is the point of this marathon road trip? It is to realize that the "tourists" invented for this introduction provide a model by which culture can be defined in its many connections. When the poetry of Walt Whitman links up with the country music of Hank Williams, when Dolly Parton and Ralph Waldo Emerson pair up and Mark Twain and Emmylou Harris are found to have a common ground, and the vacationing traveler is also involved, then new ideas about cultural relations become possible.

It is not a trivia question to ask, What does country music have in common with Thomas Jefferson, Walt Whitman, American painters Thomas Cole and Edward Hopper, and twentieth-century writers John Steinbeck and Jack Kerouac? What do these writers and artists, read in the high school and college classroom and represented on art museum walls in major cities, have in common with country music songs spanning the twentieth century but rooted even in colonial times? These questions are not whimsical, not board-game exercises, not a computer's random sorting of mismatched data, not a stunt in virtual reality. They are precisely the questions that can let us see how deeply ingrained country music is in the centuries-long traditions of American thought, art, and literature, extending from the colonial period to the contemporary moment.

Much has been written about this American country music of "pathos, miseries, happiness, life itself," including promotional fan pieces, scholarly histories, biographies of country legends, interviews with country stars, and at least one novel. As for detailed interpretation of this music — the very kind necessary to unveil its links with American culture at large — some country artists hesitate. They think it unnecessary — or worse, meddlesome and intrusive, even overblown. They shrug off the interpreter as "reading too much into it," *it* being, in their terms, a "simple tune." They seem edgy about the very notion of deep interpretation of their music, as if it were probing and prying, a violation of the natural.

Understandably. Country music prides itself on a simplicity allied with nature, meaning a style and a delivery that is not artificial, neither preplanned nor premeditated, not to be analyzed lest it be spoiled — as if some pristine and essential center of authenticity would be in jeopardy were it to be subjected to close interpretive discussion. Nobody likes the idea of dissection. Nobody welcomes the scalpel.

Yet there is a certain "deceptively simple" element in country—the accent on *deceptive* alerting us to the paradox of artistry intended to appear artless. "All you need is the tiniest movement," says Emmylou Harris of the very essence of country's challenge to achieve "simplicity and grace and unadornment." She adds, "What not to play in country music is as important as what to play. It's all understatement and how to work within that framework. People think country music is easy. It's not. It's very difficult."

Why bother with the difficulty? Why try getting at the art behind the simplicity? Country artists answer in a vocabulary that beckons us to a world of close interpretation. First, they emphasize the primacy of the story in country songs. "It's just stories told by ordinary people in an extraordinary way," says Dolly Parton. "It's plain music that tells a good story," says Bill Monroe of the bluegrass side of country. Hank Williams is quoted as saying, "A song ain't nothin' in the world but a story just wrote with music to it." Randy Travis elaborates: "Country singers tell stories . . . that people can relate to because the songs are written about their lives." Nanci Griffith likens country music to "reading a book . . . with characters and imagination." As for the shape of the stories, songwriter/singer Holly Tashian says, "If you're writing a song, you're telling a story that funnels down and it makes its point—bam!—and there's your chorus." She explains, "You've been showing this story, with examples, and then in the chorus you tell it: '*this* is what I'm trying to say.'" Emmylou Harris describes the beginnings of her concept album: "I started approaching it as a story. . . . I had to make definite characterizations. . . . I changed the story line around a little."

Story, stories, story line. Every time the term comes up, we are reminded of the difference between country music and its musical "cousin," black blues. Both country and blues sprang from those identified with rural roots and economic privation. Both express identity through music that is most often urgent, raw, soulful. African American traditions have enriched country music instrumentally (the banjo migrating from Africa), and country music masters Jimmie Rodgers, Hank Williams, and Bill Monroe all had black music teachers. The very term *honky-tonk* is evidently black slang meaning "white shack."

But the emphasis on story separates white country music from black blues. The two divide over a basic difference in form, according to the music scholar William Ferris, who contrasts the liquid form of the blues with the narrative ballad form essential to white country music. Blues, says Ferris, descends primarily from the African folk lyric. Each blues stanza can be a stand-alone entity that might or might not relate to the others in the song. In white country music, by contrast, the story is central, coming as it does through the tradition of the British ballad. And though such country music legends as Jimmie Rodgers, Hank Williams, and Bill

Monroe learned much from black musicians, their musical center, like that of all country artists, lies in the storytelling ballad.

The implications of this are momentous, especially when we consider the listener who becomes an interpreter. Terms like *story*, *stories*, and *story line* all refer to a narrative with a plot representing certain actions in the world or in the minds of characters. To tell a story is to tell of an event or a series of connected events, often being a fictitious literary composition, something deliberately made and shaped in words, something of which the listener or reader asks, What is happening? What does it mean? How does it communicate its meaning? One country album featuring Tom T. Hall and banjo legend Earl Scruggs headlines this narrative essence in its very title: *The Storyteller and the Banjo Man.*

Good stories depend on strong lyrics, country artists agree, no matter whether they write and perform slow ballads, rockabilly, or Cajun. "Country music is where strong and topical lyrics originally come from," says Steve Earle. "It was always the most important thing in country music." "It's lyrically oriented," adds Rosanne Cash, "which is what country music has always been." And Tammy Wynette remarks that country music "started out with train songs and railroads and cotton fields" but, thanks to certain lyricists, has become more urban and sophisticated ("grown up to big cities").

Strong lyrics, stories—and poetry, too. *Poet* and *poetry* are recurrent terms in country artists' comments, showing that in this music, language and form are significantly different from ordinary speech or writing. The words of a poem are more concentrated than those of ordinary speech, being rhythmic, sometimes rhymed, expressing powerful feeling—"the best words in the best order." "Poet" and "poetry" describe Hank Williams's identity and songwriting achievement, according to Randy Travis and to Emmylou Harris, who observes that the legendary country musician brought "the real" into his music in ways that are "haunting and really poetic." Harris and Rosanne Cash have also used "poet" and "poetry" to describe the music of their cohort, Rodney Crowell, while a country music journalist profiled the young Merle Haggard as a onetime "kid with . . . much poetry in him." Another journalist writes that Dolly Parton's "real strength as a lyricist lies in her novelist's eye for setting and detail [and] in her poetic imagery." *Poet* seems to be a country music keyword. "Folk poetry" is country music producer Richard Bennett's term for Kentuckian Marty Brown's song, "Wild Kentucky Skies," while Texas-based Jimmie Dale Gilmore says his commitment to country music was crystallized by a line from the poet/critic Ezra Pound: "The poem fails when it strays too far from the song, and the song fails when it strays too far from the dance." *Poet* is the term applied to musicians ranging widely in the country tradition, from the bluegrass artist Laurie Lewis to the balladeer Townes Van Zandt

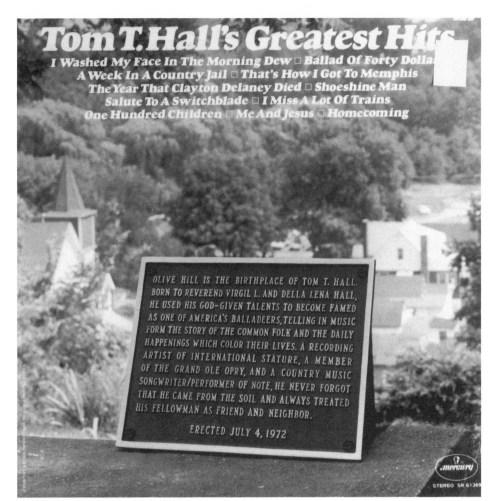

Tom T. Hall's Greatest Hits

I Washed My Face In The Morning Dew □ Ballad Of Forty Dolla
A Week In A Country Jail □ That's How I Got To Memphis
The Year That Clayton Delaney Died □ Shoeshine Man
Salute To A Switchblade □ I Miss A Lot Of Trains
One Hundred Children □ Me And Jesus □ Homecoming

OLIVE HILL IS THE BIRTHPLACE OF TOM T. HALL. BORN TO REVEREND VIRGIL L. AND DELLA LENA HALL, HE USED HIS GOD-GIVEN TALENTS TO BECOME FAMED AS ONE OF AMERICA'S BALLADEERS, TELLING IN MUSIC FORM THE STORY OF THE COMMON FOLK AND THE DAILY HAPPENINGS WHICH COLOR THEIR LIVES. A RECORDING ARTIST OF INTERNATIONAL STATURE, A MEMBER OF THE GRAND OLE OPRY, AND A COUNTRY MUSIC SONGWRITER/PERFORMER OF NOTE, HE NEVER FORGOT THAT HE CAME FROM THE SOIL AND ALWAYS TREATED HIS FELLOWMAN AS FRIEND AND NEIGHBOR.

ERECTED JULY 4, 1972

mercury
STEREO SR 61369

Album showing tribute to country artist Tom T.
Hall as a balladeer "telling in music the story
of the common folk." (Courtesy Polygram
Records)

("Poncho and Lefty," "If I Needed You," "Tecumseh Valley"). The country songwriter and singer Tom T. Hall, who has taught courses in country music songwriting, calls it "primitive monophonic poetical composition. . . . It's primitive poetical composition."

Poetry and stories can add up to opera, at least in a concept album. A country
music journalist writes that the Emmylou Harris/Paul Kennerley collaboration,
The Ballad of Sally Rose (1986), is "a country opera," and Harris also names it so, "an
opera." This means a story presented in a series of acts and acted out in the form
of a dramatic play whose text is set to music. The text can be poetic in form, the
whole opera containing numerous poems and narratives. And it is well to recall

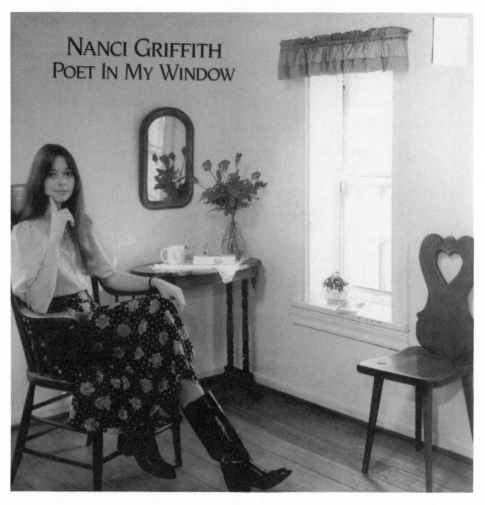

**Artist Nanci Griffith affirms links to poetry
and other literature in album designs.
(Courtesy of Philo/Rounder Records)**

that the "mother church" of country music is named in direct reference to opera, even if the key term is countrified as "opry."

So: Stories, poetry, opera. Exotic terms for country music, these, and outsiders would be laughed off the scene for using them. But when the country artists themselves speak them, they command attention. More than that, when these concepts come directly from the artists who write and perform country music from concert and club stages, from TV studios, and in album releases, then they become an invitation and a set of guidelines. They become a basis for listening.

And a basis for writing. To link country music with the long-term traditions of the country requires a special kind of listening and a particular kind of writing. It is not enough to mix verbatim song lyrics with remarks on American culture; lyrics alone are too skeletal, as is the music on the page. A song is words and notes made flesh—delivered, shaped, presented, phrased. The whys and hows of the presentation require attention. It matters that country artists, like all artists, take risks in writing and performance. "A performer is naked onstage," says Emmylou Harris. "If an artist doesn't allow the audience to see the essential truth, then it's Las Vegas time." "Essential truth" seems to be a code term for the artist's inner struggle to write and perform courageously, to "reach inward and . . . to pull out my deepest feelings, then write about them."

Fortunately, in writing *about* country music in American culture, one can take advantage of the ways in which its forms—stories, poems, opera—are written about in other venues, where they normally get close attention to technique and delivery, and where images and symbols and tonal shadings are deeply respected. Take, for instance, some recent writing on opera, on the renowned soprano of the 1950s and 1960s, Maria Callas, who recorded the role of Mimi, the seamstress living in a Parisian garret with impoverished artists in Giacomo Puccini's *La Bohème* (1896). Analyzing Callas's 1956 recording, the writer says, "When the rapturous 'Ma quando vien lo sgelo' [When the glad sun first greets me] arrives, Callas does not slur into it; her voice is gradually flooded with a warmth which at full tide is a match for Puccini's music. . . . . We are taken into Mimi's innermost fears and longings, and Callas . . . conveys a sense of the embarrassment of laying bare private feelings to a third person."

A passage like this is a good model for country music interpretation. Why not approach, say, Dolly Parton's "Jolene" with the same level of attention? Parton sings the role of a wife or lover making a desperate plea to her rival *not* to steal the man in her life. The minor key heightens the sense of discord, of emotional turbulence, and an instrumental motif of an Oriental bazaar conveys a sense of grim marketplace bargaining for human life. The voice of the woman at risk rises in fear and tension, pleading with the irresistible, ivory-complexioned, emerald-eyed "other woman," Jolene, not to commit emotional grand theft for sport. Parton sings her direct appeal in tones desperate yet dignified, reduced to begging but stopping short of humiliation. This woman's pride and integrity are intact, though fragile; her life is on the line.

What will Jolene decide to do?—we never find out, because this song-as-aria, this lyric poem, is meant to display the psyche of the narrator at a climactic stress point. The song enacts only her desperate plea. Yet it is well worth paying close attention to "Jolene." Acknowledged to be one of Dolly Parton's best songs and, within country music, recognized as a "cheatin' song," the accolade and the mere label do not, as such, convey the fuller operatic and poetic sense of the story or its drama.

To linger a moment longer with the operatic commentary is to see further possibilities for revealing the poetic and narrative power of country music. The early twentieth-century operatic tenor Enrico Caruso ("the Great Caruso") exploited the technique called a register change to achieve a sob in his signature role as Canio, the jilted clown in Ruggiero Leoncavallo's *Pagliacci* (1892). In a particular aria, "Vesti la giubba" ("On with your costume"), the singer moves back and forth between the head voice and the chest voice for dramatic emphasis; in effect, the voice seems to break as in a sob. The technique is important here because it has been common in country music at least since the late 1920s and early 1930s, when the first country music star, the ramblin' railroad brakeman Jimmie Rodgers, showed the same emotive potential for the yodeler's register change that Caruso had exploited. Rodgers made the combination of the yodel-sob and the blues into the country-style blue yodels in his popular recordings.

Hank Williams carried the style further in his landmark hits "Lovesick Blues" and "Long Gone Lonesome Blues." Chet Atkins has said of Williams's register change, "The contrast between his falsetto and his lower voice was so great; he was such a terrific yodeler." Contemporary male country vocalists like Randy Travis and Dwight Yoakam continue this technique, and women artists have also learned the power of that contrastive sob well, with Tammy Wynette using it to convey the desperation of a disintegrating family in "D-I-V-O-R-C-E" and Emmylou Harris developing it in a lament for a departed lover in Johnny Cash's "I Still Miss Someone," which opens as autumn's falling leaves foretell a stormy, cold winter. Harris's voice dips on the first line, breaks to imitate the falling leaves, then on the word *cold* it breaks again, harder, shuddering at the loss of seasonal warmth, symbolic of love's vacated warmth. The vocal breaks enact the harsh and abrupt transition, merging weather and heartache, from autumn chill to bone-cold winter.

This kind of technical attention to the poetry, the narrative, and the operatic in country music can bring to light its subtleties, its contours, and make it possible to discover how country music allies itself with kindred art forms—the stories, poems and operatic drama of American writing, thought, culture.

A galaxy of country music artists, constellated for this book, contributes tremendously to our knowledge of country music in the broader culture: Hank Williams with his soulful songs of psychological despair in America and Merle Haggard with his raw ballads of drifting, drinking, and chip-on-the-shoulder individualism; Willie Nelson, the "outlaw" commemorating cowboy life, and Johnny Cash with his work songs; Patsy Cline with her lovesick, lonely yearnings, Loretta

Lynn with her story-songs of domestic life and strife, Nanci Griffith with her songs of hometowns and old friends; bluegrass music, too, notably by Bill Monroe and his Blue Grass Boys, originators of the "high, lonesome" sound, and down to contemporary bluegrass artists like the Nashville Bluegrass Band or Laurie Lewis and her band, Grant Street. The list goes on, reaching back into the 1920s and 1930s to Jimmie Rodgers and the east Tennessee Carter Family, then moving into the 1960s and beyond, George Jones and Tammy Wynette to Garth Brooks. Decades of performers on Nashville's *Grand Ole Opry* are enlisted in a project of this kind, as are the many country artists listened to during "your" vacation trip across the country, from Marty Stuart to Pam Tillis and Alan Jackson.

Three particular artists, however, have emerged as mainstays of this project because of their songwriting abilities and styles of performance. Rodney Crowell, Emmylou Harris, and Dolly Parton are first-magnitude stars of contemporary country music. All have gone far, in fact, to define country since the 1970s. Rodney Crowell—songwriter, performer, producer—has updated country music while retaining its continuity with the past. He says, "I know eleven hundred and one of the old country songs, but you can't just reiterate the old sentiment." His critics agree: "As a composer, specifically as a lyricist, Crowell has injected real life into a genre that sometimes can seem mired in the past." Bringing contemporary complexity into country, such Crowell songs as "Till I Gain Control Again," "Shame on the Moon," and "Life Is Messy" reflect, as one critic writes, "an era of emotional ambiguity." It is arguable that the emotional complexity of certain 1990s country songs, like Garth Brooks's "We Shall Be Free" or Mary-Chapin Carpenter's "Stones in the Road," originate in the kinds of music Crowell has been writing for over two decades. Crowell himself has said, "There's a misconception about country being hay bales and laid back. . . . For me, country music has a lot of passion, a lot of energy."

Passion, energy, and impeccable subtlety mark the music of Emmylou Harris. Sometime writer and preeminent performer, Harris claims country music territory from ballad to gospel to bluegrass. In some twenty albums, from *Pieces of the Sky* (1975) through the Grammy-winning *Emmylou Harris and the Nash Ramblers at the Ryman* (1992) and the erotic yet spiritual *Cowgirl's Prayer* (1993), Harris puts listeners in honky-tonks of warm beer and cold hearts, in Appalachian hollows, in alligator-bait bayous and the open-range cowboy West. Through it all, she invigorates country music with her awesome dramatic interpretive power.

Literally *dramatic*, meaning that note by note, phrase by phrase, Harris fully enters into each role, be it the Appalachian backcountry maiden of "Sorrow in the Wind" or the tough, defiant woman-on-the-move of "Restless." The term *cover* cannot convey the power of her reinterpretation of country standards. Harris, like

▼ ▼ ▼ ▼ ▼ ▼ ▼

Pathos,
Miseries,
Happiness

Emmylou
Harris.
(Photograph
© Woody
Johnson.
All rights
reserved.)

▼ ▼ ▼ ▼ ▼ ▼ ▼

Rodney
Crowell.
(Photograph
by David
Roth; © 1992
Sony Music
Entertain-
ment, Inc.)

▼ ▼ ▼ ▼ ▼ ▼ ▼

Dolly
Parton.
(Photograph
by Sam
Emerson;
© 1993
Sony Music
Entertain-
ment, Inc.)

Crowell, deliberately embraces country music's forebears while infusing their heritage with new interpretive energy, knowing that without it, the songs become ornamental specimens stuck in amber. She uses space-age terms to make this point: "I feel like it's important to push the envelope of what we call country music without ever losing sight of the most important element, the soul."

Dolly Parton, it is tempting to say, needs no introduction—which is precisely why she really does need one here. An international celebrity, Parton has been dubbed the Mae West of country and the Marilyn Monroe of the mountains, becoming legendary for her wigs, cleavage, five-inch heels, and self-deprecating jokes ("You'd be surprised how much it costs to look this cheap"), not to mention her business acumen. Her presence in country music can be overshadowed by her very career success, by her move from the east Tennessee Smoky Mountain hollow of her birth and rearing to Nashville and the *Grand Ole Opry*, then from the Opry (where she sang with duet partner Porter Wagoner) to national network TV specials, movies (*9 to 5*, *Rhinestone*, *The Best Little Whorehouse in Texas*, *Straight Talk*), and albums like *White Limozeen* and *Slow Dancing with the Moon*—in short, from country to pop and global show biz. All this can seem to suggest that Parton dips back into country only occasionally—perhaps nostalgically, to write or sing a country song and make a video for Country Music Television (CMT) such as the 1993 "Romeo" with Billie Ray Cyrus—in order to keep up her license as a country artist while really concentrating her energies on movies and pop music and the celebrity career machine. (Parton's pop ballad, "I Will Always Love You," rode twice to the top of the charts in the 1970s and 1980s, and in 1992–93 went to Number 1 for Whitney Houston.)

Yet Dolly Parton sold out Carnegie Hall for a May 1993 performance under the concert heading "Country Takes Manhattan," and she organized an album of country standards, *Honky-Tonk Angels* (1993), featuring herself and country divas Loretta Lynn and Tammy Wynette. As this book goes to press, she joins Emmylou Harris and Linda Ronstadt in a second "Trio" album. The Dolly Parton of this book is the artist of albums like *My Tennessee Mountain Home* (1973), *New Harvest . . . First Gathering* (1977), and *Burlap and Satin* (1984), the writer and performer of autobiographical country songs like "Wildflowers," "My Tennessee Mountain Home," "Appalachian Memories," and "Coat of Many Colors." Parton's soprano, in the words of country music writer Alanna Nash, ranges from girlish and soft at one moment to raucous and earthy the next: it can "turn to a quick, high-strung vibrato and then easily glissando with extraordinary power, range, and control into a hard and high nasality." Parton's inimitable high soprano delivery is much dependent upon the recitation tradition in country music. The Dolly Parton of this book is a country music songwriter and performer of virtuosic power and unsurpassed musical ability. Like Crowell and Harris, she is an artist who has enriched, enhanced, and redirected country music.

Musically, then, these three—Dolly Parton, Emmylou Harris, and Rodney Crowell—are a pivot to the past and a touchstone for the present and future of country music. Their music, together with that of so many other country artists, is the basis for discovering the crucial role country music plays in American art and culture.

Having called country music a previously "missing" piece of the American cultural puzzle, however, I must now backtrack a bit and qualify that point. Country music does not simply complete a picture we already have well in mind. In this project, country music does not simply take its place in a familiar pattern of the arts and literature in the United States from colonial times to the present. This is not a bid to say that country music, *too*, participates in the artistic vigor of this nation, that country music can join the cultural party, so to speak.

Quite the contrary. This book says that country music, examined carefully, enables us to see vital parts of the national identity that otherwise are hidden, obscured, overshadowed, blacked out in painful self-censorship. This book works, not *toward* the music, but *from* it, taking the music as a guide into what one writer terms "the heart of the heart of the country." The discoveries are surprising.

Few have wealth, but all must have a home.
—*Ralph Waldo Emerson,* "Domestic Life"

*This, indeed, was a home,—*home.
—*Harriet Beecher Stowe,* Uncle Tom's Cabin

Be it ever so humble, there's no place like home.
—*John Howard Payne,* "Home, Sweet Home"

To the ramblers and the drifters, the seekers and the travelers and all the wanderers out there on the back roads and the highways . . . I hope that in some small way for even a minute or two I've been able to Sing You Back Home *one more time . . .*
—*Merle Haggard,* Sing Me Back Home: My Story

Home still rocks my soul, Steals my dreams each night.
—*Holly Tashian,* "Home"

Home

In July and August 1927, Ralph Peer, a New York–based producer for the Victor Talking Machine Company, drove to Bristol, Tennessee, the northeasternmost part of a state shaped like a parallelogram—or maybe a gunstock. In Bristol, Peer rented the third floor of a former furniture store, draped blankets over the walls, set up electrical recording equipment, and arguably launched contemporary country music by recording wax masters of commercially profitable ballads, spirituals, even comedy routines by figures like the Tennessee Mountaineers, Jimmie Rodgers, the Carter Family, and the Ernest Stoneman Family.

"Home, Sweet Home" is a tune in the very first release from these Bristol sessions. The voice of Ernest Stoneman says, "Here's George. He's from Iron Ridge; he plays the banjo. How about 'Home, Sweet Home'?" We wait, hearing the scratch and crackle, and then the opening chords as George obliges—the banjo as played before Earl Scruggs, Eddie Adcock, Bela Fleck. It takes a moment to make it out, but then the melody comes clear: "Be it ever so humble, there's no place like home."

"Home, Sweet Home"—the tune is virtually a country music keynote. It seems inevitable that this nationally cherished tune would help launch the Bristol sessions, called by Johnny Cash "the single most important event in the history of country music." The song's message is fundamental to the musical skit of which it is part—"Old Time Corn Shuckin'"—a skit that could just as well have been called "Home, Sweet Home" for its values and its format. As emcee, Ernest "Pop" Stoneman calls us "folks" and explains the neighborly mountain custom of shucking older people's corn "when they're so old they can't work." He goes on, "So we have shucked Uncle Joe Stoup's corn" and invites us to "a regular old corn shuckin'," which includes fiddle tunes, harmonica, jew's harp, guitar, foot-stamping buckdance, and a square dance called by "Uncle Ed." A jug, doubtless corn liquor, is passed, and its "kick" recorded in well-miked aahhs of satisfaction and reminders to share ("Give Caleb a taste . . . careful, not too much, the other boys might want a taste"). "We want everyone to take part," Stoneman says genially, closing the skit with a pleasant "good night" as we hear neighborly invitations to "come see me . . . come over to our house."

Actually written at producer Ralph Peer's request, the skit electronically validated the music and customs of those who lived in Appalachian America (and Ernest Stoneman *had* been shucking corn on a Virginia farm just before he wrote it). But the skit also consolidates a cluster of values defining the home in country music. Familial, neighborly, genial, the skit set the tone for a succession of "home" songs that would proliferate in country music for decades to come.

Songs of home, in fact, make up a premier category of country music, from "The Little Old Cabin in the Lane" through "This Ole House," "Homecoming," and "Take Me Home, Country Roads." Entire states are projected as homes, for instance, in the Louvin Brothers' "Alabama," in Karl Davis's "Kentucky," or in Boudleaux and Felice Bryant's "Rocky Top" (Tennessee). The production of "home" songs has continued unabated in the 1990s, when *Billboard*'s country and bluegrass charts offer three songs—by A. Spooner/J. Lehner (sung by Joe Diffie), by Alan Jackson, and by Holly Tashian—all called simply "Home."

In fact, nearly a half-century after "George" from Iron Ridge plucked the banjo for "Old Time Corn Shuckin'," buyers of cassettes and CDs of late twentieth-century country music can hear "Home, Sweet Home" on recordings by Dolly Parton and Randy Travis. It is the background tune running through the young Dolly's "Letter" to her family, a recitation of an actual letter written from Nashville after she went forth in her teens from the hollows of east Tennessee to seek a career in music (*Portrait*, 1985). And it is the countermelody in Paul Overstreet's "No Place Like Home," in which Randy Travis portrays a man whose marriage has failed and who lingers in his house with the stunning insight: "It hit me as I was leavin' / There's no place like home" (*Storms of Life*, 1986).

"Home, Sweet Home"—yet again. Recycled in country music, it signals country's bedrock belief in the unassailable sweetness and goodness of home. Lyrics of country "home" songs are unfailingly eulogistic in this: Alabama, so "sweet" in the spring; Louisville, the heart's "hometown"; Kentucky, the "dearest" land outside heaven; "West Virginia, mountain mama / Take me home, country roads"; and so on.

These phrases and their underlying assumptions can seem terribly old-fashioned, like a framed, cross-stitched motto hanging in the front parlors long gone from American life. And they prompt questions: What do home songs in country music offer beyond nostalgia? Aren't they sentimental yearnings for a simplistic America that, if it ever really existed, has vanished in a metropolitan and suburban age? Aren't the songs themselves rigidly formulaic in presuming a nuclear family structure and, in their message, defiant of the realities of social change? Aren't they idealistically (or blindly) unwilling to acknowledge the actual problems of home life? In an era of extended, blended, single-parent families (not all of them heterosexual), when dysfunctional homes are exposed daily on confessional TV talk shows, aren't these songs a triumph of obliviousness, if not denial? And what could be their message, beyond the obvious point that home ought to mean nurturance, shelter, and the protection given by those who bring children into the world and are responsible for their upbringing?

These questions can mount a critique of country music's idolatry of the American home. It is tempting, in addition, to take the songs at face value as peculiarly *southern*, reflective of regional yearning for an idealized home south of the Mason-Dixon line. "My Tennessee Mountain Home" or "Peach-Pickin' Time in Georgia" or "Carry Me Back to Old Virginny" bunch together like map tacks, confirming the regional focus of this music. They seem like inventory items on a list including Dixie dirt roads, grits, cornbread, the "pickin'" music of banjo and fiddle, travel by mule or pickup truck.

But there is a paradox at work in country music home songs as they relate to the national culture—a paradox that can be, so to speak, unpacked. Opened, it can show the complex role of the home song both in country music and in broad-

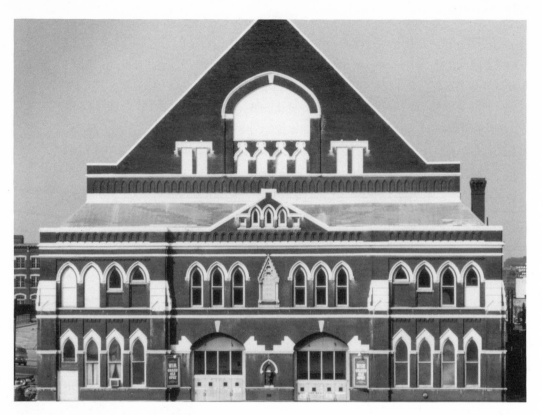

Ryman Auditorium in Nashville, Tennessee, site of the Grand Ole Opry from 1943 to 1974. Called the Home, the Mother Church, and the Carnegie Hall of country music. (Photograph © Jamie Adams. All rights reserved.) See also Plate 4.

based American cultural traditions. First, home songs are set geographically in the South, but they are only in the narrowest sense southern songs. Their focus is the southern home, but it is a mistake to think them unique to the very South they represent and celebrate in images of cabins, farm fields, honeysuckle, hills and hollers.

Put another way, these songs are set in the South, but the cultural record of the the nation suggests that their ideas of home are virtually identical with "home" images in print and the visual arts over some two centuries of cultural process throughout the United States. To recall that the ideal antebellum southern home was predicated on the repressive work of slaves is to remember as well that its northern counterpart operated on the labor of indentured (usually Irish) servants, immigrants relegated to their own stifling or freezing attic "quarters." Home, that is, maintains its ideal image only when problems of race and class do not enter in and disrupt the carefully devised and managed ideal. To trace ideas of home over time, however, is to see a remarkable consistency—even sameness—in the values

22

underlying the representations, whether "home" is located in the South, the Northeast, the Midwest or whether the year is 1852, 1952, or the 1990s. The South, it is true, figures prominently in this music of home, including Stephen Foster's "Old Folks at Home" ("Way down upon the Swanee [Sewanee] River") and "My Old Kentucky Home," but the cultural record of the United States actually shows "home" to be a national preoccupation—perhaps obsession—running through two centuries of the national experience and commanding the attention of major writers and artists. The South, in this sense, represents the nation.

In fact, we can trace to pre-Revolutionary America the basis of home's authenticity as celebrated in country music. In the 1760s, the values of the agrarian home in America were set forth in a text still read widely today by students of American literature and culture. "What Is an American?," by J. Hector St. John de Crèvecoeur, set the tone for the agrarian authenticity of the home. Writing in the persona of one Farmer James, Crèvecoeur describes the best Americans as "tillers of the earth. . . . We are a people of cultivators." He expresses the moral value inherent in this life: "The simple cultivation of the earth purifies." Crèvecoeur's point is that agrarian life is naturally pristine—in accord with the seasons, the cycles of

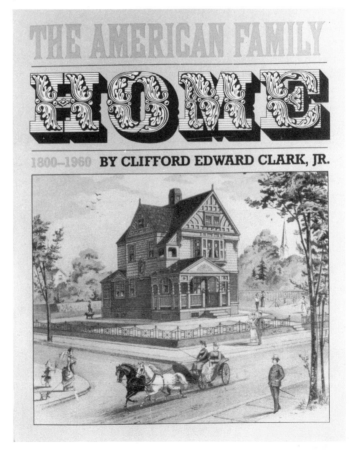

Book cover design for historical study of the American home. (© 1986 The University of North Carolina Press)

growth and harvest, and the life cycle from the newborn to the elderly. And the natural is codified in the figure of the rural farm family. Expressing the "pleasures" of being an American farmer, Crèvecoeur says, "When I went to work in my fields . . . I felt that I did not work for myself alone. . . . My wife would often come with her knitting . . . and sit under the shady trees. . . . When I contemplate my wife, by my fire-side, while she either spins, knits, darns, or suckles our child, I cannot describe the . . . love, gratitude, conscious pride which thrill in my heart."

We must remember that Crèvecoeur was not working as a precursor of documentary photography, with its insistence that certain realities be present in the image. He was, on the contrary, constructing an ideal. His farmer's infant does not wail, nor does his wife moan about the milk souring or about handling heavy wool in the summer heat. Insects do not infest his crops, nor do his feet blister or the family's teeth rot. His is a deliberately idealistic sketch of the American rural home. Inscribed quite early in American culture, it virtually makes the French emigré Crèvecoeur a forefather of the country music "home" song.

And he had company. The outlook of Crèvecoeur's Farmer James was bolstered, in the mid-nineteenth century, by the one figure who is arguably the dominant intellectual in the history of this nation. Ralph Waldo Emerson has been considered the eloquent proponent of self-reliance, democratic values, and a reverential regard for nature. His pithy sayings speak—or pontificate—from the stone and cement entablatures of public buildings throughout the United States. ("Insist on yourself; never imitate," and "He who has put forth his total strength in fit actions has the richest return.")

Emerson enthusiastically expanded the American agrarian ideals voiced by Crèvecoeur and ultimately sustained in country music. Over time, he said, it makes no difference "how you have been dieted or dressed," whether you have lodged "on first floor or attic," whether you "have been carried in a neat equipage or in a ridiculous truck." What counts, Emerson said, are "good companions" and the "marriage . . . that makes our home."

That home, what's more, is emphatically rural. "Every man has an exceptional respect for tillage, and a feeling that this is the original calling of his race," wrote Emerson in his essay "Farming." The farmer, to be sure, improves the rural land—digs a well, plants an orchard, builds a durable house. But he and his family only enhance nature; they never oppose it. Because the natural world is inherently ethical and moral, the farmer—and by implication the farm family—is equally ethical and moral, since he and his family embody the values of the natural world.

The rural life, then, is the authentic life amid "the beauty of nature [which] never hurries: atom by atom, little by little, she achieves her work." As for the

farmer, he "times [paces] himself to Nature, and acquires that live-long patience
which belongs to her. . . . He is permanent, clings to his lands as the rocks do."
This rural home evinces rocklike stability and brings that stability into a society
that is fundamentally unchanging. "He bends to the order of the seasons, the
weather, the soils and crops." He is "comparable to sun and moon, rainbow and
flood."

This legacy of American thought appears in country music's insistence that
home is more than a locale and site of family and friends—is actually the essence
of the natural world. It is made up of hills and mountains, sunlight and flowers,
and cabins hewn from wood and forest. It is the "hickory wind" of South Carolina, the "blue grass hills" of Kentucky, the "silvery moonlight," "Mockin'bird Hill,"
and a "vine-covered shrine 'neath the pines." Joe Diffie sings that home is "a
swimmin' hole and a fishin' pole," while Gene Autry sings of "home on the range,
where the deer and the antelope play."

In Dolly Parton's "My Tennessee Mountain Home," likewise, it is fireflies and
June bugs, singing crickets and honeysuckle, "A songbird on a fencepost sings a
melody." The only manmade objects are natural wood—a porch, a straight-backed
chair, a fence, and, implicitly, the church building. Life there is "as peaceful as a
baby's sigh," and the breath of that sigh becomes a summer wind sweetened by
honeysuckle. The baby, the floral aroma, the symbols of shelter and orderliness are
built from—and congenial with—nature. Like Crèvecoeur, Parton omits information that would diminish the ideal (for instance, the fact that children in large
rural families like her own slept four or five to a bed, with the mattress often wet
by morning). Conditions of hardship appear elsewhere in her songs, as in "In
Good Old Days (When Times Were Bad)." But "My Tennessee Mountain Home"
continues the tradition of rural idealism.

In fact, the Tennessee mountain home is nature itself, the Emersonian center of
authenticity in America. As Dolly Parton sings, her ebullient and cheerful voice
authenticates the lyrics. Her tone endorses the truth of every word. There are no
double meanings, no qualifications, but only wholehearted conviction behind
every note of every word.

This concept of home as nature, fundamental to country music, can seem itself
so natural, so very familiar, even clichéd, that no alternative version could even be
imagined. We can think of a contrary image of home, and American writers like
Hamlin Garland (*Main-Travelled Roads*, 1891) and Erskine Caldwell (*Tobacco Road*,
1932) have offered it up in due course, a picture of household dilapidation, filth,
and despair. In her famous antislavery novel, *Uncle Tom's Cabin* (1852), Harriet
Beecher Stowe created such an anti-home in her depiction of the Deep South
plantation of Simon Legree, whose garden is a shambles and kitchen filthy. These

Twentieth-century artist Thomas Hart Benton represents home in the same terms as Dolly Parton's "My Tennessee Mountain Home." Charcoal and ink drawing from Benton's autobiography, An Artist in America, 3d rev. ed., 1968. (Reprinted by permission of Thomas Hart Benton and Rita P. Benton Testamentary Trusts)

"homes," however, are contraries of the natural ideal and really support that ideal.

For an alternative version, therefore, it is helpful to notice a poem, "Anecdote of the Jar," published just four years before the release of the Bristol sessions' "Old Time Corn Shuckin'." In 1923 the modernist poet Wallace Stevens wrote of placing a jar in Tennessee as a symbol of civilization that would bring order to an otherwise chaotic, "slovenly" wilderness. This poetic "jar" is no corn liquor jug or home-canning Mason jar, but a ceramicist's *objet d'art* signaling the high culture of art and artifice. "It did not give of bird or bush, / Like nothing else in Ten-

nessee," says the poem, seemingly boastful of the separateness of this object from
its environment.

The value of the jar lies precisely in its power to "take dominion" over unruly nature (and perhaps over the "slovenly" hillbillies who inhabit it). Dolly Parton's Emersonian "My Tennessee Mountain Home" and numerous other country songs work in an opposite direction to affirm the value of a nature portrayed as nurturing in every way. Opposition to it is literally unthinkable, because country music evokes a world in which all that is valuable is authenticated precisely by being all of a piece with bird and bush (and, for that matter, with shucked corn).

Home involves the dwelling as well as field and furrow. One historian of architecture and culture observes that *home* brings together several meanings of refuge, ownership, and affection and also of "house and household, of dwelling." Thomas Jefferson felt farmers to be "the chosen people of God," but the American household itself increasingly came to the attention of writers and artists of the nineteenth century, ultimately making itself felt in country music.

Emerson drew the broad outline of this domestic life movement. He insisted that the real history of the world would not be found in "the state-house or the court-room, . . . not in senates or . . . chambers of commerce [but in] the personal history . . . in the dwelling-house." Two women writers, the sisters Catharine Beecher and Harriet Beecher Stowe, were activists working to prove that very point. They invested the household with the spiritual meanings that provided an important foundation for country music. Harriet Beecher Stowe actually brought her readers into a spiritually exemplary room in *Uncle Tom's Cabin*. To read Stowe's kitchen "home" passage is to dwell for a moment in a model Christian home — and to see that it belongs perfectly in a twentieth-century country music song. We enter a bustling kitchen at breakfast time, when biscuits and chicken are underway, when knives and forks clatter "sociably." And we look around this "large, roomy, neatly-painted kitchen" with its "glossy green wood chairs, old and firm, a small flag-bottomed rocking-chair, with a patch-work cushion in it . . . and a larger one, motherly and old, whose wide arms breathed hospitable invitation . . . a real comfortable, persuasive old chair."

And the woman of the house? Seen sorting dried fruit, she is the incarnation of the maternal: "Her face was round and rosy," with eyes that are "clear, honest, and loving," and her hair, "silvered by age," is parted to show a forehead on which time has written "no inscription, except peace on earth, good will to men."

An idealized portrait, of course, and exactly like those in country music. In "Coal Miner's Daughter," Loretta Lynn's mother would uncomplainingly "smile in mommie's understanding way." Spiritually the song, like the scene in the novel, shows what Stowe calls "a home, — *home*." She intends readers to grasp this scene

Currier & Ives popular lithographs representing the same home values in different regions of the nation. (Courtesy Museum of the City of New York, The Harry T. Peters Collection: Home, Sweet Home, 1869, MCNY 58.300.15; The Western Farmer's Home, 1871, MCNY 56.300.1448; American Homestead Winter, 1868, MCNY 58.300.237) See also Plate 3.

not as a dream but as the real thing; nothing less than salvation is at stake. Home has the power to banish misanthropy, despair, atheism. It is "a golden cloud of protection and confidence . . . the light of a living Gospel, breathed in living faces, preached by a thousand unconscious acts of love and good will." It is the basis on which, decades later, country artists would enshrine the home as sacrosanct.

Harriet's sister, Catharine Beecher, also defined the home as the site of comfortable retreat from the harsh world. She depicted it as the welcoming center to which one returns after travel or work or obligation in the wider world. It is the place of comfort and solace and peace to which one can return time and again because it is an abiding respite and place of one's own.

But Catharine Beecher's "home" is also the scene of work, especially women's work, which is so vivid in country music. Readers find a blockbuster dedication in the one book on which the two sisters collaborated, in which they bid to make *home* the foundation of the republic. "To the women of America," the dedication begins, "in whose hands rest the real destinies of the republic." The republic itself

is "moulded . . . amid the maturer influences of home." The book has a title worthy of its lofty aims: *The American Woman's Home: Or, Principles of Domestic Science; Being a Guide to the Formation and Maintenance of Economical, Healthful, Beautiful, and Christian Homes* (1869). With such chapters as "Good Cooking" and "A Healthful Home," the Beechers vigorously argued that the material environment of the household must manifest the highest values of the home. The dwelling must be a place of health, nurturance, and kindness from bread box to rolling pin.

Not surprisingly, about a century after these sisters worked to define the home in terms of female domesticity, Loretta Lynn's "Coal Miner's Daughter" would recount a mother who "scrubbed our clothes on a washboard every day," while Dolly Parton's "Coat of Many Colors" would describe a penniless mother who, faced with the onset of winter, reached into a rag box and fashioned a particolored coat for her daughter. Patched from rags, the coat not only is blessed by its connection to the Old Testament story of Joseph but is a symbol of maternal love. "Perhaps this coat will bring you good luck and happiness," the mother says in the song, blessing it with a kiss.

"Coat of Many Colors" deserves special attention as a parable of domestic life directly descended from the "home" movement articulated by the Beechers. Vocally, Parton takes us "back to the seasons of [her] youth," to a past now outdistanced by time and circumstance. She reenters childhood memories of walking to school with patched breeches and "holes in both [her] shoes." There is mountain dialect ("I go wand'rin' once again") for vocal transport to rural Tennessee, but no hackneyed glorification of those rich-though-poor, no martyr's appeal for sympathy. Parton's inflections tell us she would not so cheapen her song or its subject. Her tone says that, from the moment her mother reached for the needle and the rag box, young Dolly knew her coat would mean spiritual riches beyond any monetary standard. This is why she is undaunted by the ridicule of classmates, who only see the coat as a mass of rags—"rags," the very word Parton sings with such delicacy, as if she would hold them gently in hand to this day. Twice she sings of being "*so* proud," her tone emphatic, then appreciative. She knows that the coat is itself a blessing. Transcending its materials, it is not only sewn with—but *is*—maternal love so protective that the coat makes its wearer spiritually invincible.

And this kind of household is open to any man who accepts its terms. In the farmhouse kitchen of *Uncle Tom's Cabin*, Stowe has the male head of household stand off to one side, shaving (real mid-nineteenth-century men did not knead biscuits), but fully a part of the domestic circle. In country music, then, Barry Tashian can sing Gram Parsons's "Blue Eyes," about a harsh world that treats a man badly, driving him to self-punishing acts (gnawing his nails, getting stoned, pulling his hair, retreating into isolation). Tashian sings about this in clipped tones,

John Haberle, Grandma's Hearthstone,
*1890. Oil on canvas, 244 × 168 cm. Painted
in an era of rapid industrialization, this
image reaffirms traditional home values.
(© The Detroit Institute of the Arts, gift of
C. W. Churchill in memory of his father)*

biting the words as this man bites his nails. Thinking of his blue-eyed wife, however, the man heads for home, where life is love, steadying chores, sunshine, and,
in cold weather, the warmth of a "big old quilt." Tonally, there is a rollicking en-
thusiasm in this up-tempo endorsement of domestic life. When Tashian sings,
with partner Holly Tashian, of the nighttime embrace, the duet itself becomes a
statement on domestic harmony.

These values, centered in preindustrial life, continue into the twentieth century,
so often characterized by its gear-and-girder and computer technology. We might,
in fact, take a very quick inspection tour of a home linked directly to country
music and to the Beechers, Crèvecoeur, and Emerson—and yet produced in this
century. This is the home in the Little House books by Laura Ingalls Wilder
(adapted for television as *Little House on the Prairie*, starring Michael Landon and
still running nationally in syndication). First published during the Depression of
the 1930s and continuing as a colossal sales success in the eras of urban and suburban America, the Little House books of pioneering America in the 1860s–80s,
reaffirm the values of home as defined by Crèvecoeur, Emerson, and the Beechers—and, of course, by country music. Farmers, representing the natural world,
are the American heroes—patient, persevering, a bulwark against mercenary ways.
"It was farmers that took all that country and made it America. . . . It was axes and
plows that made this country."

And self-reliance is foremost, with *Little House on the Prairie* (1935) virtually a do-
it-yourself homebuilder's and home ec. handbook. The Wilder family upholds
Christian values and maintains good manners and respectability even in the crud-

Country music album designs reflecting "home" values. (Courtesy Sony Music, Warner Brothers, Inc., and United Artists)

est frontier conditions. ("You must mind your manners, even if we are a hundred miles from anywhere.")

Through all this, the family stays intact—stays home—even as it takes to the road, from Wisconsin to the Plains to the Dakota Territory to Missouri. Tested in all kinds of adversity—fire, wolves, sickness (one daughter, Mary, going blind), a severe winter in which they nearly starve—the family surmounts every obstacle. Barely escaping starvation, narrator Laura proclaims it "wonderful to be safe at home, sheltered from the winds and the cold." She adds, "This must be a little bit like Heaven."

And the world of Little House connects with country music through these traditional home values, including hard work in tough times. Loretta Lynn's "Coal Miner's Daughter" describes an Appalachian father who works night shift and farms by day; Dolly Parton's "In the Good Old Days (When Times Were Bad)" catalogs the miseries of a hapless, helpless family watching hail destroy their crops, suffering in the poverty that leaves the sick mother without a doctor's care while the workman father's hands bleed and the family goes to bed hungry. Parton's and Lynn's songs reaffirm Emerson's portrayal of the farmer as "represent[ing] continuous hard labor, year in, year out, and small gains." And Emerson's writing even links country music with the Wilder family in his phrase about "frosty furrows, poverty, necessity, darkness" and in his remark that within the household routine are "the passions that bind and sever. . . . Here is poverty and all the wisdom its hated necessities can teach, here labor drudges, here affections glow, here the secrets of character are told. . . . Here is Economy, and Glee, and Hospitality, and

**Cover art by Garth Williams for Laura Ingalls Wilder's
Little House on the Prairie. (© 1953 Garth Williams;
renewed 1981. Courtesy HarperCollins, Inc.)**

Ceremony, and Frankness, and Calamity, and Death, and Hope." The statement is unflinching in the face of hardship, but it confers a kind of benediction, too.

Music itself is a fundamental link between country music and the Little House world, especially in the fiddle on which Charles Ingalls ("Pa") plays jigs, reels, and ballads as he sings with his family and neighbors.[1] "That was the best time of all . . . [when Pa] took out his fiddle and began to play." The fiddle is synonymous with home. It soothes the frightened mother and daughters, lulls the children to sleep, leads the family into religious reverence with sabbath hymns and into the merriment of festivities. (Wilder prints most lyrics to the fiddle tunes, some of which bluegrass groups play to this day, like "Cotton-Eyed Joe" and "The Arkansas Traveler.") Because the fiddle represents every mood and activity of home, the reader is not surprised to hear it play the inevitable:

> Home! Home! Sweet, sweet home,
> Be it ever so humble
> There is no place like home.

This is home as birthright, as center of acceptance and authenticity. It is spiritually protective and stands against the inauthentic, the fake and false.

Country music puts home's enveloping love and kindness against materialism, social status, hurdles of hierarchy, and all sorts of false value systems. These are focused on the city. Repeatedly, country music positions the home directly against the opposing values represented by urbanism, itself an un-American artifice. "I'm growing tired of the big city's lights," sang Jimmie Rodgers in Bill Halley's "Miss the Mississippi and You." "You left me for the bright lights of the town," sings Loretta Lynn in the role of a young woman, a "Blue Kentucky Girl" who hopes her rural Kentucky boy ("a country boy set out to see the world") will weary of those urban lights. The husband in Harlan Howard's "Streets of Baltimore" complains of being "dragged" nightly through the city streets, and this song has been recorded by country artists as different as the rock-era Gram Parsons and the vocally smoother Bobby Bare; both versions express the plight of a factory worker recounting how he sold his farm, left kin and friends back in Tennessee, and bought one-way tickets to Baltimore so his wife could fulfill her ambition to revel in the nighttime street scene.

Bluegrass music, too, sets the authentic country world against the urban: "City heat and busy streets are wearing me down. . . . I want to go back home again"

1. The pervasiveness of songs in Laura Ingalls Wilder's Little House books is revealed in *The Laura Ingalls Wilder Songbook*, compiled and edited by Eugenia Garson, arranged for piano and guitar by Herbert Haufrecht, illustrated by Williams (New York: Harper and Row, 1968).

(Livewire, *Wired*). And in the Vietnam War years, Kenny Rogers and others sang Mel Tillis's "Ruby, Don't Take Your Love to Town," in which the paralyzed vet/husband pleads with his wife to stay home and keep him company, although we know how futile his plea will be when he describes her "painted lips" and "tinted hair." It is the artifice—the artificiality—of Ruby's cosmetics, just as it is the city lights and pavement in these and other songs, that make the critical statement. Ruby is lost to her husband because she is no longer natural (hair dyed, mouth lipsticked). And the city lights are artificial in contrast to the glow of the moon and stars.

Country music's hostility toward urbanism seems at first provincial. It seems to express the suspicion and hostility of rural naifs or innocents encountering up-

Artist Garth Williams's drawing of "Pa" (Charles) Ingalls fiddling on the prairie. (© 1953 Garth Williams; renewed 1981. Courtesy Harper-Collins, Inc.)

town sophisticates. Yet here, too, country music sustains a long-term American tradition. It is actually part of a powerful historical American suspicion of—and anxiety about—cities. From the Revolutionary era on, numerous writers have worried that North America might emulate the corrupt cities of Europe and thus re-create the very problems the immigrants sought to flee. Thomas Jefferson feared their "depravity of morals," their "dependence and corruption." In 1823 he wrote that "a city offers you . . . painful objects of vice and wretchedness." A few decades later, writers like Herman Melville and Nathaniel Hawthorne looked abroad and continued the critique of cold and squalid, evil, crime-ridden, sinful European cities.

And eventually urban America drew the same fire, as if some malignancy had entered into the authentic, natural nation. A French chronicler, Alexis de Tocqueville, worried in the 1830s about the "rabble" running riot in urban America, and

37

The city represented in American art as materialistic, menacing, and snobbish. John Sloan, Fifth Avenue Critics, 1905, from the series "New York City Life." Etching, 9⅞ × 12⁷⁄₁₆ in. (Collection of Whitney Museum of American Art, New York, purchase)

dire predictions of social turmoil continued for decades. New York City is as hard-hearted as its pavements, according to characters in a Melville novel (*Pierre*), while Melville's contemporary, Elizabeth Peabody, argued that cities originate in warfare. This antiurban bias has continued in the twentieth century. The novelist Henry James felt like a horrified Rip Van Winkle when, returning from twenty years in England, he found his old New York of church spires and schooner masts metamorphosed into a hideous industrial-age metropolis of skyscrapers and suspension bridges: a "monster . . . some steel-souled machine-room of brandished arms and hammering fists and opening and closing jaws."

Sociologists and educators were no happier, deploring the urban frenzy and impersonality fostered by new technologies. The educational theorist John Dewey observed that "the Great Society created by steam and electricity may be a society, but it is no community." The architect Frank Lloyd Wright pronounced it "impossible" to renovate existing cities: "The carcass of the city is far too old, too far gone." And Chicago sociologist Robert Park remarked that "if the city is the world which man created, it is the world in which he is henceforth condemned to live." "Cities," Emerson had said, make people "artificial."

Country music has always agreed. "I rode a freight train north to Detroit City / And after all these years I find I've just been wasting my time" ("Detroit City," Danny Dill/Mel Tillis). "It's a hard way to find out / That trouble is real / In a far away city / With a far away feel" ("Hickory Wind," Gram Parsons/Bob Buchanon). The displaced rural Tennessean of "Streets of Baltimore" laments that his urbanized wife prized the "bright lights" more than her husband. Ralph Waldo Emerson had outlined the urban/rural pattern that would emerge in country music. "The city is always recruited from the country . . . [but] poisoned by town life and town vices, the sufferer resolves: My children . . . shall go back to the land."

In this sense, country "home" songs are so often about going back to the authentic center of American life, and that center necessarily stirs yearnings that occupy a tremendously powerful place in the imagination. "Home still rocks my soul" and "steals my dreams each night," says the bluegrass "Home," by Holly Tashian (*Trust in Me*, 1988). The soul seems cradled, rocked as to a lullaby, and the Barry Tashian/Holly Tashian duet reinforces this idea with a little swoop on "rock." We can visualize the cradle or rocking chair, and the stolen dreams seem to echo the gentle spiritual, "Steal Away," with its sense of easeful movement. Performed by the Nashville Bluegrass Band (*Home of the Blues*, 1991), the same "Home" becomes an almost-jolly waltz with its lyrical resolve to return home:

> I'm goin' back where my heart still lives,
> Back to my dear old friends.
> When they reach out with welcome arms,
> It will be my journey's end.

The song tells us why home is so compelling, even irresistible, as the singers recall nights spent singing "sweet country songs." The recollection goes on, "We laughed at the good times, cried at the bad / While life just rolled along." The "rolling" itself indicates a kind of steady continuity without disruption or flux. And the comradeship of "Home" is reinforced by the very fact of the duet. As Barry and Holly Tashian sing "Home," or Alan O'Bryant and Pat Enright of the Nashville Bluegrass Band, the listener hears virtually no distinction between melody and harmony. The hierarchical "lead" and "harmony vocal" printed on liner notes are really misnomers, because those distinctions disappear as the two

Glenn O. Coleman, **Minetta Lane,** *1928,*
from the series "Lithographs of New York."
Lithograph, 11⅛ × 11 in. (Collection of
Whitney Museum of American Art, New York,
gift of Mrs. Herbert B. Lazarus)

voices become one entity. In the duet, the two are so attuned to one another's
musical styles, so aware of the singing partner and of working in synchrony, that
the two voices become one. (Family members—for example, the Everly Brothers
or the Louvin Brothers—often make good duets precisely because they are akin
and attuned, their pronunciation nearly identical, their timing the result of the
very physical knowledge of each other acquired through years of life in the same
household.)

So "Home" appears to be a classic within the home genre, its plot by now familiar: a person leaves home in the country, discovers loss, feels homesick, resolves to return. As "a light that burns so bright," the lyrics say, home is a beacon
shining forth to guide the way.

*Kenneth Hayes Miller, **Shopper**, 1928. Oil on canvas, 41 × 33 in. (Collection of Whitney Museum of American Art, New York, purchase)*

And yet "Home" can carry a cross-grained dimension within—a disturbance attributable to home's very force field. The soul can be rocked not only in an infant's cradle, but in a quake. When home steals one's dreams, it does not only slip away with them but monopolizes the mind, robbing the dreamer of other imaginative visions and projections. The home beacon in this song does not simply shine but, searing, "burns." "I never thought I'd be turnin' back," say the singers, "to a light that burns so bright." The singers seem taken unaware, perturbed, disturbed. Thoughts of home have commandeered consciousness, and the vow to return feels almost compulsory. Plus, bluegrass vocals always have an edge, a tautness that works against simple peace and quiet. Home can be obsessive, compulsive. The oppositional terms, nonetheless, are established as home's health versus urban or worldly sickness, the home-based *real* versus the false. Once these truths become self-evident, the singer/speaker has no choice to make. Home is the only place to be.

But going home is neither simple nor easy. And the problem turns out to be one of ideology, not logistics. A tangle of conflicting American values makes this problem so complex that just calling the moving van or renting a U-Haul is not the solution—is, in fact, out of the question. Turn, first, to Merle Haggard's dedication to his autobiography, *Sing Me Back Home*, named for one of his songs. The book is sent out

> To the ramblers and the drifters,
> the seekers and the travelers,
> and all the wanderers out there
> on the back roads and
> the highways . . .

This dedication is a reminder of the extent to which country music, together with American art, literature, and movies, identifies Americans as a people who value their identity as restless, migratory, and on the move. (Even in the 1990s, the average American moves twelve times.) How, then, can *home* then fit into an American world that so highly prizes those who go on the road and leave it?

One album by country musician Travis Tritt, *Country Club* (1990), sharpens the question and explores its full dimensions. The album is a good case study because it includes two songs that, put back to back, very vividly show the extent of this American dilemma about road and home, and about loneliness, too. In "The Road Home" (cowritten by Stewart Harris and Jim McBride), Tritt sings the role of a man, formerly ambitious to reach the city, who finds himself on the fourteenth floor of an Atlanta high rise, disturbed by the same urban anonymity and impersonality characteristic of anti-city texts dating back to the eighteenth century. "I just couldn't wait to get here to the city," he says, but "now I can't remember why I came." He sees the city as a hive of automated worker bees. Nobody knows his name, much less who he is.

The next lines of the song are predictable, given his new knowledge. Like the narrators of "Home," "Detroit City," "Streets of Baltimore," or "Hickory Wind," this man now knows that home is the Emersonian authentic center of the natural world, of "cattails growing by the river" and "wind in the pines." When he sings, "That old home-grown feeling's getting stronger," the phrase *home-grown* links him to the garden where growth is promoted naturally, organically. He is keenly aware of his jeopardy: "I'm gonna be a goner if I don't go back [home] someday." Health and sanity depend on his return. If he delays too long while "the road home keeps on gettin' longer," he will perish. Home is life, the city a slow drain of vitality, ultimately death. The only question remaining is whether he will get home before it is too late. His mission and goal are clear.

Travis Tritt's *Country Club*, however, includes a second song that disrupts this clear vision and makes the road back home a very dubious venture. This second song, "Dixie Flyer," presents a radically different, contradictory message about home and the flight from it, demonstrating an American dilemma of clashing values. "Dixie Flyer" (by Susan Longacre, Jim Photoglo, and Russell Smith) focuses on an American defined by restlessness and the road. Its title is the name of a train, and the singer's identity, we learn, took shape from a childhood memory of burning cinders and the steam whistle. The train's earlier route, meaning the past, is of no interest, for all focus is forward as the singer boasts that he jumped at the first opportunity to flee. Rifling toward the future, he has become airborne on the *Dixie Flyer.*

This is a song of forward, restless motion. Throttle wide open, this man surges ahead, his very soul a "driving wheel." In freedom, this flyer has even jumped the confines of the railroad track, unbounded by the steel rails. He defines his vitality by incessant motion, by restlessness and zest to absorb the wider world. He is a version of Merle Haggard's ramblin' man or Emmylou Harris's character in "Born to Run." His life is like a high-speed train, and he will roll as long as he is fired up or until he runs out of track. The fast tempo and high-energy background of electric guitars support the message of the lyrics.

"Dixie Flyer" is entirely familiar as a road song. In fact, TV viewers of the 1992 Olympics at Barcelona saw a video of Travis Tritt onstage singing "Dixie Flyer" in a Coca-Cola ad that alternates footage of Tritt with a videotape showing Olympics cyclists racing along winding Spanish roads. In aerial views, the pack of cyclists indeed resembles a long, slinky train in motion. And closeups show the "driving wheel" mentality of one American "Dixie flyer," a Texas cyclist pushing himself to the limit on the road. The corporate financial investment in an ad of this kind indicates just how deeply ingrained is the American idea of "full-speed-ahead" road life. Coke would not risk alienating consumers by presenting a message contrary to deep-seated and widely held national beliefs.

But suppose, coming fresh from Tritt's version of "The Road Home," we should ask about home values in "Dixie Flyer?" (After all, if Coca-Cola sponsors "road" messages, other corporations vigorously promote "home" values, espe-cially in connection with food products—Pepperidge *Farm*, Archway *Home*style Cookies.) So can a listener detect any signs of home in the world of "Dixie Flyer"? One approach is to ask, How does "Dixie Flyer" represent those who keep the home fires burning while Mr. Driving Wheel is on the road? How does the song regard those who stay—must we say, behind? Nearly three centuries ago the En-glish poet John Milton expressed a common Christian sentiment when he said, "They also serve who only stand and wait." Patiently, they bear witness and en-dure. Crèvecoeur's and Emerson's farm families are a version of them, as are the Beechers' homemakers. Still valuable?

Not in "Dixie Flyer," which derides them as mere onlookers foolishly "satis-fied" to sit on the sidelines as the trains roar past. This lump "some" is passive, inert, a mere odd lot of spectators who lack the vital American spirit. No listener needs instructions on what to think of them. The sedentary trackside onlookers are at best pitiable.

At first, this is puzzling, because the people sitting by the track are actually the home folks, the family members and friends invoked lovingly and longingly in so many "home" songs, including Tritt's "The Road Home." In countless country songs, they are the ones described as ready and waiting to reach out with open arms to the rovers, the ramblers, the restless wanderers—in effect, the prodigal sons and daughters. They are "mom and daddy," "home folks," "old friends," "dear friends," "sweetheart[s]." Some of them even have names, like Annie Rich in Gram Parsons's "Return of the Grievous Angel" or Barbara Walker in Tom T. Hall's "Homecoming." (Seldom is the home sweetheart a man, for the roving woman is far more apt, in social terms, to be "ruined," like Loretta Lynn's "Honky Tonk Girl" or the "Queen of the Silver Dollar," a onetime respectable girl now in the city or town and holding court from a barstool (Emmylou Harris, *Pieces of the Sky*, 1975).)

On the whole, though, we identify these home figures as the nearest and dear-est. Staying in place, they patiently abide. If the restless ramblers have experienced the harsh outside world and its monumental loneliness, these home folks are wait-ing to be the emotional, psychological, and spiritual fountain of healing. They are solace and the human face of home's authenticity. Why, then, should they be sub-jected to the disdain shown in "Dixie Flyer?" How can they be criticized for sit-ting by the track (on the porch) and watching the train (the world) pass before them while they take no active part in it?

Put bluntly, country music seems schizoid on this subject. Not that all country songs ought to be compatible; but when identities are flip-flopped—people cast as home folks one moment, sloths the next—then we can ask about a ground-level grasp of shared assumptions. Is there a cultural split that subjects the very same people to a weird American metamorphosis, in one song identified as human inertia itself, in the next as home folks and dear friends?

Yes—in a manner of speaking, there is a kind of American split or schism. For "Dixie Flyer" and "The Road Home," when brought together, confront us with a set of American contradictions. These can go unnoticed only as long as listeners mentally fence off certain songs from others. (The hard-driving electric guitars in the arrangements of both Travis Tritt songs, for instance, tend to hide the contradictory viewpoints, since the tempo and beat of "The Road Home" is similar to that of "Dixie Flyer" and seems to endorse the very city pace that the singer claims to detest.)

But once the mental fences come down, once the boundary lines drop, then a cultural divide comes into focus, and a most interesting pattern becomes visible. For country music "solves" the dilemma by offering listeners two profoundly different kinds of American worlds that can stay intact only if they never merge, never intersect, never meet each other. The first is the world of home and the home folks who belong, not to the real world in real time, but to a mythic one of nature that lies outside events marked by clock and calendar and outside the vicissitudes of human experience. To be sure, home is subject to the seasonal cycle. Yet home, this mythic American *home*, is fixed and unchanging, belonging where it always and forever has belonged and will belong—in nature. It is the "Tennessee Mountain Home," "West Virginia, mountain mama," and so on. It is a mythic space populated, in song lyrics, by "old friends" who are impervious to change, who live on and on, tending the garden or farm, and where the beloved "old folks" dwell, those already far along in years but who never become infirm. In Tritt's "The Road Home," they are described as "never in a hurry" and "never bothered by time." They could not possibly be, because they exist in the mythic home realm outside of time.

These dearest friends and family metamorphose into the trackside lumpen only when they cross through a time warp to arrive in the world of change and flux. This is a world of roads that go through actual space in actual time. This is where the Dixie Flyer sings his song of the open road. But here, in the "road" world, the home folks are redefined. When they cross over from the mythic *home* world to inhabit the road realm of change-in-process, they are assigned different identities. They are put into a new census category, so to speak. Having entered a territory where they have no legitimate place, much less a seat of honor, they become inert, sedentary figures who are foolishly content to sit still in a high-energy, kinetic America. But send them back once again into the mythic land of *home*, and their status is restored. They become "dear old friends," "mama and daddy," and so on.

Put in stark terms: The road is culture; the home is nature. The first changes; the second never does. And the two can neither meet nor mesh.

So where does that put the home-song singer? We have been viewing the strange plight of friends and relations as they switch from one realm to another. But what of the country artist who sings within a single song of both home and the road, seemingly trying to straddle both worlds?

First of all, notice that vocalists usually sing "home" songs from the road, or with firsthand knowledge of the road. This means that, according to the song, they have crossed over from the home folks' natural world and entered the America of movement and change. Having exited an American Eden, however, they now have a terrible realization of what they have lost. The Oak Ridge Boys, for instance, sing "Where the Fast Lane Ends" (Fred Koller/Sonny Throckmorton) from—where else?—the highway fast lane. They have been killing themselves, the lyrics say, chasing "fame and wealth" and "working overtime." The song is set at that moment of recognition that life on the road is injurious, perhaps lethal, not a quest but a chase. The solution? Pull off and "spend some time with my laid-back friends . . . [my] long-lost friends."

Those friends, we begin to sense, are part of the mythic "home" world. They can be found in a "peaceful place" that is accessible, the song says, "just around the bend . . . where the fast lane ends." It is just in the offing, just a short distance away. And yet the lyrics brilliantly hold the line that separates mythic nature and dynamic culture. How? By locating this peaceful place of old friends in "a photograph in all my dreams." There is no gas station route map to it, no AAA Trip-Tik. It is a photographic image from the subconscious and from memory. Powerful and emotionally real, it is nonetheless located deep within the imagination. From the culture's fast lane, the mythic world of "home" remains intact, a better world —but one in the mind, not off the interstate.

This song, like so many in country music, conveys a powerful yearning to return home, a vow to go back. But as in countless other country home songs, the singer/speaker can only yearn, resolve, prepare, and perhaps just barely begin the journey back. Actual arrival, however, is out of the question because of the culture/nature split. Home remains the place of dreams, the imaginative destination to which one vows to return—though one cannot arrive. Out of the past, real or imagined, home shimmers in the distance of the future. It is the past awaiting its future and the future awaiting its past.

But the ultimate destination is forever out of reach. At most, the two worlds can communicate by letter, as in Dolly Parton's "Letter" or the McCarter sisters' "Letter from Home" (Jennifer McCarter/Carl Jackson), a song written from the home folks to their grown children, who are country musicians on tour. "Letter from

Home" (*The Gift*, 1987) is full of family love and good will, but the song itself re-inforces boundaries. Letters like Parton's and the McCarters' can respect the separate worlds of road and of home precisely by underscoring their fundamental difference. The letter-song works as a kind of border patrol between nature and culture. Perhaps the novelist Thomas Wolfe said it best in one of his titles, *You Can't Go Home Again.*[2]

But life can be grim for those home folks who never reach the upramp. Glimpsing or intuiting the wider world of the road, they can only feel like failures if they do not venture forth. This is to glance at the so-called home folks who refuse their mythic status in Emersonian nature even though they live in its characteristic geography, the small town or farm or mountains of a rural America. Seen from the fast lane, these are "laid-back friends" or brothers and sisters. But what first-person account does country music give of them? After all, nobody wants to be somebody else's theme-park character or theatrical prop. What, then, is the outlook of those who live day by day in the world identified closely with idealized nature? What is the eyewitness report from the farm or small town?

Country music essentially continues a strain of bitter frustration felt by rural, small-town Americans consumed by thwarted ambition and a sense of failure. The written record of this covers the Midwest to New England and the South; the writers include Ernest Hemingway, Sherwood Anderson, Hamlin Garland, Flannery O'Connor, E. A. Robinson. Country music sustains that lineage of despair wherein *hometown* means claustrophobia or worse. The Bob McDill/Dan Seals "They Rage On" (*Rage On*, 1992), sung by Seals, describes men and women who, blind and baffled, shadow dance or rage "against the lives that this world gave them," including life as "a small town girl / With no room to grow" and "a reckless boy / With nowhere to go." Like caged birds with "no place to fly," they squander their life energy in back-seat sex, in due course to play out a midlife (motel room   script. "They rage on / Somehow searchin' for the answers,   s, the answers were foreclosed by limited life circumstances i   n other words, the Emersonian village has been a crushing bac

The same   n a song presented as autobiography, the McDill/ Seals "Big Wl   ight," again sung by Dan Seals (also on *Rage On*).

2. In a few co   lds do meet, and with disastrous results. Tom T. Hall's "Homecoming"   farmer father confronting one another in mutual in-comprehension   d Hazel Dickens's "The Hills of Home" shows a countryside deci   ose who must confront the consequences of their abandonment of

Here a man from a small town (one caution light at the major intersection) recalls how, as a boy, he would "slip into town" and watch the huge trucks: "To me it was a beautiful sight / Big wheels in the moonlight." Smitten with wanderlust, his life's ambition was to go on the road, to "put my life on the center line" and "see the world before I die." The bass guitars suggest the diesel horns calling in the moonlight, beckoning, stirring his dreams.

But while he cannot exactly say how or why it happened, his life took on an unexpected "home" form. He speaks to us from a living-room chair, not the cab of an eighteen wheeler. "Cain't complain about all I've got / Kids and a wife and a regular job." This is not a song of complaint, but of disappointment so deep that it amounts to self-condemnation for failure. There is a spiritual emptiness in this man stemming from a calling unanswered, a journey never undertaken. Fundamentally, he feels the waste of his life. He has not seen the world, has not been a part of the larger dynamic America. Job and family—which is to say, home—are not fulfilling. Domestic life without the experience of the wider world is barren. This man identifies himself as one of the trackside onlookers to life, not a part of its dynamic movement. Haunted by the road not taken, he thinks of himself as the homebody who is nobody. The song ends plaintively: "I know there's a peace I'll never find, 'cause those big old wheels keep rollin' through my mind."

Country music, then, presents a fundamental American conundrum. To stay home is to risk feeling dejected and thwarted. But to appreciate home, one must leave it, never to return. This dizzying puzzle means that we are caught betwixt and between, poised for voyages we cannot complete and moving from and to places that elude our arrival.

But country music goes even further, arousing strong yearnings for a kind of home so idealized that no one can actually ever experience it.[3] Country music's *home* is an unattainable ideal that exceeds any given family's best effort at love and care. Such a home provokes an unquenchable thirst, a chronic hunger, as the listener feels a homesickness that the music itself arouses from unsuspected depths. The feelings of yearning and desire become a kind of sweet pain. Above all, the

3. It may come as some surprise that Dolly Parton's Tennessee Mountain Home is actually a composite of several dwellings the Partons occupied in the Sevierville area while Dolly was growing up, from Locust Ridge to the eight miles' distant Pittman Center, then twelve to fifteen miles away to Bird's Creek, and then another five miles to Caton's Chapel—very considerable distances in mountainous terrain. Dolly has called this periodic household moving "exciting" and dubbed herself "a country gypsy," though the music room in her Nashville-area house incorporates in its fireplace logs and rocks from the cabin in which she was born, suggesting a "home" reliquary.

music announces itself as the fullest experience of this ideal home. The imagined homecoming of the condemned prisoner who recalls the "Green, Green Grass of Home" is possible only through the Curly Putnam song (recorded at least two hundred times). Merle Haggard's "Sing Me Back Home" likewise presents a death-row prisoner whose solace on the eve of execution is the guitar on which his fellow prisoner plays the old songs that stir memory and desire for home. The guitar and the songs do not merely send him back home—they *sing* him there. In some sense, any listener is that prisoner, never to experience the actual homecoming except within the world of the song.

If country music repeatedly sends this self-serving message or set of messages, it also gives us a gift unique to itself. As music, country presents itself as authenticity, as the *real* in human life, essential, unadorned, and fundamental. This music is what we have of home, the closest we can come to it. Even the instruments of country music are put forward as natural and so belonging to the authentic home. From the guitar in "Sing Me Back Home," we move to the Little House world in which Pa's fiddle is allied with nature—that is, with Emerson's natural world. When the wind howls and moans outside, the fiddle mimics it in a "deep, rushing undertone." When Pa lifts the fiddle to his shoulder, the notes can fall "like clear drops of water into the stillness": "A pause, and Pa began to play the nightingale's song. The nightingale answered him. The nightingale began to sing again. It was singing with Pa's fiddle. . . . The bird and the fiddle were talking to each other in the cool night under the moon." No wonder, then, that Wilder writes about the fiddle case or box, "Pa took the fiddle from its nest." The country fiddle is starlight, windsong, songbird—and home.

And Dolly Parton advances the same idea about the banjo, an instrument originating in Africa and sustained by slaves before whites, too, began playing it in country music. In Parton's "Applejack," an old man, Jackson Taylor, nicknamed Jack, lives in an orchard where he picks apples and plucks the banjo, drinks cider or applejack, and—whenever the singer comes his way—reaches down his banjo and plays while she accompanies on tambourine—all right in the orchard. Though the actual Jack is gone, the memories remain, and childhood's home surfaces every time a banjo sounds. The very instrument and its sound are part of the authentic and ideal home. (No wonder country music instruments are often pictured in scenes of nature.)

Country music's home, however, invariably leans toward melancholy because its cycle of desire cannot be completed. And this is the essence of "Hickory Wind" as Emmylou Harris sings it—a meditation, not on home, but on the yearning for it. Adult trouble is real, the lyrics say, as is lonesomeness. Home is an idea, intangible and ineffable—a wind redolent of hickory from a Carolina sung more as a state of

Notecard showing banjo and guitar with apples as if both the instruments and the music have just come from the orchard. (Courtesy Kay Betts and Linda Sherman/ Katydid Kreations.)

mind than a state of the union. The song evokes an unspeakable desire to feel the embrace, the enveloping caress of that hickory wind of home. But it is about the unfulfillable desire, its poignance, its open-ended ache. The more the pedal-steel and acoustic guitars build to provide company in the accompaniment, the more strongly Harris's voice speaks the solo truth of yearning that only begets more yearning. The song—the country song—is as close as you can come to home. Echoing from the road, from the Atlanta high rise, from the "far-away city," from death row, "Sing Me Back Home" is the fundamental cry of American country music.

And that way too the road happens actually to lead.
—Thomas Jefferson,
    Notes on the
    State of Virginia

Into that space went wandering a road, over a hill and down out of sight . . . [into] a land without end, a space across which Noah and Adam might come straight from Genesis.
—Owen Wister,
    The Virginian

I tramp a perpetual journey, ...
My right hand pointing to landscapes of continents and the public road.
—Walt Whitman,
    "Song of Myself"

But no matter, the road is life.
—Jack Kerouac,
    On the Road

So she left Rapid City in the blue moonlight hour With her eye on the highway and her foot on the floor.
—Emmylou Harris and
    Paul Kennerley, "The
    Ballad of Sally Rose"

I've got ramblin' fever in my blood.
—Merle Haggard,
    "Ramblin' Fever"

▼ ▼ ▼ ▼ ▼ ▼ ▼ ▼ ▼ ▼ ▼ ▼ ▼ ▼ ▼ ▼ ▼ ▼ ▼

Road

From Interstate 40 in Nashville, you can exit at Demonbreun Street and, ten minutes later, pull into the Country Music Museum, where the entrance fee entitles visitors to see Elvis's 1960 white-and-gold Cadillac limousine.

"At one time, one of the most famous automobiles in the world," intones a push-button voice, adding that Elvis customized the sharp-finned, low-slung car into a "luxurious mobile lounge." While the voice narrates, the cutaway car roof lifts back on mechanized hinges to expose the tufted-gold upholstery and the 24K gold plating on every accessory, from the guitar-shaped ID to the car phone, Elvis's comb-and-brush set, his TV, even the ice-cube trays. The half-dozen gold disks lining the roof are 45 rpm record facsimiles, the engraved titles just a tanta-

▼ ▼ ▼ ▼ ▼ ▼ ▼

lizing few feet too distant to identify. *Heartbreak Hotel?* *Blue Suede Shoes?* Surely *Hound Dog.*

Scanning the King's gold, however, a visitor registers the fact that this crown jewel symbolizes career success and, beyond that, mobility on the American road. Success and mobility merge in the material fact of the car, which itself implies the road. For Elvis, it was the road from Tupelo, Mississippi, to Memphis and Sam Phillips's Sun Studios, and thereafter the world. This King's carriages were Cadillacs, and the museum's royal treasure of American popular culture idealizes the singer's relation to the road. Displaying musical instruments, song manuscripts, stage costumes, film and kinescope performances from Hank Williams to Patsy Cline, the museum becomes an automobile showroom to make a statement—that country music is intimately connected with the American road and to the values that cluster around it.

Visitors need no push-button explanation of this, for most have come in cars, vans, motorcycles, or pickups via the asphalt and concrete of the interstates. They know that the car, being a symbol of the road, actually ratifies their culture and that of twentieth-century country music. Country artists, as some visitors also know, routinely schedule six to ten months of one-nighters in cities and towns all over the United States. Roy Acuff recalls, "I've driven hundreds and hundreds of thousands of miles." And Bill Monroe proclaims his near-perfect attendance record at the *Grand Ole Opry*, with much of the rest of each week spent performing on the road. The tradition goes deep, to the mule-drawn wagon of banjoist "Uncle" Dave Macon, who hauled lumber and his banjo, and to the medicine shows Acuff and others worked to pay their dues, to the contemporary customized buses, the forty-ton "luxury liners" clocking upward of a hundred thousand miles yearly, carrying stars and their bands on tour. Not to mention the *other* legendary Cadillac of which country music buffs are always aware—the one in which Hank Williams died en route to a New Year's performance in Ohio.

Road culture begets road music, and the most abbreviated listing suggests the decades-long flow of country music "road" songs linked to the life of country musicians. In the 1920s, fiddler/singer G. B. Grayson recorded "Lee Highway," while in recent years one can cite Eddie Rabbitt's "Drivin' My Life Away," Ricky Skaggs's "Highway 40 Blues," Ricky Van Shelton's album *Backroads*, Sawyer Brown's *The Dirt Road*, Joe Diffie's *A Thousand Winding Roads*, Native American Bill Miller's *The Red Road*. And Rodney Crowell's *Keys to the Highway* seems a driver's command performance.

In terms of the American road, then, country music seems to operate in a self-contained, closed circle in which artists write and perform songs *about* the road, songs performed on a concert circuit traveled *on* the road. Attend a country music

***Elvis's golden Cadillac, on display at the
Country Music Museum, Nashville. (Courtesy
Country Music Foundation, Nashville)***

concert, and it becomes clear that the artists even wear the insignia *of* the road. The
stage curtain for Clint Black's 1992 tour shows a highway jutting west toward the
setting sun. On the 1992 Ryman World Tour, Emmylou Harris's stage wardrobe
featured a denim vest with a Harley-Davidson "live-to-ride" trademark, the broad
wings spread across the shoulders, while a vocalist and acoustic guitarist in her
band, the Nash Ramblers, wore a motorcycle-print shirt. Open a book of interviews with country music legends and notice a photo of Steve Earle in a Harley
T-shirt. Pull out Willie Nelson's album *Born for Trouble* and observe Nelson posing
on a Harley, ready to take off. You might start humming his signature song, "On
the Road Again."

All these images imply an unbound, free life on the American road. They say
these musicians are the road itself. The names of several country music groups, in
fact, refer directly to the road: Highway 101, Sawyer Brown (a group named for
a road in Nashville), Southern Pacific (a railroad), Asleep at the Wheel. (At an
Emmylou Harris Ryman Tour concert, you can buy, as I did, a purple souvenir
T-shirt with a red-printed, circa 1956 Nash automobile, a pun on Music City,

At 60, Willie Nelson back on the road again

Newspaper headline, 1993. (From the Tennessean Showcase, May 16–22, 1993)

Nashville, and on the Nash Rambler, an American car manufactured during the mid-1950s, years of U.S. interstate highway construction.)

Country music, then, can seem like a musical mega–sales force covering the 3.87 million miles of roads in the United States, paving them with "road" music, no matter whether dirt or asphalt, gravel or concrete.

But the notion prompts questions. Isn't all this road music a genre pushed by country music insiders who insist on drafting fans into their work-related obsession? Isn't the road song a form of country music shoptalk turned into a lucrative source of income?

These are leading, deliberately skeptical questions that march us to the opening of a typical country music road song, Steve Earle's "Guitar Town." Earle remarks that road themes became part of his *Guitar Town* (1986) album "because we did 77,000 miles in '83." One of his songs can serve as a demo here, as if it, too, were a museum display. Earle warns about self-pitying road songs ("People don't want to hear you feelin' sorry for yourself because you're ridin' around in a bus that costs more than their house"). But we can put his song up on the rack, so to speak. We can look underneath to check whether it runs solely on the self-generated fuel of country music customs—or whether it gets extra power, a kind of high-octane boost, from other sources in American culture. This is to ask, in effect, whether the road song begins and ends with the tape, the vinyl, the CD of country artists identified with the road—or whether it resonates more widely and deeply in American culture.

Earle's "Guitar Town" features a singer one thousand miles out of "Guitar Town," meaning Nashville. Now he speeds through Texas between Austin and San Antonio ("smokin' into Texas with the hammer down"), on the road because, as the song says, "nothin' ever happened 'round my hometown," and he's not the kind "to just hang around." More than boredom drove him out. The road is his vocation, in the classical sense of a higher calling, for he "heard someone callin' my name one day, / And followed that voice down a lost highway." This last phrase is a tribute to Hank Williams, but it is also a "lost highway" because there

[opposite page]
Country music albums featuring vehicles and symbols of the road. (Courtesy Sony Music, Keith Case and Associates, MCA Records, and Polygram Records)

is no certain destination in the immediate future, even if the singer hopes ultimately to make it back to "Guitar Town," presumably when very successful.

For now, ambition drives his restless movement. And Steve Earle sings this song aggressively, with a jut-jawed defiance in his enunciation (even the vowels are pushy, the energy barely contained). We hear a hard-driving beat from first to last, fingers seeming flung against strings and backed by a hard snare-drum beat, as if driving not just the car but himself with the "hammer down." Earle varies the time signatures, giving the effect of skipping two beats and going on to the next measure as if in a hurry, rebelling against the rules by pushing the rhythm. This man is your "good rockin' daddy down from Tennessee," and he's serious about the road odyssey, vowing that no local cop will stop him in a speed trap. He has jettisoned excess baggage—his very own bird dog—that might slow him down. Nights, stumbling half-awake into truck stop restaurants, he wonders why he doesn't stop all this, but the voice itself surges, seeming not to stop even for breath. There are no real pauses; the tone modulates higher, its own accelerator down throughout the song.

Earle's nonstop energy tells us that coming off the road is out of the question because this singer is driven to speed from gig to gig, performing with his "back to the riser" and boots on the boards. In those moments he is not just any guy with a two-pack-a-day habit and a "motel tan," meaning a pasty complexion because he never sees sunlight. He "loves to hear the steel belts hummin' on the asphalt," and, when performing, he is his essential self, taking his stand (even if, like Custer, he should perish). One of these days he'll settle down, or so he claims. But that future point is deliberately left vague in a song otherwise filled with specifics. Road life, "Guitar Town" tells us, is his calling, his vitality, his very identity.

And Emmylou Harris's version of this same song, on *Emmylou Harris and the Nash Ramblers at the Ryman* (1992), shows that a woman's life on the road can be interchangeable with a man's. Switch the lyrics to "your cool rockin' mama" addressing her "big daddy," and the song is intact as a woman's declaration of independence on the road. In Harris's arrangement, the Nash Ramblers play an important part, amplifying the reference in the lyrics to "me and the boys . . . a rockin' little combo." Roy Huskey, Jr.'s, upright bass is resonant as a heartbeat (a Chevrolet advertising metaphor that the band has exploited onstage), and here in "Guitar Town" it's a living pulse in a song about travel in a machine. Between stanzas, Al Perkins's Dobro and Randy Stewart's guitar solos earn the very title "Guitar Town." In the lyrics on driving and defying the odds of success ("Somebody told me you can't get far / On thirty-seven dollars and a Jap guitar"), Harris's tones combine hard edges and breathlessness, and you realize that her phrasing suggests high-speed driving, where the lines of the vehicle, seen from the window,

are hard-edged but the near earth itself passes in a blur. She and the boys have "got this rig unwound," and like her male counterpart, she'll be "loadin' up and rollin' out of here tonight." Wherever "here" might be for the moment, this woman is as committed to the road as any of the boys.

57

What, then, is "Guitar Town" all about? A musician's road life backed by energy and determination. But it gains much greater significance if we step forward to ask about the abstract or symbolic issues beyond the song's particulars. In the larger sense, we might say that "Guitar Town" concerns matters of individualism, identity, ambition, activism, the quest for a wider world, the assertion of a restless spirit. We can say, in short, that this song distills certain pronounced values widely held in the United States for a long time. It indicates that when country music celebrates the road, it does much more than turn inward to praise its own rites and rituals. It really suggests that country music sustains a centuries-long tradition in which the road itself is central to American culture.

Many roads are noteworthy in American history. Great ones of national expansion come to mind, like the National Road or Cumberland Road, names memorized by school kids, or the Santa Fe or Chisholm trails of the legendary Western cattle drives, or even the "underground railroad," the route to freedom for escaped slaves conducted by sympathizers to a network of safe houses leading North through the free states and into Canada.

Other American roads are grim, like the *camino real* or King's Highway winding from Mexico into New Mexico in the era of the Spanish colonial empire and experienced as a road of subjugation by the indigenous peoples. Another is the Trail of Tears from Georgia-Tennessee to Oklahoma, named for the road traveled by Cherokee tribes forcefully ejected from their southeastern homelands by the U.S. government in the 1830s. The Trail marked what one historian calls "one of the greater official acts of inhumanity and cruelty in American history," and its roadway legacy is "The Reservation Road," a song by Native American artist Bill Miller, his album suggestively titled *The Red Road* (1993). Confined to the tribal reservation road, the singer-speaker wishes he could take U.S. senators along this road, as well as listeners who are oblivious of the historical oppression that impounds populations and turns the road into a tributary of the Trail of Tears.

Which are the roads of "Guitar Town"? Not that Steve Earle researched an atlas or history books. But meanings and messages swirl from the past to the present, and on this basis we can trace the origins of "Guitar Town" to public discussion during the American Revolution. The song's lyrical road out of Nashville to Austin and San Antonio actually started over two centuries ago with a 1770s inquiry by France, specifically by the Marquis de Barbé-Marois, about conditions in eighteenth-century Virginia. The French were trying to decide whether or not to support the American revolutionaries, and they needed some data. The man to whom the marquis directed the inquiry was Thomas Jefferson.

Notes on the State of Virginia was the result, a book-length essay covering the ecology, the geography, the social history of the New World. Abruptly, in a section on mountains, Jefferson took up the subject of the American road, speaking in terms that beckoned Americans westward for a national experience encompassing travel and national expansion—and ultimately to reappear in country music.

In *Notes*, Jefferson stands his reader on a lookout facing westward toward the Shenandoah Mountains. Like a motorist or a climber at an overlook, the reader stands just at the convergence point of two great rivers, the Potomac and the Shenandoah. This is, says Jefferson, a "stupendous" scene, though before letting us enjoy it, he insists that we notice the surrounding rock rubble, a geological record of violent upheaval. "A war between rivers and mountains."

War? Jefferson naturally would have war on his mind, writing the *Notes* as he did during the Revolution. An amateur geologist, he speculated that on this very spot, a prehistoric ocean had burst its mountain-ridge dam with such force that it ripped apart an entire mountain from summit to base. Even now, forced through the mountain pass, the two rivers rush against each other and "rend" the mountains in a scene that is "wild and tremendous."

But not to worry. The visionary Jefferson is looking past the rubble—symbolically past the Revolutionary war—to paint us a "picture" of both the American future and American space. Now the reader gazes through a notch in the Blue Ridge to see a vista both "placid and delightful." And here Jefferson becomes the artist and the director of the American future—and the patron of the road. Through the notch or "cleft" in the Blue Ridge, he sees "a small catch of smooth blue horizon . . . inviting you, as it were, from the riot and tumult roaring around, to pass through the breach and participate [in] the calm below." Jefferson says it clearly: "That way too the road happens actually to lead."

That way too the road happens actually to lead. Thomas Jefferson is conducting a miniature public relations campaign with momentous implications. "You" are issued a personal invitation to seek your future in the West across and beyond the Shenandoah Mountains. Jefferson is the guide to American space and the national future, and he sees the road already built into the topography. This is a splendid coincidence—or rather, a convergence. The road has been built by Nature itself and will soon be utilized in a blending of national goals and topographic destiny. Though he wrote so briefly of the road, Jefferson established an important idea— namely, that the road is itself a built-in geologic feature of the North American continent. This is a rather remarkable point—a New World complete with roads, at least one road on an East-West axis. Americans need only seize the opportunity to use nature's gift. On Nature's behalf, Jefferson issues both an invitation and a travel voucher.

As for difficulty of transport? No matter. Jefferson says it so clearly: "That way too the road happens actually to lead." In one sweep he overarches the specific

Tom Wilson,
"Ziggy,"
1993.
(Courtesy
Universal
Press
Syndicate)

From postage
stamps to
cartoon and
ads, popular
culture em-
phasizes the
importance
of the Ameri-
can road.

hardships of travel as recorded by diarists like William Calk of Virginia, who in early spring 1775 traveled the wilderness road through the Cumberland Gap and wrote, "This morning there is ice at our camp half inch thick we start early and travel this Day along a verey Bad hilley way cross one creek whear the horses almost got mired some fell in and all wet their loads." Between William Calk and the country singer "smokin' into Texas with the hammer down" lie two centuries of bushwhacking, flattened dirt paths, widened deer trails, rutted wagon roads, civil engineering, land grabbing, graft, greed, gravel, asphalt, macadam, poured concrete.

Not that Jefferson was oblivious to the problems of transportation (after all, during his presidency he undertook the purchase of the vast western Louisiana Territory, dispatching Meriwether Lewis and William Clark to survey it and describe it in journals that read in part like that of William Calk). But Jefferson thought in visionary terms that enshrined the cross-continental American road as an inspirational symbol and conferred on the westward-moving American traveler the larger meanings of national destiny. The road itself is already in place, waiting to take us west to the place of calm blue—in fact, to the Pacific Ocean. In effect, Jefferson named the symbolic road, grounded it in American terrain, bought it, and secured the invitation.

And the Jeffersonian symbol of the road remained so powerful that the post–World War II writer of the Beat generation, Jack Kerouac, gave the nation's founders a tradition on the road when he wrote a book of that name, *On the Road*, in the 1940s and 1950s. He assigned to Benjamin Franklin, George Washington, and Daniel Boone the "black-tar roads that curve along the mournful rivers" of the eastern U.S., like the Potomac. Kerouac imagined Franklin on an ox-cart road, Washington on Indian trails, Boone seeking the Cumberland Gap route west—as if, speeding across America's highways in a Plymouth, a Cadillac, a Chevy, he saw Jefferson and the Founding Fathers in his rearview and was driven to map their roads, too, since they belonged to the "East of his youth" as he sped to the "West of his future."

Between Jefferson and Kerouac—and Steve Earle's "Guitar Town"—others were busily filling in the cultural matrix, amplifying the meaning of the American road. Earle's song, after all, proclaims several American traits not spelled out in the *Notes*, from individuality to freedom, ambition, restlessness, etcetera. To prepare the way for country music road songs, it remained for this nation's virtual poet laureate, Walt Whitman, to complete the roadbed. "Song of the Open Road" (1867), is perhaps the best-known American road text, and it marks the era of the pedestrian. "Afoot and light-hearted," Whitman says, "I take to the open road. . . . Strong and content I travel the open road." Whitman's road, like Jefferson's, "stretches and waits for you."

Whitman's road is not for exercise but for freedom. It promises to liberate Americans from deadening routine, as if the poet anticipated the lament in "Guitar Town" that "nothin' ever happened 'round my hometown." Whitman castigates the "hometowns" for materialism, hypocrisy, regimentation, and he calls for an abandonment of conventional, routinized life:

(*Photograph © 1992 Bob and Suzanne Clemenz*)

Let the paper remain on the desk unwritten, and the book on the shelf unopened! Let the tools remain in the workshop! Let the money remain unearn'd!

He calls for rebellion: "I nourish active rebellion." But it is rebellion against the sleepwalk of conventionality (that is, of school and workplace).

In terms of personal, individual development, Whitman raised the stakes tremendously in "Song of the Open Road," arguing that individuals are woefully *in*complete if they fail to go on the road. His sojourner becomes "my own master total and absolute," with "freedom from limits." And Whitman proclaimed other attributes of the American open road, including health, freedom of choice, heroic deeds and art, above all the expanded consciousness. The road is the pathway of self-development and self-improvement. As a result of road life,

I am larger, better than I thought,
I did not know I held so much goodness.

And the possession of American space means self-possession:

I inhale great draughts of space,
The east and the west are mine, and the north and the south are mine.

On the American open road, one is "forever alive, forever forward . . . go[ing] to-ward the best—toward something great." With all these meanings intact, country music road songs like "Guitar Town" would ultimately become the sons and heirs not only of Jefferson but of Walt Whitman too. Their writings formed the cultur-al basis for such country songs as "Ramblin' Man," "I'm Movin' On," or Rodney Crowell/Keith Sykes's "Let Freedom Ring," which celebrates a woman "out on the highway," going "where she wants to go . . . burnin' down in Mexico / Freez-ing up in Buffalo"—the very incarnation of freedom as the term echoes from the quasi national anthem ("from every mountainside / Let freedom ring"). The ide-ology behind these songs is to be found in Dolly Parton's paraphrase of Walt Whitman: "This day and time, you can be what you want to be, . . . and if you don't venture out to try to be what it is you want to be, then you are a fool. You've served no purpose in life; you have failed as a person in life if you don't try what your heart says to do."

But what about home? What of Whitman's contemporaries, writers also linked with country music's heritage—like Ralph Waldo Emerson and Harriet Beecher Stowe? They enshrined the idea of home as the authentic center of national life while Whitman ecstasized about the American road. They were busy confirming the agrarian naturalness of the American home (and preparing the way for country music's multitude of home songs), even as Whitman extolled the virtues of the road and beckoned his readers to it.

Not in a gentle invitation, either, but a summons. The stay-at-homes must be re-sisted, Whitman argued. They will mock and cling, their inertial powers both a nasty irony and a clutching grasp. His contemporary, Herman Melville, seconded the motion in *Moby-Dick*, the epic nautical novel in which home is port and the road the open ocean. Home port is the domestic comfort of "hearthstone, supper, warm blankets," but it is also "treacherous" and "slavish," imprisoning the indi-vidual in mind-numbing safety. What a clash. What a mismatch. The road versus the home. Walt and Herman versus Ralph Waldo and Harriet. We can imagine the nineteenth-century authorial portraits glaring at each other from their walnut oval frames. Even now, in the late twentieth century, vestiges of their battle continue in

Thomas P. Otter, On the Road, 1860. Oil on canvas, 22 × 45¾ in. (Courtesy The Nelson-Atkins Museum of Art, Kansas City, purchase, Nelson Trust, 50-1.) See also Plate 2.

a much-subdued form. Television celebrates the road in series like *The Fugitive* and *Route 66* and continuing from the 1954 Marlon Brando film *The Wild One*, about a gang of rebel motorcyclists. (In June 1993, TV network news featured as intrinsically newsworthy the quasi convention in Milwaukee of some twenty thousand Harley-Davidson owner-riders.) On network TV from the 1970s to the 1990s, journalist Charles Kuralt has been a single male "on the road." If Kuralt presents a cozy, fatherly image of the armchair traveler in his RV, he is nonetheless a self-styled onetime "curious rover . . . for twenty-three years roaming the backroads of America."

Popular media, all the while, have continuously idolized the American home. TV has made home-based families, from the Cleavers to the Waltons to the Bradies and Huxtables a byword, and monthlies like *Hearth and Home* and *Country Living* fill the wicker magazine racks of upper-middle-class rooms papered in Laura Ashley prints.

In country music, then, is it "Guitar Town" versus "Home?" Are these the battle lines drawn in the music as in the culture at large? Face it, the country rocker "smokin' into Texas" in Steve Earle's song is not one bit nostalgic for his hometown. Wouldn't dream of going back. "Guitar Town," then, does not fit the home song paradigm in which the city, whether Austin or Atlanta or Baltimore or L.A., stirs poignant yearnings for home and sorrow for having left. Earle's

64

song, on the contrary, makes the hometown a site of boredom, tedium, dullness, inertia. No yearnings there.

So we ask again: Is it "Guitar Town" versus "Home?"

Well, not exactly.

Country music manages to avoid the head-on clash in a very cunning way. Notice, first, country's subtle, crucial distinction between *home* and *hometown*. The idea of home is sacrosanct, as we know. It calls up the sacred bonds of kinship, nature, family ideals, authenticity, the ultimate in protective nurturance. Rare indeed is the country song representing American road life as a rejection of *that* largesse.[1]

But home and hometown are not synonymous. Home*town* is another thing altogether. It can be presented as deadly dull, entrapping, smothering. Or the hometown can be exposed as intolerant, blind to the virtues of its offspring, cruelly rejecting its native sons or daughters—which is the focus of "Rollin' and Ramblin'," the Robin Williams/Linda Williams/Jerome Clark song about the death of Hank Williams (on the Williams's album, *All Broken Hearts Are the Same*, 1988). Hank Williams (no relation to the songwriters) is never named directly in the song, though the Williamses make his identity explicit in a parenthetical subtitle, "(The Death of Hank Williams)."

"Folks in Nashville slammed the door," the song begins. Williams, in fact, was a native of Mt. Olive, Alabama, near Montgomery, but the song makes his musical hometown Nashville, where he published his music, found the mentor, Fred Rose, who secured his recording contracts, and then, in June 1949, debuted on the *Grand Ole Opry* with "Lovesick Blues" before an ecstatic audience that brought him back some six times to repeat the final lines of the song: "I'm lonesome, I got the lovesick blues."

---

1. Country music's ambivalence about the split between the road and the home is both masked and revealed in many artists' favorite term, *family*, referring to the musician/employees who tour with headliners. Willie Nelson's group is the Travelling Family Band, while Don Williams has said, "We try to have a home life" on the road. Says Emmylou Harris of her acoustic group, the Nash Ramblers, "We really became a . . . family." The family metaphor is currently applied widely to American work groups from professional sports teams to juries. It has also been extended to European music, as when maestro Kurt Masur describes touring with the New York Philharmonic ("traveling together in one airplane gives us the feeling of being a family"). As for country music, one writer comments on the strategic advantage of this term: "The invocation of family . . . seems to produce immediate sympathy among tradition-minded fans." The term also obscures the fact that the band members are employees and that actual family members are not present on the road tours.

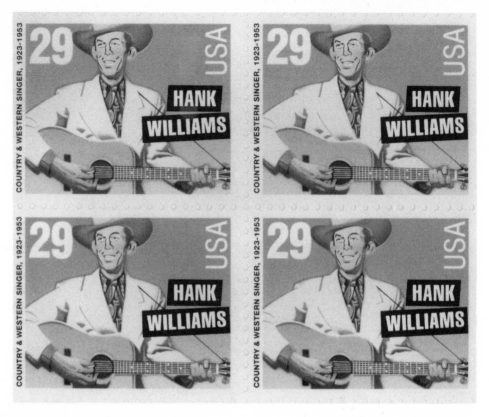

**Hank Williams stamp. American Music Series,
U.S. Postal Service, 1993.**

By autumn 1951, however, the Nashville folks "slammed the door," as "Rollin'
and Ramblin'" says, meaning that the Opry management fired the alcoholic and
drug-dependent Williams for failing to appear for scheduled shows and for performing while drunk. "We don't want you anymore," says the song in the voice of
the parental Nashville, disowning this native son of country music, ordering him
to pack up his fiddle and guitar (figuratively, his band, the Drifting Cowboys) and
to find his own way "down the road":

> Take a train or take a car
> Find someone else to keep you from the cold.

They ejected him, sent him south, back to one-nighters in high school gyms and
honky-tonks. True, "Rollin' and Ramblin'" says, Williams "sang with whiskey on
his breath," though his stage presence was by all accounts electrifying. "Women
loved him half to death," goes the song in the southern idiom, referring to his
womanizing, his troubled first marriage, and the adulation of fans, but alluding
also to the actual physical impact of his voice. Minnie Pearl has called it "animal

magnetism," and one listener explains that Hank Williams's voice could "make you laugh or cry" because it "went through you like electricity, sent shivers up your spine, and made the hair rise on the back of your neck with a thrill."

"Rollin' and Ramblin'" links Williams with all the road traditions of country music: the hobo drifter songs, the cowboy songs ("the sun has set out on the trail"), the train songs in a blues tradition, identified with the train whistle he mimicked in one of his own songs, "(I Heard That) Lonesome Whistle." The very title of "Rollin' and Ramblin'" refers to Hank Williams's "Ramblin' Man," a song in which the singer is self-identified as a figure on the road ("When the Lord made me, he made a ramblin' man").

And the automobile road is prominent in this song too, as it was in Hank Williams's life on tour, but here in special reference to his death by alcoholic cardiomyopathy in the back seat of his own Cadillac, while he was being driven in a snowstorm from Montgomery to Canton, Ohio, for a New Year's show:

> He didn't sing at all that night
> He was pale and as he dozed
> He didn't know his time had closed
> Slumped in the back seat to the right.

So in one sense the death is consistent with the life; as the song title says, Williams's was a life of rolling and rambling, a life that fittingly ended on the road.

But the unforgivable sin in "Rollin' and Ramblin'" is Williams's rejection by the hometown Nashville folks and the devastating impact on the singer/songwriter:

> His heart broke like a child's.

This line is crucial, putting Hank Williams in a child/parent relation to Nashville, blaming his fatal heart attack on the parental city. The line tells us this native son was rejected, abandoned by his adoptive hometown. He died on the road (at age twenty-nine), not as a son obeying his musical calling but as a son disowned. He is not, then, a child of Nashville who might return to "Guitar Town" at will, coming home regularly to reaffirm the old bonds. He is, on the contrary, homeless, and "Rollin' and Ramblin'" holds the hometown responsible for unconscionable cruelty, for the death of its begotten genius.

Linda and Robin Williams sing this song in part in tones of defiant anger. Her smoky voice is clipped, the pace up-tempo as if impatient to report the outrage. (By starting on A, the five-chord, the song leads a listener to expect the key of A instead of the actual key, which is D.) The Williamses give this song a Cajun beat, perhaps a reference to Hank Williams's phenomenally successful "Jambalaya."

Robin and Linda Williams. (Photograph by Irene Young; courtesy New Music Times, Charlottesville, Va.)

The tempo serves a celebratory impulse too, for the Williamses' version of "Rollin' and Ramblin'" celebrates the life of Hank Williams. Their duet gusto in the refrain endorses Hank's musical life of rolling and rambling, all the while singing the blues superbly. There is zest in their report of the fans' adoration. The Williamses sing in tones of pain for the pallor of the dying man, just as they express anger at Nashville's unwarranted rejection of him. But celebration of his life governs their interpretation in this musical eulogy.

Emmylou Harris's version is very different. No longer reporting the news of Hank Williams's ouster (Linda and Robin Williams have already done that), Harris sings in tonal astonishment that it could have occurred at all. Recounting the expulsion from Nashville (". . . said we don't want you anymore"), her voice breaks high in a kind of gasp, seeming to say that the mind cannot grasp this magnitude of stupidity and cruelty.

If the Williamses' "Rollin' and Ramblin'" essentially celebrates the country star's life, Harris's is an act of mourning (not by chance does she work that subtitle). The Harris version centers on the lyric that identifies Williams's music with the bluest note of the train whistle, "moanin' sad and cryin' low." That becomes her musical guideline. As Harris reviews the Hank Williams biography, her phrasing suggests homage being paid, if not to next-of-kin, surely to a kindred spirit. We hear the delicacy of a lullaby in the phrase, "His heart broke like a child," then experience a rich vocal slide into sorrow that "he didn't sing at all that night," the night he died. Harris slows the tempo to fit her mournful tone, and the arrangement becomes a kind of slow Cajun two-step, the reedy sound of Jo-El Sonnier's French accordion enhancing the sense of loss.

Loss, yes—but with one exception at the refrain, when the voices of singers Barry Tashian and Melba Montgomery join to form a chorus, energizing the song and preparing for Harris's ultimate image of Williams as a cowboy riding the trail of memory, his musical legacy intact. "He's taken his last ride," the lyric says, but Harris refuses the finality of *last* to embrace the idea of the ride, concluding in a kind of cowboy-song whoop. The vocalized ending might have been a mourner's funeral keening. Instead, it soars almost to a Western trailriding "Yippeee," a thanks and salute to Williams as a legend whose music lives on. Forever he rides some Chisholm or Santa Fe trail of myth. In a way, then, Hank Williams dies on the road to Canton and is mythically reincarnated on the Western road of the cattle drives. Either way, he never leaves the road.

How about ourselves? Feeling cramped and road weary, we might pull off to gas up and stretch, maybe look at the map and check some secondary routes. For the visionary Jefferson and Whitman are not the only important roadmakers on the scene. Plenty of others weigh in, surprisingly, to post warnings of hairpin curves, steep grades, poor visibility. The road can be dire and deadly, they say.

Country music tells us this in both song and biography. Patsy Cline's fatal air crash is probably the best-known country music "road" disaster, recalled especially in 1991 when Reba McEntire's entire band died in their chartered aircraft. Ira Louvin of the *Grand Ole Opry*'s Louvin Brothers was killed in an automobile accident, and Roy Acuff was nearly killed in a head-on. The list does not stop there.

These kinds of roadway disasters are duly reported in country songs. "Bad News," by Emmylou Harris/Paul Kennerley, features the highway "wreck" in which some close friend or intimate, "drivin' fast in distress / Hit a curve and died in the darkness." Dorsey Dixon's "Crash on the Highway," renamed "Wreck on the Highway" in Roy Acuff's recording, warned against drunk driving, while "White Line," also a Harris/Kennerley song (*The Ballad of Sally Rose*, 1986), describes double jeopardy, a roadway death both by accident and by drugs, lethal lines of cocaine. "White line took my baby / Led him down that lost highway."

Other routes in the atlas of American culture chart the treachery of the road to which we have been so seductively invited, summoned, directed. John Steinbeck's Nobel Prize–winning road novel, *The Grapes of Wrath* (1939), telegraphs this: "Big car. Big Cad. Hit a truck. Folded the radiator right back to the driver." Amid 1930s Depression-era dustbowl drought and farm foreclosures, Steinbeck set his poor,

**Grant Wood, Death on Ridge Road, 1935. Oil on Masonite, 32 × 39 in.
(Courtesy Williams College Museum of Art, gift of Cole Porter, 47.1.3)**

"Okie" Joad family on their own Trail of Tears, west from the Oklahoma panhandle onto Route 66, "the long concrete path across the country . . . from the Mississippi [River] to Bakersfield [California]."

Turn back a historical page, and take note of Steinbeck's predecessors. Hamlin Garland's stories in *Main-Travelled Roads* (1891) showed a "long and weariful" farm road connecting "a home of toil at one end, and a dull little town at the other." And if the American road can be a mythical waterway, a river of escape to freedom for a literary character like Huckleberry Finn, it can also be a road of oppression for slaves "sold down river" to antebellum Deep South plantations, farther and farther from the free states. Even the underground railroad from slavery to freedom was fraught with terror, as the former slave Frederick Douglass acknowledged on the eve of an escape attempt: "When we permitted ourselves to survey the road, we were frequently appalled. Upon either side we saw grim death."

This lethal road leads on, becoming graphic in gender terms in a contemporary film of the 1990s. The title characters of *Thelma and Louise* (Geena Davis and Susan Sarandon) gain personal strengths, learn survival. Their friendship deepening, they achieve independence, self-sufficiency, identity itself during their western odyssey from Arkansas to Colorado in a Thunderbird convertible. But in the view of a male society, they are disgraced—worse, criminals with no place to go. Their lost highway arcs inevitably, fatally into the Grand Canyon.

And gender has a dire relevance on the roadway, even without death. True, "Guitar Town" shows a "cool rockin' mama" easily adopting the terms of her male counterpart. But Rodney Crowell/Donivan Cowart show us a different woman's road song in "Leavin' Louisiana in the Broad Daylight" (*Ain't Living Long Like This*, 1978). Calling this "an ordinary story 'bout the way things go," Crowell recollects Texas-Louisiana bordertown honky-tonks where girls dominated by their fathers or uncles "would like to get in their car or get in a car with some stranger and just drive off, right in broad daylight." At first, then, "Leavin' Louisiana" seems like one more story of an impossible hometown and the itch to flee. Crowell relates the story as if he had overheard the rancorous mother-daughter household back-and-forth before Mary ran off with the traveling man her mother warned her against. Mary voices her own desperation: "Gotta go, gotta get out of here, gotta get out of town."

But the Louisianan has no illusions about long-term happiness or excitement waiting down that road that rolls on between the ditches of the bayou country. Her lingering memory is "mama crying with her head in her hands." This Mary cannot go back, not only because she is restless and dying to get out from under, but because she has now disgraced herself and brought disgrace upon her patriarchal family. In her father's eyes, she is a daughter "gone bad." It seemed so *right* to flee, but the number-6 minor chord brings an ache into her tone as she sings her bone-deep understanding that the road life is essentially the lifelong, incessant movement of an exile. There is nowhere to go *to*. "The highway goes on forever / Oh, that ol' highway goes on forever."

The road can be a route of emotional anguish for a man as well. "Highway 86" (by Barry Tashian/Holly Tashian) takes its title from the restaurant code for a shutdown of menu items or a general closing down—in this case of a woman's ice-cold love that sends her lover "burnin' up the highway":

> No one gets their kicks on Highway 86
> It's a long lonesome road goin' down.

Here the highway experience—"doin' time on Route 86"—is an emotional prison term served in solitary.

Even for Whitman—if we read the fine print in "Song of the Open Road." Those on his road are often "sad, withdrawn, baffled, mad, turbulent, feeble, dissatisfied, / Desperate, proud, fond, sick, accepted by men, rejected by men." On the road, Whitman's American "goes often with a spare diet, poverty, angry enemies, desertions."

Ugh.

So another question arises. Given the misery and the jeopardy, why is the road continually so alluring, even irresistible? Why are road movies so intriguing, novels of the road successful, American road art so prominent in museums across the nation? Why, in song after song, does country music exalt this nomadic pattern even as it records the perils and disappointments?

To be more specific, given two competing versions of the road—path to freedom or to trouble—why for the most part does the celebratory Jefferson/Whitman one win out? If country music and a "school" of writers say the Great American Road is a Siren song to death, danger, and disillusionment, how is it that the tradition of the warning—the caveat—has not prevailed?

The answer lies in yet another American tradition exalting the kinetic, the action-oriented. The *real* Americans, this tradition says, are mobile, migratory, questing, surging, driving, continually on the move. They are, in a word, restless. *Restless.* The very term is a national keyword, an essential concept in the American cultural vocabulary. "O resistless restless race!" proclaimed Walt Whitman of America's pioneers. "Restless" became Alexis de Tocqueville's one-word description of Americans. The nineteenth-century French social critic of American life devoted a whole chapter to the subject of "this strange unrest," Americans being "restless in the midst of abundance." Reflecting on the history of African Americans to be read in Negro spirituals, W. E. B. Du Bois identified in positive terms the "soul-hunger, the restlessness of the savage." Ezra Pound, the twentieth-century American poet and essayist, saw restlessness as the engine driving American history. Reflecting in the 1910s on "my country" ("Patria Mia"), Pound says it was "the migratory element" that founded the United States. While the "static" part of the population stayed in the Old World, the restless "pushed on to new forests, to mines, to grazing lands." The first Americans were restless men of dreams "who built railways, cleared the forest, planned irrigation." Three or four generations in, the pattern still held. The "static" part of the population was left "marooned and inert," but the restless pushed on, for instance to the pioneers' Kansas of the 1850s.

The restless, undulating road is central to a crucial event in the founding of the United States, as pictured in Grant Wood, **Midnight Ride of Paul Revere,** *1931. Oil on Masonite, 30 × 40 in. (Courtesy The Metropolitan Museum of Art, New York, Arthur H. Hearn Fund, 50.117. © Estate of Grant Wood/VAGA, New York, 1993.) See also Plate 6.*

Or the 1840s. "We yankees [are] born to rove," proclaimed the nineteenth-century New England journalist Margaret Fuller, who published an account of her own roving in the Great Lakes region. Steinbeck grabbed the term in the 1930s ("It's like a whole country is movin' . . . hungry and restless—restless as ants. . . . Every one of us . . . are descended from the restless ones"). Restlessness is crucial to Kerouac's *On the Road*, in which American highways become the refuge of the restless. It is the cherished trait undergirding the American "road" movies, including the 1940s series (*The Road to Rio*, *The Road to Bali*), extending to the 1960s psychedelic motorcycle adventure, *Easy Rider* (1969), even to *Thelma and Louise*, with the film supporting the women's journey to the fatal end. Perhaps the trait got its official stamp in the 1993 Inaugural Address at the U.S. Capitol, when incoming President William Jefferson (Bill) Clinton said, "Americans have ever been a restless, questing, hopeful people."

BY JONATHAN MASLOW

A ROAD FOR THE RESTLESS

The Natchez Trace changed from serving the necessity of transport to the pleasure of travel, but the two-lane blacktop from Natchez to Nashville still evokes America.

PHOTOGRAPHY BY LORI WASELCHUK

This restless "gene" shows itself in country music titles like "I'm Movin' On," "Ramblin' Man," "Ramblin' Fever," in Laurie Lewis's album title, *Restless, Ramblin' Heart* (1986), not to mention at least a half-dozen bands over the years who have called themselves Ramblers and the many railroad songs, from A. P. Carter's "Wabash Cannonball" to Ervin Rouse's "Orange Blossom Special," not to mention the many truck songs like Dave Dudley's "Six Days on the Road." And the very song "Restless," opening with a "country girl" at the Greyhound counter asking for a ticket to anyplace because she's "restless" and "gotta get out of town," her voice gunning like an engine ("Yeah . . . I gotta go right now"). Emmylou Harris's version of this song brings us back to her 1920s–30s country music predecessor, Jimmie Rodgers. "It's good times here, but it's better down the road," sang Rodgers in "The Brakeman's Blues," the line capturing the attitude of many of his songs—optimistic, but, as Dorothy Horstman says, "eternally restless."

The restless, however, can pay a huge price even if they don't suffer actual or emotional smash-ups. The mainstream texts of the American road tend to glide over this dark underside. It is seldom seen or heard in Whitman and Co.'s chants on American freedom, individualism, exhilaration. But Whitman aside, the price tag for roadway restlessness is firmly attached to one of this nation's most cherished ideological values. This price tag doesn't dangle whimsically like the tag on Minnie Pearl's country-comedian hat but is clamped like Kryptonite on a part of the American identity extolled in every form of expression from the visual arts to presidential speeches. The ideological value—a national product—is individualism. And country music's restlessness forces into view just how exorbitant is the price of an individual's roadway freedom.

Merle Haggard's ballad "Ramblin Fever," a direct descendant of Hank Williams's "Ramblin' Man," is the case in point. Haggard's is a report from the road, the singer-speaker representing himself as victim of an infectious illness—ramblin' fever—traceable to the sound of a "lonesome whistle" he heard long ago. The chief symptom is his compulsive, lifelong highway rambling. Like the singer in "Guitar Town," he has no choice but to travel the roads incessantly. He tells us

Merle Haggard on his **Ramblin' Fever** *album.* **(Courtesy MCA Records)**

right off, "My hat don't hang on the same nail too long / My ears can't stand to hear the same old song."

He rejects a settled life in all its guises. It can be the soft mud of highway shoulders that can only bog him down. Or an occasional romantic and domestic interlude when, lying on a sofa, he allows a "pretty lady" to rub his back, the next morning drinking coffee in her kitchen and "talkin' about when I'll be comin' back." At this point, Haggard drops back to a half-time rhythm, relaxing the song itself. But the listener notices Haggard's verb forms: "There's times that I would like to bed down on a sofa. . . ." *Would like to*, but it is only fantasy. As far as we know, he never actually allows himself the comfort, the pleasure. And here, too, he is the son of "Song of the Open Road" (in which Whitman chides his traveler, "However sweet . . . however convenient this dwelling, we cannot remain here"). This ramblin' man is so jealous of, so protective of his life on the road that his erotic and nurturant time-outs are only imagined. The most dangerous off-road trap is clearly female, and "Ramblin' Fever" is a song of macho vigilance. "If someone said I ever gave a damn they damn sure told you wrong. . . . I don't let no woman tie me down."

Like the restless in Whitman or Melville, this singer has no wish to be cured of his much-vaunted malady, boasting on the contrary that his disease is incurable, that this fever never subsides and defies any kind of treatment. In fact, when he says ramblin' fever cannot be "measured by degrees," he expresses contempt for measurement itself, not only by medical thermometers but by other such gadgets pervasive in a society prone to regimentation and standardization from cradle to grave. His, he boasts, is a passion that surpasses all quantification.

Merle Haggard, accordingly, sings this song in ways that subvert musical patterning. He proves his commitment to the message of the lyrics by varying tempo so that his rhythm cannot be measured by metronome (a musical thermometer of sorts). He drops the first beat of each measure on the chorus phrase, "*ramb*lin' fever," as if to accelerate hard. And his bass tones refuse to settle down. When he sings, for instance, that he will not leave the highway "long enough to bog down in the mud," the deep bass of the word *mud* moves by half-steps and quarter-tones, roaming the staff, evading any set pitch. "Mud" stops before the note ever settles.

Notice, however, the fevered ramblin' man's grim hope for his future: to "die along the highway and rot away like some old highline pole." Not Rest in Peace but rot in anonymity, unmourned, unmarked, un-human as a utility pole. This is not the individual's existential triumph but his obliteration. The ultimate freedom from human ties becomes an isolationist's vision of obliteration in an image approaching the brutal. Solitude, independence, self-sufficiency—all qualities coalescing in individualism—lead the restless rambler to an ignominious end. As

Merle Haggard and the road. (Photograph by Norman Seeff; courtesy Country Music Foundation, Nashville)

long as he stays in motion, he is the admirable, invincible individual. But when he stops, the liability of his restlessness shows through like the cake under the icing. Friendless, lacking companions or community, he is the individual as total isolate.

Inflexible, set in his ways, this particular ramblin' man can seem like a very extreme case of individualism. His example can send us searching for a more moderate alternative. Surely, we protest, it must be possible both to rove and to love. Surely roadway individualists can also cultivate human connections. This one song aside, surely the situation is not so bleak. Isn't there a road song of an individualist who also cares for another human being? Can't we turn up one such song?

Yes, and guess where? Right back in Steve Earle's *Guitar Town*. In the title song, remember, the country rocker "smokin' into Texas" leads an unfettered road life. He is freedom incarnate, a version of Haggard's ramblin' man and all other representations in the macho roll call of Whitman, Steinbeck, Kerouac, etcetera. But give that country music road rocker a past, and the terms change radically. Reveal that he is a father and has a little son, and the road song veers sharply in a different direction.

Steve Earle's "Little Rock 'n' Roller" is a father's pained and plaintive cry from the road, as the musician/father phones his little son from a truck stop somewhere on the Arkansas line. This dad has been logging his interstate miles while the "little guy," nicknamed "little rock 'n' roller," has been growing up so fast he can now answer the phone. The new skill measures the father's absence and leads him to ask, Has he been gone *that* long? The child makes the essential statement, that he misses his daddy. He asks, Is he coming home tonight?

No—because a couple of weeks' driving and a couple of thousand miles separate them. The rocker is a pay-phone parent, and every phrase expresses the anguish of his separation from this child. Earle's delivery of macho sensuality blocks sentimentality. He sings as a father *and* as a man, and the combination fosters the tension and conflict that make this a complex song. The heavy drumbeat of the rocker/father lightens in the bedtime lyrics to the child, then pounds again as the dad speaks of his adult life. Earle has commented that, in performance, "the better ["Little Rock 'n' Roller"] comes off, the harder it is on you." Believe it. This musician/father is in a terrible bind, committed like the truckers to a big-diesel life of the road, to knockin' 'em dead on the stage and on the interstates—but yet loving his little son, who is with him only in wallet photos and in the blessing invoked in the name of the guardian angel watching over little rock 'n' rollers and their daddies. By the close of the song, hearing both the music-box chime of the nursery and the synthesizer's throb of the big-rig diesel horn, we know what the entire song has been telling us, that the American road is both the man's individualist identity and the father's unspeakable pain. Earle's delivery says that the two parts of this man's life are as necessary as they are irreconcilable. They cannot be brought together, and the resultant pain is excruciating.

Walt Whitman was careful not to represent the American road as an easy escape from situational or psychological problems or as a quest for material riches. He said of road life, "I carry my old delicious burdens, / I carry them with me wherever I go, / I swear it is impossible for me to get rid of them." Resisting sentimentalizing the road, his term *delicious* nonetheless tends to overturn the negatives, sugaring the many burdens very nearly into a confection. Steinbeck does much the same in calling Route 66 "the mother road," the maternal image of nurturance and protection obscuring the anguish of the Okies in their roadway journey as refugees displaced from their homes. But country music at its frankest resists these palliatives, insisting instead that we face head-on the emotional costs of our most beloved national identities. It tells us how much we Americans ride a toll road.

High Lonesome

In southeastern Kansas, off State Highway 166 between Wayside and Bolton, is the site of a pioneering homestead, the Little House on the Prairie, a tourist attraction commemorating Laura Ingalls Wilder's popular prize-winning book about her own family life on the Kansas prairie in 1869–70. "Kansas was an endless flat land covered with tall grass blowing in the wind," wrote Wilder in *Little House on the Prairie* (1935). At night, she continued, "the wind made a lonely sound in the grass."

Tourists do not visit the Little House on the Prairie to listen to that lonely wind, even if it now stirs the wheat stalks as it once did the prairie grasses. They go instead to visit a world they knew as children and watched on television. They seek the actuality of American pioneer family life, which is represented in the house of hand-hewed timbers shaped to the exact dimensions named in Wilder's novel. When visitors come here to see the replica, they hope to verify themes emphasized in the novel. The very timbers, chimney, table, and stools reflect the values of the Little House world—family solidarity, self-reliance, initiative, versatility, self-sufficiency.

Certainly not loneliness.

But wait a minute. If Wilder's lonely-sounding wind seems a mere poetic footnote, look closer and you'll see a series of similar moments shot through the Little House world like light through chinks in a cabin wall. A bachelor neighbor of the Ingalls family confesses that he is sometimes "mighty lonely," and the homestead feels "empty and lonely" when Pa leaves for a few days' trip to Independence for supplies. The world again feels "quiet and lonely" when the nearby Osage Indians ride away in procession. Finally, when the Ingalls family is forced to uproot and depart (unwittingly having built their Kansas home on Osage tribal land), the Minnesota-bound family takes its last look at the Kansas house and stable and finds them "lonely in the stillness." In each case, someone who ought to be present, or used to be, is no longer there, and the absence fosters feelings of loneliness.

Loneliness is entwined with music, too, in an episode that jumps out of this novel like a scene from a pop-up book. Suddenly, in a chapter entitled "Texas Longhorns," the cowboy West thunders into this world of farming, homesteading, domestic life. The Ingalls homestead, we learn, lies on the cattle trail to Fort Dodge, and the Longhorn herds and their cowboy drovers camp so close to the Little House that the family can see the cowboys in chaps, spurs, western hats, bandanas, pistols on hips—standard fare in Western movies decades later.

And just as "Pa" Ingalls's fiddle provides music, so do the cowboys. At night when the cattle quiet down and the cowboys begin to sing, Laura listens. "Their songs were not like lullabies. They were high, lonely, wailing songs, almost like the howling of wolves. . . . The lonely songs seemed to be crying for the moon. They made Laura's throat ache."

So loneliness was present after all.

But memory plays interesting tricks. The cowboys and their lonesome songs are likely to remain vividly in mind while the other "lonesome" moments fade or even fail to register. The mournful musical wailing around the campfire is graphic to the eye and the ear; but the Ingalls family's sequence of "lonesome" moments comes and goes without much notice, as if the pioneer/novelist only needed a few stock adjectives off the shelf and reached casually for an "l" word. Somehow it seems natural for the cowboys to sing lonesome songs—and equally natural for the lone-

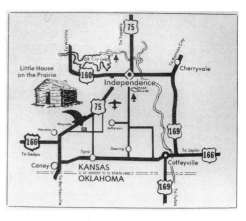

Little House on the Prairie visitor's brochure and map. (Courtesy Independence, Kansas, Chamber of Commerce and Mrs. William Kurtis)

some moments in the Ingallses' life to be fleeting and negligible, even though they crop up before the bovine hoofs ever rumble onto the family homestead and continue long after the cowboys and Longhorns have gone on to the Fort Dodge stockyards.

Did we come all the way to southeastern Kansas only to tease out these "lonely" moments and play a memory game? Of course not. We are here to confront an American enigma. Country music, the tradition in which cowboy songs belong, is ballasted by songs of loneliness. It is absolutely fitting, in the country-western tradition, for Wilder's cowboys to sing throat-aching songs of loneliness. Decades of Western movies even prime us for a soundtrack, perhaps the soulful line about "this lonesome cattle call" ("Cattle Call") or the strains of "Carry Me Back to the Lone Prairie." The onstage western wear favored by so many country artists allies country music with cowboys, from Jimmie Rodgers and Hank Williams to the so-called "hat" acts of the 1980s–90s (e.g., George Strait, Ricky Van Shelton, Alan Jackson). And any dozen country albums chosen at random yield a hefty number of "lonesome" songs, from the Carter Family's "Sinking in the Lonesome Sea," to Jimmie Rodgers's "I'm Lonesome and Blue," to Hank Williams's "I'm So Lone- 81

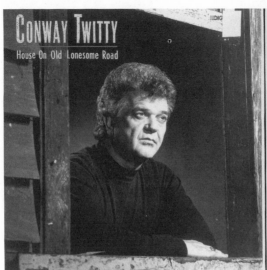

some I Could Cry," and extending to Vince Gill's "Never Knew Lonely," the O'Kanes's "Oh Lonesome You," and Randy Travis's album, *High Lonesome*.

Country music legends have all recorded songs on this theme. Johnny Cash sings in "Cold Lonesome Morning" that he "got lonely too early this morning . . . before [he] was ready to hurt," and Tammy Wynette counters with "Lonely Days (And Nights More Lonely)," the waltz time of a dance *à deux* accenting this woman's singleness. "Just Call Me Lonesome," goes a Radney Foster title, while a "lost soul" in Gram Parsons's hard-driving "Luxury Liner" cries out the identical wounding self-confirmation.

If country "owns" one American theme above all others, then that theme is surely ground-level loneliness. It is no exaggeration to say that country music is a kind of reservoir for the expression of loneliness in this nation. The Little House cowboy scene recollected from the 1870s can make Laura Ingalls Wilder seem like a canny futurist.

Elsewhere in this culture, however, loneliness seems at most to get an honorable—or maybe dishonorable—discharge. The subject appears muted, submerged, oblique, absent outright. Print texts and visual arts barely seem to register the lonely state of mind—or of heart. An occasional poem breaks the surface and sends out its ripples, as in Walt Whitman or William Carlos Williams. A passage in a novel or story may give us pause, as in Sherwood Anderson, F. Scott Fitzgerald, or Ernest Hemingway. Infrequently, a painter brings loneliness to the canvas as an overriding theme, as Edward Hopper did. And occasionally a notable social commentary appears, like Philip Slater's *The Pursuit of Loneliness* (1972), which argues that contemporary consumerism is a futile effort to overcome a

Country music albums featuring
songs of loneliness.
(Courtesy MCA Records and
Hilltop Records)

83

▼ ▼ ▼ ▼ ▼ ▼ ▼

High

Lonesome

deep-seated American loneliness. But these few examples are the exceptions that prove the rule. Considering the sheer mass and volume of written and visual production in this nation's history, loneliness survives only as a passing motif, a decorative touch, a minor subtheme. Country music tells us how deeply important it is, but elsewhere in America *loneliness*, for the most part, seems written in invisible ink.

This has not been true of other topics, like home or the road. So why loneliness?

Because, some suggest, on this particular subject the country songwriters and artists have gone off on a tangent, have overindulged and gotten themselves staggering drunk on the tears and pathos of the self-styled bereft who insist on wallowing in their own misery. Those taking this view tend to grow impatient with a musical genre they think encourages and promotes a mawkish self-pity.

Yet there is another interpretation: that on the subject of loneliness in America, country music is carrying a very heavy—a disproportionately heavy—cultural load. This means that on the whole, the nation allows country music to be the vehicle for the expression of an emotion that seems otherwise unbearable and unspeakable. It means, in other words, that country music has a special cultural license to express a feeling so deeply and profoundly disturbing that, elsewhere in society, it is muted, half-hidden, suppressed, treated like a kind of skeleton in the American closet.

To take this second proposal seriously is to take on a whole backpack of obligations. We must explore the issue, try to grasp how this state of affairs has come about, try to find out what particular forms it has taken. Where can we even begin to look? *Location, location, location,* say real estate agents of the crucial element in their work. But outside of country music, where is this emotional territory of lone-liness to be found? When a taboo of denial surrounds it, how can we gain access to that apparently vacant lot?

One approach is to go back to games—in this case, a kind of video game.

Assume the backpack contains two videocassettes. The felt-marker label on each says "AMERICAN CITY STREET." Not the road, mind you, which implies great stretches of open space, but rather the street, which indicates a societal space inhabited by numbers of people. Slip the first cassette into the VCR, and the screen is instantly ablaze with the image of a golden street. Artistic license, you might think, but the video producers would tell you different. This is a national ancestral image, they say, going deep into the colonial past, to a 1702 sermon by an influential New England Puritan minister, Cotton Mather, who was inspired by a certain powerful ancient Greek prophecy about "a city of a golden street." Mather exclaimed, "Such an *American* face upon it. . . . America is legible in these promises."

Indeed, on-screen at this instant the shimmering street wends its way up through a city on a hill. The producers know that the "city upon a hill," too, is another national trademark registered in the culture very early on, in 1630, in a shipboard sermon by John Winthrop, who was to be a New England colonial governor. In his sermon, "A Model of Christian Charity," Winthrop cautioned that the eyes of the whole world would be upon the fledgling New World society, which owed it to God and man to "knit" itself together into a snug social fabric, a commonwealth worthy of worldwide emulation. As the video images cut in and out, the soundtrack plays inspirational clips from presidential speeches. We hear Ronald Reagan say "city on a hill" in a velvety purr. The producer, we realize, hopes that as the video ends, we will be left with goosebumps of patriotic fervor. From time to time country music participates in this golden street fair, as when Presidents Richard Nixon or George Bush court votes by appearing on the stage of the *Grand Ole Opry,* and when country songwriters—especially in times when U.S. military forces are engaged in armed combat—produce titles like Barry Sadler's "Ballad of the Green Berets," George Jones's "Soldier's Last Letter," Loretta Lynn's "Dear Uncle Sam," or Billy Ray Cyrus's "Some Gave All." Some assume that country music's cultural politics begin and end with these kinds of statements.

Not so—as we see on turning to the second video, which is based on a different tradition of country music and is, in its own terms, equally street-smart. On-screen, we are suddenly on a very different sort of street, this one dark, deserted, dimly lighted. It is the location of "Heartbreak Hotel," a May Axton song whose phrase ". . . been so long in Lonely Street" gave Elvis a memorable hit line and

Carl Belew the launch for his own song, "Lonely Street." This song, in turn, comes to our make-believe video screen from a 1959 Andy Williams hit (and a song Williams still sings in the 1990s). "Lonely Street" has been a country music perennial, recorded by Kitty Wells and then by Patsy Cline on the album *Sentimentally Yours* (1962) and by Tammy Wynette (*Golden Memories, 1972–81*), finally by Emmylou Harris (*Bluebird*, 1988). There is no question about the soundtrack here: we are listening to a country music classic-in-the-making.

The story is of a search, even quest. Afflicted and burdened with a sorrowful story from the past, the singer seeks a place of emotional release to "weep" and tell all. Patsy Cline's version (like Tammy Wynette's) suggests a progression toward a street that feels very real, an asphalt strip with curb and gutters. There, on Lonely Street, this singer hopes to find a kindred soul who is also keeping a death watch over dying love and shattered dreams—but who would presumably also be a good listener. The guarded hope is to find this soulmate who might eventually draw close to the singer/speaker and enter into a new relationship, two scarred veterans of emotional wars. The tone, the tempo, the arrangement tell us this woman might be able to put this bad time behind her, if only she can locate the actual street. We can imagine the street sign, even if Lonely Street is as allegorical as the golden street in the city on a hill.

Cline conveys the feeling of being lonely, but she sings a story ballad with a message of potential change, even of guarded optimism. Posing the existence of that "someone," she continues the song with fewer catches in the throat, and the background harmonica's sweetness and the soft, almost complacent up-tempo bass line nudges us onward to a time when she might bury this painful present and reach toward a potential future. But uppermost is the idea of a physical location. Cline keeps open the possibility that the singer might find it, and that "someone" will join her there. Its "dim" lights might bring forgetfulness, but the lights hint of a neon strip, an asphalt street at night, rainslick and glistening like licorice.

Not Emmylou Harris's "Lonely Street." As Harris takes her turn on the video, the street has turned matte black. Her "Lonely Street" works as a distillation, a dark crystal of human loneliness itself. If Cline's and Wynette's interpretations take *street* as their key term, Harris concentrates instead on the crucial conceptual possibilities in *lonely*. We are in a vast, oceanic chamber of the mind itself. When Harris sings of finding "someone such as I," the grainy intonation is so exhausted, so spiritually gutted that we know there is no chance of another soul providing comfort for this person. In her inmost self, she could not possibly make room for another. The beat moves as if she were pacing, but if so, this woman walks a treadmill, for she cannot move on.

Harris's version rejects all possibilities of a progressing story. There is no way out of the unremitting bleakness and darkness—quite simply and profoundly because Harris moves the song off the street and totally into the mind of the singer. It is a one-person psychodrama in tones of a tremolo-reverb. Her sorrowful tale circulates solely within her mind, with Harris even echoing her own voice on a track that repeats the phrases on just loneliness, on forgetfulness, on "Lonely Street." The bass line underscores all this in eerie undertones and then overtones—both a floor and a ceiling pressing her in, confining her in a zone of mental sound-space. It is as if we had headphones plugged into the center of her blackest despair.

The question "Where's this place?" becomes rhetorical. The listener realizes that the singer's mind *is* the place, that no other place exists or is possible for her. In the very act of asking, she reveals her near-derangement. And Harris sings so close to it, to a loneliness-unto-insanity, that we sense her artistic risk of going over the edge, at which point this singer/speaker would become a clinical "case" instead of an extreme example of the bereft state to which all are susceptible. Harris must keep her clear of the psychiatric ward and remain instead in the inner core of that loneliness that is pure desolation. If Patsy Cline makes the song a story ballad, risking overmuch hopefulness, Harris at the other extreme risks a tone poem of outright insanity.

She succeeds in this song, which on film would look like a cross between Martin Scorsese and Ingmar Bergman. This time, our goosebumps come from dread and awe. One reviewer who heard Harris sing this song in concert wrote that "Harris got inside our memories and laid claim to them herself . . . singing about each one of us."

Everybody, from time to time at least, is a visitor to a Lonely Street of the human condition. Our video becomes a series of lyrical poems representing powerful moods, states of mind, feelings all of us enter into, at least periodically. Yet the issue is much more complicated when we put the two American streetscapes side by side—the golden street in the city upon a hill and then, just one street over, Lonely Street, U.S.A. The first is a rhapsodic symbol of opportunity for enrichment of all kinds, both material and spiritual, a land of peace, health, and plenty. The second evokes a location symbolizing a lack of companionship or society, of being alone, isolated, solitary, desolate, standing apart.

But try to pair them up, and you find that neither street can make room for the other. The zoning does not permit it. The feelings attached to the one do not transfer to the other. The lonely pedestrian or driver would be an alien on the golden street of the city upon a hill, and a "golden" idealistic optimism would be too bizarre even to take up sidewalk space on Lonely Street. The two streets are so different that they might as well be on different planets.

Consider what follows from this American split. First, think of where these videos would be shown if they were actually produced. "Lonely Street" would air on cable's CMT (Country Music Television) channel. "Golden Street," on the other hand, might be seen during a political party convention, a production of the Republican or the Democratic National Committee. Or it might be shown at a corporate business convention to inspire management or the sales force to greater efforts in the workplace. These venues are revealing. "Golden street in the city upon a hill" is the officially designated ideal image of America. For decades, even centuries, statesmen and politicians have put it forward as the American promise to which all ought to adhere and aspire. Official voices from chambers of commerce to schools make it a founding image from the past and the basis of hope for the national future.

This chasm separating "golden" from "lonely" indicates why loneliness has no authorized place in Americans' consciousness. It has never been officially recognized by those in sociopolitical power. It is not on the official map. Americans who really live their lives on Lonely Street, psychologically and emotionally, cannot give out their addresses—not even to themselves.

No wonder we don't remember the lonely times in *Little House on the Prairie*. The Ingalls family essentially claims the values of the "golden street" to which Laura Ingalls Wilder is committed in her memoir-novel. She upholds that spirit in her portrayals of daily life, from fashioning leather door hinges to staving off wolves or brushing the girls' tangled hair. The most mundane moment provides an opportunity to make the prairie homestead a Golden Street. Wilder's convictions leave her a very small margin for feelings of loneliness. No wonder she measures them out by the spoonful. And no wonder her readers cannot "hear" such moments very well. The "loneliness" frequency is jammed.

But not in country music, which broadcasts the news that loneliness is here in our culture, that it is present, important, even central. And this makes country music all the more important. Because gut-level loneliness is a particular stock-in-trade of American country music, it can point us toward a part of the national identity located in a distinct territory of the emotional life. Unrecognized by official versions of an American identity, country's "high lonesome" carves deep into the idea of what it means to be an American. In this case, country music becomes a secret map.

It takes us right back to the colonial days in which the streets-of-gold and city-on-a-hill ideas originated. The early immigrant Americans, it turns out, recorded such a profound sense of bereavement from loss, disorientation, and isolation that it seems no exaggeration to say that this nation was founded upon loneliness. The same New England Puritans who gave us those glowing images have also left traces of their deep sense of loss and isolation from the families and homes they left behind, as historians are now discovering when they read closely the poignant and wrenching statements of immigrants.

These appear intermittently in the surviving documents—again, viewed through those chinks in the colonial cabin wall. One writer sketched an English dockside scene of lamentation in 1630 as "Friends and Acquaintance" parted forever. He wrote of dearest family and friends whose speech was "strangled" from their depth of anguish. They embraced with "breast-breaking sobs" until, hand in hand, they joined the throng preparing for boarding—only to see their own scene played out within the crowd. Husbands parting from wives, bridegrooms and betrothed taking leave of brides and fiancées, fathers parting from children, "Brethren, Sisters, Unkles, Nephewes, Neeces," together with cousins and neighbors—every tie of human kinship and friendship was now to be severed by the ocean. (One minister, Thomas Shepard, after ten years in America, still could not resist "lamenting the loss of our native country, when we took our last view of it.")

John Winthrop, author of the phrase "city upon a hill," was in that dockside crowd, and he struggled to keep in his mind's eye the "lovely countenance" of the wife he had left behind. By letter he proposed that, in "griefe for thy absense," the two of them should meet in spirit each Monday and Friday at five o'clock (nothing about time zones in the 1630s).

So loneliness imbued American culture from the start. The very words, *lonely*, *loneliness*, *lonesome*, were in fact set into English by the great English poets—Philip Sidney in *Arcadia* (1586), Shakespeare in *Coriolanus* (1607), John Milton in *Comus* (1634)—and exported to the New World in the era of colonization. The vocabulary of loneliness, then, migrated to America in the language of the English colonists.

Built into the American identity from the very beginning, the lexicon of loneliness did not abate after the first surge of colonial immigrants. In antebellum America, the hope of freedom meant, for slaves, a wrenching separation from networks of kin and friends. The onetime slave Frederick Douglass recounted feeling, on the eve of his long-planned escape, the "pain of separation" at the prospect of leaving his "warm-hearted friends . . . friends that I loved almost as I did my life." These were friends he was unlikely ever to see again, as he well knew. The price of his freedom would be loneliness. Headed toward his own version of Golden Street, Douglass suddenly found himself on the curbstone of Lonely Street.

Writings on the westward movement, too, are replete with a sense of loneliness arising from the effort of dispersal and settlement. In recent years, as the history

of the West becomes better understood, we have learned much about the female
side of pioneering from women's diaries, journals, and letters that have come to
light, filled with phrases like "our hearts torn by the loss of loved ones," "nothing
that [can] atone for the loss of society of friends," or a day described as "long and
lonesome" because the pioneering woman "thought much of home—friends—
prospects—& present condition."

A historian comments, "No wonder a deep sense of loss pervades these
records," explaining that "this move [West], unlike earlier moves to nearby fron-
tiers, would separate friends by vast distances, represent[ing] what might well be a
permanent break."

Though some men spoke of living "a lonesome and desolate life" as bachelors
on the western prairie, many women left revealing passages such as this one from
the journal of Lodisa Frizzell, reflecting on embarking for the trans-Mississippi
West:

> The wellknown voices of our friends still ring in our ears, the parting kiss feels
> still warm upon our lips, and that last separating word *Farewell!* sinks deeply into
> the heart. It may be the last we ever hear from some or all of them, and to those
> who start . . . there can be no more solemn scene of parting only at death.

More than one woman represented this leave-taking in the symbolic language of
death (". . . not at all probable that we ever will meet again on this side of the dark
river"). The diarists knew how risky the pioneering life was and understood that
the emotional vacuum of separation was a kind of death.

What we hear in these voices is the price paid for an American culture of the
road, the road across oceans and a continent, the road that moved Americans
from their homes time and time again from the 1600s to the 1900s. Country music
artist and songwriter Nanci Griffith captures the terrible emotional toll taken on
this nation of wayfarers. In a song about the road, she holds us firm to the values
of the American street. "Hometown Streets" (*Late Night Grande Hotel*, 1991) could
easily become the third of our imagined videos, an overpass from Golden to
Lonely Street. "Everybody packs their goals" and "sails away for better shores,"
say the opening lines. True enough, from the Pilgrims on down. And the singer/
speaker is not exempt from the mix of hope and ambition that moved New World
immigrants from the very first. Restless, she has thus launched her own life, having seen times when her own "sails have held a brilliant shine."

But Griffith's song reveals a terrible paradox at the center of this migratory
American culture. The singer calls up the perennial image of the American streets
of gold but tells us what the precious material is truly made of:

Hometown streets are paved in gold
With faces that you've always known
But, you'll never see them
Until you pack your dreams and leave them.

Lifelong familiar faces are the real gold. Personal, human relationships are by definition the authentic golden streets, says this song. All others are merely gilded.
But that very knowledge comes after departure—too late. It comes, what is more,
to those of good faith who thought they were sailing for "better shores." Those en
route to Golden Street actually find that emotionally, unintentionally, they have
detoured to Lonely Street. It is a cruel, punishing loss of direction, unforeseen and
unprepared for. The joke is on them; they have chased fool's gold.

Griffith's chorus is the backward glance that voices a yearning for hometown
street scenes of attractive young men and true-blue friends. ("I need a hometown
street where / The love you're giving / Surely comes back 'round again—and
again and again and again.") The repeated *again*s seek a closed circle of love and
community. At this point, "Hometown Streets" becomes a characteristic home
song, in which the singer vows to return, to weigh anchor and "sail for shore."

But returning may be only a wish, as country music tells us repeatedly. And the
vast spaces of this continental nation keep the dream in that category of a wish or
a fantasy. It becomes homesickness without remedy. Emotionally, Americans may
suffer, some argue, from environmental causes—not pestilence or cataclysm, but
the loneliness endemic to American space. Mountains, prairies, deserts, pine
forests, topographical tracts of every kind, make the wayfarers feel displaced envi-
ronmentally as they are dislodged personally. In the 1830s, the writer Washington
Irving traveled to the Oklahoma prairies, "an immense extent of landscape without a sign of human existence," which Irving pronounced "inexpressibly lonely."
In the 1840s, the journalist Margaret Fuller cited the "stony loneliness" of her native New England and the "lonely heights" and "isolated spots" she had encountered in her travels westward. Laura Ingalls Wilder herself wrote that "on the
whole enormous prairie there was no sign that any other human being had even
been there." (The Ingalls family would learn soon enough of the presence of the
Osage Indians, but the feeling of emptiness was paramount.) Even in the late
1980s, the densely populous northeastern corridor of the New Jersey Turnpike
has been cited as a symbol of a suburban culture of cars and malls and condemned
for its "crushing loneliness."

America's collective loneliness has been noticed by twentieth-century com-
mentators, who argue that from the start the nation's history has been too much a
clash of human emptiness with the vast continent. The West Indian writer Jamaica

*Sculpture evoking feelings of desolate
loneliness. George Segal,* The Bus Station,
*1965. Plaster, wood, formica, metal, vinyl,
cardboard, and leather, 96¼ × 59⅛ × 29¾ in.
(Collection of Whitney Museum of American
Art, New York, gift of Howard and Jean
Lipman, 81.22a-f; © George Seagal/VAGA,
New York, 1993)*

Loneliness is the dominant feeling in Edward
Hopper, Gas, 1940. Oil on canvas, 26¼ × 40¼ in.
(Courtesy Museum of Modern Art, New York,
Mrs. Simon Guggenheim Fund.) See also Plate 7.

Kincaid, speaking of her native Antigua and its racially troubled past, hearkens back to Columbus for the root motive of slavery—and finds it to be the essential loneliness of Europeans striving to satisfy their desire for wealth and power, "so that they could be less lonely and empty." And the poet William Carlos Williams wrote similarly in a personal book on American history, *In the American Grain* (1933). A national emptiness prevailed, Williams thinks, from the time of Columbus, whom Ralph Waldo Emerson identified as quintessentially lonely. The spiritual claims of the Pilgrims and Puritans were only signs of the "intensity of their emptiness." (Early in this century, when the Jewish immigrant writer Abraham Cahan imagined a generation of immigrants collectively calling down "a curse upon Columbus," he expressed on their behalf the anger that covers loneliness, while his female counterpart, the immigrant writer Anzia Yezierska, published a book significantly titled *Children of Loneliness* [1923].)

Even that ultimate driver and devotee of the American road, Jack Kerouac ("the road is life"), wrote poignant entries on loneliness in his diary-novel, *On the*

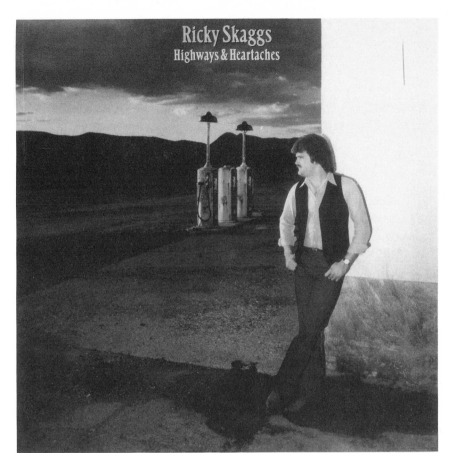

**Cover design for Ricky Skaggs's platinum album, Highways and Heartaches.
(Courtesy Sony Music)**

Road. In Denver, Kerouac feels the spatial, continental vastness: "lonesome . . . like a speck on the surface of the sad red earth." And Kerouac found musical expression of this particularly American loneliness in his beloved jazz. He calls a soft, sweet alto sax solo "a throatpierced sound in the night . . . lonely as America."

Kerouac, a jazz fan, dismissed country as "hillbilly" music and tuned it out. Too bad. Had he listened, he could have understood that country is far from immune to this environmental loneliness. Country music, on the contrary, has absorbed it, soaked it up like a sponge, and released it to listeners in rivulets—and in rivers. This message of loneliness, however, undergoes an interesting change in country music. It becomes welded and wedded to human connections. The natural environment, considered inherently lonely, is tapped to speak its message of loneliness and separation in songs on human relationships. In country music, then, the environment comes back coded in stories of personal relationships gone bad, at an impasse, hopeless, destroyed—and leaving the bereft survivor to tell the sorrowful story.

It is this kind of affliction that Emmylou Harris presents in "A River for Him," a song she wrote and recorded on the *Bluebird* album. It is a song of lament, grief, loss. And because it is not located in a particular historical moment, it transcends specifics of time and place. Freed from particular circumstance, it belongs to the entire American experience. "A River for Him" begins with a long sound-space, dead space, from which, ever so gradually, comes a sustained tone as if from a great distance, followed by another. And another, until we have a chord, then a bass cutting in like a saw. Then a keyboard arpeggio pattern over and over, like rain—or tears, at which point a baritone guitar line enters, marking another pattern of falling droplets—rain, tears, possibly blood, too, as from a wound. Just a few bars in, the song has established elaborate production values.

Then Harris enters the song with a firm attack:

> I crossed on the river,
> There'll be no returning;
> I crossed all the bridges,
> I watched them all burning.

The speaker declares herself now a "stranger," and the voice shudders in a four-stress dismemberment of the very word. Displaced by a force beyond the self, she is now "driven" to this "strange land . . . where . . . all is forgotten," yet "nothing's forgiven." The voice breaks in sorrow, and the bass line sinks into oblivion after "forgiven." Gradually one is aware of the increasing vibrato, telling us that the initial resolve is increasingly difficult to sustain in the face of a constant, incalculable pain:

> But I cried a river,
> A river for him,
> That's deeper and wider
> Than I'll ever swim.

The word *cried* is intangible, almost disembodied, until we hear "him," as if, when recollected, *he* has a solidity not possible for the singer herself. And then we learn what future she can envision for herself: "The heart, it will harden," and "the sorrow will dim." There will be no route through this mourning, only containment of pain and the desensitizing of her feelings of incalculable loss and loneliness. But not personal renewal. Never renewal. And a guitar picks the droplet pattern again, this time slightly percussive as if falling onto metal, as we realize these are not, ever, to be tears of redemption.

At some point in the song, perhaps here, it occurs to a listener that the singer does not address the lost man directly, does not sing recollectively to "you," but instead sings *about* "him." This is a third-person lamentation:

> I think of him now
> On the road I am taking,
> And wonder how long
> His heart will be breaking.
>
> But he'll never hear
> When the teardrops are fallin',
> Or the sound of my voice,
> And the name I am callin'.

The teardrops, the sound, the name—these could become an itemized list. But Harris does not sing them as a listing. Delaying the beat on each, she has the singer discovering, as if for the first time, each component of loss, only now realizing how final this separation, how great the magnitude.

The voice lingers on "callin'" as if reluctant to relinquish the hold on the act of calling his name, as if the very act might somehow keep him with her. Yet inevitably the voice (and the guitar) sinks and, in surprise, we hear it choke off into a groan and briefly stop altogether. It is a shocking moment, especially because this song is otherwise so fluid. The song actually shuts down for that brief instant and must then recommence:

> But I cried a river
> A river *for* him.

She is crying perpetually *for* him, on his behalf, not narcissistically for herself. And this prepares us for the moment when the song extends itself to global, mythic themes of loss through all generations:

> So weep for the sons
> And the dear, darling daughters,
> Oh, the passing of time
> And the parting of waters,
>
> For all who have passed
> Through this world long before me,
> To a far distant shoreline
> Where no one waits for me.

One is perhaps taken aback at the last line: "No one waits for me." No heaven, no "him" awaiting. No redemption. This song is presented in a past tense ("I cried"), but one never to be got past, never to conclude. The heart *will* harden, the sorrows *will* dim, but they haven't as yet, not even after this long duration. At this point the singer is, retrospectively, a kind of spectator of disaster, of burned bridges and an unspeakable site of ruin. "He" is gone and, with him, all action and every emotion except the state of grievous loneliness. Throughout, the chord progressions are 1, 4, 6 minor, 5, 4, 5, 4. Instead of going back "home" to the 1, the movement customary after a number 5 chord (almost an "amen" ending), Harris moves on to the 4, which propels the song forward but gives a feeling of unrest. The chord progression, however, may be less significant than the sustained synthesizer line, which imparts a bagpipe-like eeriness as it stays on the 1-chord, with other chords changing around it, and, together with the words, creating an otherworldly feeling.

We understand the American experience of this song, which reclaims a national identity based so much on journeys across great bodies of water, many unbridged and unbridgeable. Harris draws upon and continues an extensive history

Emmylou Harris in performance, 1993.
(Photographs © 1993 Woody Johnson.
All rights reserved.)

of ocean and river crossings that resonate deep in American history. And we must realize that this song is unified precisely by the cultural implications of the river of tears. There is a liquid quality not only in the lyrics but in the arrangement. The instrumental bridge includes sprays of cymbals, a fluid, sliding electric guitar, liquid keyboard teardrops. The legato guitar patterns are not fixed but seem to flow, like a river meandering. A close listener hears the singer breathing, the intake of breath audible throughout and sounding very much like a swimmer drawing breath.

The arrangement is fluid as tears, as the slipstream of time, and black as the River Styx, the principal river of Hades in Greek mythology, coupled with the river of forgetfulness, Lethe. But this song has the feel of an American Styx-Lethe, resonant of the great North American river systems so prominent in the history of this nation—and so central to the logistics of transit and the engendering of resultant loneliness. Harris's riverscape is sited in an American tradition of lonely water crossings that are both spatial and deathly.

And Harris's river draws on more than a century of commentary on the feelings evoked by American rivers. The "desolate" and "lawless Mississippi," one post-

Revolutionary writer called it, longing for the day when it might be "tamed." The most prominent American historian of the nineteenth century, Francis Parkman, wrote that the explorer LaSalle found the Mississippi Basin at the Gulf to be "lonely as when born of chaos." While America's preeminent nature writer, Henry David Thoreau, proclaimed the great unbridged American rivers (the Mississippi, the Ohio, and the Missouri) to be geographic symbols of a heroic age, other writers took a very different view. Mark Twain, in *Life on the Mississippi*, describes the predawn moment on that river as one of a "haunting sense of loneliness," finding that tourists of the late nineteenth century routinely remarked on "the deep, brooding loneliness and desolation of the vast river."

Harris's "A River for Him" really recalls the loneliness that Mark Twain has made indelible in the national literature—indelible, that is, if we set aside the "children's classic" category that has served to cover up certain issues in Twain's books. Behind the dust-jacket breeziness about "rollicking river adventures" is a Mississippi loneliness that besets one of the most appealing characters in all of American literature, Twain's Huck Finn. The story of an eleven-year-old boy's rafting down the Mississippi is a perennial favorite, with Twain's humor enlivening virtually every page of *The Adventures of Huckleberry Finn* (1882). But the closest readers cannot miss the repeated invocations of the word *lonesome* to represent Huck's feelings as an orphan and an outsider in a society that Twain insists is hypocritical and scarred by criminals preying on the innocent, by murderous family feuds, by slavery.

At times, Huck experiences the Mississippi as respite from an imperfect world and can welcome the lonesomeness best captured in the term *solitude*. Twain gives the reader, for instance, a long, lyrical scene of dawn breaking over the river, the air aromatic with woods and flowers, the currents of the river richly textured, the songbirds "just going it!" Add a satisfying breakfast of fresh-caught fish and the travelogue pleasures of passing boats and onshore scenes of daily life, like wood chopping. "So we would put in the day," Huck recounts, "lazying around, listening to the stillness. . . . We would watch the lonesomeness of the river . . . just solid lonesomeness." Here "lonesomeness" is a time-out from conflict and stress, the companionship of two souls sharing the same feelings in solitude.

Yet, more often, Huck's outsider status gives "lonesomeness" a very different meaning, a desolation that pervades the many country songs on the subject and is central to "A River for Him." This starts from the book's opening pages, when the boy retreats to his room to escape the pious hectoring of his spinster guardian. He tries to cheer himself up. And what could be more difficult?—he is virtually orphaned, his mother dead, his father an alcoholic and violent drifter. The boy is now legally the ward of a well-intentioned elderly widow and her righteous, doctrinaire, Calvinist sister. He feels his orphanage most keenly in their respectable but alien household. Retreating to his room, he is not a moody preadolescent but a soul deeply alienated from his culture when he tells us, "I felt so lonesome I almost wished I was dead."

And soon he is, in a manner of speaking. Vowing to run away, Huck stages an elaborate hoax to lead townspeople (including his knife-wielding father) to believe he has met a violent end and washed away in that lonesome river. In effect, he stages his own death. Involving an ax and pig blood, his plan is so ingenious, and Huck's resourcefulness so fascinating, that neither he nor the reader thinks ahead to the moment when it's all over, when Huck is an escapee on the Mississippi. Inevitably, the let-down comes. Then, "by-and-by it got sort of lonesome," Huck says, faced with his own isolation, the absence of community and of his only friend, Tom Sawyer. Like an insomniac counting sheep, he counts stars, drifting logs, rafts. "There ain't no better way to put in time when you are lonesome; you can't stay so, you soon get over it."

But essentially, he never gets over it. Even weather triggers the feeling of desolation. Separated from the raft he shares with Jim, the runaway slave, Huck describes the whiteout of zero-visibility fog. "If you think it ain't dismal and lonesome out in a fog that way, by yourself, in the night, you try it once—you'll see." He is not talking about weather as such, but about his state of mind. This is the isolation of disorientation, when one has no access to the world beyond the self. And the "down-hearted" feeling overtakes Huck when he sees firsthand the violence and predation of "sivilized" life. Reentry into it at the close of the novel brings back that sense of desolation. Downriver, approaching the household of Tom Sawyer's aunt, Huck says it feels "Sunday-like," dead still, "so lonesome and like everybody's dead and gone; and if a breeze fans along and quivers the leaves, it makes you feel mournful, because you feel like it's spirits whispering—spirits that's been dead ever so many years. . . . As a general thing, it makes a body wish he was dead." Within minutes, Huck hears the hum and "wail" of a spinning wheel, the signature sound of a family and household of which he has never been a part. "And then I knowed for certain I wished I was dead—for that *is* the lonesomest sound in the whole world."

Are Mark Twain's readers' ears cocked for that lonesomest sound? Usually not. *The Adventures of Huckleberry Finn* is offered as a boys' adventure novel and a masterpiece of American fiction, to be enjoyed for its humor and admired for its important themes of individualism, racial consciousness-raising, zestful colloquial language, social satire. As for loneliness, it is a motif marked, at most, in passing.

Which brings us full circle from Huckleberry Finn right back to the world of the Little House on the Prairie. Twain's river, like Wilder's prairie, is pocked with

the loneliness endemic to the vast environment and to human figures in transit. By raft or covered wagon (or four-wheel-drive Jeep), the feelings are the same. Mark Twain was too much the skeptic ever to take up residence on Golden Street, but his cloud cover of humor, adventure, and so forth only half camouflages the American state of loneliness he inscribes in his book. The subject was — as it still is — so vast and deep that Twain could only outline it in the mists of the Mississippi.

Let's not kid ourselves; country music does not always have an easy time expressing this state of heart. Country artists are not exempt from the nation's cultural taboos. Even the greatest of singer/songwriters, Hank Williams, shows a reluctance to say outright how profound is the cost of loneliness. In "I'm So Lonesome I Could Cry," Williams, like Mark Twain, projects feelings of utter desolation onto nature itself:

> Did you ever see a robin weep
> When leaves begin to die?
> That means he's lost the will to live
> I'm so lonesome I could cry.

The whippoorwill in this song is "too blue to fly," while the moon has retreated behind a cloud "to hide its face and cry." The guitar imitates a steam train whistle, and Williams's voice almost sobs on the attack. Almost unconsciously, the listener begins relying on a certain pattern of bawling, sustained crescendo beats in the three-quarter time, though Williams surprisingly drops both note and voice on "fly." And that is the point: This bird is too blue to fly. It cannot. It sinks, just as the singer's voice must do to make the point. We realize that the weeping robin, like the songbird whippoorwill, is the symbol of the singer's having "lost the will to live."

"So lonesome I could cry" is the song's key phrase — but *cry* is a code word. It is a word that pulls its punch and drives the real meaning into hiding. First-time listeners are apt to mistake this crucial word. They hear *die* — because death follows from a loss of the will to live. Those who know the song get the right word vocally, but psychologically they, too, know the essential word is *die*. This indirect message makes the song even more powerful, but it is just that — indirect, concealed, in hiding. The listener and singer agree not to state outright what both know. That is the pact between them.

And that has been the pact in American culture — an implicit agreement not to say outright just how profound is the feeling of loneliness in the experience of this nation and its people.

One might even go so far as to say that many country songs of loneliness have

[opposite page] **Hank Williams. (Courtesy Country Music Foundation, Nashville)**

a double meaning that extends beyond what they appear to be—songs of love gone bad. Such songs as Tammy Wynette's "Cold Lonely Feeling" or the Delia Bell/Bill Grant bluegrass "Lonely Violet" or songs on Kitty Wells's *Lonesome, Sad, and Blue* or countless others may carry a level of wider, unacknowledged meaning. Passing solely and exclusively as songs about failed and troubled romantic love relationships, they really use the age-old troubled romance as a way to convey feelings prompted by social and cultural conditions in America.

Pacts, codes, hints—what does it all mean? That country music is a channel of grief and mourning even now. And that tracking loneliness in American culture is a game of emotional espionage whose guidelines come essentially from country music, which is more up-front about this state of heart and soul than any other American form of expression. Country's songs of loneliness are the camouflage music by which a historically mobile nation continues to grieve the losses of departures—first across the ocean, later inland as successive generations of sons and daughters crisscrossed the three thousand continental miles, establishing their pattern of intramural mobility that continues to this day. Country, then, is arguably a grieving music for a lonesomeness bred in the American bone. If so, it may also be part of a long-term pattern of national therapeutics.

In a 1959 essay in *Esquire*, Alan Lomax, the song collector and folklorist, argued that the Appalachian Mountains had engendered a "vigorous pioneer music" vitalized by "a century of isolation in the lonesome hollows." He identified the sound of this American music, bluegrass music, as the "high, lonesome." Bluegrass music audiences know this sound well and know that it originated with Bill Monroe, the founder of bluegrass. The American high lonesome, however, extends beyond bluegrass into country music as a whole. It is not a musical tradition solely of Appalachian isolates or even of twentieth-century rural southerners dislocated by their job-related moves to northern industrial cities. It is not regional but national. The mobile nation whose population has been urged to move and move again, to continue journeying to every compass point of a huge continental space, reveals in its country music the emotional result of this restlessness. High lonesome, it turns out, is a national product, available all over the U.S.A.

Wild Wild West

Walk west through the urban canyons, west from the Avenue of the Americas and along 52d Street between money mountains—Chase Manhattan, Paine Webber, Credit Lyonnais. Then west across Broadway into New York's theater district, where you stop at a building whose facade is a red-and-silver bus, like a Greyhound or Trailways. The street address is 240 West 52d Street. It is the Lone Star Café Roadhouse, "the official Texas embassy in New York City."

How "Texas" is it? "Lone Star City Limit. Pop. 1760" reads a back-wall sign. Is this "lone" as in loneliness? Apparently not. Red neon ads for Lone Star beer decorate the bar (though the distributor has stopped East Coast delivery, and Col-

Bumper sticker.

orado-based Coors is the closest you can get in longnecks). Patrons come here for the *western* side of country-western music, and the Lone Star tries to oblige. The entryway features an oversize photo of Hank Williams at the mike in his Nudie-tailored western wear with his band, the Drifting Cowboys. And wall-mounted guitars are a major decorative motif (even a Chet Atkins-model Gibson). Texas license plates are nailed to a barroom rafter. On a Sunday night in January, a patron with a New Jersey accent is overheard to say, ". . . that's why I wanted to go somewhere that's Texas-oriented."

By Texas, she means the West—not the New Yorker's sense of "upper West Side," of course, but the mental map of the great American West. She means boots, hats, cowboys, and all that comes with them. On the job by day, she might send data through a computer, telemarket, push retail merchandise over a counter. At night, however, in boots and jeans in the Lone Star, listening to country acts like Dan Seals, Delbert McClinton, or the Marshall Tucker Band, she is somewhere and somebody else. On Country Hoedown night, she can dance the Texas two-step and line dances to DJ'd recordings of Garth Brooks, Dwight Yoakam, Rodney Crowell, or Brooks and Dunn, slipping into another identity. She becomes western, her partner at least a ranch hand, maybe even an outlaw. She feels no self-irony in this, no embarrassment as a northeasterner pretending to be a Texan. Why should she? Call it role play or fantasy, masquerade or escapism, this urbanite's western identity is, as she well knows, an American birthright. Midtown Manhattan may be an asphalt grid with yellow taxis, brass-and-glass bank doors, takeout delis, convention hotels. But that is mere exterior circumstance. It does not impinge on the way in which this urban dweller, like any American, is entitled to come to the Lone Star and be unabashedly "Texas-oriented."

The music at such moments is the *western* side of country, as in the traditional term, country-*western* (C&W, as it formerly appeared on *Billboard* and *Cash Box* charts). From this music's earliest years country artists embraced the West in song and in image. The "Father of Country Music," Jimmie Rodgers, was variously

it's never too late to be a cowgirl!

*Advertisement. (Courtesy Mongerson
Wunderlich, Chicago)*

photographed in a railroad brakeman's hat, in a straw skimmer à la crooner Bing Crosby, in a Panama straw with snap brim—but he also posed for the photographer in a classic *full cowboy*: western shirt, chaps, bandana, and wide-brimmed cowboy hat. One of his songs was "Yodeling Cowboy," another "T for Texas," and when the Mississippi-born singer drove the thousand miles from Texas to Virginia to reunite with the Carter Family and cut an album, the scripted opener was, "Why, that's Jimmie Rodgers . . . the first cowboy we've seen in a long time."

Western themes and motifs are not, of course, confined to country-western music but appear on Broadway and in the classical tradition—for instance, in Aaron Copland's 1930s ballet suite, *Billy the Kid*, and in his ballet *Rodeo* (1942) with its dance episodes written for orchestra, including *Coralle Nocturne, Buckaroo Holiday*, and *Hoedown*. Broadway featured one of the most enduring theatrical productions based on the West, the Richard Rodgers/Oscar Hammerstein *Oklahoma!* (1943), set in Indian Territory after the turn of the twentieth century, its songs celebrating the Wild West and its wide-open spaces.

But for decades country music has ardently and consistently embraced the West. "Cowboys Don't Cry" is a Hank Williams song, and the Alabama native loved playing cowboys in childhood, later naming his band the Drifting Cowboys. Preparing to debut at the *Grand Ole Opry*, Williams bought the group new stage uniforms, western-style shirts and pants "and ten-gallon hats and cowboy boots." The hats have been a country music trademark, from cowboy songwriter Bob Nolan ("Cool Water," "Tumbling Tumbleweeds"), through the jazz-influenced western swing developed by Oklahoman Bob Wills and others, to the bass and baritone vocals of Ernest Tubb and Tex Ritter. Contemporary country artists run the newest leg of this western relay—for instance, the so-called Hat Acts, Clint Black, Ricky Van Shelton, Alan Jackson—their images including broadbrimmed western hats (likely stamped "Stetson" inside).

Western music has been profitable for cowboys who show they can not only dress the part but also ride and sing (and sell records and movie tickets)—notably Gene Autry (on his quarter horse, Champ) and Roy Rogers (with his palomino, Trigger). And numerous bands have headlined western themes, like Rogers's Sons of the Pioneers, well known in their own right and also reminding us of others with western names, like the Chuck Wagon Gang, Buck Owens's Buckaroos, Little Texas, Riders in the Sky, Sweethearts of the Rodeo.

This western side of country music comes down through interlinked generations well aware of their lineage. "Outlaw" Waylon Jennings recalls reaching as a toddler for his daddy's guitar, "an old Gene Autry with a cowboy rearin' up." And Randy Travis's "Happy Trails" (*Heroes and Friends*, 1992) shows TV's influence on the western succession, as Travis sings of growing up "with cowboys [he] watched on TV"—one of them obviously the star of the *Roy Rogers Show*, which ran for six

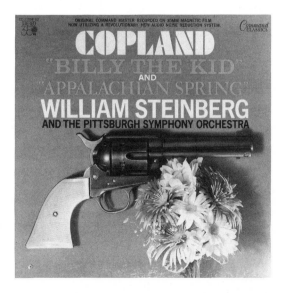

years on NBC and thereafter in syndicated reruns. "Happy Trails," a duet with Rogers, cements the western succession. A theme song written by Dale Evans, it also reminds us of women's western identity in the cowgirl tradition, a lineage traced by Mary A. Bufwack and Robert K. Oermann in *Finding Her Voice: The Saga of Women in Country Music*. The tradition extends from Patsy Montana to Lynn Anderson and a "Sweetheart of the Rodeo," Emmylou Harris, and beyond.

Specific compass points of western music punctuate the vastness of the West, too, including Merle Haggard's identification with Bakersfield, California, and Willie Nelson's with his native Texas, location of the TV program *Austin City Limits* and home base of neo-Western artists like Jimmie Dale Gilmore. But the West succeeds as an idea both specific and yet generalized in albums like Texan Nanci Griffith's *A Lone Star State of Mind* and Garth Brooks's *Ropin' the Wind*.

The western traditions have become so utterly familiar that spoofs are probably inevitable. Riders in the Sky sound earnest in their Scout-like pledge, "The Cowboy Way," for a TV children's audience ("It's the strength to say you're sorry, admit that you were wrong"), but their cowboy jokes are satirically witty, turning on product names like Frederick's of Deadwood, the Bio-Feedbag, and Prairie Lubricants, western irreverence mixing with their sincerity. Western satire goes solo in country artist Lyle Lovett's "If I Had a Boat" (*Pontiac*, 1987), in which Lovett exploits the incongruity between the West and the open water when he presents a tableau of himself and Roy Rogers in a boat, astride a pony and Trigger. And the women's version of this kind of satire is found in Karen Taylor-Good's "OBG Why Me Blues," in which a woman on the gynecologist's examining table, her feet in the stirrups, faces her male doctor and, in a line out of *The Lone Ranger*, asks, "Who is that masked man?"

He is—to make the obvious explicit—a cowboy who has come to represent the West as America. And America as the West. He is heir to a powerful ideology focused on the territory west of the Mississippi but conceptually national and rooted at least as far back as the eighteenth century, when the British bishop George Berkeley wrote a poem entitled "On the Prospect of Planting Arts and Learning in America." A much-reprinted line reads, "Westward the course of empire takes its way." Berkeley's words have been interpreted as prophecy, destiny, self-justification, cant, and God's truth. His view was bolstered by other writers and, later on, by painters. The Revolutionary-era French emigré writer J. Hector St. John de Crèvecoeur proclaimed, "Americans are the western pilgrims, who are carrying along with them that great mass of the arts, sciences, vigour and industry which began long since in the east; they will finish the great circle."

The circle went unbroken in the following century, when the New Englanders Ralph Waldo Emerson and Henry David Thoreau celebrated the West as synony-

WILLIE NELSON WITH WAYLON JENNINGS ⋆ TAKE IT TO THE LIMIT

*"Outlaws" Willie Nelson
and Waylon Jennings.
(Courtesy MCA Records)*

mous with greatness and the national future and thus sustained the ideology later
to be continued in country music. "The nervous, rocky West is intruding a new
and continental element into the national mind, and we shall yet have an American genius," wrote an optimistic Emerson in 1844. Emerson's neighbor, Henry
David Thoreau, living in or around the village of Concord, Massachusetts, said his
personal compass needle always pointed west: "The future lies that way to me, and
the earth seems more unexhausted and richer on that side. . . . Eastward I go by
force; but westward I go free." Thoreau took the arc of the sun as his guide: "I
must walk toward Oregon, and not toward Europe. And that way the nation is   109

moving. . . . Every sunset which I witness inspires me with the desire to go to a West as distant and as fair as that into which the sun goes down. . . . He [the sun] is the Great Western Pioneer whom the nations follow."

Walt Whitman made this westward ethos central to most of his poetry, but nowhere more directly than in "Pioneers! O Pioneers!":

> Come my tan-faced children,
> Follow well in order, get your weapons ready,
> Have you your pistols? have you your sharp-edged axes?
> Pioneers! O Pioneers!

Whitman defined the western spirit as venturesome, youthful, exploitive without guilt or guile, free of history's constraints, surging, a citizens' army on destiny's march. (One symbol of that march—the covered wagon or Conestoga wagon—is in the 1990s featured in the Smithsonian Institution's Museum of American History exhibition on "Road Transportation," positioned in the museum like a founding vehicle for westward settlement and expansion.)

The ideology of the American West depends on two traits. First is the destined movement toward the setting sun. From Bishop Berkeley to Whitman, the emphasis lies in an inevitable push of the population westward.

But a second feature of this ideology centers on the character of the westerner, especially the cowboy. Over time, several diverse figures have come to be identified with the American West: the Native American, the cavalryman, the white homesteader, the miner, and the trapper. All have a place in western history and in western myth. All are familiar as types from films, novels, television series. None, however, has approached the cowboy in prominence. Synonymous with the West, the cowboy became the masculine ideal of personal competence and skill embodied in a single figure who is dependent upon no one else, neither family nor team members nor peer group. Alone, he signifies the freedom of self-reliance and self-sufficiency.

The cowboy became a fixture of post–Civil War America, but he had an antebellum father, in a manner of speaking, east of the Mississippi, just as Whitman's pioneers had their sponsor in a British bishop. This cowboy "father" is a figure in buckskins, not boots. He wore a fur cap, not a ten-gallon broadbrim. And the West he represented then is more likely these days to be considered the East and Midwest. He is the fictional Daniel Boone-like character created by an aristocratic upstate New Yorker, James Fenimore Cooper, whose family gave its name to the town best known in this century as the site of the Baseball Hall of Fame. Cooper, experiencing Western America from the Adirondack Mountains, wrote a series of western novels codifying a set of values that would ultimately make their way into cowboy ideology and into country music.

Cooper's Leather-Stocking series includes *The Pioneers* (1823), *The Last of the Mohicans* (1826), *The Prairie* (1828), *The Pathfinder* (1840), and *The Deerslayer* (1841). Named for the buckskin leggings worn by the hero with the improbable name of Natty Bumppo, the tales are filled with the telling nicknames of the protagonist—Leatherstocking, Hawkeye, Deerslayer, Pathfinder, all attributes of his character and his skills. He is the sharpshooter with the eye of a hawk, the hunter who kills for food, never mere sport. He dwells on the shifting vanguard of western settlement, scouting the forest and prairie pathways, having no choice but to live "on the road" by moving ever west just ahead of the settlers who represent a misconceived, mismanaged, and materialistic "civilization." He himself is honest, courageous, temperamentally steady, fair-minded, unflinching in the face of danger, whether from a murderous warrier, homocidal settler, or ravenous beast. His "gifts," as he calls his heritage and identity, are white, Christian, and masculine. "I look forward to a life in the woods," he says, and "I only hope it may be a peaceable one. . . . Better . . . would it be if [man] could . . . take a lesson from the fowls of the air, and the beasts of the fields." Cooper, not surprisingly, calls his hero "a philosopher of the wilderness."

But he is a loner. "Days have I travelled [the woods] alone," Hawkeye says, "without feeling the want of company." For Cooper, this self-sufficient solitude is a crucial point, as it would be later on with the cowboy. This hero is not gregarious, sociable, clubby. By definition, he is independent and keeps to himself. "I am without kith or kin in the wide world," he says on the verge of his death, at more than eighty years of age. "When I am gone there will be an end of my race."

An end? Yes and no. True, the family bloodline ends with him. No family tree can be traced. A father "buried near the sea" is virtually all we know of family ties. In terms of history, Leatherstocking is a Daniel Boone figure, as his novelist/creator makes clear. And he is a sort of great-grandfather to the rovers and ramblers of the American culture of the road. It is true, also, that he is the spokesman for a way of life doomed by settlement. But his vitality depends upon his solitary self-reliance. Opposed to civilization, he necessarily must remain single. To do otherwise—to marry or in any other way to join society—would be to betray his values and himself. So Cooper's hero must remain a solo act. "Dying breed" is a built-in part of his identity. Old age alone does not kill him. From Day One he is history's casualty.

In another way, however, Leatherstocking/Hawkeye is by no means the end of his race. As the self-reliant American, he lives on in myth. Buried on the prairie, he

▼ ▼ ▼ ▼ ▼ ▼ ▼ ▼

Wild Wild West

is reincarnated in the far West as a cowboy. He swaps leather for Levis, but this independent figure lives on.

The cowboy becomes the real son and heir of Leatherstocking, a symbolic center of longtime traditional values identified in the West and considered by some to be representative of the nation. This traditional West denotes freedom, individualism, independence, hard work, a rejection of mere materialism (even in custom boots of exotic hides), a clear-cut moral code of right and wrong, a geographic scale signifying this nation at its most expansive. In a recent book, *West of Everything: The Inner Life of Westerns* (1992), Jane Tompkins analyzes the promise of the West and the ethos governing Westerns in every format from popular novels to movies. Her statements could be applied to most country-*western* songs:

> The American West . . . functions as a symbol of freedom, and of the opportunity for conquest. It seems to offer escape from the conditions of life in modern industrial society: from a mechanized existence, economic dead ends, social entanglements, unhappy personal relations, political injustice. . . . The desert light and the desert space, the creak of saddle leather and the sun beating down, the horses' energy and force—these things promise a translation of the self into something purer and more authentic, more intense, more real.

We could see country-western music as a part of the imagery dispersed in American popular culture, from Buffalo Bill's Wild West Shows, which brought cowboys

Western wear periodically popular in American clothing fashions. (Photograph by Jamie Adams)

and real Indians to Madison Square Garden in the early 1900s and to the new motion picture screen, to the cowboy and western landscapes purveyed in movies and in radio and TV series, with their spinoff toys from guns to wristwatches, pajamas, and lunchboxes, including the recycling of fringed western wear in American fashion—all to reinforce the themes of independence, freedom, individual autonomy. "Too much ain't enough," read the bumper stickers sold at the Lone Star, and this slogan might be the generalization that makes the West synonymous with America.

A few essential facts undergird the romance of the traditional West, including country-western music—one being that, measured in years, the cowboy's actual historical moment was relatively brief, from 1867 to the 1880s. (The last of Cooper's Leather-Stocking Tales was published in the antebellum 1841.) These were the post–Civil War years of what one writer calls "cowboy culture"—work techniques featuring roping and branding, bunkhouse and ranch customs, foodways, rituals peculiar to the trail and to regions like the High Plains. Cowboys, for instance, sometimes moved from the law or for luck, and one historian sees the song "The Wandering Cowboy" as an account of their culture of migration: "I am a wandering cowboy / From ranch to ranch I roam."

This was the era of the long cattle drives over famous trails such as the Chisholm or Santa Fe, drives commemorated in movies like Howard Hawkes's *Red River* (1948), starring John Wayne as the maniacal rancher relentlessly driving cattle and cowboys one thousand mostly desert miles, through Indian and bandit territory to Abilene. The premise of the film had a basis in fact, for fallen prices had ruined the Texas cattle market and motivated the drives. By the 1880s, a series of events halted the era of the cowboy West: a disastrous blizzard of 1886–87 that killed thousands of cattle, overgrazing, falling prices, state quarantine laws meant to prevent diseased Texas livestock from crossing state lines, the enclosure of open rangeland by barbed wire as farmers asserted their rights to cropland. So that short interval was the basis for all the twentieth-century cowboy western legends.

What an opportune moment for western songs, at least so it seems. Custom (and logic) would have it that cowboy songs originated from hands-on work with horses and cattle and from an emotional life of free-range solitude punctuated by mortal danger. The traditional view holds that cowboys made up songs to quiet the skittish cattle at night, lest they plunge to their deaths down arroyos and ravines. Such warnings in the song "Cowboy Lullaby" segue into a vocalized yodel of a refrain ("yah-ho, a-mol-la hol-i-day")—much like that of "Cattle Call," a hit for Tex Owens and Eddy Arnold and recently recorded by Emmylou Harris, the

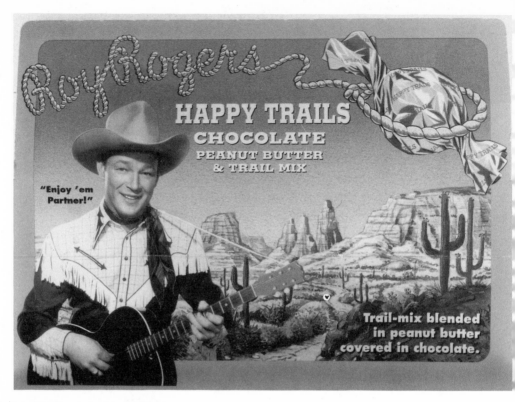

Snack food marketed in terms of the West and
cowboy hero Roy Rogers.

chorus a succession of woo-hoos sung soothingly and prettily in a near-falsetto, the vocalized tones presumably calming to the herds.

The working cowboy on the open prairie, what's more, would seem inevitably responsive to the mournful night, voicing a mournful cry of his own—like the creamy-smooth, high yodel of Elton Britt's "How the Yodel Was Born" (*Yodel Songs,* 1956). And dangerous, even deadly work with livestock in foul weather would seem to find commemorative expression in songs like "Little Joe the Wrangler" or "Blood on the Saddle," both cowboy work songs recounting fatal accidents in which cowboys are killed by falling horses, slathered with "gore" and "smashed to a pulp." Common wisdom, then, says that the cowboy songs originated on the range as cowboys worked the herds and sought to keep their half-ton charges from . . . well, from charging.

And yet revisionist history has been at work on the cowboy songs, and the truth of the matter is that relatively little of this western music was written or sung by cowboys. Dorothy Horstman, a student of country music, writes that "few of the 'western' songs that comprise a large share of country music literature are authentic relics of that celebrated quarter-century following the end of the Civil War when the great cattle drives took place." She explains that the repertory of popular cowboy songs was based on folksongs and popular songs of the nineteenth century and that they fall well within the definition of "commercial country music." Douglas P. Green corroborates the point that "sentimental songs and poems of real-life cowboys [mixed] with the strains of Broadway, the hot jazz from Chicago, the deep blues, dashes and dollops of Mexican, Czech, and German ethnic strains . . . and the stately, sentimental songs of the Gay Nineties." He concludes, "The real-life songs of the working cowboy played only a relatively small part in the formation of [western swing and the western songs of the singing cowboys], other than image, the same image the cowboy and the Westerner gave to popular literature and art."

Image, then? Mere image? So has the *western* side of country music been a fabrication?

Yes, and so too has country artists' western wear, which Horstman and numerous others identify as mere theatrical costuming, since countless country singers have no biographical connections whatsoever to the West. Cowboy clothes, we learn, were a shortcut out of the hillbilly's overalls, an image makeover with a certain advantage in terms of status. Again, Horstman: "The cowboy image . . . was more appealing to the country singer than the costume of the mountaineer or the farmer. Many singers who seldom sang cowboy songs gave themselves titles like the Cherokee Cowboy or the Yodeling Ranger. . . . 'Tex,' 'Hank,' 'Hap,' and 'Slim' became common nicknames, whether a singer was from Macon, Georgia, or Mason City, Iowa." (Hank Williams was baptized Hiram.) New York clothier/designer Ralph Lauren learned in the later twentieth century that a middle-class man with some disposable dollars — say, a Pittsburgh accountant — could go western by riding his plastic charge card to the Lauren "Chaps" line of sportswear and aftershave. But country music knew from the 1930s on that an image makeover was as close as the nearest western outfitter, that it was possible to move from a hick to a hero in one change of clothing.

We must face the fact, moreover, that the whole Western myth, cowboy songs and all, has fallen on hard times lately. A spate of well-researched studies are debunking the myth of the American Old West. The recent revisionists' West is no center of freedom and national destiny but a site of greed and ethnocentrism. The "destiny" of writers like Whitman and Cooper now is exposed as imperialism. Onetime inspirational imperatives like "the Winning of the West" and "Manifest Destiny" now sound like windy slogans as historians cite the exclusion of Native Americans and of women in western histories that too long ignored mixed-race western actualities and blithely trumpeted the triumph of Anglo-American democracy over the western territories. The contemporary historians' cowboy, not surprisingly, has been exposed as a corporate hireling, powerless in his lack of property and wealth, a kind of emasculated figure, a two-legged steer in a ten-gallon hat. As one historian writes, "The corral built to contain Western history [has] been knocked apart."

Amid the scattered slats, we return to the western side of country music. The cowboy songs, seen in this light, become just a pack of wish-fantasies buckled into saddlebags, and country-western music just one more product of an image factory promoting the West. To grasp one source of the appeal of this figure and this music, one might turn again to the songwriter/artist/student of cowboy songs, Douglas P. Green, better known as Ranger Doug of Riders in the Sky. Green believes that the "primary, profound appeal" of cowboy songs has been their "escapist lyricism." Surely such a trait underlies Roy Rogers's promise to keep the Old West alive in music: "I've sold my saddle for an old guitar." This is to say that the new, revised history of the West lives side by side with—or maybe gulf-by-chasm with—a powerfully residual "escapist lyricism." Perhaps it is this that motivates the New Jerseyite to pull on western boots and journey to the Lone Star Café Roadhouse on a wintery New York night. If so, she is heir to an invented West, a construction of western ideology's own Edisons and Alexander Graham Bells.

It might seem, then, that interest in the cowboy songs of country-western music diverges like a Texas river forking in two directions. One branch meanders through a sympathetic appraisal of its poignant nostalgia ("escapist lyricism"). The other cuts swiftly through an iconoclastic exposé of the musical "West," and along its banks we see the factory turning out a kind of machine product called the Old West.

But a third current reveals itself, an underground river as it were, flowing from the Adirondack Mountains of Cooper's Leather-Stocking novels to the Cimarron and Rio Grande of country music. This current, too, needs mapping, and a good place to start is with a cowboy song, "Mamas, Don't Let Your Babies Grow Up to Be Cowboys," the lead song on *Waylon and Willie*, the so-called Outlaws' album. The song upholds the cowboy code in its address to mothers, the proper audience. Those listening "mamas" are apparently urged to block their sons' ambitions to become cowboys, to raise them instead to be conventional professionals, "doctors and lawyers and such."

But no court of law could match the cowboy life in these lyrics, no surgical greens compete with the "Lone Star belt buckles and old faded Levis," the tactile stuff of multimillion-dollar ad campaigns for jeans makers. And the cowboys' tastes are compelling:

> Cowboys like smoky old poolrooms
> And clear mountain mornings,

Little warm puppies, and children
And girls of the night.

Though hedging on whores, the profile is still evocative and sensuous, from the puppy fur to the green felt through a tobacco haze to the bracing morning mountain air. "Mamas, Don't Let Your Babies Grow Up to Be Cowboys," seems to illustrate the notion that "the primary, profound appeal of the music of the singing cowboys [is its] escapist lyricism," and that the music endlessly reproduces the imagery serving this impulse.

Another familiar trait in this song, however, should give us pause because it links up with James Fenimore Cooper's independent and self-reliant forester, Leatherstocking, and with other American representations of individualism. Waylon and Willie's "Mamas . . ." works to present the self-reliant psyche of the cowboy. "He's not wrong, he's just different," say the lyrics. How different? Different from all others, refusing to be conventional, being instead a loner, a man apart. As a stranger, the song says, the cowboy is disliked, and as a familiar figure, baffling. Essentially, the cowboy is elusive: "Cowboys ain't easy to love, and they're harder to hold / . . . They never stay home and they're always alone / Even with someone they love." It is this very loneness, this solitary state, that ought to stop us in our tracks. Inside those faded jeans, the song says, is a figure of psychological complexity who goes right back to Hawkeye/Leatherstocking. He is not social, gregarious, or convivial. A loner, he stands apart by definition, a figure all by himself, noncommunicative, an isolate.

He is the strong-but-silent cowboy, and we know him on sight from Cooper and numerous other popularizers, right down to the Marlboro Man, whose very silence is a measure of his strength (he will light up in defiance of the "doctors and lawyers and such"). This loneness of the cowboy has important implications. On the one hand, he is a figure of American competence itself. He can ride, rope, shoot, camp, herd cattle. His pain threshold is higher than mesas and bluffs. He squints into the horizon and knows the weather, knows what might spook the herds. Nightlong, camping in the open, he endures cold, heat, physical pain. But mostly in silence, uncomplaining. He holds his thought and feeling inside. As for his inner life, we are led to believe it in sync with the values he represents. He is independent and self-sufficient. He is the exemplar of self-reliance, a deeply respected, long-term American value. Great-grandfather Hawkeye would be proud.

But this cowboy also has literary uncles who set their own bootheels in American soil long before the post–Civil War cowboy era. The self-reliant American man appeared on the horizon not only in the Leather-Stocking Tales but at other points leading up to the heyday of the cowboy West, of the West*ern*, and of country-western music. Within American culture, the self-reliant hero was invented and reinvented through the nineteenth century. The man of whom Waylon and Willie sing in "Mamas, Don't Let Your Babies Grow Up to Be Cowboys" is actually a relative latecomer in American culture.

To look more deeply at the western hero's self-reliant psyche, his underground stream of consciousness, is to find that the western side of country music involves much more than hats and fringe, much more than costumes or even lyrical escapism, powerful as that motive might be. To grasp the deeper significance of the western side of country music, we must really reverse Leatherstocking's westward journey and travel East, back to the New England world of Ralph Waldo Emerson, that champion of the American farm and home, the very writer who argued that life's authenticity lay in the exemplary model of the natural world.

Emerson, as it happens, also gave his blessing to the ranch. In effect, he became an ideological champion of the cowboy before there were cowboys. He not only prophesied the glorious West but projected onto it the figure who came to symbolize it in the twentieth century. The traditional western hero, put in play in the Leather-Stocking Tales, is very much an exemplar of self-reliance, as if Emerson took up where Cooper left off and projected this man onto the plains and deserts, the trails, the saddle, in the essay-address entitled "Self-Reliance" (1841).

Ne te quaesiveris—"Do not seek outside yourself." This is the motto with which Emerson began his essay, the Latin epigraph indicating a timeless classical endurance of the message. And indeed Emerson filled the essay with his own epigrammatic sayings that serve the ideology of self-reliant individualism. "To believe your own thought, to believe that what is true in your private heart, is true for all men,—that is genius." Or: "Trust thyself: every heart vibrates to that iron string."

Emerson's world of the self-reliant is distinctly masculine. He warns that social convention is castration. ("Society everywhere is in conspiracy against the manhood of every one of its members. . . . Whoso would be a man must be a nonconformist.") The entire essay exhorts American men to break free of a stifling dependence on tradition and to develop values not based upon material property or money. And Emerson linked self-reliance with the natural order. His "true man . . . is the centre of things. . . . Where he is, there is nature." This self-reliant man is a solitary figure by definition, standing majestically apart from the general population, that human herd who only play a "blindman's-bluff game of conformity." Instead, the individual—self-aware, independent, self-reliant—achieves greatness by being in possession of these very traits. "The great man is he who in the midst of the crowd keeps with perfect sweetness the independence of solitude." Worldly status is irrelevant. The self-reliant great man can be found—or find himself—

anywhere, north/south/east/west. He can be anybody, sailor or cobbler, herdsman or tailor.

Or cowboy.

In the twentieth-century world of the Western, he is very much a cowboy. He is Waylon and Willie's self-reliant man, who is "always alone, even with someone [he] loves."

And it must be said that this very self-sufficient autonomy is the state sought by women in country music. The western image not only frees the female from the gingham and ruffles that signaled her domestic subservience but offers terms approximating the man's. "I want to be a cowboy's sweetheart," sings Patsy Montana, this familiar opener seeming to affirm the traditional subordinate role. But in the next breath she says why: "I want to learn to rope and ride." She wants to do what the guys do. Skill and action are her goals, even if she can achieve them only through a romantic indenturing to the cowboy. As sweetheart, she gets lessons and, later on, becomes the cowgirl of Laurie Lewis's "Cowgirl's Song" (*Restless, Ramblin' Heart*, 1986), riding along with her "hat thrown back," her pony her only companion as she camps and "rides the wide prairies with the greatest of ease."

But what is country-*western* music's relation to this self-reliance? In part, country music's job is to profile over and over again the figure who embodies it. To ratify that figure by repeatedly singing him alive. "Don't Fence Me In," goes the cowboy song of the self-reliant individual who is a law unto himself. He is not to be contained or restricted. Nor ought he to be, this individual who is *all* in one. He (or she) is literally an outlaw, that is, outside the humdrum laws dreamed up by the mundane hordes. (Even Leatherstocking was turned into an outlaw when he was found guilty of violating game laws to which he should never have been subjected.) The self-reliant American is rightfully an out-law from those petty "laws" that do not apply to him.

Cover design for Willie Nelson album, A Horse Called Music. (Courtesy Sony Music)

And country music presents itself as the pipeline to this figure. Country has the studio franchise to paint his portrait, to be his official photographer. "Hankering to be / With a banjo on my knee," sings Gene Autry in "Take Me Back to My Boots and Saddle." "A guitar for a cowboy way out in Arizona" is on the inventory of merchandise in "Mule Train." "Cowboys . . . they'd rather give you a song than diamonds or gold," sing Waylon and Willie to the Mamas. The cowboy/musician rides Wayne Carson's "A Horse Called Music," as Willie Nelson sings him in a portrait song. His cowboy has ridden a trail from Boston to Bozeman, Montana, "riding along on a horse he calls music / With a song on his lips and a tear in his eye." This musician *is* the cowboy and vice versa. Cowboyness is his musical credential, which in turn authorizes his western outlook. These snatches of song lyrics all reaffirm country as the western music entitled to represent the self-reliant.

Were the westerner only the human face of a self-reliant America, however, this music would be just another engine of ideology. But in fact western music offers something more, something unique. In essence, country-western music gives voice to a figure otherwise silenced, ironically, by Emerson's definition. For country music responds to a terrible dilemma that Emerson failed to see but that another writer, a contemporary of his, faced squarely in the 1830s with a shudder. French traveler Alexis de Tocqueville noticed American self-reliance all about him as he traveled from New York City to Boston, then westward to Green Bay, Wisconsin, north into Canada and south as far as New Orleans—all the while taking notes on social conditions as well as governmental structures of the new American democracy. His two-volume, much-reprinted, and endlessly quoted cultural study was immediately translated into English as *Democracy in America* (1835, 1840).

Tocqueville, like Emerson, noticed the American tendency toward self-reliance, though he coined another name for it—individualism. Americans preferred to live apart, not together, he noticed. The custom disturbed him. Individualists, he said, "owe nothing to any man [and] expect nothing from any man; they acquire the habit of always considering themselves to be standing alone, and they are apt to imagine that their whole destiny is in their hands." From Emerson, such a statement would glow with approval. Not so from Tocqueville, who offered a terribly sad and poignant silhouette of individualism: "It throws him back forever upon himself alone and threatens in the end to confine him entirely within the solitude of his own heart."

To confine him entirely within the solitude of his own heart. Where Emerson saw self-reliant genius, Tocqueville saw unsocial isolation. Where Emerson saw majesty, Tocqueville saw a lonely confinement. Where Emerson saw self-sufficiency,

Tocqueville saw loneliness. The one saw cause for affirmation, the other for desolation.[1]

But the two overlap in at least one crucial respect. In both camps, human beings are quite literally speechless. Separate from others, they necessarily fall silent. Tocqueville's individualist is beyond calling distance, while Emerson's self-reliant American is hushed by his very superiority, cut off from others so different (so inferior) that they lack the capacity to understand him. Tocqueville's individual is walled off, Emerson's sealed in. Neither can speak. Each is incommunicado.

Enter country music. With its western identity, its songs can give voice—literally, provide a voice—to this individualist American typified as a self-reliant western hero. Country-*western* songs, that is, become the voice of the American who otherwise is mute. In his guise as western hero, the self-reliant individualist gains a crucial voice in song. Through music, he can give expression to his inner life. Country music becomes his voice.

A demonstration of this is as close as the nearest video rental store. From the *Western* section, select a classic that offers a typical showdown story—and an Oscar-winning country-western song sung by Tex Ritter. The film is *High Noon*, the song title the same (but best known for its opening line, "Do not forsake me, oh my darlin'").

High Noon (1952) stars Gary Cooper as an American individualist, Marshall Will Kane, who retires to take up storekeeping at the urging of his pacifist Quaker bride, Amy (Grace Kelly). The couple has wed just as news comes that lunatic outlaw Frank Miller has been freed from prison—unexpectedly pardoned—and is heading toward Hadleyville on the noon train to seek revenge on Kane, the marshall who sent him up. The new town marshall is not scheduled to arrive and take up his duties until the next day, so that in twenty-four hours the new lawman will have his hands full, both with Frank Miller and with his gang of three who have ridden into town and are waiting at the train depot for their boss. In the nick of time, it seems, Kane will elude the avenger, for he heads out of town with his bride.

---

1. Tocqueville's insights were updated nearly a century and a half later in the 1980s, when a group of sociologists borrowed a phrase from the Frenchman and used it as their book title, *Habits of the Heart*, meaning social practices and customs. Their book concerns individualism and commitment in contemporary American life. They found that Tocqueville's fears were justified. Conducting extensive interviews with individuals in many walks of life, the sociologists found that citizens of the United States inherit ways of thinking that "leave the individual suspended in glorious, but terrifying, isolation."

They get as far as the open prairie. Then, reining in the horses, Will Kane says, to himself as much as to his wife, "They're making me run. I've never run from anybody before." In the face of her bafflement ("I don't understand any of this"), he turns back to town, saying he's not trying to be a hero and that he knows his decision violates Amy's religious principles. (This showdown Western is edited to take place in "real time," the actual countdown measured by a hotel lobby grandfather clock edging toward high noon. Each shot of the clock ratchets up the tension.)

Most of the film's action involves Kane's failed attempts to get help from the very townspeople he has so faithfully served. By purging Hadleyville of outlaws, Kane has made this former "wide-open town" a safe and peaceful family haven of picket-fence yards and flowering shrubs. Yet now, in this hour of crisis, the judge who sentenced Frank Miller to death packs his portable scales of justice and flees, signaling the demise of the rule of law. One by one, all the men desert Marshall Kane: the immature deputy who resents being passed over for marshall; the veteran retired lawman and onetime mentor of Kane, who refuses to help "because it's all for nothin'"; but also the men in the tavern, in the church, in their households. Kane goes from one to the other, from public place to private dwelling, seeking but not begging, and all to no avail. Cowardice, hypocrisy, smoldering resentment—all surface among the citizenry to augur Kane's death in this upcoming four-against-one gunfight.

Most painful of all, Kane's pacifist bride has deserted him, repelled by the violence she has forsworn since the senseless deaths of her father and brother in gunfights. Recoiling from her husband's decision to stand and fight, she has bought a train ticket to St. Louis. While Kane tries to form a posse, she waits in the hotel lobby for the very noon train that brings her husband's killer.

Essentially, *High Noon* is an allegory and a psychological case study of Will Kane, whose character must be tested and proven this one last time—not for the townspeople but for himself. His self-respect is on the line. "I'm not trying to be a hero," he says matter-of-factly to his uncomprehending wife. And indeed he is not. "You scared?" asks the deputy whelp in the face of Kane's inability to raise a posse. To which Kane replies, "I guess so," too busy seeking help to ponder the question deeply, but too self-aware to delude himself. The camera moves in repeatedly to give us a portrait of a stoic under pressure. It registers the depth of Will Kane's emotion, and Gary Cooper shows Oscar-winning muscle movements around the mouth and jaw, signaling pain, disappointment, forbearance, determination. In the movie, Will Kane is a page right out of James Fenimore Cooper and Ralph Waldo Emerson, a portrait of quintessential American self-reliance.

Yet the on-camera close-up cannot adequately convey the psychic dimensions of Kane's mind. And the marshall's scripted one-liners ("Go on home to your kids, Herb") do not even attempt profound vocal expression. Besides, talk itself is suspect in *High Noon*. The best public speaker in Hadleyville makes a stirring speech about Will Kane's exemplary service to the town—then uses a debater's twist to urge Will to flee and spare the town the dangerous showdown, which is to say, to leave the town in the hands of mad Frank Miller. Talk, then, is cheap, treacherous, cowardly.

Yet viewers must have access to Will Kane's mind. Otherwise, the psychodrama turns into mere melodrama. We need to feel the depth of his turmoil, the nature of the conflict as Will experiences it. We need to know that *he* knows the terms of his own fight. What are the crosscurrents in his own mind? Is it Will Kane versus the feckless citizenry? Kane versus archenemy Frank Miller? And bride Amy—to what extent is she a presence in his thought? This film claims to be psychological, not merely situational.

How, then, to gain access to his mind? When facial expressions and terse one-liners have failed to convey sufficient complexity, when stark camera shots of the deserted town and of Frank Miller's outlaw sidekicks have provided all the tension possible but *still* not established this as a psychodrama, then what can a filmmaker do? The answer is, work the soundtrack, provide access to the hero's mind via his song—the theme song as sung by country-western artist Tex Ritter, whose voice opens Will Kane's mind in "High Noon" by Dimitri Tiomkin/Ned Washington.

The chorus opens the song ("Do not forsake me, oh my darlin'"), as if the singer cannot wait for the preliminaries of scene-setting and musical storytelling. Will Kane's hope, his wish, his deepest secular prayer is that he will not be forsaken by this bridal "darlin'." She will "grieve," we learn in a subsequent verse, if her husband shoots the vengeful gunman in an act of violence, but a grieving beloved is better than none at all. Ritter's voice, speaking Kane's mind, outright begs that Amy not abandon her husband for the action he must take, committed to his new life yet straddling the unfinished business of the old one. His voice breaks on the word *forsake*, expressing his worst fear that he will be utterly abandoned, not by the feckless townspeople, but by this morally pure beloved. He asks only for time. "Wait along," he asks repeatedly in the refrain, begging her to abide, the musical notes sounding like steady but faint hoofbeats.

It is in a full-bodied narrative that Tex Ritter sings Will Kane's situation:

> Oh, the noonday train will bring Frank Miller.
> If I'm a man I must be brave.
> And I must face a man who hates me
> Or lie a coward, a craven coward
> Or lie a coward in my grave.

Coward—the term repeats, as if vocally the marshall is testing the identity-as-epithet. The term threatens to brand him. Kane knows he might be in the grave by early afternoon, but Tex Ritter's voice says, as well, that should he fail to confront Miller, he will be a coward for all eternity. Ritter's voice breaks again in a kind of sob on the word *craven*, as though to tell us how unutterably despicable he would be. The conflict here is not between life and death, or good and evil, or even between bravery and cowardice, though those are crucial terms. In a phrase of varying rhythm, Ritter sings Will Kane's plaintive cry: "I'm not afraid of death, but oh, what will I do if you leave me?"

He has no answer, only the question that opens up Will Kane's terrible dilemma. If he shoots Frank Miller, he loses his bride; but if he fails to confront the gunman, he loses his self-respect, which is to say, himself. Kane is in a double bind, a lose-lose situation in which death is just one subordinate variable. Deep-chested, full-bodied, sobbing, but resolute too, Tex Ritter's voice sings Will Kane's psyche. "Do not forsake me, oh my darlin'."

What is happening here? Quite simply, Tex Ritter's song has become a soundtrack of the hero's mind. The western song becomes, in effect, an audio version of the psyche. This loner, this self-reliant individualist hero, speaks his mind through the song. Tex Ritter is his spokesman (and so effective that an early 1950s parody of this Oscar-winning song went, "Do not forsake me, oh Tex Ritter"). Gary Cooper cannot burst into song, but his mind is opened to us by it. "Do not forsake me, oh my darlin'" is the vocalization of Will Kane's very being. It makes the melodrama a psychodrama. The self-reliant man in his magisterial solitude speaks his mind in the song.

But why couldn't Gary Cooper sing his own song? Why can't the hero speak? In part because drama and musical theater are of separate worlds. *High Noon* is not *Oklahoma!*. But more important is the ideological reason. Because he is self-reliant, Will Kane is severed from the world of ordinary mortals. He has nothing to say to them. They are unworthy of any words he might utter. The Emersonian drama proves this scene by scene with the townspeople, who are in effect conspiring against their marshall's manhood in urging him to run away.

Let us think for a moment about the self-reliant western hero. He is a man of deeds, not of words. The laconic Will Kane is typical. Like other western heroes, he really mistrusts language, and his mistrust is a deeply ingrained American trait, historically inherited from New England colonists who were suspicious of ornate speech and writing and committed instead to a "plain style." Will Kane is also the heir of Founding Fathers like Benjamin Franklin, who warned against poetic "eloquence." And heir of James Fenimore Cooper's Leatherstocking and of the Ralph Waldo Emerson who denounced streetside conversation as "superficial and treacherous," social evenings as "tedious," society at large as "vulgar." Mere talk, Emerson argued, quickly degenerates into factionalism, and he saved his highest commendation for the "exquisitely made" man who can and must live alone. He exalted the "necessity of solitude," a condition essential to the self-reliant.

The western hero is the embodiment of this ideal. "Westerns distrust language. . . . The western at heart is anti-language." This is Jane Tompkins's insight, and absolutely correct. Bona fide legends of the Old West may have helped to establish this pattern. In his autobiography, Buffalo Bill (William F.) Cody remembers Wild Bill Hickok as a man who "seldom spoke himself unless requested to do so." Westerns virtually engrave this trait in every hero. The cowboy in Owen Wister's classic Western, *The Virginian* (1902), is nature's gentleman, a "handsome, ungrammatical son of the soil." *Ungrammatical*—not simply flawed in grammar but without it, unable to express his most powerful feelings ("the Virginian rode beside me, so silent in his volcanic wrath that I did not perceive it").

Other Westerns are cut from this mold. Lassiter, the gunfighter/hero in Zane Grey's *Riders of the Purple Sage* (1912), appears at a crisis point "like a man in a dream. Hunger was not with him . . . nor speech." The speechlessness signifies a true western hero, a man of few words:

> "Lassiter, will you be my rider?" Jane asked him.
> "I reckon so," he had implied.
> Few as the words were, Jane knew how infinitely much they implied.

Jane can know and tell, but not Lassiter. And the same holds in *Shane* (1949), the Jack Schaefer novel featuring a mysterious gunfighter/savior, Shane, who is "reserved, . . . withdrawn beyond a line of his own making," both in town and with the farm family who learns virtually nothing about him, not even his full name. When the wounded Shane rides out of town at the novel's end, having vanquished the farmers' enemies in a blazing gunfight, he is as much a mystery as the day he appeared.

The western hero thus operates under a code of virtual silence and separateness. Louis L'Amour's Flint (*Flint*, 1960) says, "I am a man who minds his own affairs, and that's all I ask of others." Readers meet him as a man who believes himself mortally ill: "He was seeking a dark and lonely place where he could die in peace, and in his own way. . . . He would die as he had lived—alone." The hero of the twentieth-century American West, then, is the self-reliant man and the lonely individualist of Cooper, Emerson, and Tocqueville. In a world hostile to and suspicious of language, he is confined to the solitude of his own heart. Emotionally, it is as if he belongs forever to the silent movies.

What might the cowboy say about his life if he could? That he is lonely, home-

Thomas Eakins, Home Ranch, 1888. Oil on canvas, 24 × 20 in. (Courtesy Philadelphia Museum of Art; given by Mrs. Thomas Eakins and Miss Mary Adeline Williams)

less, in pain. Roy Rogers sings that in a life of cattle and dust, the cowboy seeks so-lace in the music that speaks his state of mind: to ward off loneliness, he'd "strum" his guitar ("How the West Was Swung"). "Lonely but free," says the "rovin' cow-boy" of "Tumbling Tumbleweeds." And cowgirls too. "Even cowgirls get the blues," says the Rodney Crowell song, while Laurie Lewis's cowgirl ("The Cow-girl's Song") admits sometimes, "I'm as lonesome and blue as a coyote's cry."

And loneliness recurs in other fiction of the American West, for instance, in Jack London's story, "All Gold Canyon," in which we meet a gold prospector whose eyes show Emersonian "calm self-reliance and strength of purpose," but who is shocked when he climbs a Sierra mountain peak at dawn and, expecting splendor, encounters "loneliness." It is the central trait for the settlers scattered in the Cascade Mountains of the Pacific Northwest in H. L. Davis's *Honey in the Horn*. Although lonely, they nonetheless resist any efforts at community. "What loneli-ness . . . had lost them was the habit, not of talking, but of listening." Perhaps it is significant that the prolific Louis L'Amour expressed this theme in titling three of his books: *The Lonely Gods*, *The Lonely Men*, and *High Lonesome*.

It seems as though we are simply recycling here the American loneliness of Lonely Street. It feels like a reprise of the loneliness we explored earlier in coun-try music and in such American writers as Mark Twain. Aren't we only citing the regional, western version, as in "Bury Me Not on the *Lone* Prairie"—the very prairie that writers like Washington Irving had labeled "inexpressibly lonely"? Aren't cowboy songs just the boots-and-spurs version of the same thing?

Certainly, yes—if Westerns are one more database for a national theme. But the western side of country music gives a very different slant. The music becomes the voice of the individualist otherwise consigned to silence. He (and usually it is a *he*) gains the power of speech through the song. The song makes him conversant, communicant. The song lets him speak, lets others hear him.

And on a whole range of subjects, sacred and profane, trivial and profound. Through song, the individualist can break his silence and release a flood of thought and feeling. On his Country Music Foundation Hall of Fame album, didn't Gene Autry sing about falling in love "South of the Border" yet bidding farewell to his "Mexicali Rose," about unrequited love ("Someday You'll Want Me to Want You"), about his "Home on the Range," about being "Back in the Saddle Again," about his "Silver-Haired Daddy," about a "Mule Train" carrying mail, boots, a Bible, tobacco, calico, cotton thread, shovels, and rheumatism pills? Was any subject off-limits to this almost-garrulous cowboy, who used song as a pipe-line to broadcast his passing thoughts, observations about the jimson weed, the cement sidewalks, the one person who is nothing less than the singer's very "sun-shine" ("You Are My Sunshine")? Imagine Shane or Lassiter or the Virginian saying, "Come and sit by my side if you love me." Unimaginable. And yet the singer in western wear is entitled to voice such thoughts and wishes, whether they are passing notions or deepest convictions.

The costuming of country music becomes important here. It both certifies the West and frees the artist to sing geographically beyond it. Specific western geography—trails, cactus, canyons—can become unnecessary, as was evident when Hank Williams, dressed up in his cowboy suit, sang about love and loneliness, the American individualist telling us he's "so lonesome [he] could cry." When artists perform in western garb, their stage clothes mean West, and that West, in turn, is an individualist, self-reliant America speaking its heart and soul. The cowboy suit becomes a license to sing about—in effect, to talk about—anything under the sun.

The western song is thus the voice of a jailbreak from solitary confinement. It seems not at all coincidental that Johnny Cash recorded albums in prisons, Folsom and San Quentin, implying that all are imprisoned, psychologically if not actually. On a symbolic level, every listener is a prisoner given voice in the songs. The Wild, Wild West in country music serves to free the self-reliant American from an imprisoning solitude of the American heart.

▼ ▼ ▼ ▼ ▼ ▼ ▼ ▼ ▼ ▼ ▼ ▼ ▼ ▼ ▼ ▼ ▼ ▼

Red Red Rose

The Biltmore Estate in the mountains near Asheville, North Carolina, opens to visitors every day of the year except major holidays. "House/Gardens/Winery," reads the brochure enticing travelers to George Vanderbilt's 8,000-acre, onetime summer home, a Gothic-revival French chateau of 285 rooms, with gargoyles and mansard roofs, reflecting pools, a palm court, indoor swimming pool, billiard room, banquet hall, art ranging from medieval tapestries to portraits by John Singer Sargent.

And a stunning formal rose garden. In sunny, hot late June, you can stroll the graveled paths of this rose fancier's paradise where three full-time gardeners tend the beds. The rose species, of course, are highly bred, and the varieties impressive—King's Ransom, Tiffany, Saratoga, Dresden. There are singles and doubles, staked and climbing arbors and trellises, every hue and color imaginable from white to burgundy, cream to peach. From the pathways you can bend close, cradle the flowers, and sniff the heavenly aromas.

The rose garden, like the estate's architecture and furnishings, testifies to the American devotion to all things European. The highest order of Western civilization is symbolized in those roses, which hearken back to the great gardens of England and France. They also echo historically from European cathedrals' stained-glass rose windows and from the ducal houses of Lancaster and York, whose feud became the War of the Roses. As for music here, the program would predictably include carols and madrigals at Christmas, string quartets, a flute-harp duet playing Palestrina. Opera?—for this garden, of course, it would have to be *Der Rosenkavalier.*

But just for fun, how about a country music concert? Imagine it—those gorgeous roses inspiring a special events program of country "rose" songs, from Lynn Anderson's "I Never Promised You a Rose Garden" to Holly Dunn's version of "Blue Rose of Texas," Eddy Arnold's "Bouquet of Roses," Rose Maddox's "My Rose of Old Kentucky," Dolly Parton's "Yellow Rose," Conway Twitty on "The Rose," Emmylou Harris doing the bluegrass "Roses in the Snow." Also "The Bramble and the Rose," "Ramblin' Rose," "Second-Hand Rose," "The Hobo and the Rose," "Two Dozen Roses." Plenty of songs. So how about a concert?

Is confusion the first response? Or maybe a smile touched with skepticism? Bluegrass and country in the rose garden? Fiddles, guitars, a banjo amid the hybrid tea roses? The special events coordinator would probably pale at the thought and, straining for tact, murmur something about country music being widely available in this area of the southern Appalachians—of course, for those who like that sort of thing. Bluegrass on Asheville's town square on the Fourth of July weekend: fiddles and Dobro guitars, cloggers and buck dancers. Delightful public festival, fireworks. Take the children. Corn dogs and slushies.

But country music at the Biltmore Estate? We think not. Oh, maybe a few bars of a slide guitar on a groundskeeper's radio or a tourist's tape deck before they park and cut the engine. But a banjo and slap bass by the Damask and Province roses? Out of place, literally. George Vanderbilt rolling over in his grave.

Country music, then, is not entitled to a place in the garden despite its repertory of "rose" songs. *Yes* to a chorale singing "Lo, How a Rose E'er Blooming," but *no* to the bluegrass "Roses in the Snow." Bluegrass becomes a weed in the formal garden.

Roses in country music can seem like a topic far afield of the great American

themes of the road, home, loneliness, the Wild West. The rose, however, provides
tremendous flower power. It can open up certain American public attitudes toward country music—ironically, considering the beauty of the flower, the negative
ones. The rose can show why country music suffers from a cultural bias against it,
even in times of tremendous popularity. This is not to put a rosebud in the lapel
of country music, not a boutonniere for the gentlemen or a corsage for the ladies.

The rose, in other words, is not to decorate or commemorate but to teach. It
shows us biases and prejudices against country, how they started and why they
have dragged on and on. They start coming to light precisely when we shift familiar categories around. As the Biltmore scenario shows, country music represents
roses in the "wrong" way. It uses the steel-string instead of the classical guitar, the
fiddle instead of the violin.

In high-culture terms, country even represents the "wrong" roses. And where
do they grow, if not in a formal garden? Our gaze shifts beyond the estate walls to
the mountain ridges to the south and west. There, in sunlit thickets growing by
stands of hickory, maple, or cherry at the edges of meadows and on hillsides, grow
country music's roses. Botanists would say they are the *Carolinae* roses native to
eastern and central North America, upright but low in growth, their deep pink
blossoms "with wide-spreading sepals, borne singly or in few-flowered corymbs
on slender canes that are usually armed with bristles." No beds, however, and no
gardeners. No tending or feeding or pruning.

Wild roses.

Let's cut a few to show what country music is up against, a kind of war of the
roses in class terms. For American towns, cities, and even rural routes have plenty of self-styled respectable and upstanding citizens ready to fire salvos at rural
people who live in the outback where wild roses grow.

The term is *hillbilly.*

A hillbilly is "a person who lives in or comes from the mountains or backwoods, especially of the South," according to *Webster's Dictionary of the American
Language.* This definition emphasizes the regionality of the term. And many country musicians so define themselves—for instance, Loretta Lynn in her signature
song, "Coal Miner's Daughter," adapted for a feature-length film of the same
name and an autobiographical statement about growing up in rural poverty in Ap-
palachia. Country musicians may proclaim their backwoods hillbilly identity long
after they achieve financial and popular success. Merle Haggard reportedly told
President Richard Nixon to "just let [him] know . . . if there was anything a hillbilly
singer could do for him."

Webster's, however, goes beyond region to the emotional reverberation of the
word. "A somewhat contemptuous term," it says. Turn "hillbilly" from a noun to

an adjective, states the dictionary, and the best example is "hillbilly music." The word is not solely geographical, then, but emotionally loaded, its negatives hammering country music. Logically, by the dictionary definition, hillbilly music is "somewhat contemptible." Thus the barbs at the music of hicks, rednecks, lowlifes. The meanings branch to include ignorance, bigotry, the crude and the coarse. And even a low level of musical skill.

Now we are in name-calling territory. *Woods* and *mountains*, which ordinarily are positive terms, now become denunciations. L. L. Bean and other merchandisers have built fortunes on products directly linked to woods and mountains, but "hillbilly" is no mail-order catalog theme. We pause at this juncture to ask, Who gets to call somebody else a hillbilly? Identity is tricky. When Ralph Lauren markets a Log Cabin line of home furnishings, the last thing the Lauren designers want to suggest is "hillbilly" bedding. Lauren strives, instead, for an image of affluent rusticity, and buyers of Log Cabin flannel sheets know they are playing a game of lifestyle from within their realm of comfortable respectability. They play, in short, by the rules of the conventional social order. It is from *inside* those conventions that they can look outward and, if they wish, pass harsh judgment on those who fail to conform in ways that make them, as citizens, uneasy. The conventional citizenry of insiders can express their hostility in hierarchical terms. From on high, as insiders, they can look down-down-down and dismiss the outlanders as hicks, rednecks—hillbillies.

Seen from the world of traditional civility, then, the hillbilly is uncouth, in the very worse sense *primitive*. All kinds of negative associations come tumbling in—foul, degenerate, stupid. No redeeming qualities whatsoever. *Hillbilly* is virtually synonymous with everything that civility loathes and deplores. It is altogether repellent.

These negatives characterize the class-based antagonisms besetting country music from its beginnings. The music has consistently been disparaged in language setting class against class, and country music has fought back at the class-war front lines. Customs, material goods, and occupations that stratify us top-down and bottom-up become armaments in the lyrics. A "simple man," for instance, is the narrator in Frankie Miller, Jr.'s, "Black Land Farmer," which contrasts the smooth-faced (i.e., too-slick) banker and the lawyer to himself, a hard-working, warm-hearted, dutiful, devotional farmer. The song "Rednecks, White Socks, and Blue Ribbon Beer" positions country in white working-class terms, turning labels of contempt into a boastful and patriotic badge of identification. Lyrically, country's class-war songs often pivot on sociological homonyms. The private country club of golf and swimming pool becomes, in Travis Tritt's "Country Club," a bonding of pool-shooting buddies with pickup trucks. Friends in high places, the phrase indicating access to power and influence, becomes Garth Brooks's pledge of allegiance to his "Friends in Low Places." The *real* people, country music says, are those who value honest labor, loyalty, independence, and fairness over and against the false values of the opportunists, social climbers, snobs, materialists, and the well-to-do whose lives are backed by undeserved wealth and white-collar crime.

Typically, then, country responds to class-based hauteur with a self-defensive and aggressive stance of pride and defiance, though sometimes the poignance of the have-not shows through. In "Amanda," a poor husband laments that his lovely wife was cheated of the chance to be a "gentleman's wife." He struggles in vain for worldly success, his wife's facial lines a calendar of his futile striving. "Take This Job and Shove It" expresses in its title the pain and anger of a worker trapped in a dead-end job. Such songs seem haunted by the economics-based conviction of a Harlan Howard song: "The rich is smart and the poor is a fool" ("Mississippi Delta Land").

Spoofing hillbillies: Henry Haynes and Kenneth Burns as "hick" comedians Homer and Jethro. By the 1950s, they preferred suits and sportswear to the hayseed image emphasized here. (Courtesy Country Music Foundation, Nashville)

Sociologically speaking, much could be revealed by mapping the lyrics on country music's economic consciousness, including the irony that some of its artists and writers have become very rich from music about class-based privation.

Yet even more can be gained from looking at these matters through cultural symbols that include economics but extend into realms of art and imaginative expression. Let us return to that biting epithet—*hillbilly*—aware that the term can have socioeconomic meanings of poverty, lack of education, social unruliness, and the like.

For starters, notice that within country music, the term *hillbilly* has a wide set of associations made possible by its floral symbol, the wild rose. The very delicacy and subtlety of this flower enable a range of positive meanings about hillbilly life in country music. The wild rose seems to grow randomly and spontaneously in the American environment and, accordingly, lends itself to a certain idealism about hillbilly America. By its very nature, the wild rose suggests a beauty and delicacy whose origin and growth are centered in the natural world. The hillbilly wild rose becomes, in this sense, a musical celebration of a free spirit.

We are talking, really, about symbolic possibilities that open up when we read flowers instead of demographics and economics. We are also talking about two vastly different conceptions of the rose as an American cultural symbol. The hybrid tea rose represents a highly structured and disciplined civilization based on long traditions and practices. The tea roses whose names are registered with the American Rose Society belong to the cultural world represented by the Biltmore Estate.

The wild rose, on the contrary, is identified with the idea of unbounded personal freedom. It expresses the vitality and beauty of the natural world. One early twentieth-century genteel city lady admired this kind of wild rose for growing "across the mountains . . . without tendance, or skilled labor, or tags to tell their varieties," growing on "dew and sun and rain and love." Strictly speaking, this lady was writing about a hillbilly flower. She envied the living thing that flourished in nature without human intervention. She grasped the basis on which country music would celebrate its hillbilly rose.

The rose, then, can become an American cultural symbol representing ideas that are poles apart. These opposing ideas have been put forward in American writing, in decorative arts—and in country music. Depending on its cultivation or its wildness, the rose fluctuates drastically in its message about society and the individual. Wild or hybrid, however, each rose symbolizes the highest ideals of beauty. The bred rose is the badge of civilization, the wild the insignia of unfettered nature. Each competes for our approval. Each seeks to be desired.

The wild rose, country music's hillbilly rose, flourishes on the Grammy-win-

Trio *album cover design showing rose-theme costumes of Dolly Parton, Linda Ronstadt, and Emmylou Harris. (Courtesy Warner Brothers Records.) See also Plate 8.*

ning, platinum album *Trio* (1987), by Dolly Parton, Linda Ronstadt, and Emmylou Harris. Their collaboration, recorded in Nashville, resulted in an album whose cover design shows all three in color-coordinated western wear—festooned with roses. Embroidered roses are massed on all of their costumes, cascading over the shoulders and bosom of Dolly Parton's weskit, encircling Linda Ronstadt's skirt and scalloping her upper chest, rambling across the yoke of Emmylou Harris's jacket. All together, the roses are white, pale pink, scarlet, flowering in various states from buds to full blooms.

The roses—wild ones—are crucial to the album and to the identities of the artists. Dolly Parton's "Wildflowers" is a song about nonconformity, flight, freedom, individuality. In seasonal terms, it is a song of spring and summer, for the

▼ ▼ ▼ ▼ ▼ ▼ ▼

hills are covered with wildflowers, "alive" with them, as the cheerful voice of the autoharp seems to say from the introductory chords. These hills are a wildflower garden, says the lilting melody.

The singer knows, however, that to remain in the garden is to perish. This is a floral population "lost" in anonymity, its seasonal cycle fating these flowers to wither in the harsh sunlight. The singer/speaker alone can escape because she is different from the others, a flower much wilder than her companions: "I was wild, even wilder than they." While the others were contented with their lot, she was imbued with dreams, eager to run, fearless, and constantly aware of her difference:

> I grew up fast and wild and I never felt right
> In a garden so different from me.
> I just never belonged, I just longed to be gone.

By now the theme of this song is familiar, taking its place in the American pattern already known to us. "Wildflowers" is a song of the American road. The point of origin, the hometown, is insufficient, and the individual must depart and travel. We can predict that this woman, this wildflower, must go, and she says it directly:

> I uprooted myself from home ground and left,
> Took my dreams and I took to the road.

"Wildflowers" thus fits the pattern of "Ramblin' Fever" or "Restless," though instead of taking a Greyhound, this wildflower hitchhikes. In keeping with the imagery, the masculine wind picks her up, a "friend" to this wild rose who is as fearless as she is optimistic about her destination. At this point in the song, the drum comes in with a half-time, relaxing rhythm, a technique often used in country songs. The tactic works to particular effect here: her escape successful, this wildflower can relax a bit. She explains in the refrain, "When a flower grows wild, it can always survive," and says her particular destination doesn't matter, since a wild-growing flower can always survive. Survival is impossible only on the home soil.

In some ways, "Wildflowers" is a most radical statement about the relation of the hometown to the ambitious individual. The consequence of staying is not merely tedium but fatality. The threat is not of failure to thrive, but failure to survive. One remains in the home garden on penalty of death. The home ground is lethal.

Perhaps it is the very frankness of the message, its bold statement about life and death, that leads Dolly Parton to sing it so very prettily. When the song begins with the delicate chords of the autoharp, it signals a longtime tradition, referenc-

Dolly Parton with handcrafted mountain dulcimer. Note the sound holes carved in Dolly's signature butterfly pattern. Dulcimer designed by Dan and Ethel Doty. (Courtesy Dan Doty's Dulcimers, Memphis, Tennessee; photograph © Dan Doty. All rights reserved.) See also Plate 9.

ing the Carter Family, the country music group who performed from the 1920s to the 1940s and are called the patron saints of traditional country music. It is Sara Carter's autoharp to which this song hearkens from the very beginning, its sound a kind of many-stringed cousin to the mountain dulcimer that Dolly Parton has strummed onstage in live concerts, itself a reference to traditional mountain music and her own Smoky Mountain origins. The 1-4-5 chord pattern is standard for a country song, and appropriately so, given the Carters' electronic voyage on recordings beyond their rural southeastern Virginia homes. Embracing the autoharp, Parton is claiming that she has carried something of that wildflower garden

**Dolly Parton sings with her sisters
accompanying on autoharp and guitar
at Dollywood, Pigeon Forge, Tennessee.
(Courtesy Dollywood Foundation)**

with her. She has not rejected it, even though driven to leave it. It remains an important part of her. (It is noteworthy that Dolly Parton's childhood nickname was Blossom and that she has considered writing a novel entitled *Wild Flowers*.) "Wildflowers" is sung so prettily, in addition, because the flower is so beautiful. The singer *is* this flower, a wild rose singing herself as the most lovely of flowers. The voice curves like the very petals.

Extended to the entire *Trio* album, the theme of "Wildflowers" encircles all three musicians, all three singers being wild roses here, their costumes proclaiming that all of them are wildflowers. They have all left the scenes of their origins. They are all thriving in realms beyond. The embroidered flowers are emblems of their identity. The very fact that they stand before us on the album photograph proclaims their identities as wild roses in the Wild West.

These roses, then, fled the places of their origins to seek growth and vitality elsewhere in the wider world. They live outside the orderly garden bounds of do's and don'ts, protocol, tradition, custom. In that kind of regimented, conformist space they would "wither." As is, they have eluded the pruning shears of those who would teach them to "behave." They remain beyond the boundaries—wild.

And the audience wouldn't dream of denouncing these "wildflowers" as hillbil-lies. Absolutely not. We cheer for the wild rose who cheated circumstance and did it her way. We identify with, admire, support, wish we ourselves, etcetera. Thus we celebrate this renegade individual American. At the same time, we are endorsing the very idea of the wild, the socially out-of-bounds that holds a certain fascina-tion, especially when life is humdrum and full of rules and regulations. Henry David Thoreau proclaimed, "I love the wild not less than the good," having turned his back on American middle-class conventions and taken up a disrep-utable life alone in a shack by a pond in the woods. Hippies did this same thing in the sixties. The idea of free wildness has been vivid and continually attractive in this nation. And the hillbilly rose is a central figure in that wildness.

But she is not an American original. Dolly Parton's wild rose is actually part of a long-term and prestigious American cultural tradition. Her wild rose heroine has an American founding mother, as some *Trio* listeners will recall from their en-counter with *The Scarlet Letter* (1850). Nathaniel Hawthorne's American classic was a bestseller in its own time and still is, in the 1990s, the most frequently taught novel in all of American literature. Hawthorne, like Dolly Parton, drew upon the North American *Carolinae* roses, seeing surefire symbolic value in what he called "a wild rose-bush, covered, in this month of June, with its delicate gems" of "fra-grance and fragile beauty." The wild rose, Hawthorne saw, was perfect for his story of passion and desire that led a young married woman parishioner into an adulterous love affair with her minister. For Hawthorne, wild roses offered a sym-bol for a lush life force surging amid—yet outside of—society and existing as a law unto itself.

Rose-red in its title, *The Scarlet Letter* opens with a critique of the grim and somber townspeople gathering on the site of their failed Puritan American utopia, their major structures a cemetery and prison, that "black flower of civilized soci-ety." They will see the emergence from prison of Hester Prynne, the adulterer who has given birth, while in jail, to a baby of unknown paternity. In addition to her prison sentence, Hester has been sentenced to wear a scarlet "A" on her breast, identifying her as an adulterer. HESTER WAS A SEXY WIFE!

Hawthorne's narrative shows tremendous sympathy for the suffering minister/lover/father who is trapped in his hypocrisy. But his view of the scarlet woman, Hester, is ambivalent as he shows this social outcast wearing on her breast an or-nate, richly embroidered, sexy, rose-red "A." Mentally, Hawthorne says, she is as wild as the untamed Indians in the woods, radical to the point of anarchy. Her very nature, he insists, is "wild," the perfect match for a forested American environ-ment in its own state of wilderness. What better symbol, then, for wildness in fe-male form than the American wild rose? Hester is that wildflower, the embodi-

▼ ▼ ▼ ▼ ▼ ▼ ▼ ▼

ment of natural passion, beauty, spontaneity, life force surging beyond the bounds of social constraint.

Hawthorne also has an audience participation game for his readers: "We could hardly do otherwise than pluck one of its flowers and present it to the reader." Clever Hawthorne—for surely he knew that when he offers us a wild rose and mentally we reach for it, we also reach for the wildness it signifies. We become involved in American wildness, just as we do in supporting the singer of "Wildflowers" when we enter into the mentality of flight, escape, radical individuality.

And an actual hike into wild rose territory is not required, as Hawthorne's flower show proves. His book reveals that wildness does not necessarily mean flight to or from a geographic location. His readers, like those of today, were a literate lot with enough time on their hands to get comfortable, turn up a sitting-room lamp, and settle in with a good book. They qualify as vicarious wild roses, just like listeners playing *Trio* on a car stereo. Wild, then, can be a state of mind.

And a state experienced in a movie theater. Beyond book and song, the wild *Carolinae* blooms yet again in American culture, this time in a 1991 movie, *Ramblin' Rose* (based closely on a 1972 Calder Willingham novel and featuring Laura Dern as Rose). We hear "Ramblin' Rose" on the soundtrack, see roses climbing a trellis, notice the rose motifs in her clothing and on the wallpaper of Ramblin' Rose's room. The Blockbuster Video summary describes the film: "A man reminisces about the sexually liberated young woman who threw his traditional Deep South family into an uproar when she was hired as a governess in the 1930s." Uproar? This Ramblin' Rose threatens the entire social order. In its terms, she is a corruptor of children, a would-be adulterer, a nymphomaniac, an incompetent unfit for work, shiftless and feckless, and a liar, just as the "wild, wild rose" of "Wildflowers" is a deserter, a renegade, a subversive.

But as we root for "Wildflowers" and identify with Hawthorne's wild rose, so we love this wild hillbilly Rose, who represents not only sex in this film but "positive energy on the planet." She is female vitality incarnate in low-cut, see-through clothes, the embodiment of love not only for men but for children, for the family whom she serves as housekeeper, for all humanity. Some forty years after the events of the movie, we learn that Rose is deceased, but the survivors reject that mere fact. "Rose lives!" is their concluding and celebratory requiem for Rose and for the lives she has transformed forever.

From inside the confines of society, however, Rose has threatened the social order. Like Hawthorne's Scarlet Woman, she has showed herself beyond the law, beyond regulation. She threatens those citizens committed to upholding discipline, conventional morality, tradition, rules, regulations, all the hard-won traits of "civilization." Made anxious by Rose's flouting of their world, the citizens lash out, especially the men in positions of social power. Disturbed, they hurl insults that keep them safe by putting the errant "wildflower" in her place ("over-sexed," "near nymphomania"). According to "civil" traditions, the backwoods Rose poses a certain threat. Like the Wildflower and the Scarlet Woman, she lives beyond the reach of regimentation and regulation. She is a hillbilly. (Not by coincidence did the 1980s–90s all-female acoustic/electric/bluegrass group almost dub themselves Miss Behaving before deciding on another name: Wild Rose.)

Hillbilly disruption divides along lines of gender. Women hillbillies like Rose threaten sexual chaos, but the male hillbilly signals violence. In W. J. Cash's classic, *The Mind of the South*, the hillbilly is represented as "storing power as the air he breathed stores power under the hot sun of August, and then to explode, as that air explodes in a thunderstorm, in a violent outburst of emotion." Latent and sporadic violence, then, is one threat the hillbilly man poses to society. And though the South is most often linked with the term, at least one writer, the aristocratic New Yorker Edith Wharton, in the novel *Summer* (1917), denounced hillbilly mayhem, squalor, brutality in upcountry New England (New Hampshire). At the turn of the century, the wealthy Mrs. Wharton wrote novels in her study at The Mount, her summerhouse estate with its formal gardens in the Berkshire Mountains of western Massachusetts. From The Mount, she used the fictional voice of a New England attorney to denounce the mountain hillbillies for living beyond the church-steepled civility of the village. "A gang of thieves and outlaws," says the attorney-character, "defying the laws of their country."

Warnings against hillbillies, in fact, were posted as far back as the post-Revolutionary years, when J. Hector St. John de Crèvecoeur railed against the "back settlers, . . . ferocious, gloomy, and unsociable . . . lawless." Their children, Crèvecoeur said, "live in sloth [and] grow up a mongrel breed, half civilized, half savage." This vision, too, has been brought to the movie screen in *Deliverance* (1972), based on a novel by James Dickey and starring Jon Voight and Burt Reynolds as two of the four Atlanta businessmen who canoe into hillbilly territory, encounter rednecks, and must fight for their lives. Interestingly, country music provides one of the most memorable scenes from that movie—featuring the banjo legend Earl Scruggs in "Dueling Banjos," a virtuoso performance of "Foggy Mountain Breakdown." (Scruggs's music had also provided the soundtrack for *Bonnie and Clyde*, the 1967 film about outlawry and violence.)

"Dueling Banjos" brings us back to a question: Where does all this mixed emotion, from admiration to terror, leave country music? What is the status of this "hillbilly" music that is embroiled in American social conflict, as expressed in film, fiction, and social commentary for some two centuries? From Dolly Parton to "Dueling Banjos," what is country's place?

The answer is: on a seesaw. Wild and wonderful on the one hand—and danger-ous on the other. But who gets to apply the labels? Who, on this playground, gets to tip country music up or down? The listeners, of course, though that term is too big and vague to include all who tune in. Those who grew up on country as their one-and-only music, for instance, are apt to be puzzled by all the fuss, even if their defensive hackles rise over the derogatory *hillbilly*.

Other listeners, however, experience country in a more complicated way. They are themselves in some state of oscillation. When boxed in by routines, rules, and regs, they can follow the lure of honky-tonk or Cajun or rockabilly or bluegrass. This music satisfies a craving for the wilder, freer side of life. This is the music of the wild rose.

But the attitude changes when the listener feels tugged toward the citizenly side, the realm in which duty and obligation take on their veneers of virtue. At that point the civic self gains ground, defined by credit ratings, insurance policies, voter registration, sobriety of every sort. Then the wild side can seem disrep-utable, even menacing. It is not alluring but encroaching. It becomes a disturbance of the traditional social order of things and warrants reproach. At that point, country music can feel like a threat and be blasted—as, of course, hillbilly.

In a very special sense, then, country is mood music—depending on the mood of the listener who is oscillating between two cultural realms. When one is hemmed in on all sides by jobs, rules, strictures, it becomes a wonderful fantasy of radical freedom—running wild and raw in the honky-tonk, the bayou, the dive. When the world of tradition becomes one of rutted convention, country music's wild rose beckons irresistibly.

But country becomes crude hillbilly music when social rules that are broken or go unheeded start feeling like earth tremors. At that point, the very grammar of country ("she done me wrong") feels like a violation of respectability and a potential undertow that might suck the unwary into the lower depths. *Webster's* "backwoods and mountains" has a symbolic implication after all. The *back*woods and the steep elevations to the very "timberline" are places beyond the reach of regulation, and the very idea of such places can be threatening. "Hillbilly" is name-calling meant to disarm that threat, to banish and ostracize the outlanders and to reassure those tucked into conventional society that they are safe within the norms of respectability.

Country music, for its part, has not stood still like some sort of wallflower while this back-and-forth blows around it. Its artists have not simply produced and reproduced wild rose music for radio and video for the delight and dread of American neurotics unsure of who they are at any given moment. Coun-

PLATE 2. *Thomas P. Otter,* On the Road, *1860. Oil on canvas, 22 × 45⅜ in. (Courtesy The Nelson-Atkins Museum of Art, Kansas City; Purchase, Nelson Trust, 50-1)*

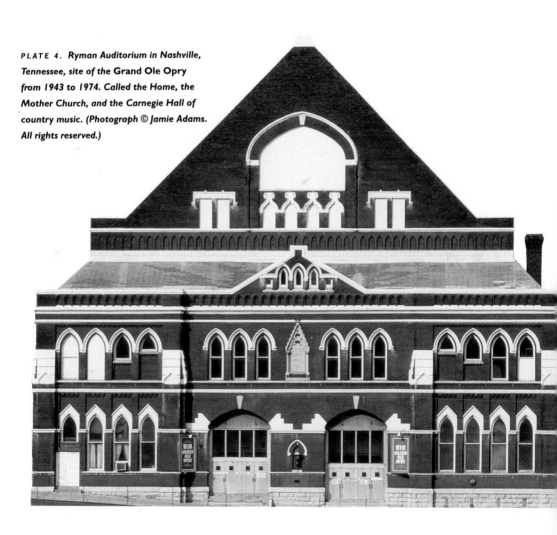

PLATE 4. *Ryman Auditorium in Nashville, Tennessee, site of the* **Grand Ole Opry** *from 1943 to 1974. Called the Home, the Mother Church, and the Carnegie Hall of country music. (Photograph © Jamie Adams. All rights reserved.)*

PLATE 5. Dolly Parton, onstage at the Grand Ole Opry to celebrate Roy Acuff's fiftieth anniversary on the Opry. (Grand Ole Opry photograph by Donnie Beauchamp. Reprinted by permission.)

PLATE 7. *Edward Hopper, Gas, 1940. Oil on canvas, 26¼ × 40¼ in. (Courtesy Museum of Modern Art, New York, Mrs. Simon Guggenheim Fund)*

PLATE 8. Trio *album cover design showing*
rose-theme costumes of Dolly Parton, Linda
Ronstadt, and Emmylou Harris. (Courtesy
Warner Brothers Records)

PLATE 9. *Dolly Parton with handcrafted mountain dulcimer. Note the sound holes carved in Dolly's signature butterfly pattern. Dulcimer designed by Dan and Ethel Doty. (Courtesy Dan Doty Dulcimers, Memphis, Tennessee; photograph © Dan Doty. All rights reserved.)*

PLATE II. *John Stuart Ingle,* **Still Life with Rose and View into the Landscape,** *1984. Watercolor on paper, 60 × 40 in. (Private collection; photograph courtesy Tatistcheff Gallery, New York)*

PLATE 12. *Thomas Cole, The Voyage of Life: Childhood, 1842. Oil on canvas, 52⅛ × 77⅛ in. (© 1993 The National Gallery of Art, Washington, D.C., Ailsa Mellon Bruce Fund)*

PLATE 13. *Barry and Holly Tashian, 1993.*
(Photograph by Jim McGuire)

PLATE 14.
Rodney
Crowell.
(Photograph
courtesy
Columbia
Records, Inc.

PLATE 15. *Lin Barber,* **American Road,**
1993. Watercolor tint on photograph.
(Photograph © 1993. All rights reserved.)

PLATE 16. *Edward Hopper, Nighthawks,*
1942. Oil on canvas, 76.2 × 144 cm. Friends
of American Art Collection, 1942.51.
(Photograph © 1992 The Art Institute of
Chicago. All rights reserved.)

try, in fact, has been extending its reach and making its bid to set foot on Biltmore turf for quite a while, claiming a place in the formal rose garden and stepping out in formal footwear. The American Rose Society, for instance, has bred roses named for several country music artists whose work in some way connects them to the flower: Lynn Anderson, Minnie Pearl, Barbara Mandrell, Patsy Cline, and Dolly Parton.

Careful country listeners, what is more, can hear a cultivated rose song that runs—or grows—contrary to the wild ones. This bred rose, too, has social and cultural significance. And country has claimed it at least since the late 1940s, notably in Eddy Arnold's version of the Nelson/Hilliard song, "Bouquet of Roses" (1948), one of Arnold's top-ten records in a career spanning the 1940s to the 1990s, with record sales of over sixty million. "Bouquet of Roses," Arnold's signature song, is a forerunner of what came to be known as the Nashville sound in the 1970s, a smooth sound avoiding roughness or distinct edges. This song shows the influence of the crooning style of singing most commonly identified in the 1940s with Bing Crosby, and it suggests the basis of Arnold's crossover success in pop music.

"I'm sending you a big bouquet of roses," says the despairing lover at the start, "one for every time you broke my heart." The song proceeds as a rationale and an explanation. This man has "begged" her—his lover, perhaps his wife—to change her ways, to be true to him. And countless times he has forgiven her for repeated infidelities, though this is once too often. She has taxed his powers of forgiveness, and the "door of love" between the two is closing, the singer/speaker knowing that "tears will fall like petals" when they part.

Whose tears? Possibly hers, tears of remorse or regret. But his tears for sure. His is the broken heart; he is the one wronged. And the falling petals most clearly signify the tears he will shed for the love she could not or would not give him. "You'll always be untrue"—this is the bedrock fact of their relationship, and he cannot continue on those terms. He is "tired" of forgiving her. The chord sequence (1-5-4-1, with the pull on the last two chords) enables Arnold to lean vocally on "roses" and "closes," binding the two in the irony of a floral tribute to failed love, while the bridge, a part of the song that amplifies the dimensions of the story, widens our sympathy for his plight. Interestingly, this song has no chorus per se but in effect begins with its chorus. This bouquet of roses actually reverses the customary gift symbolizing continuous love or courtship. Each flower a marker of pain, this is a bouquet of anguish, loss, final separation.

Yet the roses in this song are a *bouquet*. They are not plucked from a bush but sent from the florist. They are not growing wild but in a greenhouse, for they are cultivated flowers, perhaps the American Beauties so proudly developed through complex grafting by American rose growers late in the nineteenth century and named in honor of celebrated actress Lillian Russell. In Eddy Arnold's arrangement of "Bouquet of Roses," there is no instrument like an autoharp or dulcimer to suggest rural wildflowers such as Dolly Parton's, even though Eddy Arnold was known as "The Tennessee Ploughboy" from his farm-family beginnings. Instead, one can picture the bouquet prepared for delivery, either a long box for long-stemmed roses nested in white or green tissue or perhaps a florist's vase in which the bouquet has already been arranged.

The point is this: country music also seeks to claim a different rose tradition, one that runs counter to the idea of the wild. This other tradition actually works against the wild, cherishing instead the carefully cultivated rose grown under controlled conditions, as in the hothouses and beds of the Biltmore Estate. This is the rose of civilization, and it has a foundation in European and American culture. When "Bouquet of Roses" meets "Wildflowers," then, the contrast is much more than botanical. It is one of clashing values in which the rose itself becomes a symbol of the struggle over individual, social, and artistic values. Behind the "*Bouquet of Roses*" lie centuries of all the symbolic roses of the tradition we call Western civilization.

Eddy Arnold, the "Tennessee Ploughboy," in formal wear. (Courtesy G. W. Purcell Associates, Ltd.)

And what values does this cultivation suggest? The list would be very long indeed, for entire books have been written about the symbolism of roses in the tradition of Western civilization. The public gets bits and pieces of the story in annual Valentine's Day features in major metropolitan newspapers. Roses signify the power of love in the human heart, they say, extending from ancient Egypt through classical Greece, emphasized in Greek and Latin poetry. They are ritualistic, too, from the rose petals of the newlyweds' bed, to the shredded petals in wine cups to accent the meanings of godly ecstasy, to roses on graves symbolizing the brevity of human life and, later on, in the Renaissance, inevitable decay. Troubadours throughout the Middle Ages made roses the basis of their tributes to love, beauty, and springtime, and this secular meaning was highly codified in terms of the symbolic rose of courtly love in *Roman de la Rose*, in which love holds transcendently romantic power.

Journalists point out, too, that Christianity elevated the rose to new levels of spiritual meaning, in which the flower became a symbol of love incarnated in Christ. It became the chief flower, the rose of heaven, in the garden of Paradise, appearing in complex symbolic form in Dante's *Paradiso*, in which it is queen of the flowers and refers to Christ, Mary, Paradise, and Divine Love.

**Country music albums featuring the
cultivated rose of Western civilization.
(Courtesy MCA Records)**

*Rose
window
in the
medieval
cathedral of
Notre-Dame.*

Valentine cards annually bloom with roses, of course, and with quotations from romantic poets. These draw upon the ancient meanings and continue a poetic tradition from the Renaissance, when the rose was employed as a sexual symbol by numerous poets. Christopher Marlowe wrote, "Come live with me and be my love . . . / And I will make thee beds of roses," and Shakespeare especially enlarged upon the beauty of the flower ("the deep vermilion in the rose"). The romantic poets' preoccupation with nature led them to invoke the rose anew as a metaphor of love, beauty, joy, and the transience of human affairs—Robert Burns, for instance, saying, "My love is like a red, red rose" to express the beauty of his beloved. February is the season for all these quotations to bud and flower on stationery racks throughout the United States.

It comes as no surprise, what's more, to see that just as "Wildflowers" has a lineage in American writing and art, so does "Bouquet of Roses." Hawthorne's rose counterpart is a fellow writer, the essayist Margaret Fuller, who decided to write a travel book describing her impressions of the Territorial Midwest of 1843. At thirty-three, Fuller knew she was venturing into an exotic America of Indians, wide-open spaces, pioneering. She was, in *Webster's* dictionary terms, heading for the hillbilly country of the day and was determined *not* to confront all this with a "stupid narrowness," but to be open-minded about everything she saw. After all,

this was "a new form of life," which "we must learn to look at by its own standard." Her book, *Summer on the Lakes, in 1843* (1844) would attempt to report events
according to this new standard.

Fair enough. But it proved impossible when Fuller confronted the astonishing
thickets of wild roses in pioneering Milwaukee, Wisconsin. They made such an
impact that she could not dispatch them with a mere phrase. They demanded so
much more. Fuller even takes us, the readers, to the very bushes: "A few steps will
take you into the thickets, and certainly I never saw so many wild roses, or of so
beautiful a red." What sort of flowers were they?—botanically speaking, the *Carolinae* roses of Dolly Parton and Nathaniel Hawthorne.

As a wild-rose writer, however, Fuller was blocked. After *wild*, *beautiful*, and *red*,
her supply of adjectives ran out—though not her intellectual resources. Wildness
was really alien to her classically trained mind, so she resorted to the standard she
knew best, that of classical antiquity, of England, and of Europe. For Timothy
Fuller, her father, had taught his very smart Margaret to read classics by age six,
Shakespeare by eight. She had studied European languages, English literature, ancient and modern history. It was a virtual certainty that Fuller would feel most at
home in the world of the Biltmore roses of Western civilization.

"Of such a color were the first red [roses] the world ever saw," says Fuller, eas-
ing into her mental territory, Greek myth. Mentally she left the American backwoods and receded into ancient Greece, presenting the Wisconsin roses in terms
of the story of Venus or Aphrodite, goddess of love, who was herself in love with
Adonis, the classical Greek embodiment of male beauty. When Adonis was killed
by a boar while hunting, Venus caused his blood to color the white roses red. Seeing an opportunity to provide a picture of sorts, Fuller even inserts a description
of the painting *Venus and Adonis*, by the sixteenth-century Venetian artist Titian.
Titian's "Venus herself is very beautiful," reads the description, "especially the
body is as lovely as can be; and the soft, imploring look." The quoted passage, in
turn, refers us to the Venus of Shakespeare, including a comparison to Shakespeare's poem, "Venus and Adonis" ("This Venus is not as fresh, as moving and
breathing as Shakespeare's").

By now, Fuller has put us at several removes from the immediacy of these wild
American roses of Milwaukee, Wisconsin. The flowers are screened through
Shakespeare, Titian, and classical Greek mythology. Wishing to do them justice,
Fuller evidently felt stymied on the bluffs of the lakes of this Wisconsin Territory
in a kind of seedling society ("nearer the acorn than we were"). Her friend, Ralph
Waldo Emerson, was calling for American writers to use the language of the com-
mon people, the vernacular language, the very kind of language Dolly Parton
would use in "Wildflowers."

But instead Margaret Fuller does exactly what she had been taught to do: recite the lessons on roses passed down through history. And this is ironic, because Fuller, wishing to convey the essence of these native roses, essentially shows that she cannot bear to show them as "wild." She draws a blank at the very idea of backwoods roses or the "wild mountain rose." Presenting them through the high-cultural tradition, she uses Greek myth and Titian and Shakespeare to prune and shape and graft and transplant, so that, in her prose, the roses move out of the thicket and into the formal garden. Even though the mythical story of these roses is one of sexual desire, of passion run wild, Fuller really makes the roses worthy of respect by very careful cultivation in the arts. She encounters the wild roses in thickets, but in her writing she makes them respectable by transplanting them to a formal garden. She moves the wild roses out of hillbilly territory into the beds of the Biltmore Estate.

Without the slightest intention of doing so, Fuller established one set of terms by which roses would make their way through American culture. These are the terms of the bouquet, of roses cultivated, brought into conformity with certain prescribed traditions and practices and rituals, with knowledge and formal education. And assigned a certain social status. To know roses is to know the arts of Western civilization, and vice versa. Those who are educated and knowledgeable about art and the finer things can incorporate roses into their cultural vocabulary. For them, it is essential to be cultivated. The only legitimate roses are those under cultivation—Biltmore roses.

One thinks this tradition belongs *naturally* to those with much formal schooling and a certain affluence, those with an inclination toward poetry and the arts. In fact, by the later decades of the last century, all the cultivated roses were, so to speak, being grown for this, the affluent and elite segment of the population. This "rose bouquet" tradition was, in effect, being roped off in the United States, reserved only for those considered worthy of it, principally those of much formal education and/or wealth, which is to say the ruling classes of the cities. Recently, the historian Lawrence Levine has showed in great detail how this social segmentation or stratification was accomplished, for instance by newspaper reviews that called opera audiences "the better class, the most refined and intelligent of our citizens."

Levine calls this "the emergence of cultural hierarchy," and it was occurring in all American cities: Boston, Philadelphia, New York—and Nashville, Tennessee, soon to become the capital city of country music, that hillbilly music, even as the city fathers strove mightily to foster its image as the Athens of the South. Indeed, when Tennessee opened its state museum, the curators made certain that the roses of civilization were on full view in display cases, along with the rustic buckskins and homespun. Visitors can trace the history of the state in the cultivated rose motifs in a lady's handbag, in portraits of children, on the cover of a young lady's diary, in parlor furniture from a rose-patterned carpet to a rose needlepoint piano bench—all intended to suggest that from the earliest pioneer days, the very highest standards of civilization were in place. If it wasn't the Biltmore Estate, it was close enough. "A symbol of refinement," reads the placard explaining the objects in one rose-theme room. As if we didn't know.

But in these same display cases, imagine coming upon Eddy Arnold's tuxedo and a 78 rpm recording of "Bouquet of Roses." And why not? His formal attire and his signature song are also symbols of refinement, are they not? Didn't this country artist become a part of the bouquet tradition when he fastened his studs and cummerbund and slipped into the satin-lined jacket to sing "Bouquet of Roses"? Isn't he at least an honorary elite?

Sort of. Somewhat. Up to a point. Suspicion arises, you see, that deep down, underneath the tuxedo, he is really wearing something else—country garb, perhaps the bandana and denim farm overalls of the kind Roy Acuff wore for many years of singing and fiddlin' with his Smoky Mountain Boys on the *Grand Ole Opry*. (Eddy Arnold is, after all, the Tennessee Ploughboy.) Is the tuxedo, then, really Eddy Arnold's masquerade? Is he only trying, unsuccessfully, to "pass"?

Anybody thinking so would be astonished to know that the Ploughboy's tuxedo is actually part of a long trajectory of "bouquet" rose clothes in country music. The "tuxedo" tradition came into country quite early on, in the late nineteenth century. In those days, country musicians dressed up to the bouquet, as Charles K. Wolfe has shown in his research. Surviving photographs tell the story. Take the Market House Fiddlers of 1886, four men wearing trousers, vests, shirts with neckties, all sitting on parlor side chairs against a backdrop of draperies and shelved books in matched bindings—and looking for all the world like a European string quartet on a concert stage. Or see the country music string band organized by Dr. Humphrey Bate. In a 1926 photo, Dr. Bate's group poses with their instruments, six men in business suits with a huge carbon radio microphone at the center, the background a window drapery and a reading lamp with a pleated shade.

Yet two years later, in 1928, Bate's band are a-settin' 'round a rustic bench against a painted backdrop of farm fields and timbered cabin with stone chimney. A new member has joined the six, and all have shed their suits for farm pants and work shirts with shapeless felt hats. The polished oxfords have been swapped for dirt-caked work boots. Dr. Bate has abandoned his patriarchal pose to settle in at the center wearing work pants, a slouch hat, and an open-neck shirt. The group is now a visual match for its name: The Possum Hunters.

Before: Dr. Humphrey Bate's string band, dressed in suits and ties for 1926 radio concert performance. (Courtesy Country Music Foundation, Nashville)

Who did the makeover? And why?

The "who" was a wardrobe master in the person of the powerful radio announcer George D. Hay, who rechristened the *WSM Barn Dance* with the copyrighted name *Grand Ole Opry*. It was Hay who understood that country music needed a dress code, one in keeping with its own identity as rooted, literally, in the natural world. Hay understood that if country music based its authenticity in nature, then it had better look the part. The stage clothes had better be as earthy as the music seemed to be. If country was "down to earth" and "close to nature," as Johnny Cash has said, "as fundamental as sunshine and rain, snow and wind and the light of the moon peeping through the trees," as Hay himself ventured, then the suits and ties and vests and white shirts had to go. They belonged to civilization, not to nature. Left to their own devices, country musicians had been performing in their Sunday best, looking virtually indistinguishable from classical musicians in the European tradition. Looking, in short, too much like the bouquet. Hay coaxed and cajoled them into the agrarian garb of nature. The "bouquet" coats and ties went into mothballs, while the local dry-goods merchants

**After: Dr. Bate's same string band, the Possum
Hunters, two years later in 1928, now dressed in
homespun country-music farm "uniforms."
(Courtesy Country Music Foundation, Nashville)**

profited handily from sales of bib-front overalls and muslin work shirts.

Eddy Arnold, then, was reclaiming an old country music tradition when he donned a tuxedo and went on to sing about a bouquet of roses. But decades of newer traditions had intervened and made their claim. By the 1950s, Eddy Arnold owed it to himself and his audience to signal his earthy origins. He had better have a twang in his voice, a country music teardrop, a down-home anecdote to recount. The point, then, is not to suspect that at heart Arnold might be wearing overalls under his tuxedo—but to know that deep down, he had better be. He is a descendant of the country artists who became Hay's hayseeds—and the other "H" word, too.

Is this war of the roses one of absolutes? Not at all. The two sides struggle against each other, but not always in mutual exclusion. The territory shifts with claims and counterclaims. Clothing styles remain suggestive here. The gorgeous stage clothes of country performers like Reba McEntire and Dolly Parton make a bid for the elegance of the rose bouquet, and yet the highly suc-

**American art upholds the division between
high culture and vernacular music. Jefferson
David Chalfant's The Old Violin (1888)
represents the instrument against a background of printed music by a European
composer. Oil on canvas, mounted on board.
(Courtesy Delaware Art Museum, Louisa
du Pont Copeland Memorial Fund, 1940)**

**Thomas Hart Benton's drawings, Hill Man
and Father and Daughter,** *show the same
stringed instrument, here called a fiddle, in
informal settings and played by ear. Charcoal
and ink drawings from Benton's autobiography,* **An Artist in America,** *3d rev. ed., 1968.
(Reprinted by permission of Thomas Hart
Benton and Rita P. Benton Testamentary
Trusts)*

cessful, Los Angeles–based Dwight Yoakam claims the rustic, hillbilly association with faded jeans conspicuously split at the knee. The donated costumes on display at the Country Music Museum show the pull and tug of identity, from the plain, battered boots of Millie Goode to the green sequined matching costumes worn by Dolly Parton and Porter Wagoner in their 1970s duo days at the Opry. Interestingly enough, the most "hillbilly" side of country music, bluegrass, has a deep tradition of consistently dressing *up*, the suits and neckties a legacy from the 1930s, when Bill Monroe rejected the hayseed image and dressed the Blue Grass Boys in jodhpurs and trooper hats that gave them a quasi-military, dignified bearing.

As for country music itself, it continues to work both sides of the Biltmore garden wall. The group Shenandoah records "Two Dozen Roses" (by Robert Byrne/Mac McAnally), a song that asks whether a reluctant lover would relent if presented with a bottle of wine and "two dozen roses." And the fine-arts rose tradition lives in the Rodney Crowell/Larry Klein song, "Alone but Not Alone" (*Life Is Messy*, 1992), which opens with an image directly from the modernist Georgia O'Keeffe's southwestern paintings:

Chet Atkins, "Mister Guitar," photographed in informal and formal attire. (Courtesy Country Music Foundation, Nashville)

*Red Red
Rose*

Dolly and
Porter re-
unite briefly
at the cele-
bration of
Roy Acuff's
fiftieth an-
niversary on
the Grand
Ole Opry.
(Grand Ole
Opry photo-
graph by
Donnie
Beauchamp.
All rights
reserved.
Reprinted by
permission.)

I'm stretched out like a canvas 'neath a blue and endless sky
Staring up through cattle bones as cotton balls roll by
I swear I see a rose up there so beautiful and white.

Referencing O'Keeffe's painting, *Cow's Skull with Calico Roses* (1931), this song embraces the wild and stark as they are encountered in a prominent painter's American West. But the reference extends beyond the work of art to its prestigious position in American culture. The song associates country music with the fine-arts tradition of museums like Chicago's Art Institute, in which O'Keeffe's painting is exhibited. The song is linked as well with the expensive, oversized books of art reproductions purchased by those self-identified with the "bouquet" population of the elite.

But what about that hillbilly mountain wildflower? It lives too, vigorously. In music, this wild rose thrives not only in Dolly Parton's "Wildflowers" but in the Emmylou Harris/Paul Kennerley "Timberline" on Harris's quasi-autobiographical country opera, *The Ballad of Sally Rose* (1986). The major character, Sally Rose, has the flower's name as well as its identity as a mountain or country rose—a "wild, wild rose." She is a hillbilly. "Timberline" begins as a kind of folksong, the singer accompanying herself on guitar (the chord progression is 1-4-5), recalling the past when her true love swore undying love and kindness. The young man, however, swore on "that Shenandoah hill," the very notched mountains in which Thomas Jefferson envisioned the road summoning Americans to travel. This singer obeyed that summons ("our love bloomed until I went away and left those promises behind").

The promises may be left behind, but not the memory, and certainly not the hold on her imagination. And as the song progresses and the harmonica, mandolin, and bass come in, we learn that one day Sally Rose imagines returning to reclaim that identity as wild rose, rising up from the timberline and reclaiming that love. She tells how she pictures herself at that moment, with a ribbon in her hair and "a gown of calico." And her reunion with this true love is imagined in wildest floral terms:

And the sweetest kiss will be the tie that binds
Like the wild, wild rose and the columbine.

She yearns not for the cultivated bouquet, but for "that place . . . where the wildwood flowers go." The bass and drum here change the tempo to a half-time beat, relaxing the song as Sally Rose imagines her life as a kind of timberline pastoral idyll. She now vows to return ("I'll go back, I swear I will"), to become the backwood, mountain rose—the wild, hillbilly rose.

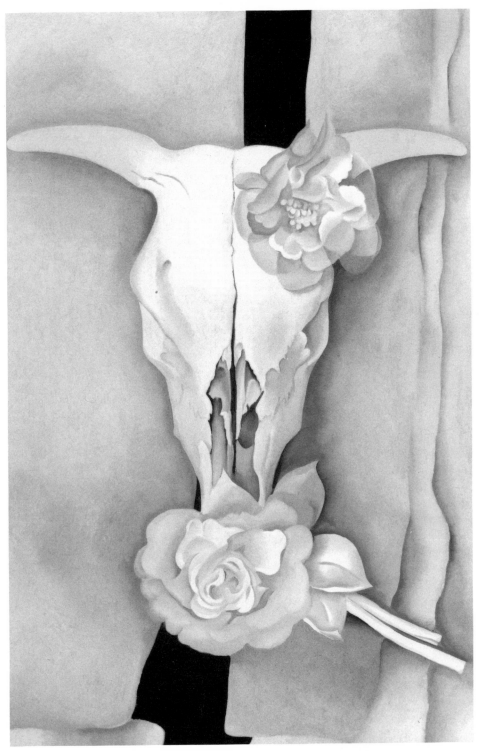

*Georgia O'Keeffe, **Cow's Skull with Calico
Roses**, 1932. Oil on canvas, 91.2 × 61 cm. Gift
of Georgia O'Keeffe, 1947.712. (Photograph
© 1993 The Art Institute of Chicago. All rights
reserved.)*

American artists show their own divided
attractions to the rose as wild and/or civilized.
Here, William Merrit Chase's late-nineteenth-
century Portrait of Miss Jessup, The White
Rose (n.d.) affirms a classical purity. Pastel
on paper mounted on canvas, 69 × 39 in.
(Courtesy Phoenix Art Museum, Phoenix,
Arizona, gift of Miss Margaret Mallory.)

The calico and ribboned hair somewhat domesticate the hillbilly wildness (and rebuke the notion of hillbilly squalor). But this particular country artist has chosen symbolically to sustain her identity with the hillbilly idea. It was fantasy to imagine Eddy Arnold's tuxedo in the Tennessee State Museum, but move to another Nashville museum, the Country Music Museum, and there is the wild rose on actual display. The black guitar, a Gibson J-200, has a very large, bright-red rose emblazoned on the top. It looks almost iridescent, certainly flamboyant. The guitar, in fact, is the original of the instrument Emmylou Harris plays in performance and is thus the guitar of "Sally Rose," that wild rose of "Timberline."

But in another of Chase's paintings, his sensual, bare-armed Carmencita dances seductively onstage in Georges Bizet's opera, Carmen. The roses strewn at her feet suggest that the opera's protagonist, a cigarette factory girl, is the artist's version of a hillbilly wild rose. William Merritt Chase, Carmencita, n.d. Oil on canvas, 69⅞ × 40⅛ in. (Courtesy The Metropolitan Museum of Art, gift of Sir William Van Horne, 1906)

The guitar's rose is large enough to be visible from the back of a concert hall. Close up, it is wild in its very brightness, insistent, flaring, gaudy. This is not, however, a wild rose simply because of its size and hue. It proclaims its wildness, instead, by its location on the guitar and by the nature of the instrument, which in and of itself deserves attention.

The acoustic guitar, says bluegrass historian Robert Cantwell, is an instrument working as an analogue of the human body: "The resonant body of the guitar . . . models the resonant human breast, and a vibrating string . . . the voice." With the idea of the guitar-as-body, we look again at that "human breast" of the Gibson,

*Philip Leslie Hale, The Crimson Rambler, ca. 1908. Oil on canvas, 25¼ × 30⁵⁄₁₆ in.
(Courtesy The Pennsylvania Academy of the Fine Arts, Philadelphia, Joseph E. Temple Fund)*

*Marsden Hartley, Wild Roses, 1942. Oil on Masonite, 22 × 28 in.
(Courtesy The Phillips Collection, Washington, D.C.)*

John Stuart Ingle, **Still Life with Rose and
View into the Landscape,** *1984. Watercolor
on paper, 60 × 40 in. (Private collection;
photograph courtesy Tatistcheff Gallery,
New York.) See also Plate 11.*

Red Red Rose

with its florid, floral statement. Pause to register the meaning of the big red rose imprint. It strikes you most vividly as—a tattoo. That guitar is tattooed. And the very idea of a tattoo proclaims the exotic, personal daring, an imprint on the body proclaiming it to be beyond the pale of routine respectability and defiant of conventional order. Wild—just like the Wildflower and the Scarlet Woman and Ramblin' Rose. Wild like Thoreau when he embraced "the wild not less than the good." Hillbilly wild.

Emmylou Harris performing with Gibson J-200 ("Red Rose") guitar. (Photograph © Woody Johnson. All rights reserved.)

But here, too, the country artist refuses to be walled out of the formal rose garden, with its rich resources of meaning and symbol. Emmylou Harris insists on also claiming the tradition of the cultivated rose as a musical treasury. Her performance venues cross from the intimate country music club to the symphony hall, and, like some other country artists, Harris regularly appears in concert with symphony orchestras.

The Harris recording, however, belonging most emphatically to the bouquet tradition is David Mallet's "Red, Red Rose" (*Brand New Dance*, 1990). This is country's ultimate bouquet song, both in lyrics and in production. The opening chord of mandolin and acoustic guitars sounds most like the symphonic harp, and the cello takes a melodic line within the instrumentals, pushing the boundaries of the country music format with a complex bridge and chord structure. The key phrase, "This love is like a red, red rose" comes directly from Robert Burns's poem, "Red, Red Rose," and another phrase, "heart of darkness," references Joseph Conrad's novel of that name in the European and British tradition. And the entire song is emphatically a Valentine in alliance with the world of art and culture extending to the erotic roses of the romantics and the Renaissance and back into classical antiquity.

The singer in "Red, Red Rose" has come to insight and knowledge that her lover does not as yet have, and she sings to him at a time when reflection on their relationship is possible, "between the tough times and the tender." Calling herself a "dreamer," she addresses his doubts about her—whether he really knows her, whether she cares enough not to leave him "sad and lonely," whether his loving her will bring him more than the limbo of an endlessly receding "someday." She is frank about her own weaknesses, stating outright that she may "stumble" from time to time in their relationship, and that she has a "heart of darkness." All this aside, she now seeks to allay doubt and to assure him:

> This love of ours is no common flower
> You know this love is like a red, red rose.

Harris presents this Valentine by combining the delicate and the full-throated, the filigree and the palpably passionate. The word *rose* is sung with lacy gentleness throughout. When this singer/speaker sings, "It all comes down to you and me," she draws the couple together, "you" being sung as if his heart were in her palm, cherished and protected and drawn toward her until they become one being.

At other moments, admitting that she may stumble, that hers is in part a heart of darkness, the personal confessions are so wildly flagrant that they come close to subverting the idea of a Valentine. But that is the point, that this is no mere greeting card, no heart-shaped box of creams. This, in short, is not a token but the real thing. How real can Harris sing it? Conventional wisdom would bet that *rose* would beam the energy from this woman to her lover. But that would come too close to the February Hallmark rack. Refusing the conventional, Harris displaces the passion of this woman's conviction to *red* itself.

Red. It is no mere adjective, but encompasses every possible shade and tone—crimson, vermilion, fuchsia, garnet, scarlet. It is love incarnate, heart and flower and emotion all in one. As Harris sings it, the one word becomes tangible, a sculptural form shaped anew each time, until you realize that it is, after all, the Venus Aphrodite, the cultivated rose—this time with the passion intact. This song resonates passion's wildness within melodic form. The wild rose of "Timberline" is domesticated in calico, but the bouquet-bred flower of "Red, Red Rose" throbs with underlying intensity as the music and the musician extend this American Beauty into the realm of modern romance. This is passion brought to the formal rose garden. This is Biltmore erotics.

Early in this century, the writer Gertrude Stein said, "A rose is a rose is a rose," intending her audience to understand that with each utterance, the word changes, that the emphasis shifts. You cannot say it the same way twice, Stein argues. Or sing it or live it. Roses, then, are dynamic flowers, as territorial in country music as in the country itself. Wherever they are, they bear close watching. They bear close listening. In the formal garden, they can be more erotically subversive than their custodians intend; on the hillside, more beautiful than those who tremble to say "hillbilly" can believe.

If they looked behind them, there was the mighty ocean . . . to separate them from all the civil parts of the world. . . . What could now sustain them but the Spirit of God and His Grace?
— *William Bradford,*
   Of Plymouth
   Plantation

"Our burdens are here, our road is before us, and the longing for goodness and happiness is the guide that leads us through the many troubles and mistakes to the peace which is a true Celestial City. Now, my little pilgrims, suppose you begin."
— *Louisa May Alcott,*
   Little Women

So the train came, and he pinched his little sister lovingly, and put his great arms about his mother's neck, and then was away with a puff and a roar into the great yellow world that flamed and flared about the doubtful pilgrim.
— *W. E. B. Du Bois,*
   The Souls of Black
   Folk

They found they must live like strangers and pilgrims.
— *Cotton Mather,*
   Magnalia Christi
   Americana

I am a pilgrim and a stranger
Traveling through this wearisome land.
— *"I Am a Pilgrim"*
   (trad.)

I am a poor wayfaring stranger
Traveling through this world of woe.
— *"Wayfaring Stranger"*
   (trad.)

▼ ▼ ▼ ▼ ▼ ▼ ▼ ▼ ▼ ▼ ▼ ▼ ▼ ▼ ▼ ▼ ▼ ▼ ▼

Pilgrims on the Way

Reservations for Thanksgiving dinner can be made at Plimoth Plantation, the recreated colonial New England Pilgrim village with thatched roofs and narrow sandy lanes, livestock, and authentically costumed "Pilgrims." When the day arrives, you drive Routes 3 and 3A to Massachusetts's Cape Cod, enjoying November's sky of low gray isobars while feeling hungry and a little smug for planning months ahead. And feeling pious—no, make that reverential. You expect to enjoy a meal like the first Thanksgiving in 1621, a harvest feast of "cod and bass and other fish, waterfowl, venison, Indian corn"—the closest record we have to a menu of that first Thanksgiving. Still, you don't go to Plimoth Plantation for the food. Culinary interest takes a back seat to the reenactment of one of the most familiar and beloved rituals in the nation's holiday cycle, a harvest meal symbolizing gratitude, abundance, ethnic and racial harmony in the vast space of North America ultimately to become the United States.

At first, nothing seems farther from country music than the fourth Thursday of November, with its turkey dinners and elementary school cutouts of Pilgrims and Indians. But recall the very word—*pilgrim*—that underlies those cute caricatures in tall hats and big square buckles. Pilgrims. It means those who journey through this world toward a future life. The pilgrimage in this sense becomes any mortal life conceived as a journey. "Pilgrim" becomes a term extending beyond colonial specifics. To identify with the Plymouth settlers is to accept a part of that identity within oneself and one's nation. Even in the 1990s, the idea of American life as a spiritual journey is made vivid when, on any given two days, the *New York Times* quotes a college student calling his life a "tremendous journey" and a minister calling his "the journey I am on."

Journeying in America—in fact, the very notion of travel—can seem to swing us right back to the American road, both fast lanes and slow, U.S. Route 6 or 66, a whole atlas of asphalt. Journeying, what is more, brings up the departures from home and the lonesomeness and yearnings so striking in country music and in related American writing and art back to the colonial and Revolutionary periods. The American journey can suggest conflicts between the free-ranging individualist and the dear ones "back home." It brings up the vexed relation between home and hometown, the ambivalent feelings toward those who stay, so to speak, behind, these being "friends" and "loved ones" but also figures pitiable for their timidity or inertia. The journey, then, becomes a knot of cultural complications in the record of this nation.

Yet the roadway of a pilgrimage changes everything. This road is not concrete or asphalt, not linked to worldly ambition or success. It is, instead, a higher pathway connected solely with the spiritual life. And this higher road pervades country music as it does the cultural record of American literature and art. Consider, for instance, the New England poet Robert Frost's well-known poem, "The Road Not Taken," representing American life as a symbolic spiritual journey. Or the Negro spiritual "Road to Heaven," from the musical tradition the African American writer W. E. B. Du Bois calls "sorrow songs" of "an unhappy people [expressing] their unvoiced longing toward a truer world." Or the song, "Precious Memories," the country spiritual that calls up "life's pathway." Or Leon Payne's "Lonesome Highway," popularized by Hank Williams, which depicts the path of a wayward soul lost to vice and temptation. All these are based on the idea of life as a journey along a spiritual path. Actual travel may play a part, but not necessarily so, for this is an inward journey.

Country music, like other areas of American culture, inherits this rich spiritual legacy from earliest Christianity. And no country music tradition has been more emphatically linked to the South, with its evangelical Christianity expressed in the gospel music of that region. The southern foundations were perhaps laid in the African American "sorrow songs." As Du Bois writes, "Before the Pilgrims landed we were here," and in *The Souls of Black Folk* (1903) he selects such spirituals as "Swing Low, Sweet Chariot," "The Wings of Atalanta," and "Steal Away" as the music of "trouble and exile, of strife and hiding," songs that "grope toward some unseen power and sigh for rest in the End."

But southern gospel also emerged in part from early eighteenth-century British border county "holy fairs," forerunners of the camp meetings that Scots-Presbyterians held in the American backcountry later in the same century. One historian lists these ingredients in the American southern gospel tradition: "the camp meeting, the Christian fellowship, the love feast, the evangelical preacher, the theology of Protestant fundamentalism and born-again revivalism." Country music historian Bill C. Malone adds that southern gospel music further developed out of nineteenth-century evangelical revivals and shape-note singing schools (which taught melodies using notes whose shapes, such as diamonds or squares, indicate their relative places on the scale).

Southern gospel has been a commercially important part of country music since the 1920s and is echoed, in the 1990s, in a song like Garth Brooks's "We Shall Be Free," its themes of freedom, racial justice, and equality supported with the gospel sounds of a church piano and organ, tambourine, background choir. When the poorest and most vulnerable are fed and housed, then and only then will all be free, say the lyrics, which ask listeners to keep "a little faith."

This song, stylistically rooted in gospel, is nonetheless sufficiently secularized for airplay on commercial stations throughout the U.S. It qualifies for market-driven radio precisely because it does not reflect a world of born-again fundamentalism sharply divided between the kingdoms of Christ Jesus and of Satan. That fundamentalist gospel tradition survives throughout the South in churches and small meeting halls, the singing groups sometimes being families who might record an album in their living rooms. Their music merges doctrinally with personal Christianity and, as Malone reminds us, presents the Savior as "a shepherd tending his flock or as a loving father watching over his sometimes-erring family," while Heaven is "an abundant Beulah Land traversed by flowing rivers and fragrant with the aroma of eternally blooming flowers." No music, he says, has been more "cherished by southerners than such gospel songs as 'Precious Memories,' 'Farther Along,' and 'If I Could Hear My Mother Pray Again.'"

Southern gospel in this sense is an expression of faith in a personal savior, as when the Carter Family sings that "Jesus will protect and shield" surviving family members after He has "carried" the wife/mother "home" to Heaven in "Just a Few More Days." Or when the Cooke Family sings of Jesus or the Jordan River in "King Jesus" or "Banks of Jordan." The listener hears the vocal incarnation of a deeply personal Jesus and of a river flowing, not in the Middle East or even in the Scriptures, but in the mental-spiritual realm of the Pentecostal and evangelical mind of each musician. The musical expression is an act of worship in which the physical is inseparable from the spiritual—no, in which the physical act of singing and guitar playing *is* the spiritual act. As Dolly Parton recalls her religious-musical background: "I was brought up in the Church of God. It's a very free church. If anybody wanted to get up and sing or shout out an emotion, they would do it. There was a freedom there." Songs sung as such godly acts are not stage or studio performances but open-throated prayers and acts of faith.

Seemingly particular to the South, the spiritual side of country music actually extends much more broadly to the nation, as the Thanksgiving theme at Plimoth Plantation indicates. The national origins, in fact, go back to the sixteenth- and seventeenth-century Christian Reformation. That religious movement stressed that every individual, without exception, is a pilgrim. Each is obliged to try charting the course of the soul's journey. Spiritual salvation, it goes without saying, is the goal, and the Christian's life is seen as one in constant movement. The Plymouth Pilgrims understood this well, for the Massachusetts colonists saw themselves as spiritual wayfarers. William Bradford, the Pilgrim governor who described the first Thanksgiving, searched for biblical parallels to authenticate the Pilgrims' journey to the New World. Bradford quoted the New Testament Book of Corinthians II, in which the Apostle Paul recounts the wayfarer's travails ("In journeyings often, in perils of waters . . . in perils in the wilderness, in perils in the sea" [11.26]).

The New England governor recited this litany to comfort the New England Pilgrims in an identical state of transit. And Paul's phrasing continued about colonists landing in a New World, "in which they found they must live like strangers and pilgrims . . . [afflicted with] solemn trials . . . to remind them that they were pilgrims and strangers upon the earth." Country music inherits and renews this idea. In "I Am a Pilgrim and a Stranger" or "I Am a Pilgrim," or when Fred Rich writes of "life's journey" and "your pilgrim way" in his song "Jordan," the Christian sentiment traces a particular American part of the Reformation and recommits it to an ongoing present.

And what could seem more hopeful? One might backslide, inch forward, detour, get sidetracked—but overall, the sustaining faith lies in a pilgrimage toward redemption, toward spiritual salvation. What belief, further, could be more sustaining in a nation in which so much of the population, including slaves and Plymouth Pilgrims, has arrived by ship or rickety boat via a dangerous, often traumatic oceanic voyage? It was probably inevitable that writers and artists would characterize the spiritual dimension of American life in terms of travel or journeying, given the patterns of migration to this continent from Europe, Britain, and Africa. The fact of transit and the spiritual meanings attachable to it were central to the national experience from colonial times onward.

Travel brochure from Plimoth Plantation. (Courtesy Plimoth Plantation, Plymouth, Massachusetts)

PLIMOTH PLANTATION

Explore Another World in Another Time

In 1620, America's most famous immigrants— the Pilgrims— set foot on the land which would be their new home. Today their lives, experiences, concerns and those of the Wampanoag Indians on whose land they settled come alive again at Plimoth Plantation. Enjoy the time of their lives in the **1627 Pilgrim Village**, at Hobbamock's (Wampanoag Indian) Homesite, the **Carriage House Crafts Center** and aboard *Mayflower II*.

"Wayfaring Stranger," a traditional folk-country song, speaks directly to this experience. Its verses make up a spiritual autobiography of the kind any number of American immigrant groups would find accurate to their own experience:

> I am a poor wayfaring stranger
> While traveling through this world of woe.
> Yet there's no sickness, toil, or danger
> In that bright world to which I go.

The singer is a kind of everyman or everywoman, a wayfarer because life is a journey, and a stranger because the earthly world is only transitory, never a home in the highest spiritual sense of the word. In Emmylou Harris's version (*Roses in the Snow*, 1980), the song opens with a guitar and bass pacing the footsteps of the wayfarer. The pathway through life has not been cushioned, and fittingly, the spiritual melody is in a minor key. The singer/speaker struggles essentially to keep faith while journeying in a woeful world. This person, we learn, is going "over Jordan . . . over home," meaning crossing from this world over to the next, to Heaven, the ultimate home. The wayfarer will at last be united with the heavenly (and also earthly) father and be reunited with the deceased mother who "said she'd meet me when I come." The singer reassures herself that "I'm only going over Jordan / I'm only going over home," the word *only* a reminder that in Christian terms, the inevitable is also the natural. Death is a passing-on, a uniting and reuniting. All the yearnings for home will be fulfilled.

Meanwhile, life is an incessant journey in a world of relentless trials. The voice of the Wayfaring Stranger is steeped in knowledge of this world's "sickness, toil, [and] danger." She sings late in life, knowing from long experience how terribly "rough and steep" the way. This is a world so trying, so arduous that the voice requires every atom of strength to sustain the effort. Harris's entrance makes a firm announcement of identity—"I am a poor wayfaring stranger." But the life-journey is taking all her effort. Musically, Harris cannot flat the notes, and yet she sings to the downside of the tones, the listener aware that this weary stranger is struggling just to sing her story. She is giving all and yet nearly giving out. The pained, almost strained vibrato, the bursts of energy, then near-collapse, the renewed push—all tell us this wayfarer has nearly run out of the breath of life, yet has no choice but to push on. She simply must be resilient because the journey is not yet done. At the concluding verse, the strings—acoustic guitars, gut-string guitar, Dobro, and mandolin as well as bass—express the beauty of hope, as does Ricky Skaggs's backup vocal. The "beauteous fields . . . where God's redeemed their vigils keep" is here suggested by the arrangement. The wayfarer's mission is to keep this vision before her, not to despair as she approaches that final crossing.

"Wayfaring Stranger," then, is a traditional American folk hymn that portrays life as a difficult pilgrimage. But Americans were not the only ones representing life in these terms. Literature on the spiritual pilgrimage also came ashore to America from England in the form of a published book by a self-made Puritan preacher, John Bunyan, whose *Pilgrim's Progress* is the best known of all spiritual biographies. The book recounts the story of a figure named Christian, who journeys through earthly perils and trials toward the Celestial City.

The very subtitle of *Pilgrim's Progress* provides the storyline or plot: *Wherein Is Discovered the Manner of His Setting Out, His Dangerous Journey, and Safe Arrival at the Desired Country*. First published in England in 1678, the book is part religious allegory, part novel, part romance, moral dialogue, folk story. It was extremely influential in America, threading its way through writings by Benjamin Franklin, Ralph Waldo Emerson, Louisa May Alcott, Harriet Beecher Stowe, Mark Twain, John Steinbeck, and certain utopian visionaries. (Bunyan has been so thoroughly assimilated in American Protestant culture that the lyrics of "Wayfaring Stranger"—for instance, those about the "rough and steep" journey—echo *Pilgrim's Progress*: "I looked then after *Christian* . . . clambering upon his hands and his knees, because of the steepness of the place.") Though Bunyan never set foot in America, his book would prove exemplary for country music and other American art forms envisioning life as a spiritual journey. If American country music owes Governor Bradford and his descendants the image of the pilgrim, it is indebted to John Bunyan for the fully developed pilgrim story.

To linger a moment longer both with Bunyan and the Plymouth Pilgrims is to see the ways in which American culture—including country music—was to work out the whole subject of the spiritual journey. Bunyan's *Pilgrim's Progress* is set in "the wilderness of this world," in which a ragged Christian, aided by Evangelist, leaves his family to follow the shining light he hopes will be eternal salvation. The allegorical figures who block his progress reveal themselves by their names (Obstinate, Timorous, Mistrust, Sloth). Their polar contraries help him (Prudence, Charity, Piety, Good-will).

The spiritual environment of that dangerous journey is revealing and ultimately important to country music. The way leads by a swamp called the Slough of Despond, the Hill of Difficulty, the Valley of Humiliation, byways of Danger and Destruction. Yet the heavenly city—that "Desired Country" or "Celestial City"—is always the goal, and it is previewed in locations like the Celestial Gate, the Palace Beautiful, the Delectable Mountains.

In all these allegorical names, we find an approach or technique called spiritualizing. Literally, it means to attach spiritual meaning to something, to elevate it from the mundane and material realm, to interpret it in such as way as to make it spiritual. In so doing, the object or situation becomes connected to the immaterial part of human life, the soul. The nineteenth-century poet Emily Dickinson, herself a descendant of the Pilgrim-Puritan tradition (many of her male family members being ministers) demonstrated very clearly the technique of spiritualizing:

> I cross till I am weary
> A Mountain—in my mind—
> More Mountains—then a Sea—
> More Seas—And then
> A Desert—find—

This is a mental, not physical, act of negotiating mountains, seas, desert. The trek —all within the mind—is self-evidently arduous, difficult, daunting, as in "Wayfaring Stranger." Geographic specifics are not uppermost for Dickinson, nor for the Wayfarer. Neither seeks actually to scale mountain peaks, swim seas, survive Death Valley. The struggle of each is a kind of spiritual triathlon, a struggle of the inner life. Dickinson, like the Wayfarer, uses familiar geographic features in order to express the magnitude of her inner struggle. And her list is implicitly open-ended. It could extend to deserts, ravines, swamps, and so on, just as the Wayfarer could sing further stanzas on storms and hills and fair meadows. There is no end to the trials and travails or to the sources of hope and faith that can be represented in geographic terms.

The entire geography, nonetheless, has moved into the mind of the individual. "Wayfaring Stranger" and Dickinson's poem teach an important lesson. In order to represent the journey, even an entirely spiritual one, a writer or artist must provide a context, a scene, a place—an environment. The very task of representation requires it, and Christian art from the Middle Ages onward shows it, with castles and trees and mountains and flowers representing various states of the inner life. In Emily Dickinson's poem, the mind is a realm made up wholly of symbolic geographical features. These can be visualized because they originate in scenes of worldly topography. The journey of the Wayfaring Stranger, likewise, with its "dark clouds," "rough and steep" way, and "bright fields," can be grasped readily because all of these features of the landscape are already well known. In short, in order to be presented in an understandable way, the spiritual state must include familiar features of the physical world *out there*. The artist or poet or songwriter borrows from the geography of the earthly in order to represent the spiritual. It is the very familiarity of the elements of the outer world that makes the representation of the inner one accessible.

These environments are not chosen at whim. Where do they come from? Originally from the Bible, which provides the ultimate in spiritually symbolic sites (gar-

Thomas Cole, The Voyage of Life: Childhood, 1842. Oil on canvas, 52⅛ × 77⅛ in. (© 1993 The National Gallery of Art, Washington, D.C., Ailsa Mellon Bruce Fund.) See also Plate 12.

dens in Eden, Canaan, Beulah Land, contrasted with harsh and hostile environs in the East-of-Eden world of toil after the Fall—not to mention the rigorous biblical wilderness). The Negro spirituals understandably link the American South with the biblical Egypt, whence Moses led his people out of bondage. A southern Egypt is the basis for spirituals like "Go Down, Moses," "Didn't Old Pharaoh Get Los'," and "Ride On, Moses." Americans from poets to songwriters increasingly made the particulars of North American geography into places with spiritual significance. Constant encounters with North American terrain over decades and centuries inevitably led to a spiritualizing of American space.

Like the road. This most secular and profane—and crucial—of national places becomes a spiritual, virtually sacred site in writing, art, and country music. John Steinbeck hinted this in *The Grapes of Wrath*, in which many things happen to the American refugees on Route 66, "some so beautiful that the faith is refired forever." And Walt Whitman's "Song of the Open Road" bows, if awkwardly, to the "efflux of the soul." The Negro spirituals incorporate the railroad as a "gospel train" with a full head of steam ("git on boa'd, little children"). Country music sends a spiritual roadway message in songs like Roy Acuff's "The Highway to

Thomas Cole, The Voyage of Life: Youth, 1842. Oil on canvas, 52⅛ × 76¾ in.
(© 1993 The National Gallery of Art, Washington, D.C., Ailsa Mellon Bruce Fund)

Heaven," in which the singer walks with his Savior toward the heavenly home. And the railroad is spiritualized in "When Jimmie Rodgers Said Goodbye" (Dwight Butcher/Lou Herscher), a song in which Rodgers's death becomes a freight-train ride to Heaven.

Or listen to Allen Reynolds's "Someday My Ship Will Sail" (Emmylou Harris, *Angel Band*, 1987), which defines life as "a passing moment / On a never-ending trail." Once again, the minor key signals the burden of mortal life even as the lyrics promise a steady, even cheerful resolve to follow the earthly "pathway":

> But I will walk this road a while
> I will walk it with a smile.

This country song joins up with others that state their meanings directly, like the Christian hymn, "Just a Closer Walk with Thee," predating the era of rail and automobile. All such spiritual road songs have a cultural foundation going back to Scripture and coming down through *Pilgrim's Progress*.

And coming to country music by way of their American cultural cousins' master classes on how to spiritualize the road. "Jes' git me on de road to go to Heav-

Thomas Cole, **The Voyage of Life: Manhood,** *1842. Oil on canvas, 52⅛ × 79¾ in.*
(© 1993 The National Gallery of Art, Washington, D.C., Ailsa Mellon Bruce Fund)

en," sang African American spiritualists, but in the Northeast, Henry David Thoreau also enlisted in the American pilgrim band when he wrote, "Every walk is a sort of crusade. . . . by the grace of God." Thoreau's essay, "Walking" (1852), describes his daily journey on foot:

> When the spring stirs my blood
> With the instinct to travel,
> I can get enough gravel
> On the Old Marlborough Road.
> Nobody repairs it,
> For nobody wears it;
> It is a living way,
> As the Christians say.

Thoreau was not a doctrinal Christian, but the term *living way* quickens that Old Marlborough Road into spiritual vitality.

The road is now a full-fledged spiritual site. At the conclusion of "Walking," Thoreau walks "in so pure and bright a light . . . so serenely bright, I thought I had   177

Thomas Cole, The Voyage of Life: Old Age, 1842. Oil on canvas, 52½ × 77¼ in. (© 1993 The National Gallery of Art, Washington, D.C., Ailsa Mellon Bruce Fund)

never bathed in such a golden flood." This moment becomes transcendently spiritual: "So we saunter toward the Holy Land, till one day the sun shall shine more brightly than ever he has done, shall perchance shine into our minds and hearts, and light up our whole lives with a great awakening light, as warm and serene and golden as on a bankside in autumn." The Old Marlborough Road, bypassed in the name of commercial progress in rural New England, becomes a pike spiritualized as a highway to Heaven.

Thoreau's successor—also kin to the country music tradition—is the twentieth-century poet Vachel Lindsay, who intended to make actual road travel a spiritual experience. In the opening years of this century, when country music's string bands played in local festivals and holiday gatherings, Lindsay tramped the nation's secondary roads in the Carolinas, the Midwest, and the West. In the 1910s he became immensely popular, a kind of evangelist reading and chanting his poetry before large audiences in theaters and high school auditoriums. Lindsay was the pilgrim "afoot and penniless," expounding a gospel of spiritual beauty. He made journal notes as he went: "Splendor after splendor rolled in upon the . . . highway of our God." Lindsay's stance: "Better to die of plague on the highroad, seeing the angels, than live on iron streets playing checkers with dollars forever and ever."

And Vachel Lindsay even tried to elevate an American legend, Johnny Appleseed, into a symbol of the spiritual road. Going alone and barefoot, the story goes, Johnny Appleseed (actually, the New England–born John Chapman) walked ever westward, cultivating apple orchards and dispersing the seeds across the land that became the United States of America. While Paul Bunyan axed the forests and John Henry bested machine technology as a steel-drivin' man, Johnny Appleseed became the patron of American agriculture and horticulture—and of the spiritual benevolence of the American road, according to Lindsay: "He kept moving for a lifetime toward the sunset, on what we would call 'The Mystical Johnny Appleseed Highway.'" Historically, the mystical and legendary highway has merged with governmental actuality, for in 1950, the Ohio State Department of Highways officially named three state routes, going north and south across the state, the Johnny Appleseed Highway. Secular, yes, but spiritually an important part of American space.

Almost tempting us, in fact, to speculate on the spiritual possibilities of Elvis Presley Boulevard in Memphis and Nashville's Roy Acuff Place, both roadways commemorating country artists who have recorded and performed songs of Christian spiritual journey.

But country music claims a very subtle spiritual road, too. Rodney Crowell's "Many a Long and Lonesome Highway" shows the pilgrim's way on a road of the automotive era. Cowritten with Will Jennings, this song says that a man will live life *his* way, on his terms:

> Many a long and lonesome highway lies before us as we go.
> In the end I'll do it my way; look for me where the four winds blow.

This song of the masculine spiritual road dangles a set of "keys to the highway"; the phrase is both the album title and a tantalizing promise of mobility and freedom.

Yet the song rejects adolescent car-key fantasies, replacing them with a far more solemn definition of male spirituality in terms of the American highway. This man has moved beyond the day-to-day world of men's and women's lives into the larger realm of Nature. He seems freed into the everywhere-and-nowhere of the four winds, the currents of air being his ever-shifting locale. Repeatedly he tells us, "In the end I'll do it my way." His credo maps the way ("I believe in love and danger, I believe that truth is stranger"). And he expresses a guarded optimism: "I believe the best will find me / When I leave the rest behind me."

But he faces a life's highway of solitary spiritual journeying. The refrain speaks directly to the pain of a man traveling with the vivid memory of his father's death ("though I was there, he died alone"). Crowell's use of the 6-minor and 2-minor chords creates a feeling of the lonesome, of a lament. The singer's highway, we realize, has become an involuntary journey through time, an adulthood less of independence than of loneness: "Many a long and lonesome highway lies before us as we go." In his delivery, Crowell extends the word "long," enacting the very length of the road, and pronounces "highway" with a strong long-*i* sound, so that the highway and the "I" become one. This man *is* the very road, his route the journey of life.

One additional spiritual roadway winds its way through country music, and to recognize it, we ought to return to the Pilgrim village of Plimoth Plantation. Before their Thanksgiving dinner, visitors not only can tour the village, with its English-style houses, its hay barn and blockhouse, but also see the reed-mat and ash-bark-covered structures of "Hobbamock's Homesite," a re-created household of a seventeenth-century Wampanoag Indian. Hobbamock lived with his family of "above ten persons" just south of the Plymouth settlement in the 1620s. Counselor to Chief Massasoit, Hobbamock may have been assigned to keep the English Pilgrims under surveillance—though the doleful history of Indian-white relations in U.S. history makes the very notion of such vigilance at best poignant. Hobbamock's Homesite might strike some as a minireservation and a reminder of whites' relentless suppression and destruction of the Native Americans. Certainly the homesite reminds us that the Thanksgiving image of a Pilgrim-Indian peaceable kingdom only masks a history of discord, violence, theft, killing—and, on the part of those historically culpable, guilt.

Country music has wished to ally itself with the Native Americans, not only historically but in spiritual terms. This alliance is consistent with the populist inter-

Detail from Plimoth Plantation visitor's map.
(Courtesy Plimoth Plantation, Plymouth, Massachusetts)

**Peter
Rowan.
(Photograph
by Rick
Gardner;
courtesy
Keith Case
and Asso-
ciates)**

ests of music identified with poor whites or hillbillies. Country has long been a music sympathetic to "Dust Bowl children," to borrow from the title of a Peter Rowan album whose songs include Native Americans among the hapless, the oppressed, the unlucky.

But country music, in addition, shares the Native American belief in spirituality immanent or indwelling in the natural world. Having embraced Ralph Waldo Emerson's view that the rural American is comparable to "sun and moon, rainbow and flood," country artists accordingly express an alliance with a spiritual outlook based in the Native American relation to the natural world. This is to say that country artists can move from the Christian-based views of writers like Emerson into the Native American conception of nature as a world peopled by what one scholar calls "other-than-human persons, often of mysterious powers and dispositions." Native American spiritual names—Thunder Grandfather, Spider Grandmother, Corn Mother—reveal this outlook. Spirituality, for the Native Americans, lies in the relationship with the earth itself, and thus country music identifies the spiritual pathway as inherent in the earth.

"Trail of Tears," by Peter Rowan (*New Moon Rising*, 1988), shows this relation well, its title referring to the infamous, forceful removal by the U.S. government of the Cherokee from their southern homelands to Oklahoma in the 1830s. Rowan's song, however, is less about history than spirituality, though it begins as a secular folk-country road song of rambling and sad memories. The fiddle-guitar-Dobro opens with a sense of loneliness—then comes Rowan's tenor:

> In the Great Smoky Mountains
> Of North Carolina
> That's where I have rambled
> For many long years
>
> In the Great Smoky Mountains
> Of North Carolina
> I've followed a trail of tears.

At first, "Trail of Tears" seems appropriated for private use, grabbed from history for an autobiography saying that any individual's life can be an unfortunate trail of tears. The song risks trivializing the Cherokee disaster and blurring lines of culpability—except that the lyrics reveal this man's keen awareness of a terrible historic irony: his North Carolina mountain cabin sits right on the infamous trail. He is burdened not only with private loss and sadness but with historic memory as well. He knows the Indian removal did not clear the land for whites like himself, did not start a new time clock for pioneer settlement. On the contrary, it made the North Carolina site one of continuous, irremediable tragedy. The singer/speaker must live with his private loss ("Now I wander all alone") and with history's too. The abrupt change of rhythm in the second verse signals his double consciousness, for Rowan moves into a 6-minor chord and a dactyl tom-tom beat that brings the Cherokee experience into the world of the song. "Red Cloud said he saw you / On that path to Oklahoma," says one line, the identity of "you" unspecified—perhaps the actual person in this man's life (someone who appears to have deserted him) or perhaps the Cherokee on the forced march. Whether this singer heard or overheard the Sioux chief of the Oglala Dakotas, Red Cloud's presence melts away boundaries of linear time and of space. Divisions between one century and another (or one lifetime and another) are false in the world of this song, as are geographic distinctions between, say, Middle Atlantic and Far West. Heard or overheard, the name of Red Cloud, renowned for bravery and prominent in treaties and councils, extends the Native American reference across the continent in a "trail" of widened consciousness that transcends calendar years and survey lines.

But the geographic path becomes a spiritual one as well. Thunder, rain, and lightning summon the spiritual presence of the Cherokee ancestors. They are ghosts here in the North Carolina Smokies, spirits haunting this place with their presence. Behind the lyrics—or beyond—is a mystical spirituality to which the words refer but which transcends specifics. The trail is a mystical pathway toward a painful enlightenment, and its spirituality is based upon the ghostly presence of the Cherokee in these North Carolina mountains. The song says that "no one remembers anymore," but the mind of the singer/speaker is all memory. His sense of self—past, present, and future—is bound up with the Native American spiritual presence.

The place name of the "great Smoky Mountains of North Carolina" nonetheless signals the crucial role of the American landscape in the soul's journey—even when the journey does not bear upon the Native American tradition. Spiritualized America, in the tradition of Christian thought, is most prominent in country music and in numerous texts in American culture. This America divides into two kinds of space, as "Wayfaring Stranger" shows us. On the one side is the land of "beauteous fields," indicating the splendor of eternity, the hope for the soul's arrival at a realm of utter happiness. The other spiritualized space, however, is dire and dangerous—described by the Wayfarer as a world of sickness, toil, danger, woe. Such is the space of the Negro spirituals. It serves as a constant warning about human weakness and waywardness, temptation and the evil threatening to lure the traveler to eternal damnation.

So we really have two kinds of Christian spiritual environments. The Pilgrim Governor Bradford gave us both, writing first of "a good harbor, safe arrival, the God of Heaven who . . . set their feet on the firm and stable earth." The words are pictorial enough for anybody to grasp the security of the good, the safe, the firm ground. This is the autumnal Cape Cod, a land mass shaped like an outstretched arm holding the Pilgrims in its sheltering embrace. This is the environment of God's providence and blessing. American literature and art—and country music —abundantly carry forward this tradition. Not surprisingly, the spiritual landscape is distinctly regional, based on writers' and artists' personal affection for particular places. For instance, the romantic poet William Cullen Bryant, an amateur botanist and sojourner, wrote "A Forest Hymn" (1825), a poem in which he pictured the New England forest as a cathedral, its green branches, massive trunks, roosting birds, soft wind as conclusive evidence of God's presence in nature. The New England forest, says the poet, is a place of "continual worship."

From New England, American spiritualized space moves westward in art and literature as in settlement, emerging, for example, in the middle western plains of Willa Cather's novel *O Pioneers!* (1913), in a scene of spring plowing: "The brown earth, with such a strong, clean smell, and such a power of growth and fertility in it, yields itself eagerly to the plow." This land, Cather continues, "gives itself ungrudgingly to the moods of the season, holding nothing back. . . . The rich soil yields heavy harvests. . . . The grain is so heavy that it bends toward the blade and cuts like velvet." These lines are erotic in their spirituality, and so visually evocative that the scene was brought to the television screen in the 1992 TV production of *O Pioneers!* (starring Jessica Lange). Cather's midwestern plains represent plenitude and abundance—the very idea of an American Canaan.

Move still further West, and the American spiritual environment becomes California. Frank Norris's *The Octopus* (1901) compares the industrial-age spread of the railroad to the tentacles of a grasping, sucking beast in a story of corporate greed and heartbreak that nonetheless features a spiritual landscape in the vast wheatfields of California's San Joaquin Valley. Norris returns to William Cullen Bryant's idea of nature's sacred space: "A cathedral hush overlay all the land, and a sense of benediction brooded low—a divine kindliness manifesting itself in beauty, in peace, in absolute repose. It was a time for visions." The vision is largely a spiritualization of the California wheatlands: "There it was. The wheat! The wheat! In the night it had come up. . . . The earth, long empty, teemed with green life. Once more the pendulum of the seasons swung . . . from death back to life. . . . 'Oh death, where is thy sting? Oh grave, where is thy victory?'"

Country music continues this tradition of spiritualized American space. Its regional focus, not surprisingly, is the South, one excellent example being Dolly Parton's "Appalachian Memories," a song of the landscape of strength, promise, hope. The song opens as it closes, with a woodwind melody in the style of composer Aaron Copland's *Appalachian Spring* (1945), cleverly paying tribute to Copland's own tribute to Appalachian ideals (quiet strength, simplicity, fundamentalist faith). The prelude and postlude of Parton's "Appalachian Memories" also carry a fragment of "Wayfaring Stranger," thus promising listeners a story of an Appalachian family journeying in their own spiritual pilgrimage—though one that began as a most secular venture:

"You ought to go North," somebody told us,
" 'Cause the air is filled with gold dust,
And fortune falls like snowflakes in your hand."

Living too long in debt, the "poor Appalachian farm folks" have been seduced by this glittery promise, and Dolly Parton sings these lines in throaty, whispery tones that capture both the allure of the siren song and also her full sympathy for these credulous pilgrims who "headed out to find [the] promised land."

Their hopes are dashed. There is no land of promise, no America of golden streets, for in economic terms "our dreams all fell in on us." Still poor, the family is virtually stranded ("Oh, these northern nights are dreary"). Displaced, they are much worse off than before. Parton sings a crucial line: "It's a struggle keeping sight of who you are." Far from home in an alien land, this family has a crisis of identity, dignity, self-respect. The singer/speaker, herself a family member, strives not to cave in to despair ("my southern heart is weary . . . my southern eyes are teary"), not to go crazy, not to buckle spiritually even as her family is succumbing economically. "Life's a mill," this woman tells us, "and I've been through it. . . . It takes all I've got to give what life demands."

Yet her personal Christian faith provides solace, comfort, strength:

I'll keep leanin' on my Jesus,
I know he'll love and guide and lead us.

This is not testimony about doctrine or dogma but about a personal faith in a personal savior. Singing about leaning on Jesus, Parton's voice leans fully and heavily on the very phrase. Her voice enacts this woman's need to be supported by her Savior—and we learn how fundamental a source of abiding strength *He* is in her daily life. (Dolly Parton notes the inspirational power of gospel music: "It lives inside you. . . . It lets everything out, all you hear, all your feelings. When I write gospel songs, it's a way to sing praise.") The refrain of "Appalachian Memories," one of the most spiritually powerful in all Dolly Parton's music, completes itself with this line:

Appalachian memories keep me strong.

The musical intervals, first a fourth, then an octave (B-flat/E-flat/B-flat) move ever higher, Parton trilling a bit, reaching toward the tonal peak, and falling away —the pattern almost that of the singer/speaker leaning on Jesus. And we come to realize that the melodic pattern is also a visual one. The notes are a graphic, pictorial outline of the mountains seen against the sky. Parton is profiling the skyline

The Smoky Mountains of east Tennessee, the peaks and valleys profiled in Dolly Parton's "Appalachian Memories." (Photograph by William Tichi)

of the Appalachian Mountains and the spiritual faith originating in that home-place. To sing this song is to re-create the Appalachian skyline from memory, to live there again with each vocalization of that refrain. The steep pitch of the octave is the steep pitch of the mountain. And the personal savior is present within a spir-itualized landscape of those mountains, of that place. The inner life of this Way-faring Stranger remains vital in a wealth of Appalachian memories. These provide the strength, the support, the courage to endure and continue life's journey.

The Appalachians, then, like the California wheatlands or the Midwest at plow-ing time—all lend themselves to portrayals of spiritual hope and strength.

Yet never far away is the cautionary American landscape, al-lied with the harsh biblical wilderness. It warns, it unnerves, sometimes terrifies. And all to good purpose, namely, the reminder that temptations lurk, that faith will be tested, that every human being must be vigilant—and humble and faithful, too.

From Governor Bradford, once again, we hear the voice of spiritual admonition. No sooner does one take comfort from the stable earth than its perils loom. Those Pilgrims who pass the "vast ocean" now face grim realities of circumstance and spirit: "The whole country, full of woods and thickets, represented a wild and savage hue. . . . What could now sustain them but the Spirit of God and His Grace?" This part of the pilgrimage is fraught with danger. Only the Lord's grace and spiritual gifts can provide comfort in so perilous a place. Death and destruction lurk. "Sharp and steep" is the pathway.

Documentation of this view is everywhere, even in the most secular of texts. Ralph Waldo Emerson's essay "Fate" cautioned the U.S. to be mindful of the "terror of life," because Nature, warns Emerson, is no sentimentalist. "The world is rough and surly, and will not mind drowning a man or a woman, but swallows your ship like a grain of dust." The cold "freezes a man like an apple." The "sword" of the climate in New Orleans "cut off men like a massacre." "Our western prairie shakes with fever and ague." He sums up, "Famine, typhus, frost, war, suicide . . . must be reckoned calculable parts of the world."

American writing was already documenting this environmental peril. Diaries and letters would record personal tragedy, like the mid-nineteenth-century mother's letter telling a grown daughter in Illinois that son and brother Hiram was dead: "He swam Across the river and the Watter run very fast and he could not rach the shore. . . . The other boys Cald to him and said O hiram O swim and he said O My god I cannot. . . . O My god O Lord Jesus receve my Soal for I am no More." The mother continues, "It has Al most kild Me," adding, "If we are good per hapes then we can meet him in heven."

Wrenching accounts like this had long been a part of American literature — drownings in *Moby-Dick*, in Kate Chopin's *The Awakening*, in Stephen Crane's "The Open Boat," in which the strongest swimmer in a lifeboat dies in the shallows while his mates survive. And in Jack London's fiction, tornadoes and cyclones, riptides and lightning, earthquakes and volcanoes are liable at any point to snuff out human life. One of novelist Edith Wharton's midwesterners recalls the tornadoes that flatten entire towns and villages of her home state. Drought and pestilence destroy the lives of American farmers in Hamlin Garland's *Main-Travelled Roads*. And freezing weather invades Upton Sinclair's *The Jungle*: "A grisly thing, a specter born in the black caverns of terror; a power primeval, cosmic . . . cruel, iron-hard." The fictional characters "cringe in its grasp, alone, alone."

Add to these the historic natural disasters, the San Francisco Earthquake of 1906, the great Galveston Hurricane of 1900 (so well known that a Coney Island amusement attraction was based on it in the 1910s), with other storms bearing ironic human names through the century, Camille to Andrew. And the volcanic blast of Mount St. Helens in the Cascade Mountains of the Pacific Northwest. The uncontained fires that have swept cities (Baltimore, Boston, Chicago) and raged over brush and forest (the Yellowstone fire of 1991). Not to mention the great midwestern flood of 1993. One writer pondering the influence of *Pilgrim's Progress* in the United States has noted that its portrayals of evil gained special urgency for Americans because of the "harsh realities of severe climate . . . and a literally trackless wilderness." If so, the fictional and meteorological record of U.S. history continues to provide data for spiritual journeys fraught with deadly peril.

And American history has incised certain landscapes—not only Native American but those of the Slave South—with meanings of peril and woe. The antebellum South underlies the spiritual dimension of songs of sojourners "walkin' long, Lord, wid head hung down . . . [and] an achin' heart," sojourners who will "die in de fiel'," sojourners who yearn to "lay down my heavy load," who compare themselves to "a po' inch worm . . . a inchin' along."

The spiritual dimension in this is self-evident in its faith that the "weary traveler" will find an ultimate redemptive respite. Du Bois speaks of "the Negro folk song . . . as the most beautiful expression of human experience born this side the seas," on a continent characterized by "rude grandeur" and inhabited in a spirit of utilitarian ingenuity (the Caterpiller tractor dominating the musically expressive "inch worm"). But what of the *spiritual* dimension in the many secular texts? Some of the writers chronicling environmental havoc reject any notion of spirituality, in fact consciously react against it. Their mission is iconoclastic. How, then, can there be a higher purpose behind their reportage?

The question is important because, in terms of the soul's journey, the mere recital of environmental peril and catastrophe without a metaphysical message is pure melodrama. Titillating, maybe, but finally trivial. When country music itself produces "Amelia Earhart's Last Flight" (by Dave McEnery) and "The Sinking of the Titanic" (Robert Brown), is it only showing a tendency toward tabloid sensationalism? Or crass sentimentalism?

It is not. Actually, it is putting into play the most traditional form of spiritualizing. One way to see this clearly is to revisit Henry David Thoreau—once again while walking, but this time on the Pilgrims' own turf, Cape Cod. Were we ourselves to venture to the town of Wellfleet on the outer Cape, in fact, we could get some idea of what awaited Thoreau on his own Cape walk in autumn 1849. Visitors' placards on the Massachusetts Bay side of Wellfleet remind one of maritime peril in treacherous waters. The Cape's shoals, tides, uncertain winds, sudden storms, submerged rocks—all have spelled danger and marine disaster. Some of these are recorded on the stainless steel placards charting the locations where this

Environmental havoc and spiritual travail in John Steuart Curry, The Mississippi, 1935.
Tempera on canvas, 36 × 47½ in. (Courtesy The Saint Louis Art Museum, purchase)

brig or that schooner sank with terrible loss of life. The placards' engravings are coolly tactile, and the visitor runs fingertips over them with pleasure even while reading of watery mayhem and death just offshore.

Thoreau needed no plaque in October 1849, when he began a walking tour of Cape Cod, hearing the news of "Death! 145 lives lost at Cohasset!" The brig *St. John* from Galway, bearing Irish immigrants seeking livelihoods in America, had sunk in a storm, and the bodies had been washing ashore. In the Cape Cod town of Cohasset, Thoreau mingled with relatives of the victims, walking among the hastily constructed coffins and seeing the poignant belongings—"a man's clothes on a rock . . . a woman's scarf, a gown, a straw bonnet." Relics.

He asked, "Why care for these dead bodies?" then overarched the rituals of interment to proclaim that those drowned were—and are—voyaging spiritually. The owners of these bodies, Thoreau wrote, were coming to the New World as Columbus and the Pilgrims did:

Before they could reach [New World] shores, they emigrated to a newer world than ever Columbus dreamed of, yet one of whose existence we believe that there is far more universal and convincing evidence . . . than Columbus had of this; not merely mariners' tales and some paltry drift-wood and sea-weed, but a continual drift and instinct to all our shores. I saw their empty hulks that came to land; but they themselves, meanwhile, were cast upon some shore yet further west, toward which we are all tending, and which we shall reach at last.

The language is solely of marine experience, but spiritualized, the metaphysical meaning drawn out in terms that turn into spiritual lessons applicable to all. Nothing could be more important than the spiritual journey of life and its transcendence to the spiritual world beyond the mortal. The journey of life is a democratic one in which class and caste are made irrelevant.

(No wonder, then, that country music offers its spiritual lessons from misfortune in a hostile environment. Amelia Earhart has landed happily in a faraway heavenly field, while those drowned on the *Titanic* are indeed "nearer my God to thee.")

This marine and maritime emphasis in country music in no way clashes with its heartland geography, once we understand the underlying spirituality. Country music, of course, has represented itself mainly in terms of the *country*, both farm and ranch, and often its imagery is agricultural, as in Floyd Jenkins's spiritual, "I'll Reap My Harvest in Heaven."

Thus the country music superstar Garth Brooks sings about sailing his boat ("The River," cowritten with Virginia Shaw, on *Ropin' the Wind*, 1991) without arousing a sense of incongruity in his cowboy hat, western shirt and belt, jeans, posed on the album photo against a big sky that looks for all the world like Montana or North Dakota. This, after all, is a song about a "dreamer" on the voyage of life, battling daily to navigate between the "shores" while also venturing outward, onward.

And these terms hold for secular life. The Christian tradition both established and now underlies the American conception of spiritual life as a journey. But the terms of wayfaring or journeying are remarkably tenacious in expressing the secular side of spiritual life in this nation. Du Bois, for instance, writes of African Americans' struggle for "book-learning" or literacy-based education as "the mountain path to Canaan, longer than the highway of Emancipation and law, steep and rugged, but straight, leading to heights high enough to overlook life."

Even those who are not Christians, who consider themselves secular in outlook, tend to express the dynamics of the inner life as a spiritual journey. Herman Melville's *Moby-Dick* casts the idea in terms of an ocean voyage in which "all deep,

earnest thinking is but the intrepid effort of the soul to keep the open independence of her sea." Contemporary writers and their audiences continue to use and
encounter the life-journey as terms communicating the processes of the inner
life—for instance, in Natalie Goldberg's Zen-influenced *Long Quiet Highway* (1993)
and in M. Scott Peck's *The Road Less Traveled* (1978), subtitled *A New Psychology of
Love, Traditional Values and Spiritual Growth*. The inward, spiritual/emotional personal experience is uppermost in such texts as they respond to the secular in their
conception of human life as a spiritual journey.

And a song of spiritual wayfaring, like "Let Me See the Light" (Barry Tashian/
Holly Tashian, *Ready for Love*, 1993), is the secular version of such "pathway" texts
in country music. In the minor key customary for country and bluegrass songs of
spiritual travail, we see life represented as travel down a rough road, through a
wide valley, the lights of home receding far behind. There are cold nights, long
days, storms, waters rising, strong currents overpowering the hapless soul—all elements of the spiritual environment of peril, and all faithful in allegorical terms to
life's problems. Barry Tashian sings this narrative in taut, open tones, his voice
breaking at the memory of an anguished moment when "the wind began to cry
and moan." At the verge of drowning, the soul is joined in the duet by the alto,
Holly's voice introducing the realm of womanly travail. The cry goes forth from
both—"Lord, let me see the light"—and the prayer is answered, for in dawn's
light the waters recede. The singers speak the lesson learned: "Then I knew I was
not alone."

The lyrics then state the spiritual message of redemption: "Lord, I can see the
light." This is illumination unprecedented in these individuals' experience. The
Tashians' close-edged harmonies, however, never suggest newfound bliss. The
voices never bend toward the saccharine or sentimental—in part in faithfulness to
the musical tradition of predecessors like the Louvin Brothers, but also in keeping
with the conception of life's journey as one of struggle. As for the actual language
of the lyrics, we know as listeners that the individual need not actually come near
drowning or suffer a shipwreck or boating mishap to understand and to experience this spiritual world, its peril and its hope. But we know as well that the
singers/speakers need not be doctrinal Christians. Their language of spiritual expression has, so to speak, overflowed the boundaries of doctrine and of Scripture
to be embraced as legitimately expressive of nonsectarian but spiritual life.

Such language lends itself to myth, says the psychiatrist Rollo May, defining
myth as "a drama which begins as a historical event and takes on its special character as a way of orienting people to reality." The myth is vitally important, May
argues, because "it carries the values of the society." What is more, "By the myth
the individual finds his sense of identity." Much has been written about American

myths and the American identity, though the legitimacy of the very term *American identity* currently is cast in doubt in a multiculturalist era when different groups within this nation protest that no overarching myth can speak adequately to the particularities of their special experience.

Yet the idea of the spiritual journey comes close. It lends itself to the experience of immigration per se, to the idea of diasporas, and it is sustained by the very mobility and even by the restlessness that have continued to be defining traits of cultural and ethnic subgroups within the nation. Given a Pan-American mentality of journey, the country artist Kathy Chiavola presents a medley of the traditional "I Am a Pilgrim" and "We Are Pilgrims on the Way" (by Marcus Humman). Chiavola's linkage of the two songs gives listeners a paired, traditional-and-contemporary conception of the life pilgrimage. The first song, "I Am a Pilgrim," is much like "Wayfaring Stranger" in its scriptural references to the "wearisome land," to the spiritual home in "yonder city," to the River Jordan as a river actually in the Holy Land and metaphorically a boundary between the living and those who have "passed on" to heaven.

Chiavola sings this traditional song in a sensual blues style, moving it away from its evangelical roots. She intends these two "pilgrim" songs to be complements, not a before/after history lesson in the American sacred and secular (much less the sacred and profane). Her recording features step-out guitar solos in the inimitable signature style of Chet Atkins, whose jazz-country licks respect the spiritual even as they ride the listener to its thrilling outer edge. Chiavola's own blues style segues nicely into the jubilant warmth of "We Are Pilgrims on the Way," a Walt Whitman-ish, up-tempo celebration of American ethnic and regional diversity. (And fiddler Randy Howard journeys through country styles from swing to bluegrass on an instrumental musical pilgrimage all its own.) Kerouac-style, from the road ("raindrops thumpin' on my white-wall Chrysler"), the singer/speaker catalogs an America of young and old, blacks, whites, Latinos, cowboy to fireman, school to church to trailer park, hot dogs and beer keg and baseball. This is the chorus:

> You don't know me, but I know you
> We are pilgrims, we are pilgrims on the way. And
> I could love you, you could love me
> We are pilgrims on the way.

Traditional? Absolutely. Old-fashioned? Maybe. Outmoded? Not when, in the 1990s, individuals are quoted in news stories describing their own lives in terms of a journey. Not when one of our most esteemed contemporary writers, Annie Dillard, titles her autobiographical sojourn in the natural world *Pilgrim at Tinker Creek*.

Not when National Public Radio runs a tape of Malcolm X describing his life as a "pilgrimage." Even in a secular age, the voyage of life is a serious matter, the vessel of that voyage an image of great spiritual power.

The idea of the voyage of life is entrusted to country music, as it has been entrusted to other arts in American culture. The symbols of this tradition appear uncomplicated, even simplistic, but to borrow a phrase from a Shaker hymn: "'Tis the gift to be simple." Simplicity, in this sense, is profundity. Country music's straightforward songs on wayfaring, journeying, sailing for better shores express the most profoundly spiritual beliefs many continue to hold and to find strengthening. As the fourth Thursday of each November reminds us, in America the pilgrims are still wayfaring.

*. . . Fundamental as
sunshine and rain, snow
and wind, and the light
of the moon peeping
through the trees.*
—*George D. Hay,
founding announcer
of the* Grand Ole
Opry, *on country
music*

. . . Close to nature.
—*Johnny Cash,
on country music
(wall placard,
Country Music
Museum,
Nashville)*

*Sometimes we'd have that
whole river all to ourselves
for the longest time.
Yonder was the banks
and the islands, across
the water . . . and some-
times on the water . . .
you could hear a fiddle
or a song coming over.*
—*Mark Twain,*
The Adventures of
Huckleberry Finn

*Country music? They all
sing through their nose.*
—*Nashville bank officer*

*I don't know music,
I just do it.*
—*Emmylou Harris,
stage performance,
First Church Unity,
Nashville*

▼ ▼

Nature's Music

In southwestern Kentucky, take Routes 62, 68, 31-E to see
white fences and rolling hills of bluegrass from your car windows. The great horse
farms are there too, Whitney Stables, Calumet. And the other farms for which the
state is notable, the fields of Kentucky burley tobacco, the leaves turning from
green to yellow over the summer—at which point they are cut and, by August,
hanging in tobacco barns that look like open-air cribs. Dried, they will go to a
stripping shed, the leaves pulled by hand from the stalks. One can travel these
highways over a growing season and see a time-lapse version of the entire cycle.

You need not, however, actually motor along these roadways to have seen this
agricultural scene. As with much else in the nation and world, television has al-

ready taken you there—that is, if you watched CBS's *48 Hours* on March 13, 1991,
when viewers got a good look at these fields, sheds, and tobacco warehouses in a
special program entitled "A Song and a Dream." The show dealt with Nashville
and country music, and one segment, "The Kentucky Kid," featured a young
country artist named Marty Brown, a tobacco warehouse worker and homegrown
singer/guitarist/songwriter with the gumption to head his pickup down I-65 to
Nashville's Music Row, the publishing and executive-office center of country
music. For young Marty Brown, most of the Music Row doors at first stayed shut
tight as he pounded the pavement and accumulated the rejections that seem part
of the dues any artist must pay. Too broke to pay the highway tolls back to Kentucky, Brown even slept in a cardboard box in Nashville before finally finding a
record producer willing to listen and provide encouragement.

The upshot of all this is success—in the form of an album, *High and Dry* (1991),
coproduced by two of the most prominent names in country music—Tony Brown
(unrelated to Marty), who in 1992 was named in *Newsweek* magazine's list of America's cultural elite, and Richard Bennett, producer of Emmylou Harris and Marty
Stuart. The struggle has paid off. Young Marty Brown has had the good fortune in
the early 1990s to be launched by major producers and a major label, MCA. The
album showcases a very interesting voice, rough-edged and vocally textured, like
the burlap pictured in the album photo. We ought, in fact, to linger with that
photo. Tempted to think about the impressive voice and the songs, we need to pay
special attention to the album, the actual CD or cassette. A tangible mark of musical ambition and accomplishment, the album certifies Marty Brown's achievement—but also shows a certain country music dilemma.

Ironically, the graphic design for *High and Dry* provides a window on a very serious problem in country music, a "public relations" problem that plagues country and its performers. From Cajun to bluegrass, no matter how successful they
are, whether kings or queens of country music, legends, fathers of . . . , stars with
megasales, or sidemen whose names are known only to insiders, country musicians share a problem common to all. It is a problem of country music's status as
serious music worthy of respect—not enjoyment only, but respect. It is a problem
of musical snobbery and hierarchy. For country, face to face with other musical
traditions, classical to pop, all too often scrapes bottom, with the public assuming
a low level of musical skill ("hicks with picks . . . and most of them can't even read
music"). Ironically, this is a long-term problem for which country music is also
largely responsible. And the problem is not one of musicianship but of stereotype.
It feeds much more on images than on performance or composition.

To understand it, let's begin with the album graphics for *High and Dry*, which
show the decision of Marty Brown's promoters to link him with his rural Ken-

**Marty Brown
in a tobacco
field. Album
cover photo
from High
and Dry.
(Courtesy
MCA
Records)**

tucky origins. The compact disc includes a foldout, four-color glossy of Marty, in jeans and workshirt, in a Kentucky tobacco field on a clear day. It is spring, and the plants are sprouting like rows of little green fountains in the chocolate-brown earth extending to the horizon. Never mind that tobacco has become an infamous crop or the fact that it is planted mechanically by a machine designed to regularize spacing between plants. Never mind the fact that not one of these plants was set by hand. The photographic emphasis, instead, is on country music's link with the country, the rural roots, the world of nature. The tiny plants have taken root, and Marty Brown hunkers down in the field, literally down to earth in tan-brown boots, surveying the scene as if he might have planted every seedling by hand, the very hand that picks and strums his guitar. And that, of course, is the essence of the photographic message, that Marty Brown is down-to-earth country, as if he and his music, like tobacco, were a crop.

The founders of commercial country music would have approved. Down in that field, Brown is a graphic illustration of the terms in which, in the 1920s, the founding *Grand Ole Opry* announcer, George D. Hay, characterized this music:

"Fundamental as sunshine and rain, snow and wind, and the light of the moon peeping through the trees." For decades Roy Acuff spoke of country music as "down to earth," while more recently, Johnny Cash affirmed this music as "close to nature."

We know about this already. It is Ralph Waldo Emerson's legacy. Country music defines itself as belonging to, and united with, the natural world of earth and sky and seasons. Nature is its foundation and its source of sustenance and strength—its very *inspiration* in the linguistic root meaning of breathing in. Nature is the bedrock of its authenticity. (It is no coincidence that over several years Willie Nelson has launched and supported Farm Aid, the annual televised benefit concerts supporting the American family farm. A Who's Who of country artists have lent their support from the stage, including George Jones, Dwight Yoakam, Loretta Lynn, Alan Jackson, Alabama, Ricky Van Shelton, K. T. Oslin, Kathy Mattea. Soliciting donations from viewers, Nelson emphasizes that Farm Aid seeks to support the American *family* farm—not international high-tech corporate agribusiness, but farms legitimately of the natural order.) It seems natural, in Marty Brown's case, that the images on the album cover reaffirm the young musician's place within the heritage of country music. It makes sense to present him within country's most cherished images of itself. (For that matter, why shouldn't a country music artist who comes from a rural background legitimately be represented in scenes characteristic of his or her life?)

The point is not merely to "read" the album graphics in minute detail. It is to notice the images in which the young artist comes, if you will, packaged: Marty Brown and his music as nature's own creation. Taking this example as a guide, we can widen the search for similar kinds of messages, noticing the extent to which the entire culture of country music, from journalists to artists, sustains and promotes this music as indigenous to nature.

To read through a file of reviews on an artist, for instance, is to see a pattern of images belonging to a preindustrial world of handicrafts and rural life. Recurring phrases describe Emmylou Harris's "mountain-minor twang," the "mountain-spring purity of her haunting voice," the "comfortable dirt road [she has taken] with her music," which is "hand-hewn." Not a word indicates an industrial or postindustrial world, even though Harris, like other country artists, works onstage and in the studio with the most sophisticated available recording and sound reproduction equipment. A few reviewers of Emmylou Harris, in fact, have ventured to describe her voice in terms outside the world of nature ("like bevelled glass," "clear as Waterford crystal," "like a scalpel cutting into a knot of regret"). These terms imply something hard, vitreous, steely. But the reviewers, perhaps anxious about breaking the bounds of conventional country music writing, soon scurry back to more familiar terms, like "angelic" ("If angels elected a singer on earth, they'd choose Emmylou Harris . . . [the] Alabama Angel"). The country press persistently naturalizes the voice in this musical tradition. Journalists and reviewers identify the voice of the country artist with aspects of nature, including its spirituality. They perpetuate the idea that country is, above all, the music of the natural world.

Country songwriters, too, support the notion of the natural as they describe the process of writing. They downplay any rigor, difficulty, or problems of composition (word choice, rhythm, rhyme). Instead, they present their work as if technique were not required. We hear this over and over again from songwriters quoted in *Sing Your Heart Out, Country Boy* (1975), by Dorothy Horstman. One important feature of this useful collection of twentieth-century country songs are the remarks by the writer or a close companion explaining something about the origin of each song. Hank Williams's second wife, for instance, recalls driving from Nashville to Louisiana in a top-down convertible as Hank described marital problems with his first wife, whom he characterized in that moment in the car as a "cheatin' heart." Billie Jean Williams Horton recounts Hank's exclamation, "Hey, that'd make a good song! Get out my tablet, Baby; me and you are gonna write us a song." Horton recalls Hank Williams dictating the song, "Your Cheatin' Heart," in a matter of minutes.

The speedy song is virtually a staple of country music songwriting—that is, as the writers report it. It is said to be the product of an offhand phrase or an overheard chance remark. Harlan Howard, the legendary Nashville writer and member of the Country Music Hall of Fame, recalls overhearing an arguing couple, the woman flinging the line, "Well, you can just pick me up on your way down." A year later, Howard recalls, "All of a sudden, I sat down and just wrote the song from beginning to end, and I've never changed a word. It just kind of fell into place." Anecdotes like these make country music songs sound like natural processes. No struggle is required. The writer does not fret or agonize over lyrics or the melody line, does not shift phrases around in the search for coherence or for the most satisfying form. The writer, in this account, meets no resistance. A key phrase is simply overheard or spontaneously spoken, and the song immediately takes shape. Thus Merle Haggard recounts that "Okie from Muskogee" "probably took twenty minutes to write," while Jay Miller recalls that he pulled his car over and took a tablet from his glove compartment in order to write down the lyrics to "It Wasn't God Who Made Honky-Tonk Angels." Holly Dunn claims that her signature song, "Daddy's Hands," entered her mind one morning and was "a reality" by nightfall. Numerous songs are similarly described, including Ted Daffan's "Headin' Down the Wrong Highway," Mel Tillis's "Ruby, Don't Take Your Love

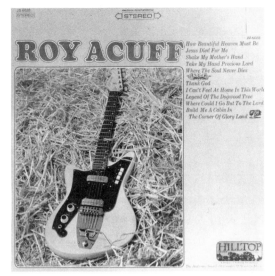

Country music albums showing artists and instruments as belonging to the world of nature. (Courtesy Hilltop Records, Capitol Records, MCA Records)

to Town," John Volinkaty's "Satin Sheets." The writers all say the same thing: "It took about ten minutes including the melody. . . . I wrote the story in about an hour. . . . It took thirty minutes to write." And so on.

But speed of composition is not really the essential issue. The important thing is the notion that the song is a whole entity, intact, virtually existing before it is written down. The act of writing only formalizes what already *is*—or what already is gestating. The writer becomes something between stenographer, spiritual chan-

199

nel, and incubator/midwife. "I give birth every time I write a song," says Dolly Parton. Roy Acuff elaborates, "Nobody really writes our music, you know. If we write a song, we're only writing what we've felt and heard."

Country music writers who reminisce about the short time it took to get the song down on paper are really speaking out of a romantic-era belief—a belief of the era of Emerson—in the organic form of the song or poem. Their conception of the song is best stated by Emerson's friend, Henry David Thoreau, who said that "poetry . . . is a natural fruit" and that "man bears a poem . . . as naturally as the oak bears an acorn and the vine a gourd." The country music song is a version of Thoreau's poem—and we recall how often country artists use the terms "poem" and "poet" to describe songs and artists, from Hank Williams to Rodney Crowell, who has said, "I'm just here with a butterfly net, catching . . . the music." Country songwriters who use stopwatch terms to describe their work are essentially committed to Thoreau's viewpoint. Their songs, like his poems, are organic entities that come into being in the moment of ripeness. In this sense the organic or natural song is "picked" or harvested. "I caught a song and set it free," goes a line in the Rodney Crowell/Will Jennings song "Many a Long and Lonesome Highway," representing the country song as a creature trapped and then released into the world. Marty Brown, the "Kentucky Kid," used the same maternity image we heard from Dolly Parton when he explained on TV: "Writing a song's just like . . . having a baby. If it's going to come, it's going to come. And when it does, you'd better have a pen and pad around just like you'd better have a doctor around delivering that baby."

Harlan Howard gives some indication that matters are really more complex, that country music songs like "Pick Me Up on Your Way Down" have a more complicated relation to the writer and the production of the song than is usually acknowledged. "I carried [the title] around mentally for about a year," he says. "I wrote it subconsciously." Howard adds, "That's how songwriters say they 'wrote that song in two minutes.'" These comments acknowledge what all self-conscious writers know, that the work of writing is to a great extent invisible, conducted indeed at a subconscious level, battled out in the mind as much as on the page (or on the word processor screen). And that work goes on in the course of mundane actions—not only at a desk or table but while sipping coffee, driving, stopping at the laundromat or cleaner's, staring out a window. All the while the writing project is going on, churning, invisible, and often stubbornly resistant. Yet country music songwriters do not often divulge this side of their work.

They do not acknowledge, what's more, that their sources sometimes come from involvement in other arts, although Rodney Crowell likens his music visually to a Van Gogh painting, *Café Terrace at Night*, while a critic compares his songs to the street photography of Henri Cartier-Bresson. Crowell's "Alone but Not Alone" is lyrically indebted to a Georgia O'Keeffe painting and to *Hamlet*, while Mary-Chapin Carpenter's "Halley Came to Jackson" concerns the fiction writer Eudora Welty, and Texas-based singer/songwriter Jimmie Dale Gilmore identifies himself as a neo-Beat figure whose musical influences include Jack Kerouac and the English writers Aldous Huxley and W. Somerset Maugham. The list goes on. Guy Clark's "Picasso's Mandolin" directly links his song with Picasso's cubist *Girl with Mandolin* (1910). Kris Kristofferson's "Here Comes That Rainbow Again" is taken directly from a scene in John Steinbeck's *The Grapes of Wrath*, and Michael Anderson's "Maybe It Was Memphis" literally situates a character in the literary tradition of the South ("Read about you in a Faulkner novel / Met you once in a [Tennessee] Williams play"). Nanci Griffith directly acknowledges the influence of writers like Eudora Welty, John Updike, Flannery O'Connor, Truman Capote. (The album photo on *Once in a Very Blue Moon* shows her with a copy of Welty's *Delta Wedding*, while her 1993 *Other Voices, Other Rooms* borrows the title of Capote's story collection of the same name.) These linkages suggest country music's enmeshment with other arts. To listen to most songwriters tell it, however, they are beating the clock by doing what comes naturally. The music of nature can only emerge without tinkering or mechanics—which is to say, according to nature.

The country music "genius" is also conceived as a creature of nature, arising as a natural phenomenon. The patriarch of country music, A. P. (Alvin Pleasant) Carter, is said to have been "marked" by a ring of fire, that is, by the lightning that cracked tree branches and played at his terrified mother's feet in an Appalachian apple orchard while A. P. Carter was eight months *in utero*. He was born weeks later, in December 1891, with a congenital tremor:

> Little A. P.'s trembling hampered him in school and virtually everywhere else—until he found the one thing that transformed his handicap into a blessing: singing. For when he sang, the tremor became almost a shimmer, an effect that became more profound as he grew older and his bass voice ripened, filling the songs he wrote with an urgent, heartbreaking quality. . . . And A. P. Carter never stopped trembling until the day he died.

The above account was written in 1991 by a *Life* magazine journalist retelling Carter's story. Interestingly, the journalist does not approach the story from a viewpoint in modern neuroscience, but from country music's origin in romantic nature. A. P. Carter is not only his parents' child but is sired by lightning. The *ripening* voice is nature's own, its origin a natural phenomenon.

Country music really participates in a long-term American tradition in which genius, considered to be male, is regarded as a phenomenon of nature. Ralph

Waldo Emerson, in "The Uses of Great Men," declared, "It is natural to believe in great men. . . . Nature seems to exist for the excellent." He named Plato, Shakespeare, and Napoleon Bonaparte as exemplary natural geniuses. By the turn of the twentieth century, Emerson himself was serving as such an example, at least for the environmental activist John Muir, who, in *Our National Parks* (1901), recounted meeting his much-admired Emerson and crying, "You are yourself a sequoia. Stop and get acquainted with your brethren."

The idea of the natural country music genius continues in the career of Hank Williams, with his biographer (also named Williams) calling Hank's songs "rough diamonds" (quarried rather than picked). At least one country music writer argues that the mythology surrounding Williams has made it virtually impossible to learn the facts about Hank Williams's songwriting collaboration with his mentor/publisher, Fred Rose: "Because the Williams myth has hardened with time, it's guesswork to say what he wrote and what came from Fred Rose, the northern sophisticate."

Indeed, the commitment to the idea of nature's American genius makes Hank Williams's biographer edgy about the degree of cooperation between the country genius/poet and his publisher and mentor. Nature's own genius must, by definition, write nature's own songs. He might need jeweler's rouge to polish the rough stones to a "high gloss," but a songwriting partnership of equals would threaten the idea of the natural genius. It is thus acceptable to say that Rose, a successful pop songwriter, provided finishing touches for Williams's songs (the term is "lend a helping hand"). And the two men do share cowriting credit on at least one song. But the idea that Rose, the onetime Chicago-based professional songwriter and arranger, would actually cowrite Williams's songs in a collaborative partnership is out of the question.

So is the notion that Vic McAlpin, another Country Music Hall of Fame songwriter, would share credit on classic Williams songs — though country music journalist Chet Flippo says that in 1940s-50s Nashville, "songs traded hands like playing cards in a poker game." Flippo elaborates: "Hank had cowritten 'Long Gone Lonesome Blues' and 'I've Been Down That Road Before' with Vic McAlpin and then bought out McAlpin for $500 per song so Hank could get full writing credit [which] meant more to him than money in his pocket." No wonder the solo credit was prized. This very notion of collaboration, if widely publicized, would challenge the concept of Williams as a natural country genius. Williams's biographer concludes, "It is clear that Rose's contribution was craftsmanship, while Williams's was genius."

Within country music, what is more, musicians and writers present the instruments themselves as living creatures of the natural world, like the nightingale fid-

*Country music instruments—mandolin,
upright bass, banjo, fiddle, guitar—harmonize
with the world of nature in this postcard
scene. (Courtesy Tennessee Department of
Tourist Development.) See also Plate 1.*

Lin Barber, Rising Storm with Mandolin.
(Photograph © 1993. All rights reserved.)

dle and apple orchard banjo we noticed earlier in the discussion of "Home." "Screams like a bayou wildcat," says one writer of Cajun artist Doug Kershaw's fiddle. "Light as the ribcage of a hawk," says a bluegrass historian of Bill Monroe's Lloyd Loar–designed Gibson F-5 mandolin. Rodney Crowell recalls his late band-leader father calling the teardrop-shaped mandolin a "taterbug" (shaped like the potato bug insect). Patsy Montana recollects sleeping with her head against the "doghouse bass" crammed into the car beside her on road trips.

The idea of the organic instrument propels at least one entire country-folk song. "I was the child of earth and sky," laments a maple-turned-fiddle narrating the bluegrass artist Laurie Lewis's "The Maple's Lament" (*Restless, Rambling Heart*, 1986). The story, played mournfully by Lewis's fiddle in keening, Celtic tones, laments the live tree's metamorphosis from its natural state, when birds nested on its boughs, storms swirled in season, and the sun drew the branches upward, like arms. As a fiddle, the onetime maple now feels imprisoned ("bound so tight in wire strings") and subjugated ("but the slave who sings when master draws the bow"). Laurie Lewis sings the lament in open, nasal tones, the voice of the one-time tree coming, so to speak, through the "walls of time," the veil between the dead and the living. The fiddle is now a tree-spirit, speaking posthumously:

> But sometimes from my memory, I can sing the birds in flight,
> And I can sing of sweet dark earth and endless starry nights—
> But oh, my favorite song of all, I truly do believe,
> Is the song the sunlight sang to me while dancing on my leaves.

These lyrics about sweet earth, starry nights, and birds aloft are countered by the minor key for fiddle and voice. The song is thoroughly one of lamentation, the fiddle's enslavement stated in the virtually unvarying repetitions—seven of them —of the melody. One feels that symbolically the central subject is youthful freedom lost to the constraints of adulthood, when one is restricted in numerous ways and many masters call the tune.

The central image of "The Maple's Lament," however, is the tree/fiddle as nature and as song. Lyrically, the singing and dancing sunlight becomes a part of the maple and, in turn, of the fiddle itself, which sings its own origins even after the violin makers have done their deed. (Laurie Lewis follows the country song-writer's tradition in declining to describe the composition as a constructed or even written effort. On album liner notes, she says that the "silent fiddles" in her violin shop "gave me the song"—that is, presented the organic being in its entirety.)

But the naturalization of country music instruments may have its limit. On a re-cent Robin and Linda Williams album (*Live in Holland*), Linda Williams praises band member Kevin Maul's performance "on the hound dog Dobro."

Hound dog?

The country canine lets us consider the fuller meanings of these nature similes as they apply to the instruments of country music. Back in the 1920s, Dr. Humphrey Bate's string band, renamed the Possum Hunters, was photographed with Bate posed scratching a hound dog. To hunt 'possum (or 'coon) in the country, you would want a good hound dog. But the notion of the resonator or Dobro guitar as hound dog seems odd, given the history of the development of the Dobro. Back in the highly industrial 1920s-30s, steel-string guitarists were calling for louder instruments, and experiments in amplification led to the development of resonating aluminum cones fitted inside the guitar body. Some of these new resonator guitars have all-metal bodies, while others, of wood, have a dishlike metal plate over the front and look rather like a standard guitar with a hubcap clapped to the front. The name *Dobro* is actually a shortened nickname for the inventors, five Czechoslovakian immigrant brothers named Dopyera (thus DOpyera BROthers or Dobro). The instrument is played in a horizontal or "tabletop" position on the lap or, if the musician stands, held by a neck strap, with arms and hands working inside, the rich sound produced by a combination of plucking and a metal steel bar depressing the strings while sliding over the fingerboard. (Virtuoso Dobro player Jerry Douglas wittily has named one of his albums *Slide Rule* [1992].) The sound of the Dobro is, as Linda Williams's simile suggests, mournful in the way a baying hound can be. (Her phrase comes from a model of the instrument called "Original Hounddog.") Spoken on the album as a compliment to a performer, the phrase "hound-dog Dobro" sounds down-home, a typical country-music phrase.

The Dobro, nonetheless, is no more grown from a litter than the banjo is ripened like a winesap or the fiddle hatched in a nest or birthed by bayou wildcats. Of course not, one protests, ready to agree with the notion that musical instruments are objects of human design—even handcrafted machines.

But in fact the Dobro, "hound dog" aside, represents a distinct technological development (as are the lap steel and pedal steel guitars). It dates from earlier twentieth-century high modernism, sometimes called the machine age for its emphasis on machine-produced products and for a certain celebration of machines in the arts. Aluminum, the metal of the Dobro resonator, was being developed for numerous industrial and household uses and was used in artful, high-style design in architecture and sculpture. To this day, the patterns etched on the Dobro "dish" echo the Art-Deco geometric juts and recesses as they appeared in skyscraper-style architecture and Cubist art earlier in this century. Even though some Dobros have scenes of nature etched on their metal bodies (leafy trees, palms, clouds), physically the instrument *looks* like what it is, a machine-age design of the 1920s—30s.

**Dobro
guitar.
(Photograph
by Jamie
Adams; guitar
courtesy
Gruhn
Guitars)**

**Dobro
guitar
showing art
deco design
influence.
(Photograph
by Jamie
Adams; guitar
courtesy
Gruhn
Guitars)**

A hound dog, it is not.

But when the Dobro is compared to a dog, the instrument is being naturalized. No longer a machine, it becomes a natural phenomenon, a living being in nature. What does this mean?—that the Dobro is removed from the world of technological development and social process, which is to say a world of historical movement. The Dobro is put, instead, into a world of unchanging nature. It becomes a country music instrument precisely by being so naturalized.

Country music also confers a kind of honorary natural status on certain other machine-manufactured objects, like trains and trucks. The many train songs from "Orange Blossom Special" to "Wabash Cannonball" show this, as does a contemporary country song like Alan Jackson's "Home," which lauds the father, a mechanic so honest and ethical that neighbors drive many miles just to have him look under their hoods. (These are not merely customers in a fee-for-service transaction, but members of the community, hometown folks.) Jackson's song continues a tradition in which certain objects of industrial technology are accorded the status of the natural, especially if they fit with major themes of country music, like the road or the West. It is natural for a good father to earn his living repairing nature's own pickups.

Certain categories of work are similarly naturalized—if they are the "right" work, like railroading or ranching. Within the honorary natural, it has been perfectly plausible to characterize Jimmie Rodgers as the ramblin' railroad brakeman, or Gene Autry as a singing cowboy. Both those categories were naturalized in country music in the 1920s and 1930s. "It's not unusual for a country artist to work at other jobs while waiting for the big break to come," writes one journalist, "but usually those jobs are appropriately earthy—farming, truck driving, even working on the railroad." We notice the emphasis on *appropriately earthy*—that is, natural.[1]

Why bother about all this? Why take a tour through country music's nature im-

---

1. It is interesting to see what happens when a country artist's former occupation does not conform to the "earthy" category. Such was the case with Nick Nixon, a onetime optician. A country music journalist points out how silly it sounds to describe Nixon as "the singing optician"—though just why country music and optical work should be incongruously laughable is open to question. The country music scholar Charles K. Wolfe tells us that many of the musicians of early country music, occupationally speaking, came from artisanry and trades like locksmithing and engine repair. Would it have been plausible, in the 1920s, to present a roster of Opry performers billed as "the Fiddlin' Ford Mechanic" or "the Guitar-Picking Locksmith?" Why not?

ages? The artists, journalists, production workers have all succeeded in "rooting" this music in nature, authenticating it as the American music of the natural world. Country music workers have set the terms, adhered to them, largely remained consistent from the 1920s onward. Theirs are the terms in which country music has successfully presented and represented itself. They have done a very good job.

Maybe too good.

And that is why we have taken this tour of images—in order to see the troubling, unforeseen consequences of a musical tradition that holds copyright on nature. Endlessly promoting its genesis and nurturance in nature, country music has kept silent about its developmental side. Omitted from farm field and other rural scenes is the *art* of this musical tradition, even though its performers, like Marty Brown, are routinely called artists. *Artists*. The very word embraces the idea of artifice and implies a certain level of skill, musicianship, technical proficiency. Artists have gifts that are developed through training, application, practice. They work to develop their gifts; they exploit their aptitude. Tobacco field aside, Marty Brown was not born playing the guitar.

Country music wants to have it both ways—as nature and as art. But the two concepts do not work in sync. They are, in fact, largely irreconcilable. The natural simply *is*, while the artful must be made, shaped, created. Country is caught in a bind. If it discloses the terms of its art—the schooling of its musicians, long hours of practice, auditions, vocal coaching, etcetera—then it risks forfeiting its claims to being natural. It risks being seen as learned rather than bestowed, developed instead of given like the moon and the stars. It risks showing itself to be a music far more humanly complicated, deliberate, schooled than the images of nature permit it to be. Country music is really caught in an internal contradiction of its own making. It is both perpetrator and victim of its own ideology.

This fault line could stay buried or could surface as a mere curiosity, except for the serious consequences. These might be collectively dubbed country music's "public relations" problem. It involves difficulties of status, esteem, reputation, and respect, difficulties that uniquely beset country music in the United States.

These problems become clear as we listen to the late Roy Acuff's introduction to *Nashville's Grand Ole Opry* (1975), a coffee-table book lavishly produced to celebrate the Opry as the living foundation of country music. Acuff was called the king of country music because of his faithfulness to earlier styles of play and because he was the first national country star. Repeatedly he terms country music "down to earth," invoking the soil and the music's attachment to it. Here are the opening remarks of his introduction:

There is something about our kind of music that is different from anybody else's, I've always thought. I know that none of our boys can play a violin as perfectly as people who play symphony music, and I know I could not attempt to sing a classical song. Symphony music is beautiful music, played correctly by note. Our boys play by ear, and we slide into and slur some of the notes.

But what we do is pretty to us. We put a lot of feeling into it, and we reach the hearts of our audiences.

The people who watch us understand that we're not really professional at it. They understand that we're not trained. But they also understand that what we do is part of a sort of inheritance. In a way, nobody really writes our music, you know. If we write a song, we're only writing what we've felt and heard, the way we've been raised and the way our people have lived. Those things are not created, they're inherited. And we sing them with a feeling of sincerity, because they are part of ourselves.

At once, readers recognize the appeal to nature. The musicians play, not technically by note but organically by ear, based not primarily upon skill but upon feeling and sincerity, upon upbringing and traditional folkways. And this music goes to the audience's "heart," the center of feeling. It is not created, Acuff emphasizes, but inherited. Country performers come by their abilities naturally ("these things are not created, they're inherited . . . they are part of ourselves"). It is understood to be a legacy, one that is virtually genetic. Acuff's terms are based in country's naturalistic idea of itself. His statement subtly critiques European ("classical") music as "beautiful," though too technical to go to the heart—played by "note" through "training," resulting in icy professionalism.

Yet Acuff's statement is also defensive. The very terms setting country apart from classical music threaten to become a critique of country: "None of our boys can play a violin as perfectly as people who play symphony music. . . . I could not attempt to sing a classical song." We "slide" and "slur" — "but what we do is pretty to us."

Why the *but*? Why qualify the sense of beauty, confining it to the *us* who are emphatically *outside* the world of classical music, excluded from it because "we" cannot play "correctly by note"?

Why would the notion of singing a classical song even come up? Why would the king of country music open this lavishly produced book by half-apologizing for imperfect instrumental performance and for the inability to sing European music?

Acuff's introductory remarks are all the more extraordinary if we imagine counterparts in other musical traditions. Imagine coffee-table books on jazz, folk, rock music, each with an introduction by a "legend" in that field. Would Charles Mingus ever have positioned himself in contrast to the principal bassist of the New York Philharmonic? Would John Lee Hooker regret that he does not play guitar as well as Andrés Segovia? Would Joan Baez lament wistfully that she is no Maria Callas or Joan Sutherland? Or John Lennon that he was no Luciano Pavarotti? It is simply out of the question for these artists to think in such terms. It is inconceivable that a jazz, folk, or rock artist would make an unfavorable comparison between his or her own music and some other musical genre.

Why does country? Was it simply the unintended curse of announcer George D. Hay, naming country music as contrary to grand opera (and symphonic music, too)? Did Hay unknowingly tag country forever as the antithesis of "classical" music, putting it in bondage to European music even as he strove to free it with terms of nature? Or is it country music's own inferiority complex, bending inwardly to the class-based bias against it as upper-class southerners erected their classical Nashville Parthenon, founded their symphony, and turned a deaf ear to "hillbilly" music? A recent country song, "Blue-Blooded Woman" (Alan Jackson/Keith Stegall/Roger Murrah), pits an upper-class, "blue-blooded woman" against a "red-neck man": she adores the violin, he the fiddle. To some extent, the defensiveness that lingers in the country music tradition must result from this history.

But there is another reason why country squirms defensively about its own artistry. This reason shows up in Roy Acuff's remark that country music is natural (from the ear to the heart), as if inherited like right- or left-handedness or eye color and therefore *requiring no developmental skills*. From this view, the country musician comes into the world—the rural world of nature—endowed at birth with the traits that will emerge as part of the developmental process. Like crawling and walking, babytalk and speech, the music, too, will come in time. This is the notion expressed in Emmylou Harris's onstage remark, "I don't know music, I just do it." When outsiders hostile to country music sneer that "all you have to do is sing through your nose" or "just twang your guitar," they are flinging back a version of country music's own representation of itself. The very idea of country music *artists* thus becomes either a tribute to a rare "natural" genius, like Hank Williams—or a taunt meaning just the opposite, meaning that country is a music without art.[2]

2. This argument on "natural" musical development is only rarely made in connection with European music, one such instance being a review of conductor/pianist Daniel Barenboim's January 1993 recital of the music of Franz Schubert. *The New York Times*'s music reviewer wrote, "Occasionally one comes across human beings who seem to have been created by music for music. Mind, muscles and nerve endings are preordered genetically into a smooth, well-oiled vessel. Through it, musical impulses flow: unimpeded, natural and direct."

Nonsense. We can laugh at the naïveté of anybody's harboring such foolish notions. This is not to deride country music's ideology of nature, but instead to clear a space for an appreciative understanding of the musicianship of country vocal and instrumental performers and writers. It is to raise the level of consciousness precisely for the sake of, shall we say, art appreciation. A useful model for this is already present in *Mystery Train*, the book in which the rock 'n' roll writer Greil Marcus explodes the myth of the "natural" musician through his work on Elvis and the Sun sessions, proving how unrelentingly Elvis worked to develop his music.

But what about the training of a country musician? Anyone who has held a guitar or banjo or mandolin for the first time knows, to understate the case, that they are not holding a kazoo. The instrument does not play itself. The novice fiddler, like the novice violinist, makes the instrument sound tortured. If we seek country artists' own statements about musical development, however, we are apt to elicit reflections based in the "home" world of nature. Ricky Skaggs sketches such a picture of his musical training: "My mom and dad was singin' Appalachian music, or eastern Kentucky old-time music, back before it was called bluegrass—back before it was nothin' but just ol' hillbilly, back-porch, livin'-room, kitchen, whatever you wanna call it, pickin' music. You know, you just set around and play and sing."

Set around and play and sing—but how many hours, days, years of this? How many patient moments initiating each child into the mysteries of playing an instrument, singing harmonies, memorizing words in an environment no less rigorous for being naturalized in family life? One country song, Iris DeMent's "Mama's Opry" (*Infamous Angel*, 1992), capsules this traditional, indigenous musical education. DeMent's vocal style puts her in the so-called "primitive" country-folk tradition of singers like Hazel Dickens and Wilma Lee Cooper, though her voice carries a special elegiac poignance. The autobiographical "Mama's Opry" hearkens back two generations to a country-fiddler grandfather, to the household phonograph recordings of the Carter Family and Jimmie Rodgers, to the Saturday night radio broadcasts of the *Grand Ole Opry* (on which the young Iris may have heard Wilma

---

Notice in this language the emphasis on this phenomenon as "occasional," anomalous, unlike the representation of country as populated widely by musicians genetically endowed with their musical skills. The "genetics" argument is not ordinarily made in relation to European musical families, such as the Bach family (Johann Sebastian, Johann Christian, Carl Philipp Emanuel) or, in this century, the father-son pianists Rudolf and Peter Serkin. The "classical" tradition has always emphasized the arduous practice and development necessary even for its prodigies, for example, Wolfgang Amadeus Mozart.

Lee Cooper). All these are a heritage passed down to the singer's mother, who as a girl "dreamed about singin' at 'The Grand Ol' Opry.'" Instead, as a housewife hanging out the family wash, this mother found herself singing those old songs while the young Iris "was a kid just hummin' along."

The nostalgic song lyrics also take us indoors, where daughter Iris recalls singing along when her mother played old gospel records like "Sweet Rose of Sharon," "Abide with Me," "The Gospel Ship to Heaven's Jubilee," "He'll Pilot Me." Years later, the song tells us, as a songwriter and performing and recording artist, the adult Iris DeMent came to realize the depth of this musical education— "I was singing on the grandest opry. . . . And nothin on this earth is half as dear to me / As the sound of my Mama's Opry." (In tribute to her mother and her musical legacy, the final track on *Infamous Angel* features Iris's mother, Flora Mae DeMent, as lead vocal on the traditional "Higher Ground.")

To hear this kind of family musical tutelage in action, we can turn back to Marty Brown, the country musician just out of the Kentucky tobacco field and on his way to another splendid album, *Wild Kentucky Skies* (1993). You glimpsed a crucial dimension of Marty Brown's musical education if you were present at Ricky Skaggs's 1992 open-air Fan Club picnic at Nashville's Belle Meade Mansion, where Brown performed by invitation as fan clubbers sat on folding chairs under a caterer's tent, enjoying picnic dinners of pork barbecue, southern green beans, baked beans, rolls, iced tea, and chocolate cake. First, Marty sang a few solos with his father onstage beside him playing guitar, while Marty told how, in boyhood, he couldn't wait to get his hands on his father's off-limits Martin guitar when his father went off to work his factory shift. Now, onstage at the picnic, he sang with his father (who sounded something like a dour Johnny Cash), then summoned his mother to the stage for a song, "There's a Hole in the Bottom of the Sea," in close, three-part harmony, accompanied by his father on that once-forbidden Martin. And finally the brother who, we were told, had commandeered Marty's boyhood Christmas-gift harmonica and made it *his* instrument. All four of them playing and singing—a family band. They could be The Browns.

And at that moment you knew that Marty Brown's musical education had begun virtually at birth, not by genes but by schooling. He was born into a music school. Family members were his music teachers, youth symphony, and conservatory combined. You knew that his musical training had been part of the household life, steady, thorough, constant. And, over the years, rigorous.

It is the example of Marty Brown that led me to seek out a young country-musician-in-the-making. At age eleven, Cody Kilby (born 1981) of Cowan, Tennessee, had won juvenile national championships on banjo, guitar, and mandolin. With his family's help, he had produced two albums on cassette, a solo banjo *Trib-*

ute to *Earl Scruggs* and *Cowan Jubilee,* named for his own composition in honor of his hometown. Cody had twice appeared on TNN's nationally televised country music interview program, *Crook and Chase,* and a half-hour television production solely about him, entitled "Finger-Pickin' Strings," had been taped for national broadcast on PBS in 1993, hosted by the mandolin virtuoso Sam Bush, of the Nash Ramblers and the New Grass Revival.

What is this child's musical pathway, his educational route in country music? What is the curriculum? Were Cody to study European music, his schooling would lead through individual lessons into recitals and competitions sponsored by state-wide organizations of music teachers and by manufacturers of instruments, such as Selmer and Yamaha. He would pack off to summer music camps and seek conservatory training, thereafter perhaps to audition for an orchestra seat or to concertize as a soloist. What, then, is the comparable structure in country music? Piano and violin child prodigies solo with symphonies; but what is the counterpart for the debut of the precocious country musician? Where does a Cody Kilby come from?

Geographically, he comes from Cowan, Tennessee, a pleasant rural town off I-24, reached by a steep state road (41A) of hairpin curves down Monteagle Mountain. Cowan's main street has one traffic light, and on the left, in the middle of town, is Kilby Bi-Rite, a full-service supermarket that retains the small-town feel, friendly and pleasant. It is owned and operated by Cody's parents, Ronny and Sharon, and much front wall space is devoted to their son's award plaques and certificates—and color photographs of Cody posed with stars and aristocrats of country music, especially bluegrass: Bill Monroe, Roy Acuff, Sonny Osborne, Jesse McReynolds, Ralph Stanley, Carl Jackson, Ricky Skaggs, Porter Wagoner, Grandpa Jones. One photo shows Cody seated beside Earl Scruggs at the Scruggs family dining-room table, signing a contract with the Gibson Company agreeing to play the Gibson banjo exclusively. Cody later acknowledges that meeting these legendary figures makes his own future in country and bluegrass music feel more "real."

But how does all this come about? Are the Kilbys, like Marty Brown's family, steeped in country music? Have they taught Cody? In the evening darkness of early December, we drive from the store out to the Kilby home, a spacious, large house with white columns and a circular drive, and a front entrance with the name Bluegrass Farm and an incised emblem of banjo and fiddle. In the warm, paneled family room, we settle in, Ronny and Sharon Kilby and Cody who, at eleven, is a slender, blond boy with a crewcut and impeccable manners. (The Kilbys' daughter, Scarlet, is introduced, still in her cheerleader's uniform after a basketball game. Ronny points out her fiddle, displayed over the mantel, turned into a decoration because, though talented, Scarlet disliked public performance and so quit the instrument to take up piano.)

How did Cody get started in music? The Kilby's naming their home Bluegrass Farm suggests a longtime love of country music. Is it a family tradition? The answer is *yes* in appreciation, *no* in performance, for Ronnie and Sharon Kilby grew up with country music in their own family homes, with Nashville's WSM radio (broadcasting country music and the *Grand Ole Opry*) and a morning eye-opener, the *Eddie Hill Show*, popular in an agricultural area in which many arise well before first light. As a dating couple, Sharon and Ronny were fans of Tammy Wynette and Patsy Cline—and both feel lingering regret that neither had the opportunity to play instruments as children.

But Ronny Kilby had always liked the sound of the banjo ("banjer," as pronounced in the Tennessee inflection), and the couple enjoyed having a neighbor's amateur bluegrass band come over to practice in their house (as Sharon says, "We just liked to be around the music"). A turning point came through their business, when a merchandise promotion for Martha White Foods, a baking-products company, brought a banjo into the household as a sales bonus premium. Ronny rounded up two of his employees for weekly lessons to be given by the bluegrass-band neighbor, the lessons taking place in the Kilby store. Every night after supper, Ronny Kilby faithfully practiced his banjo, as "awful" as he and his wife admit it sounded at first, until he could play "O, Susannah," "Cripple Creek," "Blackberry Blossom." "I would practice every day," Ronny says, "and when I'd lay it down, Cody would pick it up," the eight-year-old saying, "Show me something, Daddy."

Though Ronny Kilby became discouraged and let his lessons lapse (as did Sharon, who tried briefly to learn guitar), their son persisted—"absolutely begged, 'Daddy, find me a teacher.'" At first, the parents were at a loss, knowing no one in country music. Ronny began asking around at the various bluegrass festivals scheduled all summer long in the area. Word of mouth brought them a name, Benny Williams, a *Grand Ole Opry* house band fiddler from 1957 to 1975. Benny Williams had played with Bill Monroe and Flatt and Scruggs and was now earning his living as a kind of musical circuit rider, teaching five country music instruments (fiddle, guitar, banjo, mandolin, Dobro) in a route covering middle Tennessee. At Ronny Kilby's invitation, he agreed to come to Cowan weekly to teach Cody and others who signed up for lessons, tots to adults. Local newspaper ads and word of mouth brought some twenty students, and once again the Kilby Bi-Rite became a music center and studio. This continued for two years, with Cody surging ahead on the banjo (and sister Scarlet showing great promise on fiddle).

Between lessons, Cody practiced his banjo fingerings, not from lesson books with horizontal staff lines, clefs, notes—but from what is called "tablature," a fin-ger-patterning chart showing the five strings in vertical arrangement. At the top of each string, a numeral indicates where the finger should be placed in relation to the frets (for instance, a "2" indicates the second fret). The tablature patterns dia-gram the drills fundamental to mastery of the instrument. Dexterity and speed are to follow. From the beginning of his work with Benny Williams, Cody practiced daily, usually an hour or more, though success requires the ability to play by ear. Especially in bluegrass music, which Alan Lomax called "folk music in overdrive," the ability to read music is irrelevant. As a Nashville Symphony flutist/piccoloist

Cody Kilby.
(Photograph
by Doug
Smith)

observed to me at a bluegrass performance of the Del McCoury Band, the ability to read music would be futile for bluegrass play. The music simply moves too fast to be read off the page. So Cody Kilby's success depends upon his ability to be extremely agile in picking and fingering—but also upon his ability to hear musical intervals, dynamics, tempos, note values (all mentally), to memorize songs, and to modulate and transpose not from the page but in the mind. The term *to play by ear* is shorthand for all this.

The Kilby family agrees that Ronny Kilby has "pushed" his son, in the best, encouraging sense of the term. He scours the Nashville newspapers for notices of auditions and registers his son in instrumental competitions held at country music festivals, especially bluegrass. (He lists the numerous country stars whose pathway to stardom led through bluegrass, including Ricky Skaggs, Vince Gill, Marty Stuart, Travis Tritt.) When Cody played for Roy Acuff in his dressing room at the Opry, the king of country music advised the boy to learn to sing, and father Ronny arranged for weekly voice lessons from Nashville-based country vocalist Kathy Chiavola, each lesson involving a four-hour drive. Noticing at festivals that many younger players were adept at several instruments, Ronny encouraged Cody to begin the guitar, which he still studies, and also to take up Dobro and mandolin, a sign of his seriousness being that within the next two years, Cody will receive his limited-edition, Bill Monroe signature model mandolin currently on order and under construction—especially meaningful because Cody played with Monroe at a Christmas benefit in 1992. The new mandolin will be paid for largely from the boy's winnings in country music competitions.

These competitions occur at festivals from March through October all over the South and elsewhere (upstate New York, the upper Midwest, New England). On weekends, Sharon takes over the Kilby Bi-Rite while Ronny drives Cody the hundreds of miles through Tennessee, Alabama, Georgia. The winners' plaques tell the story: "To Cody Kilby, Mandolin, 2d Place, the Georgia State Championship Fiddlers Convention, Hiawassee, Georgia." And: "To Cody Kilby, 1st Place, Bluegrass Banjo, the Annual State Fiddling and Bluegrass Convention, Cahaba Shrine Temple, Huntsville, Alabama." Ronny Kilby's hope is that at any given competition, a notable figure in country music might be present to hear his son and widen the network of his acquaintance. And this has happened. At the 1992 Merle Watson Festival, Cody jammed with the bassist in the distinguished Nashville Bluegrass Band, Gene Libbea, who in turn invited the boy onstage to play with the band when they performed, as usual before a packed house, at Nashville's bluegrass mecca, the Station Inn. On another occasion, banjoist and songbook writer Pete Wernick heard Cody play and gave the family Earl Scruggs's telephone number, while Opry star Porter Wagoner appeared as a surprise guest at a holiday party at which Cody played. "Maximum exposure" is Ronny Kilby's guideline for his son's career in music.

For the future, the Kilbys express the concern of many parents of musically talented children. "He's practiced a lot. . . . He's been faithful to practice," Sharon Kilby says of Cody's daily hour each on banjo and guitar, and she hopes the music world will give her son the opportunities he has earned. Ronny frets aloud about music politics in Nashville ("You know there's all kinds of good talent that doesn't make it"), and he worries that as Cody moves into adolescence, he could become just "another sixteen-year-old banjo player or guitar player or mandolin or Dobro player." Both lamented the death of Roy Acuff just weeks before Cody's twelfth birthday, at which Acuff had promised to put Cody and his banjo on the Opry stage. As for Cody, his ambition is to play the Opry, to appear on TNN's *Nashville Now*, and to go on the road in a customized tour bus. His favorite instrumental musician is bluegrass Grammy winner Carl Jackson, and his favorite vocalist Randy Travis. Meanwhile, there is the school basketball team, homework, the normal activities of an eleven-year-old. Before I took leave of the Kilby household, Cody eagerly played his flattop Martin guitar for me, a solo full of runs and rapid-fire chording up and down the neck. Too polite to protest the tedium of an interview, he came alive with his instrument. Talking to adults on a sofa has been dull, but the "finger-pickin' strings" are life itself.

And listeners to the *Grand Ole Opry* on January 16, 1993, heard those fingers flying at the strings. Just minutes before midnight on Cody Kilby's twelfth birthday, the young artist debuted on the Opry playing "Foggy Mountain Breakdown," a banjo showcase, after which he had the opportunity to chat with country star Marty Stuart, who more or less grew up on the Opry stage himself. So Roy Acuff's promise was fulfilled, and Cody Kilby was launched from the stage of the Mother Church of country music.

Artists' Art
Country Music Profiles

From Cowan, Tennessee, I-24 North leads back to Nash-
ville. Chances are, when Cody Kilby gets his driver's license, he will log many highway miles in roundtrips to this so-called musical Third Coast city to which so
many country music artists have come from Kentucky, Indiana, Missouri, the Carolinas, New England, the West Coast. And it is tempting to leave off here, with a
young, developing country artist approaching his teens. To hear Cody Kilby is to
feel confident that country music of the future is held in trust. He works hard to

develop his art, his musical education involving teachers, practice, performance, more practice, lifetime practice.

In the years ahead, however, Cody will most likely downplay this hard work and contribute to country music's nature lore whenever called upon to discuss his art. It is probable that, having grown up on Bluegrass Farm, Cody Kilby will speak of his music in the nature vocabulary other country artists use. He will explain his artistry by resorting to the terminology of the natural world. This is the available language, and he will speak it.

To pry open the artistry of country music a little further, then, we need to find some bilingual country artists, those born and raised in other musical worlds before they crossed over into country. We need, that is, to locate artists whose musical autobiographies show a certain pattern of immigration across musical borders. We cannot simply ask that musicians raised in the tradition of country explain their art. Why?—because country music presents itself in terms of the natural world, its artists growing up thinking of what they do as "down to earth," their musical vocabulary not extending one branch or brook or fishing hole beyond this realm. Most country musicians—Ricky Skaggs is one, and so is Marty Brown, and, for that matter, Cody Kilby—have lived lifelong in the worlds of country and bluegrass. Chances are, their statements would fall well within the naturalistic terms in which the music is so pervasively characterized. They are not likely to be able to articulate the essentials of their art. They can speak the language of nature but fall silent when asked to reflect on—to analyze—the musicianship of country music. They lack the distance or detachment to reflect analytically because they have lived solely in one musical country, which is country itself. Born and raised in this one musical "nation," they inhabit it without self-consciousness.

Those who have immigrated to country music are different. Like newcomers to a strange land, they are in a position to notice differences in styles and techniques. As naturalized citizens, they speak at least two musical languages, whether they have come into country from rock 'n' roll, rhythm-and-blues, classical. As immigrants, they are good informants because they have lived in at least two musical worlds. These are the bilingual country artists, and the interviewer's tape recorder lets them provide their own insights into the artistry of country music. Because they hold dual citizenship in different musical realms, these musicians are best able to raise consciousness on the *art* of country music. It is especially timely to hear their voices just now, at a point when different musical traditions are becoming resources for each other. In Carnegie Hall in fall 1992, for instance, the Saint Louis Symphony, conducted by Leonard Slatkin, performed William Bolcom's oratorio, *Songs of Innocence and Experience*, based on the poems of William Blake. Beyond the expected complement of sopranos, mezzos, tenors, and baritones, it featured a madrigal group, reggae and rock bands—and "Lee Anna Knox, country singer." The oratorio shows different musical genres complementing one another through musical integration across traditional musical boundaries.

Here and now, however, it is the distinctness of separate musical styles that allows country to show its art in a kind of ABC's of musicians with dual citizenship. The profiles that follow feature country musicians with roots in other musical forms. Each was willing to reflect on the art of country in relation to his or her musical tradition of origin. Each musician brings the art of country music into sharper focus by speaking about country *and*. . . .

Country and Rock 'n' Roll—Barry Tashian

With three country duet albums with his partner, Holly—*Trust in Me* (1988), *Live in Holland* (1991), and *Ready for Love* (1993)—Barry Tashian's country credentials are anchored deep. The *Los Angeles Times* praises the duet's "extraordinary vocal blend reminiscent of the Everly Brothers at their best," while *Rolling Stone* lauds their "openhearted songwriting" and *Billboard* calls the *Ready for Love* album "an incandescent piece of country vocal work in the grand manner of the Louvin Brothers." Add to this Barry's 1980s stint as lead harmony vocalist and instrumentalist with Emmylou Harris's Hot Band (a slot held also by Rodney Crowell, Ricky Skaggs, Vince Gill) and his presence through the 1980s on Harris's albums (*Last Date, Thirteen, Bluebird, Brand New Dance*), and it seems that Connecticut-born-and-raised Barry Tashian was destined for Nashville as a country singer, guitarist, songwriter. Look for prophetic moments in Tashian's career in country music, and you discover that the first song he recalls playing on guitar was Hank Williams's "Your Cheatin' Heart," picked out note for note from sheet music.

Yet the route to country has been much more complex, and we could locate a milestone on the December 26, 1965, *Ed Sullivan Show*, when one of the most enduring personalities in American network television announced the next act, the Remains, a young rock 'n' roll group out of Boston and New York. "Let's have a nice welcome for them," says Ed Sullivan. Flanked by go-go dancers in cheerleader outfits, a rock group appears in coats and ties and long hair, singing a hard-driving "I want you, open up your door / You got to let me through." Their beat is surging, pounding, electric-loud, with instrumental licks that locate them squarely in the tradition of the Beatles and Rolling Stones. Their leader and lead singer is Barry Tashian, and the group has already been recording for Columbia Records and will open the following summer, 1966, for the Beatles on their last tour, fourteen cities in eighteen days—soon after which the Remains would disband, musically having "run its course."

The Remains wrote and performed the rock music Barry Tashian had loved from the age of ten when, each late afternoon, his classically trained pianist mother set the timer for twenty-five minutes, the mandatory practice period for an eleven-year-old taking classical guitar lessons on the instrument that had "hooked" him from the moment he saw it on TV. Describing himself as someone who "took to music," Barry bent to his mother's insistence that he "get educated, with written music," including several years of piano and keyboard theory. Beginning in the eighth grade, however, Barry Tashian had garage bands, all rock music ("It was always rock with me . . . since I was eleven or twelve. . . . [I] didn't want anything to do with classical music").

Needless to say, country was nowhere on the Tashian musical map.

Looking forward to learning theory, composition, scoring, Barry nonetheless was thwarted in his early sixties effort to enter a bastion of classical music, Boston University's School of Fine and Applied Arts. He actually tried to put music behind him by entering a liberal arts program at the university instead. But a mystical, visionary experience ("one of those transforming experiences") in a London music club moved Barry Tashian to recruit college friends to form a rock band. The Remains consisted of electric guitar, electric piano, bass, and drums, and they hired a specialist to set up the highest-quality amplifiers for the vocals. "It was loud," Barry admits. The band was "enthusiastic about what we were doing and didn't want to give the [audience] the chance to talk." From Boston, the Remains played New England, then cut ties there and moved to New York. Recording for Columbia, yet dissatisfied with their sound quality on recordings, at one point they were sent to Nashville to try to capture "an earthier, funkier sound" from the studios there. Producer Billy Sherrill, later to win fame as producer of Tammy Wynette, was assigned to work with the Remains and tried, unsuccessfully, to persuade them to play more softly. He also offered to try arranging an appearance at the Opry.

The young rockers responded with contempt: "We thought country music was square; it did not fit into our mindset. We were Rolling Stones [people]. Yes, Chet Atkins is a great guitarist, but the whole setting was unacceptable at that age."

But so, at a certain point, was rock 'n' roll. If the Remains lay low in Nashville for fear that their politically subversive, counterculture long hair might get them into trouble on the city's conservative streets, Barry Tashian nonetheless reached the point in rock music when he felt, "If I played another Chuck Berry song with the same chord pattern . . . basic blues 1-4-1, 5-4-1 . . . I felt like I would die if I had to play that again. . . . I was so fed up with that progression."

Yet within a few years, Tashian had found another three-chord musical structure—country music—and embraced it. How did he move from contempt to love? How did country music so capture his energies that by 1993, he and duet partner Holly Tashian had moved toward the bluegrass side of country music in albums and performance touring in the U.S. and abroad?

Tashian's musical gateway to country was Gram Parsons, a key figure in vitaliz- ing country music for the age of rock 'n' roll. A brilliant songwriter and musician who died before achieving stardom, Gram Parsons is widely credited with bring- ing country to the age of rock, working to synthesize the two within a succession of bands, including the International Submarine Band, the Byrds, and the Flying Burrito Brothers. (Two Parsons albums remain available, a *GP/Grievous Angel* [1990] double album and a key neocountry album showing his influence, the Byrds' *Sweetheart of the Rodeo* [1968].) Barry Tashian had befriended Parsons while in New York and then, when the Remains broke up, moved to the West Coast, where he "moved in with, camped out with . . . Gram Parsons's group, the Inter- national Submarine Band. . . . We were buddies in New York; they had a house in the Bronx. . . . They'd be rehearsing, and they were playing Buck Owens's stuff. It was just wonderful."

What made it wonderful to Barry Tashian was that it was country music played with "a rock attitude," meaning "a rhythm-and-blues attitude, a more rhythmic ap- proach." Tashian explains, "They had drums, bass, two guitars. Gram was one, singing lead, and the bass player sang harmony. They had long hair, they smoked pot, and the drummer, a native of Baltimore, had come from a rhythm-and-blues group out of Boston's Washington Street. He was used to playing James Brown, so he was throwing in a lot of kicks and stuff on the bass drum. His touch was rhythm-and-blues. The bass player leaned toward syncopation and a percussive style, too."

Tashian rests his case for Parsons's bringing a "rock attitude" to country music mainly on Parsons's reconceiving its percussion. (If this does not sound suffi- ciently innovative, one can take a crash course by listening to country artists' own failed efforts to accommodate their styles to the rock 'n' roll era largely by chang- ing their beat—for instance, Faron Young's change from his Hank Williams-era "If You Ain't Lovin'" to the rock effort of "Goin' Steady," or, for that matter, the shift in the country vocal duet of Wilma Lee and Stoney Cooper from the blue- grass rhythms of "The White Rose" to the attempted rock beat of "It's Started Again." The problems of accommodating to a new age dominated by rock are au- dible in these "before" and "after" songs, in which country artists severely com- promised their sound trying to update it. In each case, the newer "rock" sound be- came an unintentional parody both of country and rock and thus occupies a musical limbo.)

It was in working with Gram Parsons that Barry Tashian grasped the formal possibilities within country music. (In fact, it is Barry, not Gram Parsons, who sings "Cry One More Time" on Parsons's *GP/Grievous Angel*.) The three-chord pattern felt not like constraint but freedom. This sense of variety is perhaps analogous to poets' attraction to the disciplined freedom of the sonnet form. "What I saw in country songs was the possibility of using three chords in an infinite number of ways," says Barry, and the song that brought this insight was a trucker's road song, Dave Dudley's "Six Days on the Road." Says Tashian, "It just opened up a whole world of infinite possibilities, and that reoriented me towards a style of country music which I've been on ever since."

Still, rigorous practice is required, and continuous learning. "I hope and pray to continue to be inspired, motivated, disciplined enough to take lessons, to pick things up—techniques—from record[ings] and then integrate them into my playing." Tashian muses on the idea of *natural* talent, citing the virtuoso British electric guitarist, Albert Lee, whose cohorts report that he played brilliantly at sixteen. "So there's a case of someone who's just *so* natural, so gifted." Tashian shrugs. "Other people, like me, while I have the gift, I feel I have to work at it, develop it. . . . The people who are great *practice*."

Barry Tashian, however, is careful to say that mere doggedness is not the prime motivation, but spirit. "It takes spirit and desire and a willingness to want to do this. . . . When I hit a day when I don't feel like practicing, I must do it anyway. It pays off in the long run." He cautions, "If I don't play guitar for two days, my guitar playing ability drops 30 percent. The same with singing. You have to do it every day. And when you don't have a concert or recording session, it can be very challenging to sing at home for an hour or more each day. It's really hard just to stand in your own house and sing for an hour like you meant it. . . . But practice raises the performance level for the listening audience. It creates a higher, more enjoyable listening experience for everyone. That and honesty are what I enjoy most of all when I hear music. . . . I admire and love to listen to people who are really accomplished at what they do."

At present, Tashian's musical identity is centered in the folk and bluegrass side of country: "While I still *love* rhythm-and-blues, I view it as another mindset," meaning a younger mentality energized more by anger and rebelliousness ("some artists have it until they die"). But Barry Tashian has moved on. "In my heyday of rock 'n' roll, I was angry," he says, "and that's what I was feeding on to perform. And now I don't use anger." Asked to reflect on the central difference between rock and country, Tashian characterizes rock as the music of anger, country as the music of beauty. In performance, he experiences "an element of wanting to give something away [to others]." The music he writes, performs, and records is conceived in this way, not as a musical assault but as a communicative gift.

Barry and Holly Tashian. (Photograph by Jim McGuire; courtesy Rounder Records)

Country and Madrigals — Holly Tashian

In duets with partner Barry, Holly Tashian's alto rides over and under his baritone in harmony vocals and solos occasionally in album cuts (instrumentally, she is heard on rhythm guitar). Her songs, many cowritten with Barry, rise high on the country charts in England, and her "Home" won a bluegrass Grammy nomination. In the 1990s, Holly's duet work and songwriting with Barry, especially on *Ready for Love*, earns praise for its strength and simplicity that "reflects a confident maturity that comes from the couple's extensive musical background." An Austin, Texas, music journalist writes, "Even in a city as rich in possibility as Austin, it's rare that one gets the chance to hear music as exquisite as this . . . the purest of musical pleasures." *Bluegrass Unlimited* says Holly's voice "kick[s] the duet's sound into the realm of . . . astoundingly powerful vocal harmonies."

Yet this native of Westport, Connecticut, might have been a painter, a dancer—or, in music, a violinist. The projection for her musical future, based on her upbringing, would place her somewhere in the classical tradition with no more than a dilettante's interest in American vernacular musical forms like folk, jazz—or country.

Holly's family home was musically multilingual—up to a point. Her father's record collection included show tunes and "race music," a euphemism for black jazz and blues, from Louis Armstrong to Johnny and Baby Dodds, and her parents played that music late into the night and hired jazz musicians from New York City to play an annual barn dance in suburban Tarrytown. Holly liked it all, including popular rock (synonymous with Elvis) and folk (Doc Watson). And she recalls listening to Bo Diddly albums with fellow high schooler Barry Tashian. But Holly's mother, Jeanne Kimball, had received formal voice training at Radcliffe College and was deeply involved in classical music ("Saturday afternoon was the [Metropolitan] Opera"). She started a madrigal group in the Westport area, a suburb of New York City, and Holly sang in it for a short time. Like her sisters, Holly studied an instrument, in her case both piano and classical violin.

What brought Holly Tashian to country? "I danced ballet, and I loved classical music," she says, but "I wanted to play the fiddle." Hearing Roy Acuff on the family collection of old 78s, she thought, *That's for me!*" The identification was instantaneous. A Tex Ritter album of cowboy songs cemented the bond ("The fiddle on that was terrific") and so did Tammy Wynette's vocal on "Stand By Your Man" ("Wow!").

The pathway was not unobstructed. Holly tuned in country radio's *Jamboree* on Wheeling's clear-channel WWVA, but the mandatory classical violin lessons made the term *second fiddle* more than slang. The family's classical mandate, in fact, deprived Holly of the kind of training young Cody Kilby is getting, the training required for the country instrumentalist who *must* learn to play by ear. Eventually Holly would turn to the autoharp as an intermediate step into country. Though the instrument felt awkward to hold, it helped her "to learn how chords work . . . [and to learn] some [country] songs."

Guitar, fortunately, was a different matter. Several years of what psychologists call random learning, in this case watching the chord fingerings of partner-to-be (and husband) Barry, worked to good effect. Within a few months this "mirror vision" succeeded, and Holly Tashian was feeling her way around her first Gibson, amazed at how quickly she "picked it up," playing rhythm guitar to Barry's lead.

Was her vocal development a parallel track? After all, it was Roy Acuff's fiddle and not his voice that was galvanizing—and no, it was not Acuff's singing "Wabash Cannonball" or "The Great Speckled Bird" that provided inspiration.

Instead, Holly recalls that hearing the Gram Parsons/Emmylou Harris harmonies on Parsons's *GP* was "a turning point" in her resolve to sing—songs like "We'll Sweep Out the Ashes in the Morning" and "That's All It Took." Hearing those harmonies in the early seventies, Holly knew, "*That's* what I had to do." She elaborates on her first country vocal efforts: "When Barry and I began seeing each other in the early seventies, he would sing country songs, and I loved trying to sing harmony. . . . I knew enough about harmony to know where the harmony lay."

She knew this from her voice-coach mother, who, when Holly was eight, began teaching her daughter rounds and catches and *a cappella* choral music as well as English and Italian madrigals. Now Holly began working on country vocals, with Tammy Wynette and Emmylou Harris as models. From her background in vocal groups, she was drawn to the duet, listening closely to Tammy Wynette and George Jones, and to Dolly Parton and Porter Wagoner, and later to the Louvin Brothers and the Everly Brothers. She says, "I started singing [because] I happened to love to sing harmony."

But vocal development has taken serious effort, and increasingly Holly Tashian has come to appreciate the voice coaching a classically trained instructor like Jeanne Kimball provides. The issues are several: how to support the voice; how to pronounce vowels so as to keep an open throat; how to pronounce consonants so as to be understood. There are vocal "techniques involved in all singing across the board," Holly concludes, "not just classical or pop or country, but basic rules for everybody." Her coaching has proved very valuable for both Tashians, Holly and Barry. In the process, Holly has come to terms with the myth that country singing is natural rather than cultivated (nature versus art yet once again). "It took me a long time to fully appreciate my mother's advice. I'd say, 'I don't want to sound like an opera singer.'" The vocal-coach mother would rejoin, "'You've got to open up your throat,'" insisting that the best country singers have an "open throat" and support their voices. Holly agrees. "It has taken a long time to [feel] confident enough in my voice to allow . . . the restricted sound to drop away so that I could get . . . a good open vowel sound, which any good singer's going to have, no matter what style." Some country singers, like Brenda Lee or Irish country artist Daniel O'Donnell, tend to do this intuitively; others need professional help. Holly does regular vocal exercises "for the health of the whole voice," and she (like Barry) states that "anybody who uses their voice seriously for a living has got to have training." She concedes that her mother would probably have preferred that she sing classical, but "we meet in the middle [and] she's been very helpful."

One main question remains unanswered. What, essentially, is the appeal of country to this singer and songwriter who grew up "loving" classical music? Why was Roy Acuff a young New England girl's musical inspiration? Holly Tashian answers that it is the "simplicity" and "directness" of country, the accessibility of meaning. "I keep coming back to the idea that [country music and bluegrass] are accessible, and they are direct." She admits to using the term *simple* in a sophisticated way. "I absolutely do not mean mundane; I mean simple in the way a plant is simple. It's a line, and it has leaves—nothing more." But its complexity reveals itself to anyone attempting to replicate it in a drawing. "You'd discover the many dimensions and think, 'How can I possibly draw it?'" She regrets "that dumb hillbilly act" as "unfortunate for country," whose artists are "not hillbillies by any means. There are a lot of sophisticated people in the field. A *lot*." She names Lyle Lovett and Nanci Griffith as the kind of country artists who, coming under the umbrella of country, are "very knowledgeable" and "really making an impact." "In my opinion, some of the best musicians in [the U.S.] are in the country and bluegrass field." This is the musical territory where Holly Tashian has chosen to make her home.

Country and Rhythm-and-Blues—Mike Lawler[1]

A "bad attitude" is Mike Lawler's self-styled relation to country music. Oddly negative, given Lawler's current titles of Arts-and-Repertory Manager and Staff Producer for Mercury/Nashville. Behind the businessman is the musician. The first synthesizer player on the *Grand Ole Opry*, Lawler is now "one of the three kings of Nashville studio keyboards," according to *Keyboard* magazine. "I've been playing on hit records since 1985," he says—and after playing on a hundred number-one hit records, he quit counting. A fellow keyboardist, another "king," John Jarvis, jokes that Lawler was "the first musician to get a permit from the Tennessee Valley Authority to run a [synthesizer] rig." Lawler's work can be heard on Hank Williams, Jr.'s, *Born to Boogie*, Tanya Tucker's and Conway Twitty's *Greatest Hits* albums, Kenny Rogers's *Something Inside So Strong*.

But Lawler is also featured on the likes of Etta James's *Sticking to My Guns* and James Brown's *Body Heat* and *Get Up Offa That Thing*. The "bad attitude" may well originate in Lawler's steadfast devotion to the rhythm-and-blues traditions of these artists. It is telling that Mike Lawler, who toured with Brown for several years, laments the decline of the once-vital rhythm-and-blues center, Memphis. As Beale Street became Memphis's musical desert, Lawler feels artists like himself were forced east to Nashville's Music Row. (One great advantage to the Third

1. Most of this profile was based on an interview with Mike Lawler in December 1992. Some of his quoted statements come from Doerschuk, "Country Keyboards."

*Mike Lawler.
(Photograph
courtesy
Mercury/
Polygram)*

Coast city, in his view, is that it saves him from the dire fate of living in L.A. or New York.)

A native of tiny Cooter, Missouri, Mike began music with piano lessons as a boy and, like so many musicians, loved his first (and "brilliant") teacher, who recognized Mike's "downfall," a certain inattention to the printed music. "I wasn't a great sight reader," he admits, saying that he took up guitar on the side. "I figured you played piano by [printed] music, but you played guitar like the Beatles. . . . I was playing guitar with chords and piano with music. [But] one day, when I was a junior in high school, I figured out that you could play piano the way you play guitar, with chords. As soon as I found that out, I went out and got a gig." With his mother signing the minor's permission slips, the fifteen-year-old Mike was soon gaining experience playing in honky-tonks.

"The Beatles came out and changed my life," he says. Their music ultimately led Mike Lawler to play the synthesizer as an artist thinking like a guitarist. Working on the synthesizer, he says, "I became the guitar player I always wanted to be." (And in the basement of his home, he has installed his synthesizers in a state-of-the-art recording studio.) Mike defines his place in country music this way: "I come at it from a different perspective, not being a piano player. I'm able to do these home tracks by myself, and overdub, with real instruments over the top."

If current country music relies "more on synthesizers than on fiddle," as one recent writer claims, then surely Mike Lawler is one of those responsible for the new direction. He rejects any notion that a synthesizer keyboardist is an electronic metronome: "If somebody told me a track I did sounds like a machine, that would be like a slap in the face. It would be like telling me I failed." Lawler "pulls out some sound you wouldn't think would work, but does," says Matt Rollings, a keyboardist colleague (the third of the "kings").

Still, Lawler feels country music is far too limited in structure and adamantly resistant to change: "Country records are just the same thing." The chord structure Barry Tashian finds artistically liberating has the opposite effect on Lawler: "For the most part, man, they are milkin' that format." Lawler is on record as claiming that the country song structure has all the variety of a fast-food salad bar. Basically, he warns, as far as country music is concerned, "you are talking to a troubled person."

Mike Lawler's country music troubles began early. It was the bluegrass Opry the six-year-old Mike Lawler loved, the Opry of Flatt and Scruggs. The soulful balladeers, however, turned him off, and they provoke him to this day. "When I listen to the Jimi Hendrix Experience's *Electric Ladyland* [1969], [I] might tell myself, 'I'm thirty-nine years old and shouldn't like that. [Instead,] I should like [the current country superstars].'" Having played the Opry and feeling personally very grateful to Porter Wagoner for giving him his start, Mike Lawler worries about his impulse to bite the very hand that has fed him well, not just the Opry but Music City.

But shoulds and oughts don't work for Lawler. "You can't help what you feel," he recalls a friend saying—a homegrown aphorism consoling to this musician with deep convictions. What sends Mike Lawler into near despair is what he calls "that phony element" in country, that "double-knit element" (seventies-era slang for rube clothes and a general put-down of the unhip, the uncool, the mediocrity of middle America). He cites a country song he loves, "White Line" (Emmylou Harris/Paul Kennerley), the hard-driving song punning on the lethal risk of cocaine and the lost highway. "But how high did it get [on the charts]?" he asks rhetorically, implying that the song is beyond the reach of the "double-knit" mentality and therefore commercially doomed. (His favorite female country vocalist, Emmylou Harris, is simply "too cool for the double-knits.")

Mike has a country music formula for simultaneous commercial success and artistic failure. Every country hit that climbs high on the charts contains what he calls "a major irritant." This is not the sand grain that promotes a pearl's growth but a flaw that grates upon his musical ear. If he felt differently, Lawler thinks, he could not be happy with himself, meaning that if he could be satisfied with the country music status quo, he would not work to "come up with something that's new and different and cool." He would be like the average country music listener, mindlessly pleased and oblivious of that demon, the "major irritant."

Mike's major frustration is that country is "ten years behind," that it has failed to exploit the resources of pop and other musical styles that could help it reinvent itself ("I don't care what anybody says, it's true"). Mike Lawler can be called a resistant insider, one who critiques and protests from within a structure or organization, committed to changing it if at all possible. At the same time, he becomes angry at the country audience's ignorance of the musical tradition. He speculates that Hank Williams—Hank Williams, Sr.—is an unknown to fans of Garth Brooks and Billie Ray Cyrus who neither know nor care about country's musical lineage. And he faults some country music producers for musical provincialism and some fellow studio session musicians for a lazy cynicism: "There are studio players now, especially on country records, who will play a lick right out of 'Midnight Train to Georgia' because who's gonna know? This country producer who's only listened to country? Or this nineteen-year-old kid who just bought the Billy Ray Cyrus album?" (Playfully, Lawler once overdubbed the Beatles' "Here Comes the Sun" in a country studio session—and nobody noticed.) But Mike is also unforgiving of older musicians who have lost sight of their musical values ("They started spending more money on buying a new boat than on buying new keyboards").

This is not misanthropy or sour grapes, you realize talking with Mike Lawler, but a certain level of frustration that masks his idealism and ambition ("It's weird being a session player because you can't stop and say, 'Hey, that's me on the radio'"). Lawler much appreciates the keyboard legacy of his forerunners, notably Floyd Cramer, who brought jazz resources into country. And he cites exceptional songs, like "Stand By Your Man," saying, "I get the same chill listening to that as I

do . . . the Rolling Stones." And that's the intriguing thing: that "some [songs] *every*
now and then pop through," meaning that occasionally a country song rockets out of
the realm of the "major irritants." When it does, "it is cool all the way down and

winds up being a hit."

This is Mike Lawler's model for country music opportunity—the songs that
might "pop through" with his own musical integrity intact. This is what lures and
drives him as he moves into the role of producer. For Mike Lawler's musical ambition runs deep. He has a particular country music sound in mind, and he is moving to go public with it. Actually, that goal took shape as he began guiding some
young bands out of Arkansas (one of them, from the state's tornado belt, naming
itself and its first album Twister Alley). These are "three different little groups . . .
of kids I found out in the sticks," as Mike puts it, groups green enough to believe
they needed to pay thousands up front to get recorded. Mike has steered them
away from the "Music Row sharks" and has been shepherding them. "They're all
real young. . . . I cut 'em some basic tracks to practice with on my [equipment].
. . . They'd come in on weekends and work [in Lawler's studio]. . . . I said to 'em,
'Y'all get good enough, I'll get my buddies that play on hot records to play on
[yours].'" After two years of this apprenticeship, Mike listened closely and decided the kids were ready. The booming popularity of country music dance clubs and
the 1992 Billie Ray Cyrus ("Achy Breaky Heart") phenomenon has made the record labels receptive to young country artists. For Mike Lawler, the moment feels
right to push. "I'm cowriting my songs with them. I'm playing [and] producing."
He says they will record on three different labels.

But their sound is his main focus, a sound he has developed, a sound originating in Mike Lawler's own head and nowhere else. The sound of these bands is *his*
sound, the uncompromised and uncompromising sound to which he is committed. Adventurous country music producers must worry about "getting too far
out," and the Mike Lawler sound is musically "all the way to the right." He is
working with the same label executives who signed Cyrus and K. T. Oslin. "Time
is gonna tell . . . if I'm too far beyond the folks."

Sometimes, after all, the irritant is found inside the oyster shell.

Country and Classical—Andrea Zonn

Is it fiddle or is it violin? *Both!* says Andrea Zonn without a nanosecond's pause.
Calling herself "musically bilingual," this young woman dwells as much in bluegrass and country as in classical music. She is dead set against an either/or choice.
And in her early twenties Andrea Zonn has already slalomed smoothly from a stint
as harmony singer and fiddler for country superstars Vince Gill and Ronnie Mil-

sap to soloing with the Vanderbilt University Orchestra (She played the Mozart A-Major Concerto as her prize for winning a concerto contest at the university's Blair School of Music, now her *alma mater.*) You can catch her bluegrass act— Andrea Zonn and the Zonbies—at Nashville's Station Inn in the winter of 1993. Reach back some ten years, and you could have heard her at New York's Lincoln Center and at the Library of Congress, playing a violin part in an ensemble performance of her composer-father's commissioned composition, *Prairie Songs.*

It was a "family affair," Andrea Zonn reminisces, as if chronicling a commonplace event. It came about this way: Joel Krosnick, cellist of the Julliard String Quartet, commissioned a composition from composer Paul Zonn, head of the Composition Department at the University of Illinois, Urbana-Champaign. Zonn's score called for violin, cello, acoustic guitar, oboe, mandolin, and bass— and what fun to have daughter Andrea onstage playing with her musical parents and their colleagues! After all, wasn't Andrea the principal reason why avant-garde composer Paul Zonn included bluegrass music in *Prairie Songs* in the first place? Musically speaking, hadn't his commissioned composition come directly out of his determination to find some kind of decent music to keep his daughter interested in the violin? Hadn't the threat of ten-year-old Andrea's abandoning her classical violin actually led the composer serendipitously into country and bluegrass music?

And should anybody be surprised when, ten years later, Andrea Zonn appeared on the stage of the *Grand Ole Opry*, televised to the world as the fiddler and harmony singer for Vince Gill, her voice blending with his so beautifully on the heartwrenching refrain, "Nobody answers when I call your name"? Should it be surprising that Andrea, determined to have a solo performing career, would since have given up the security of touring with Gill and begun working for herself, vocally and instrumentally, and writing songs, too?

Not at all, is the inevitable answer when you hear the fuller story. At age ten, a frustrated Andrea had wanted to quit violin because of her inability, after five years of lessons, to play the classics of Mendelssohn and Tchaikovsky. Her composer father was thankful when a local violin repairman suggested a book of "old-time" fiddle tunes as the sort of music that might interest the child sufficiently to bridge the next developmental years. (This fiddle book proved to be the entire family's introduction to bluegrass, an interest that soon became so compelling that in his forties, Paul Zonn, a pianist and clarinetist, would begin the mandolin, and the whole family would hit the interstates to attend summer bluegrass festivals in Illinois and neighboring states—Ohio, Kentucky, Kansas—including Indiana's Bean Blossom Festival.)

Unknown to bluegrass newcomer Andrea or her parents, however, their intro-

duction to the bluegrass notation in the "old-time" fiddle book was at best skeletal, since bluegrass inflections are so complex they cannot be fully notated. The crucial improvisational dimension of bluegrass was nowhere indicated on the printed music. Unaware of this, Andrea began learning the tunes in the most literal, note-by-note way.

What then? A fiddle contest at the county fair, and her dad asking, Did Andrea want to enter? Only reluctantly, because it seemed "stupid and hokey," conjuring "backwoods" images to this sophisticated child of a university town. Still, Andrea agreed to work up the tunes and compete. And the rest, as they say, is history. The seventy-five-dollar second prize was nice, but the real bonus was exposure to veteran fiddlers who spoke the stellar bluegrass names unknown to the Zonn family, names like Kenny Baker and Paul Warren. "Listen to Paul Warren," said one, "he plays with Flatt and Scruggs." Andrea recalls thinking, "Flatt and Scruggs, who's that?" and then feeling somewhat at a loss when first she heard the two, needing time to understand that microtonal inflections are "absolutely" a part of the blue-grass musical interpretation. She laughs at her own childish perplexity ("I was just a shallow-minded little kid").

Andrea Zonn moved out of those shallows fast, working on the bluegrass music that proved irresistible. "The neat thing about the fiddle contests," she recalls, "was these sixty- and seventy-year-old guys who'd been playing fiddle their whole lives . . . who'd sit down and show you their tunes and play them over and over again and get their left hand right in your face so you could see exactly what they were doing. . . . [They'd] play them until you learned the tune. And that's how the tradition is carried on. You learn it and work on it at home . . . and change it up a little . . . until it becomes your own. . . . [Though it] hardly ever sounds the same way twice." The older players are very generous, says Andrea, suggesting that bluegrass music, never commercially successful, is haunted from one generation to the next by a fear of extinction.

She reflects on her musical development in those years when, as now, she was playing both classical and bluegrass. "The nice thing about starting bluegrass so young is that I didn't know what I was doing." From her violin experience, Holly Tashian has described bluegrass fiddling as "taking a leap of faith . . . sort of like parachuting," and Andrea Zonn indicates that youth itself protected her from knowing how daunting the musical task was. "[Take] the way you hold the instru-ment," she muses. "When I play bluegrass, I slouch a little bit more. . . . And the way you think about time: In classical, you've got a constant beat divided into ab-solutely metronomic divisions. You never slur it around. Bluegrass is a much more rolling rhythm. When classical players try to take on bluegrass later on in life, they want to know, What is the [note value]? [You could say] it's kind of like a triplet" (three identical notes having the value of the first two beats). "But it's *not* a triplet. If they do a triplet as in classical music, it sounds too rigid."

Zonn emphasizes, however, the value of musical training, rejecting any notion of the "natural" player: "Without some proper technique, you just can't play some things." She says, "Being a classical player [gives you] certain basic principles and knowledge of certain techniques . . . that provide facility and speed and tone." She adds, "I can look at other fiddle players without formal training and see that they are blocked at a certain level." Zonn then remembers the exceptions that prove the rule. "I look at Stuart Duncan, who I don't think has had any training, and [see that] he's figured it out in his mind." As for Kenny Baker, the name first heard at that Illinois county fair: "I don't know how he learned to play, but he's wonderful." Zonn recalls watching Baker from a first-row festival seat at age twelve or thirteen. "I learned a lot from watching him play, that I didn't learn in classical music. He has one of the most fluid right arms I've ever seen . . . an arm like spaghetti . . . and you can hear that, no tension, nothing rigid about his playing. And that was something I tried to emulate." Though Baker was not "formally schooled," Zonn says, "fiddle players watching him play get [an] education."

What of her own education? How did she cohabit the two musical worlds? Not easily. Years were passing, and Andrea Zonn entered the University of Illinois under an early admissions program, leaving high school after her sophomore year. As a university music student, she was soon confronted by her classical violin teacher, who objected to bluegrass's "interfering" with Andrea's musical education. The teacher gave her student an ultimatum: bluegrass *or* classical music. The timer was set—Andrea had one summer to make up her mind, a summer in which she admits to crying much of the time.

Then the sixteen-year-old Andrea took action. "My decision was to pack up and move to Nashville and do both. My decision was *not* to make a decision." Nashville had a symphony, she knew, and a university. And bluegrass bluegrass bluegrass. With her parents "fully supportive," Andrea made the move. Her first job in music was playing in a show at Opryland, the musical theme park adjacent to the Grand Ole Opry. "And I've been really, really blessed."

But what about her singing? It was not only the fiddle but a vocal tape that got her the job with Vince Gill. How did she learn country singing, which she terms "very difficult"? Not from formal instruction initially (though a series of recent lessons with country-bluegrass vocalist Kathy Chiavola—"a wonderful teacher" —has helped Andrea correct some problems with pitch control and phrasing). "When I think about it," she says, "I can't think of anybody that hasn't studied in one form or another." Andrea faults herself for an inability in her young teens to appreciate the classic female country vocalists like Kitty Wells, Patsy Cline, Loretta Lynn, Connie Smith, whose music now gives her "chills" when she listens to them. Andrea, however, had always liked the more "weighty" male vocalists like Tony Rice and Ricky Skaggs, whose tonal shaping she especially admires ("It takes years to emulate that. . . . [It] doesn't sound hard but is tremendously difficult").

Most radio top-40 female country vocalists of the 1980s nonetheless struck the teenage Andrea as pallid ("Dolly Parton [was] trying her pop thing . . . like 'Islands in the Stream'"). Once again, it was father Paul Zonn to the rescue: "My dad said, 'Here, listen to Emmylou Harris,'" handing her *Quarter Moon in a Ten Cent Town*, *Elite Hotel*, and *Luxury Liner*.

"And *wow*! listen to this gal. . . . She [did] these songs that had meat to them."

It is not simply the themes in Harris's albums but the level of musicianship. "The people who learn to play [and sing] this music study inflections; they don't take it lightly [but pay attention to how the musicians] play each note. They may scoop into a note, or put [in] a little trill or pronounce a word [in order to] really draw attention to minute details." Zonn concludes that the best country artists pay intense attention to the details to achieve "a sense of balance, a sense of perspective, a sense of phrasing and really giving direction to the verses." Zonn knows musicians who play a country music tape at half-speed and "pick it apart note for note . . . to find out what people are doing . . . like Earl Scruggs's banjo playing." She says, "It's a studied thing."

As for the country song as an art form itself, Zonn emphasizes that the most successful artists understand the coherence of the song, the integrity of all of its parts, and that the best artists are those conscious of the interrelation of the whole. She compares learning a country song to learning a poem: "You have to continue and continue. . . . You have to make the audience understand the weight of the lyrics [over some twenty-four lines]. The audience has to know what you're singing about." And each song must have "its separate identity—and you really have to listen to the lyrics and make the song relate to the lyrics. . . . The music should be an extension of the song instead of a bed for the song to rest on." She adds, "I think certain singers like Emmylou Harris make you feel the music and make it mean something to you . . . and that's not something that comes naturally." Mary-Chapin Carpenter is another country artist whom Zonn much admires for the superb differentiation of her songs, from the "fun" of "Sometimes You're the Windshield, Sometimes You're the Bug" to the "ethereal mood" of "Come On, Come On."

Zonn worries, as Mike Lawler does, about the homogenization of country music. Too many producers, she finds, seek country star soundalikes instead of searching out new and different talent. They resort to sound replication instead of innovation, using the same players repeatedly in studio sessions so that the music sounds much the same from one cut to the next, one album to the next. She quotes a friend's remark that country is becoming "so formulated and processed that it's possible for any wannabee to walk in and do it and look good." "You wouldn't play Mozart and Sibelius with the same articulation," Zonn says, "so why would you do that with a song that Guy Clark wrote and a song that Jim Rushing wrote?" Such matters press in on Andrea Zonn's mind as she turns from "dabbling" in country songwriting to devoting serious attention to it ("You've got to sound like you're speaking it. . . . It's really hard").

Zonn knows how formidable the challenge before her and is keenly aware of the steps necessary to move from backup or harmony singer to soloist. She is utterly determined, bringing to her musical ambition the indomitable will that brought her to Nashville at sixteen with her violin and her fiddle.

Country and Opera—Kathy Chiavola

"Terrifying," says Kathy Chiavola of the day she took her guitar and three country songs to sing for her voice teacher, the former Metropolitan Opera star, soprano Eileen Farrell. Everything was at stake for Chiavola: her future in music, her family's expectations for her career, her decision on whether or not to complete her doctoral degree in vocal and voice pedagogy at Indiana University's renowned School of Music. Appealing to Farrell as "the only voice teacher who can possibly relate to this situation," Chiavola admitted, "This is terrifying to me, but I may change careers, and I want your guidance and your input." Then Kathy Chiavola, a lyric mezzo-soprano, summoned the courage to sing Buffy St. Marie's "The Piney Hills" and two country songs she had written, accompanying herself on guitar.

Perhaps Chiavola sensed that she had come to the right person. Eileen Farrell was not only a star at the Metropolitan but somewhat of a musical maverick who had caused a stir in classical circles in the 1960s when she broke ranks to sing Broadway show tunes. Committed to musical diversity (she taught a course in jazz singing at Indiana), Farrell listened to her student and then gave her the authorization for radical change. Says Chiavola, "I owe a very big debt of gratitude to [Eileen] Farrell."

And what did Professor Farrell advise? Chiavola recalls the opera star saying, "The hell with a classical music career, forget it. . . . Follow your heart and do what you love."

What Kathy Chiavola increasingly loved was country music. Cherishing the classical tradition, she nonetheless was reaching beyond its boundaries to embrace country, ultimately to record with artists like Ricky Skaggs, Vince Gill, and Emmylou Harris and to cut an album of her own, *Labor of Love* (1990), which showcases a voice moving effortlessly, or so it seems, from western swing to honky-tonk to country blues and folk (and backed by a galaxy of front-rank country instrumentalists). The *Tennessean*'s country music writer, Robert K. Oermann, has written, "Kathy has the ability to 'cry' like a country star, moan like a blues mama, and maintain the clarity and purity of tone of a folk soprano, often all in the same song." "Born to sing," says the British/Irish *Country Music Round-Up*, commending Chiavola's "awesome vocals" and stylistically linking her with Linda Ronstadt. Chiavola tours in Europe and Britain and performs regularly with her band in Nashville-area clubs before notoriously tough audiences peppered with fellow musicians. Finally, she has also become a voice teacher for country music hopefuls and professionals alike.

But the country music route of her heart's desire was nonetheless tortuous. A good stretch of it involved Chiavola's revolt against the increasing "confinement" and "rigidity" of classical training, starting with the Oberlin Conservatory faculty who forbade her—a scholarship student and budding soloist—to sing in the college choir ("We're training you to be a soloist. We don't want you singing in the Oberlin College Choir; that's *out*"). Kathy recalls "sneaking around" in Early Music groups.

Such musical segregation was foreign to Chiavola's experience, indeed to her very nature. As a child, her only musical "sneaking" was the parentally forbidden rock 'n' roll on the radio as Kathy grew up in Kansas City, the niece of a founder of the Kansas City Lyric Opera and daughter of "amateur classical musicians" who encouraged every "legitimate" musical interest. She studied classical piano and voice, took the lead in school shows, and sang around the city, both opera (later performing with the Kansas City Lyric Opera and with the Saint Louis Municipal) and rock too ("I was the Grace Slick of Kansas City"). She recalls early exposure to a wide variety of musical styles, including the folk music of Joan Baez, Peter, Paul, and Mary, Pete Seeger, Phil Ochs, Tom Paxton. And she recalls buying compilation or sampler albums on Vanguard or Electra and enjoying folk artists in what she calls "the Woodie Guthrie . . . and Doc Watson . . . tradition" ("Bob Dylan wasn't really out yet when I was twelve"). At fourteen, she got a Martin D-18 guitar from her mother, an instrument she still uses and a gift she commemorates in the title song from *Labor of Love*.

But Kathy "loved" Delta black blues, too, therapeutic music for a young person whose parents were divorcing. "I could identify with acoustic black blues," she says, "Mississippi John Hurt, Odetta, Lightnin' Hopkins, and also the [Paul] Butterfield Blues Band." These eclectic tastes seemed natural to a native of Kansas City, a blues and jazz crossroads.

But what about country? Or bluegrass? "Actually," Chiavola admits, "the old-timey country stuff I was exposed to—Flatt and Scruggs, the Greenbriar Boys, [other] Newport Folk Festival album cuts—it sounded curious to me. The high singing sounded very foreign. I had not heard that in Kansas City, [and] when I heard it, I thought it was funny, peculiar. . . . I didn't really know how to 'file' Bill Monroe [either]."

Her first entrée to country came through the David Grisman Quintet, which played bluegrass-inspired acoustic instrumental music often described as jazz ("dawg music," as Grisman termed it from his own nickname, Dawg), and also through the music of Ricky Skaggs, Emmylou Harris, Tony Rice. A crucial musi-

Kathy Chiavola. (Photograph by Dennis Carney)

cal door opened through early Stanley Brothers recordings: "[They] made the hair on the back of my neck stand up. I loved it." Ralph and Carter Stanley were catalysts for Chiavola, who vowed, "This is a whole tradition and world, and I want to learn about it. I want to assimilate."

Assimilation meant moving to Nashville, where she cut a demo the very first day in town and got a gig with an all-girl band, the Bushwhackers, including bluegrass vocalist Ginger Boatwright. Chiavola has also traveled to rural Tennessee and other border-state communities to perform under the auspices of the Old

Time Music and Dance Foundation, headed by Jacky Christian ("Jacky has done so much for traditional dance [like buckdance] and music, it's just unfathomable"). In addition, Chiavola found Nashville to be a musically open environment that enabled her to continue an involvement in classical music: directing a church choir and singing in a quartet that performs an eclectic mix, from songs of Debussy (transcribed for guitar, strings, recorder) to the Spanish composer Rodriquez to *Peter Pan*. Chiavola is also an active member of Nashville's Opera Guild. Like Andrea Zonn, Chiavola refuses to confine herself solely to one musical tradition, no matter how much she loves it.

From the first, however, Nashville was a country music conservatory for newcomer Kathy Chiavola: "After being immersed in classical [in college and graduate school], I was basically a student back in school again." The Station Inn, Nashville's center for acoustic music, became the new "university" where Chiavola went to night school ("I spent almost every night of the week [there] before it was popular to do so"). Her seminar instructors? "Every touring band, [and] Alan O'Bryant and Pat Enright," now of the Nashville Bluegrass Band. As for her "commencement," Chiavola feels she got her country music diploma in 1982 in the form of an invitation to record with a bluegrass purist, the late Red Allen, a Kentuckian who has worked with the Osborne Brothers and is perhaps best known from appearances on the WWVA *Jamboree*. (Chiavola is the only female vocalist ever to have been invited to record with Allen.)

In a speaking voice that *sounds* trained ("I don't disguise it"), Chiavola reflects on issues of musicianship and musical training. Her views originate in large part from practical experience, starting in adolescence when she realized, "Screaming my lungs out in a rock band was not helping my voice, and the classical training was." She cautions that within musical categories like "classical" or "country," there is a very wide range of musicianship and skill. "On the topic of finesse in [both] country music and classical," she says, "there are classical players who can read and know the repertoire, but . . . some are more gifted with subtlety and finesse in their music than others. It doesn't matter [what the genre], there's a tremendous variety of talent within all styles of music." She warns against generalizations based on limited listening: "There's a great wealth of talent [within country as well as classical]. It just happens that when you have a more organized tradition [as in music schools throughout the U.S.], you're taught dynamic awareness, taught ear training skills, taught basic music skills you might not come by as easily in a traditional [i.e., informal] sense."

Nor is Chiavola a wholesale worshiper of country music. Much as she loves it, she sees justification for some criticism of its musical failings. "Sometimes there are minimally talented people who do not sing [even] close to being in tune," she says—"whose phrasing is off, who [lack] a basic good sense of rhythm, timing, pitch. And that makes it unappealing for people to listen to." In these terms, some of the "old-time singers are not up to par with [current] commercial music."

Yet Chiavola cautions that music is largely a matter of personal taste, that beyond a certain point, objective standards cannot be applied. It's "such a personal and subjective thing," she says, adding that, for a variety of reasons, "A person might be singing with a great deal of soul and authority and technique and *still* not appeal." The baseline is liking and disliking on an individual basis.

But Chiavola feels that current technology, together with widely available and affordable recordings, have led to a significant degree of musical overlap in every genre in recent years. Even those living in remote places—places like Mike Lawler's hometown of Cooter, Missouri—have access to contemporary musical developments. Ask who the newer country artists have listened to in their youth, says Chiavola, and they reply, "The Beatles, the Opry, Rod Stewart." "Everything is more available these days with the technology we live in [*sic*]. . . . If a person has a true hunger for music, they'll find their way around and be able to have a pretty broad base. . . . [For instance,] you'll go into a fiddle player's home and find some classical recordings." Chiavola cites the example of her own band's fiddler, the superb Randy Howard, who in youth got hold of some Paganini recordings: "He locked himself in his bedroom and copied them note for note for hours on end, and he figured out the techniques himself for playing this virtuosic music."

As for the general listening public, "They take what they're fed." Like the others interviewed for these profiles, Kathy Chiavola takes a dim view of the top-40 country music menu, worrying that in order to ensure mass popularity, country music is becoming "diluted" and "generic." Unfortunately, she says, "I can only listen to [top-40 radio] country music half the time." The big record labels, she observes, are run with a mentality oriented toward business, not music. The frequent result is country music generated in a self-perpetuating cycle of musical banality.

Given the current popularity of country music, however, it is perhaps no surprise that many of Chiavola's current students are classically trained vocalists yearning to sing country. What does she teach them?—first, basic techniques like posture and breathing, after which they work from certain model recordings. Teacher Chiavola recommends imitating a favorite country song note for note.

Which artists does she recommend to her students as country music masters? Chiavola lists this essential artistic roster: Dolly Parton, George Jones, Merle Haggard, Emmylou Harris, Vince Gill, Vern Gosdin, Linda Ronstadt, and Ricky Skaggs, whom she singles out as a musician's musician ("A great vocal technician embod[ying] the soul of eastern Kentucky and the Stanley Brothers tradition [along] with a great technique and a great ear and a great sense of musicianship.

His sense of timing and phrasing and pitch is extraordinary"). Chiavola emphasizes that she is talking about much more than technique: "When you talk about singers, you're not just talking about pitch and phrasing; you're talking about the soul. That's what I lock onto, and that's what these people have." She does not mention that critic Oermann has said that her own "heart and soul is in the bluegrass/acoustic scene" of Music City.

Chiavola continues to value her classical training and feels it contributes to her country music work, calling it "a bonus" in studio sessions and performance ("I've learned to use my ear to . . . mimic and blend. . . . I'm really grateful for the classical training I've had"). As for her students' own vocal changeovers from classical to country, she says, "I've had to undo what they've been taught."

Saying this as the interview draws to a close, Chiavola pauses a moment, looks thoughtful, begins to laugh. She leans forward and, still smiling, comments with a certain relish, "If my old teacher from Oberlin knew, she'd have a heart attack."

Bluegrass/Country—Laurie Lewis

"I did not grow up with this music."

Across the oak pub table, spoken in the fast-paced tones of a northern Californian, it is a statement of fact: "I did not grow up with this music." No exclamation point needed.

Startling nonetheless, when you consider that the speaker is Laurie Lewis, the 1992 International Bluegrass Music Association's Female Vocalist of the Year. More startling still if, the previous night, you had been part of the studio audience of a TNN *American Music Shop* TV taping featuring a bluegrass duet between Lewis and the three-time IBMA male vocalist of the year, Del McCoury, whose own musical bio includes tenure as a Blue Grass Boy for Bill Monroe.

Kentucky's bluegrass country is very far from Laurie Lewis's home. Her musical hills ("The Hills of My Home") are no southern Appalachians but the Pacific coastal topography of Berkeley/Oakland/San Francisco, where she grew up and makes her home yet. And Lewis's musical surprises only start there. Elitist bluegrass fans apt to be disdainful of commercial country music, for instance, will find another of her pub table statements provocative, if not outrageous: "Bluegrass is country music."

A remark like this is not solely a First Amendment exercise for Laurie Lewis. Speaking freely on country music/bluegrass, she is stating a conviction earned through years of vocal and instrumental performance and songwriting, rave-review albums, awards, and master-class workshops she offers in fiddle.

Lewis's triple-threat credentials as vocalist, songwriter, and fiddler surfaced

with *Restless, Rambling Heart* (1986) and continued with *Blue Rose* (1988), a collaboration of five women artists, followed by *Love Chooses You* (1989), voted best country album by the National Association of Independent Record Producers, then
Singing My Troubles Away (1990), *Together* (1991), a collaboration with a fellow artist,
vocalist and guitarist Kathy Kallick, and most recently another solo album, *True
Stories* (1993). Reviewers praise Lewis's band, Grant Street ("polished," "savvy"),
commending each musician individually. And newspapers from San Francisco to
Tucson, in addition to periodicals like *Billboard, Frets, Bluegrass Unlimited, Sing Out!*

(these last two featuring Lewis in cover stories in the 1990s), all praise her voice as "stunning," "gorgeous," "clear and true whether she's delivering a burning bluegrass song, a soulful Nashville duet, or a haunting, traditional-style dirge." Lewis's compositions are termed "charming," "topnotch" (her "Love Chooses You" recorded by Grammy-winner Kathy Mattea), and her award-winning fiddling is "fine instrumental work . . . just stunning on all fronts, a superb singer, fiddle player, songwriter."

One writer, however, states a basic fact: "Lewis paid a lot of dues before she got her shot at a solo record."

She paid those dues, in part, in fiddling championships and stints with West Coast groups like Pat Enright's Phantoms of the Opry and Good Ol' Persons. But Laurie Lewis's dues also include some five years of shunning music altogether, five young-adult years in which Lewis neither played nor sang, her fiddle gathering dust under a bed.

Reclaiming that fiddle is actually a connect-the-dots moment in a musical biography that begins with Lewis's father, a physician who worked his way through medical school playing flute and piccolo in the Dallas Symphony and who, when Laurie was twelve, suggested violin lessons as part of the education the Lewis family expected of their children. Why violin?—because a sister had already claimed the flute and "because I had a really good ear," a trait essential for learning an unfretted instrument. The self-styled "dutiful daughter" let herself be signed up, although Laurie already considered herself somewhat of a musical "flop" from piano lessons that were aborted when the seven-year-old could not crack the code of written music ("If I had to go home and figure it out from a piece of paper, I couldn't do it").

The California elementary schools, fortunately, had done a good job instilling in Laurie the pleasure principle of music, notably with folksongs like "Old Joe Clark" and "Old Dan Tucker." Says Lewis, "I knew all the words to those songs 'cause I learned them when I was just a kid in school, and I just remembered 'em." Good thing—because unknown to Lewis, those folksongs were actually fiddle tunes. And this time around, the instrumental lessons succeeded. From age twelve, the violin became an ally, even if notes on a staff still make Laurie Lewis's eyes water and redden ("I can't learn anything from written music"). Instrumentally, what's more, the teenage Laurie was branching out, becoming interested in banjo ("My dad bought me a banjo, and I took bluegrass banjo lessons and started listening to bluegrass") and guitar, too.

But back to the hard-core fact that Laurie Lewis did not grow up with the music that identifies and defines her now. She reflects, "If somebody did grow up in the tradition, whether they're musical or not, . . . it's in their head in a very deep way in the first place. With somebody coming at it from the outside, you have to listen to it enough to get it in your head. You have to internalize it."

For Lewis, the internalizing proceeded in adolescence as her friends pursued dance, theater, and folk music while she listened to bluegrass artists Bill Monroe, the Stanley Brothers, Flatt and Scruggs, "a little bit" of the Osborne Brothers and Red Allen.

"And not too much else." Getting "into" bluegrass, she heard performances by Monroe and Kenny Baker ("who made a big impression on me"), Lester Flatt and the Nashville Grass, Ralph Stanley "with one of my all-time favorite bands, with Roy Lee Centers, Jack Cooke, Curly Ray Cline, and Ricky Lee—a really great band." Lewis explains that the music "has to catch your ear in the first place and make you want to listen to it. And it helps if you're younger because you have more time to do these things. . . . You have the time to seek out this [music] that you love, and just listen to it incessantly."

Which she did—though upon high school graduation and a parental breakup, Lewis snapped shut the locks on her instrument cases and quit singing, too. The next five years passed in college semesters (at two University of California campuses, San Diego and Berkeley) and in managing a dance studio. No music at all. But when the dance director's husband learned of Lewis's instrumental background, he took her to a San Francisco bluegrass bar, Paul's Saloon, having decided she ought to play the fiddle. The strategy worked; Laurie was "smitten" and, by now, sufficiently mature to make a new commitment—as she puts it, "enough like my own person" that "my interest in music reawakened."

Lewis has never looked back. Her primary allegiance to the bluegrass tradition does not mean parochialism for this artist who credits influences from Bob Wills to Billie Holiday and mixes western swing ("Texas Bluebonnets"), torch ballads ("I'd Be Lost without You"), and folk with bluegrass standards like Bill Monroe's "Cry, Cry Darling." But Lewis's heart belongs to bluegrass—and bluegrass, in her judgment, belongs in the realm of contemporary, avant-garde music, even though its practitioners are not accustomed to analyzing it in such terms. "It's very advanced music," says Lewis. "It's just that the people who've been involved in it, who more or less invented the musical form, didn't have the vocabulary [in which] to analyze it, to say, 'We're purposely making these tensions in the music.'" She adds, "The social traditions from which it springs are not big on the communicative arts . . . so consequently [bluegrass] has got this reputation as a music that's unconscious."

Lewis is reminded that artists in every medium resist and resent the summons to provide explanation, from sculptors who refer inquiring audiences to the object itself down to poets who refuse to supply a vocabulary for work they already have cast in words. She nods. "I'm sure [Bill] Monroe, when he's writing a song and singing it, the way he hears it in his head, he doesn't want to have to sit down and explain it as he's doing it. And he shouldn't have to. It's a piece of art."

Yet the verbally adroit Laurie Lewis consents across the oak table to reflect on the structures of bluegrass music—for instance, its harmonics. "What's really interesting in terms of bluegrass harmonies," she says, is the relation between the instrumental harmonies and voices. "What makes it a deceptively simple music is the chord structure. . . . The open chords on the guitar are very 1-3-5 [major triad] types of open chords. They almost never add a flatted 7th . . . no 6ths, no 9ths. They never go for denser chords.

"However, the [vocal] harmonies sing those [denser intervals] all the time. In the Stanley Brothers, that's what's so great. You hear Ralph Stanley singing 9ths all the time, but against these giant, open 1-3-5 chords, so there's this incredible tension in the music. And to me, the music doesn't sound right without it, although there's plenty of bluegrass that doesn't take advantage of that. But the real mountain-y stuff, the stuff that *I* love, really has that in it. It's much more advanced in terms of the chords that they're hearing . . . and that they're creating. It's the juxtapositioning of this very simple style of playing the guitars and open instruments—the bass is playing a 1 and a 5, and the guitar's playing chords made up of all 1's and 5's, and most of the other instruments are, too—and then the voices and the lead instruments are hitting these intervals that frequently are flatted 3ds and 6ths and 9ths."

And Lewis elaborates on what the term "playing by ear" involves. "For one thing," she says, "there's so much nuance in playing a fiddle tune, let's say, playing 'Leather Breeches.' There can be so much nuance and individuality [in] the pitch of the notes. It's not like the [half-step] difference between a C and a C-sharp. It's a blurred thing, but it's tonally correct for the music."

Lewis feels doubtful about the possibilities of notation for bluegrass. "I don't think there's a real notation system yet to write all that stuff down so somebody could read it and make it sound right." She explains the complexities in notational terms. "I don't think there is the written vocabulary in terms of notes, and rests, slides, slurs, and the little jumped beats. It would be *very* difficult music to read." Lewis emphasizes that she is not talking about tempo ("you can always learn to play something fast") but about the richness of subtlety: "It's more the nuance that they haven't learned to get down exactly." She compares bluegrass to the music of India, in which the half-tone chromatic scale does not apply. "It's more like an Indian scale," she says, "especially the old-time fiddle tunes." She warns that listeners to Western classical music may misjudge bluegrass. "It's not necessarily sloppiness where the [performer] is putting that note. You think, 'Oh God, he's playing that flat' or 'He's playing that sharp every time.' But no, he's not. He's going for . . . the right thing."

Lewis offers an example from a conversation while jamming with virtuoso fiddler Stuart Duncan. "We were playing around on 'Uncle Pen,' and he started doing it like a Swedish fiddler, [the way] he was putting his 3d. It wasn't sharp, it wasn't flat, but sort of in the middle. We were talking about it, and [Stuart Duncan] said, 'There [are] these flutists that play along in Swedish fiddling music, and they do exactly the same thing. They're half-covering the holes so they get that same intonation.' And that is . . . correct." Lewis sums up the point: "It's not like Western classical music, and it's not meant to be. And if you try pushing it into that standard, you're missing something."

Lewis readily acknowledges that bluegrass is emphatically vocal music, and that the pitch of individual voices requires instrumentalists to be masters at transposition. "It's vocally based music," says Lewis. "Forget about the fiddle tunes that all have standard keys, [because] the bulk of this music is vocal music. . . . Every song's got a different singer who's gonna find the right place in their voice to do that song. That's what Bill Monroe did with those old-time songs originally, which is what invented bluegrass music. He said, 'Well, I just started singing it to where it suited my voice.'"

Lewis explains the momentous implications of a cryptic phrase like "suited my voice," using the example of an old-timey song, Sam and Kirk McGee's "Blue Night." Bill Monroe, she says, "sings it in the key of B, [which] completely changes the tone of it because . . . the stringed instruments which are used to playing open are now playing in closed positions—and it's simply because [Monroe] decided vocally to pitch it where he could really show off his voice, then pulled all the instruments with him, specifically the mandolin and the fiddle, because they don't have capos. So they're the ones that really have to change the way they play, dramatically, to play in those closed keys. So that's a *lot*."

Lewis pauses, then injects further complexity into the subject by proposing other keys, like B-flat or C, in which different vocalists might sing "Blue Night." Or "some woman might come along and do it in E," she says. "And you might want to get that same [essential] feel, but you've got all these different possible keys. [And you've got to be ready to do it in] whatever key the vocalist wants, unless you're a complete jerk and say, 'No, I have to do "Can't You Hear Me Callin'"' in G because that's the way it was originally.'"

Lewis pauses again, having come to the border of controversy over commitment to the authenticity of original or early versions of songs versus the argument favoring flexibility in interpretation. "To tell you the truth," she says, "I ride the fence here, [on the one hand] as a bluegrass purist, somebody who really likes bluegrass music that *sounds* like bluegrass music." On the other hand, Lewis admits, she speaks "as a singer who happens to be female," knowing that her vocal presentation can be better if a song is shifted from its original key into one that favors the female voice. "I'm [thinking], 'It's too low for me in the key of G. If I'm going to do that song, I'm going to do it in a different key.'"

Caught between compromising her own art or that of the original song, Lewis may simply steer clear of the dilemma. "I just say, 'Okay, that's a song I'm not going to mess with [i.e., not going to sing it], because I love it so much originally, the way it was in the key of G. That's fine.'" She shrugs.

The conversation turns to the culture of bluegrass music, in particular to its overall reputation as distinctly masculine. Is bluegrass a "macho" form? Lewis nods, admitting there's "a lot of that," and referring back to the early decades of country music, when a man's domain was the world of work and of music, while a woman's was domestic. (The Carter Family may be the exception that proves the rule, though Sara and Maybelle Carter were, publicly at least, very much in the roles of the wife and sister-in-law under the care and protection of the patriarchal figure of A. P. Carter.) Even today, "there's definitely a gender issue," Lewis says, and she identifies a "gunslinger attitude among a lot of instrumentalists, [notably] bluegrass banjo players."

Lewis explains the point in terms of onstage behavior. "It's far more a male thing than a female thing to go for that [combativeness], you know, 'I'm gonna shoot this guy down, play hotter licks, and faster, and louder.'" Few women, Lewis says, invite that pressure. Laughing, however, she suggests women bluegrass artists need not get trapped in that macho game. "The world is a big wide place, and you don't have to hang around with those people. And there's plenty of great players who don't feel that way, who want to just play music for music's sake. So you just choose who you play with, and your audience picks you. . . . And it has not been a problem for me, 'cause I haven't wanted to go out there and gunsling with anybody."

Describing these gender problems, Lewis is not talking about ducking the highest musical standards or avoiding the highest caliber artists. Quite the contrary. She cites virtuoso mandolinist/fiddler Sam Bush, for instance, as a most "demanding" onstage colleague who requires the utmost from fellow musicians in performance but who generously gives back "musical strokes" and is "incredibly supportive." Playing with Bush is "extremely exhilarating."

But what about playing the same songs repeatedly? How does an artist on a grueling tour schedule of some two hundred days per year sustain freshness and vitality in performance? One key, says Lewis, is playing for different audiences. "The material becomes new for every audience." And those who have heard the recorded versions might be hearing songs live for the first time. Lewis also admits to choosing her material with great care. "I don't sing anything I can't get into. . . . And I change my set list all the time. And then . . . it's like acting. I'm sure you've heard actors say they throw themselves into the part, and then the part takes over. That's exactly what happens when you sing. . . . It sounds really schmaltzy but it's really what happens. You get inside it, and it's like good acting. You learn the techniques to get inside it. . . . You start singing the song, and then you *are* the song."

The Art of the Country Music Producer—Richard Bennett

"My goal is to make passionate records, with integrity."

Richard Bennett's adjective is well chosen. *Passionate*, it becomes clear, is his key-word, a litmus test, alchemist's stone, kindling temperature for musical power. Offer this individualistic country producer an album project, and his response is clear-cut and immediate: Does he love it or does he hate it? "It's strictly a gut thing for me, and it's right away. It's that basic." His fingers snap. "There's something there for me or there's not, whether it's a passion in the voice or the songs—but it has to be *that* strong." He adds, "It's not a matter of filling up a month in my calendar."

Producer Bennett's calendar has been chock-full since he moved from L.A. to Nashville to coproduce Steve Earle's pathbreaking *Guitar Town*, a landmark album in country music's renaissance of the mid-1980s, when artists like k. d. lang, Lyle Lovett, the O'Kanes (Kieran Kane and Jamie O'Hara) were invigorating country. Readers of this book, in fact, have already made Richard Bennett's musical acquaintance. He is the producer behind the driving energy of Steve Earle's road song, "Guitar Town," and behind the liquid sounds of Emmylou Harris's high lonesome "A River for Him," in addition to her "Red, Red Rose" with its classical orchestral arrangement. He coproduced Marty Brown's *High and Dry* (the album showing Brown in the tobacco field) and also Brown's *Wild Kentucky Skies* (1993). He is the producer of the group Prairie Oyster, of Cajun artist Jo-El Sonnier's RCA albums, of Becky Hobbs's *All Keyed Up* (1988). Bennett is also credited as a major player in the popular upsurge of Marty Stuart's music in the 1990s, with albums like *Tempted* and *This One's Gonna Hurt You*. His production of Native American artist Bill Miller's *The Red Road* (1993), with live recordings of powwow chants and tribal flutes, positions Native America in popular music as never before. His devotion to country music traditions, what's more, moves Bennett to involve himself in the producer's equivalent of a lawyer's *pro bono* work: He does the stereo engineering, gratis, for the German Bear Family's reissues of country legends like Faron Young and Johnny Horton. Finally, Bennett maintains an active presence

*Richard
Bennett.
(Photograph
courtesy
Richard
Bennett)*

onstage and in the studio as a guitarist, both acoustic and electric. Listeners can hear him on recent albums by Hal Ketchum and Jimmie Dale Gilmore—and in a lovely solo on Emmylou Harris's "You Don't Know Me" (*Cowgirl's Prayer*).

Richard Bennett's name on a country music album means two things: first, a deep and abiding respect for the longtime traditions of country music, and, second, newness or innovation, which is to say an exciting expansion of the sound

parameters within that music. Listen, for instance, to Marty Brown's "She's Gone"
(*Wild Kentucky Skies*), a lover's bereaved and suicidal cry at the grave of his dead
beloved. (Actually, Brown says it commemorates his grandmother's death.) The
arrangement includes Bill Miller's tribal flutes, harmonium, and certain eerie, otherworldly chords produced, literally, by hoses and tubes (garden hoses and Clorox
jugs blown like trumpet and tuba) in an adaptation of the vocal sound of a Tibetan
Buddhist monastic order, the Gayota Monks, who have toured the United States
and recorded their extraordinary vocal music. Their deep, pulsing, strange—to
Western ears—chords are physically unnerving, and, brought to Marty Brown's
"She's Gone," this sound heightens the terrible tension of the lover's primal cry.
The anguish of the song is traditional, a part of what Rodney Crowell calls the
longtime "Gothic" strain in country music. The innovation lies in the instrumen-
tation. "She's Gone" is a lesson in inviolable tradition carried forward through invigorating presentation—and this is Richard Bennett's stamp on country music,
one extremely difficult to achieve, since tradition can easily become mere repetition and newness collapse into novelty.

Given all this, it is ironic that audiences can be largely unaware of the producer's work. Most radio and album-buying listeners think only of the country star
performer(s) whose voice is the trademark. But *how* that voice sounds, in what
arrangements, with what instruments, even in what song sequence on an album
(the wrenching "She's Gone" is followed by the restorative sweetness of the title
song, "Wild Kentucky Skies")—these are largely the producer's work. It is the art
of the producer, in fact, that embodies each song, molds it into a unique presentation. The producer is the behind-the-scenes costar.

And a figure of tremendous power, dating from the very earliest days of country music, when the New York Victor executive, Ralph Peer, set the criteria for
country music production by dividing pop from country, dissuading Jimmie
Rodgers's group, the Tenneva (*Tenne*ssee and *Va* for Virginia) Ramblers, from recording pop songs of the 1920s. Peer instead insisted they "find older, more
down-home songs" and likewise disapproved of Rodgers's own repertoire of
"fairly new pop songs," requesting "older ones" instead. This may sound unre-
markable until you realize the implications. Rejecting certain categories of songs
as not country enough, approving others as old, traditional-sounding tunes, the
New Yorker Peer was really establishing the producer's prerogatives. He was
demonstrating the producer's power to define country music and to direct its
course in ways that would have a momentous impact. The city-bred Yankee was
shaping and defining country music in the 1920s and casting a long shadow
through twentieth-century country music to fall on producers inheriting his
mantle.

Like Richard Bennett.

Though much has changed, the choice of songs and performance style are still very much the producer's territory, and inevitably Bennett joins this "Peer group." He lists the many hats a producer must wear—first, as logistics expert ("pulling the threads together of the players, the studio, time schedules") and as A&R person ("You have to listen for songs, both seeking and listening to songs brought to you. If an artist writes his own material, you still have to sift through a bag of their stuff. Not everyone writes gems all the time. The ratio of good to mediocre is, if you're lucky, fifty-fifty"). Add to these the roles of psychologist, babysitter, hand-holder, taskmaster (Bennett has differed with Marty Stuart on sequences—"Between the two of us, we'll hash out a sequence we're both pleased with").

Above all, this producer is the champion of the artist, never an adversary. "It's the artist first. If there's something passionate I can connect with, contribute to, and a bit of a challenge to me as well, then I'll get involved. I make music for, first, my artist, and a very close second, for me. If the company likes it too, great. But it's really for the artist."

Most artists, Bennett reflects, have strengths in three or four areas, and the producer's challenge is to build on these—to be creative in and around them. Planning an album, Bennett works to individualize each song so that it is "as unlike any other as you could possibly imagine."

How does a producer hear the possibilities of a song? Responsible for submitting a finished product to the company, the producer must rely not only on technics but intangibles. As Bennett says, "In the end, it's your taste, whether you think a performance is good enough or whether it needs scrapping or rethinking completely." What equips the producer to make such decisions? And how can he (most producers are male) bring to a song the sonic dimensions even the writer and artist may not have grasped? What, in short, makes up the artistic credentials of a producer? What is his schooling or pathway?

In Richard Bennett's case, a Chicago childhood in which his mother sang light opera on the radio and his amateur-musician dad played the accordion. There was always music in the household ("all kinds"), including pre-rock music of Frankie Laine, Patti Page, Rosemary Clooney, Perry Como. Bennett recalls his parents' dancing in the living room to 78s during the mambo and cha-cha crazes of the mid-1950s.

But Bennett's earliest Chicago musical memories also include a nightly hour-long broadcast on WJJD of *Suppertime Frolic*, a hillbilly music show running continuously since the 1930s. He recalls listening nightly from the age of two: "That's where my first taste of country music came from, people like Webb Pierce and Hank Williams, Lefty Frizzell, the early Faron Young. And a hundred more."

This country schooling continued when the family moved to Phoenix, where, at eleven, Richard tagged along with a school pal en route to his guitar lesson at a music shop. Seeing the shop walls covered with the signed-and-framed photos of the hillbilly radio heroes of the *Suppertime Frolic*, Richard "went ballistic" and realized, "Here was my mecca." Shop owner and teacher Forrest Skaggs hit it off "very well" with the visitor. And a good thing, too, for Richard's soon-to-be guitar teacher was Phoenix's "kingpin western band guy." Through the fifties, this man had hosted *The Arizona Hayride*, a Saturday night live barndance and a venue for major country acts of the time ("Ernest Tubb, Johnny Horton, Hank Snow, *all* of them").

It was Skaggs who gave Richard Bennett his "great love for the *older* music." Through the senior man's influence, Richard began collecting the beloved 78s that now line his music room shelves (some six thousand). Bennett points out the "bizarre" twist of his musical autobiography, that he came up playing guitar in the sixties but "never played with his contemporaries, never even played their [rock 'n' roll] music." Instead, it was the music of his teacher's era that he learned, music of the thirties and forties. "So I came up loving Hawaiian music . . . and Bob Wills, and hillbilly music of the forties. And when I started playing gigs as a teenager, I was playing beer joints. I was always the kid, and the next youngest guy would be forty years old. They were playing music of *their* youth, which was twenty years earlier." Bennett smiles, recalling that through his mentor, he "learned to love that music and not think of it as some kind of antiquity or . . . weird-sounding, scratchy junk." He concludes, "So my rooting is fairly deep."

Yet Bennett's "passion for guitar" came in part from "Elvis and Carl Perkins and the early rock 'n' roll." By age twelve, foreseeing his future solely in music, he was studying printed music and mastering chords to prepare himself for Los Angeles ("Nashville wasn't a consideration for me"). Through Skaggs, he had an important L.A. connection, a first-call session guitarist, Al Casey, who helped the new high school graduate work his way into studio work. "And that's what I did [in L.A. as of 1968]. I was a session guy doing two-to-three record dates a day."

Looking back, Bennett calls the experience invaluable. "You didn't know if you were gonna walk in on a four-piece rhythm section date or a forty-piece orchestra date. Sometimes you'd just be handed a chord chart, and you'd create your own part as [studio musicians] do now. But you were just as likely [to be handed] a piece of paper black with notes. You had to play it all, and I did. It was a great training ground, and I've worked under some great arrangers. I've recorded with artists as diverse as the Ventures and Peggy Lee, Johnny Mathis, Barbra Streisand, Tennessee Ernie Ford. I did literally thousands of record dates . . .

". . . until I just couldn't stand it anymore." At last, Bennett found himself burned out, in personal rebellion against the routines of studio work that became a grind and a mill. His own evolving musical tastes, moreover, conflicted with his studio work—an interest in British art rock like Pink Floyd, nowhere satisfied on the L.A. musical landscape. It all got "a bit frustrating," says Bennett in tones of understatement. Fortunately, he was also working onstage and in the studio with Neil Diamond. Reporting this fact, Bennett's voice sounds awed at the very calculation that he worked with Diamond for all of seventeen years.

So what prompted the leap into producing in Nashville? Bennett recalls first producing garage albums for a friend ("also a hillbilly nut"), then coproducing "a couple of things" for Neil Diamond in the late 1970s. Having virtually retired from session work, Bennett was newly drawn to recording work by the early eighties, just as keyboards and synthesizers transformed the work of recordmaking. Not being "a keyboard guy" or "terribly technical," this self-styled "basic guitar player" began commuting to Nashville to play on record projects. He got catalytic advice from friend and musician Emory Gordy, Jr., who said, "When it gets to the point that you think you can make better records than what you're playing on, it's time to produce." Bennett admits to feeling that way for years.

Both Bennett and country music were then at a crisis point—*crisis* in the Chinese meaning of danger and opportunity. "I felt I had something to offer," Bennett reflects, "and to give back to country music and to Nashville, because even though I'd been off doing other things, I'd learned so much from it." More than that, Bennett admits he "felt somewhat of a mission." He smiles. "Of course, you don't come into town and say, 'I'm here on a mission.' They'd bounce you right out. I just felt it was time for me to make some records here." So much for opportunity.

But country music itself was endangered, Bennett felt. "There was very little country left in country music. To me, it had turned to pap in the seventies." Essentially, Richard Bennett meant to help reroute country to its roots. He had a few Nashville contacts (Tony Brown, Emory Gordy, Jr., Jimmy Bowen), but it was Steve Earle's *Guitar Town* project that precipitated the move. A friend and occasional L.A. houseguest of the Bennetts ("We wrote, ate Mexican food, and just hung out"), Earle arrived in the Bennetts' living room in 1985 "wielding this tape, full of energy, saying 'You've gotta hear this, I've just written an album!'"

There were about seven demos of *Guitar Town*, Bennett recalls, the "nucleus" of the album. Earle said, "'Listen, you need to move to Nashville, and that's it, man. I want you involved in this record.'" Bennett recalls exchanging glances with his wife, Tina (the couple had been "toying" with the idea of a Nashville move), and saying, "Well, okay." It was "that quick."

The fledgling producer admits he "couldn't have asked for a better entrée to the town" than *Guitar Town*, "a commercial failure but a critical explosion. It was a great album." Bennett's guitar playing on the album earned him respect as a distinct musician ("beyond walk-in session guy"). And *Guitar Town* launched his new career: "It gave me instant credibility as a producer."

But how does Bennett work? He rejects the notion of the dictatorial producer: "I don't do anything without the approval of the artist." (Just how crucial is a good working partnership between artist and producer came to light publicly in the 1970s in Dolly Parton's much-publicized breakaway from her longtime producer and duet partner, Porter Wagoner. The final split was attributed to irreconcilable differences over the production of Parton's music, which Wagoner claimed he would not produce to her specifications ["It would not have worked"]. Parton rejoined that her former producer "took away the joy of recordin' the song at all," adding that "without Porter, at least I can write the songs and get them down the way I hear them.")

Bennett, then, collaborates with the artist ("I consider an artist's input first"), deciding what songs to record ("your bagful of tunes, which, by the way, is arrived at with input from the A&R person at the label as well") and putting the band together. Then Richard Bennett does something virtually unique to commercial music recording in Nashville: He rehearses his projects. "I like to know what I'm going in *with*," he says, "to go into the studio personally secure about being able to achieve the complete picture, so I'll take the whole thing into a rehearsal studio for a few days or a week."

The rehearsal itself signals that music professionals "will have to dig a little deeper" into their talent and skill. But Bennett insists, "I don't stand over people with whips either." In rehearsal, he says, an odd lot of musicians actually becomes a cohesive band ("I'm very much into band-sounding records"). The rehearsal studio, Bennett explains, is a "cheaper clock" than a studio, its atmosphere "much more relaxed and casual, more of a workshop." "I don't care how many record dates you've done or how many years you've been at it," Bennett says, "there is a tension in the studio [where] you're always aware that the [budget] clock is going." Reminded of how different this is from his L.A. session days, Bennett nods and observes that without rehearsal, "You sometimes get run-of-the-mill [musical] street currency of the day, [mere] licks and perfunctory performances." He issues his ultimate indictment, "There's little passion there," and adds, "I demand a lot more of the people who play."

And Bennett demands much of himself. Hearing a song for the first time, he sometimes envisions its production. And he feels free to experiment beyond categories, cherishing the "freedom" he finds in a diverse range of styles. Labels like "country" or "rock 'n' roll" are immaterial, he says. "Anything that works is okay.

It's happening or it's not. Whatever the music calls for—string section, Tibetan bells, musical saw, anything." Yet Bennett admits to a musical combination that may underlie his success as an innovative traditionalist in country music: "I come from all over the map musically. There are no rules, no confines. However, having a very deep root in hillbilly music from the 1920s to the early 1960s, I know what that's about."

Bennett questions whether those currently making recordings in Nashville ("running the business these days") and paying lip service to names like Hank Williams or Jimmie Rodgers have really listened to their music. "How many people will admit to loving hillbilly music of the 1950s, when everybody at that time was ashamed of it, even the people making it?" He finds it painfully ironic that although the *Grand Ole Opry* participants could not wait to shed the musical "rube" image, it is the pallid mutant musical successors who are in fact truly laughable.

Country music, Bennett regrets, has lost "its heart and its passion, and its roots," becoming overpopulated by hackwork "briefcase writers" and by performers and producers so focused on top-40 radio and video play that these very boxes have boxed them in. Market-driven radio is, he implies, a kind of electronic vampire sucking the lifeblood of musical talent and energy ("I think as soon as you start thinking in terms of radio music, you're cutting yourself off"). "Believe me," Bennett says, "I'm not opposed to being on the radio," but he cites himself as "probably one of the few people in town that doesn't pander [to it]." Denying that he seeks art at every turn, Bennett nonetheless feels dismay that this music is usually mere "wallpaper to people's lives." He would agree with the *New York Times* writer who comments in 1993 that "young country wants to prove it's steeped in tradition while aiming for hits and jettisoning most of the tradition's subtleties. Often, it ends up picking up rock's leftovers and shifting country's heartfelt sentiment toward sentimentality."

"But I don't have to make that kind of music," says Bennett. Indeed he does not. And if top-chart country is seldom a useful source of musical stimulation for this producer, he takes an interest instead in the music at the margins (on the independent labels like Rounder, Sugar Hill, Flying Fish), in a wide range of pop music, and in ethnic and world music. And Bennett applies certain tests of his own. "Has it got a melody, or does it just meander around? Can you hum a guitar solo, or is it just 'a flurry of licks?'" Pausing in a jam-packed work schedule, he reflects on his career in Nashville: "I take a great deal of pride in the enigmatic and eclectic nature of my work. I get a lot of projects sent over to me ('Give it to Bennett, he hates everything')." But "they let me do my records," he says in tones of appreciation. "They don't mess with me. Nashville's been very good to me. They took me in as a musician, they took me in as a producer. They are very supportive. So I'm glad to be here."

All the artists in these profiles are clearly glad to be here, *here* being country music as they understand and pursue it. All have made a life-commitment to country, which divides them from those merely eager to ride the radio/video gravy train or join the feeding frenzy during country music's cycles of great consumer popularity. These artists, then, have not ventured into country music as opportunists, but rather as practitioners open to the opportunities of this American musical tradition. From the producer to the bluegrass vocalist/instrumentalist, whether working as soloist or ensemble performer or duet partner, male or female, and whether the musical point of origin is classical, rock, rhythm-and-blues, whether at the beginning of a career or full maturity, all these artists show a kind of patterning in their biographies. Diverse as they are, their profiles show certain viewpoints held in common: That country music has a history and a repertoire that its practitioners must learn and master over a long period of intense concentration. That an education in country music is an education in taste and discernment. That musical richness in country, as in any other form of music, can only be achieved by careful study and preparation. That country music quotes itself historically even as it moves toward the twenty-first century with new interpretations, arrangements, sounds that are guided by the long-established country canon. For each of these individuals, the artistry of this music must meet the highest, exacting standards. For all of them, country music is emphatically an artists' art.

I'm really a country singer at heart. . . . I don't try to categorize my music, but it's always been the same—real honky soul. . . . It doesn't bother me to be labeled "country." . . . Elvis was a country singer, so were the Everly Brothers. . . . Those that think it's a problem are misinformed.

I feel an obligation to carry on the music of my dad's time, the music of Hank Williams and Jimmie Rodgers. Their talents and their symbolism forged the style, and we draw upon a kind of universal storehouse of country music knowledge.

Younger people really owe it to themselves to trace the roots of this stuff [country music] back to where it came from. And by the same token, the country fans . . . owe it to themselves not to have closed minds about such cool things as came out of England in the early sixties.

The real gratification comes from writing and singing the song. It's like painting a complete picture from start to finish.

Songwriting is my form of keeping a journal.
—Rodney Crowell, newspaper and magazine interviews

10

▼ ▼

'What Serious Songwriting Is All About'
An Interview with Rodney Crowell

"I stand by my words."

It is Rodney Crowell's parting line. Hair tousled, wearing sleek black running pants and an ivory sweatshirt, he is saying farewell, bound now for the lakeside trail he will walk after spending a spring Saturday morning recording a cassette full of words—words reflective, critical, analytical, even whimsical on the subject of country music songwriting.

The tape is worth its weight in gold to a student of country music because Rodney Crowell is a country music Olympian and the rare artist willing and able to reflect on his art and his craft. The triple-talented Crowell—Grammy-winning songwriter, performer, producer—is a country music artists' artist. Musicians crossing into country from other traditions, like rock, rhythm-and-blues, opera, Euro-classics, can become fluent in the language of country music, but only the occasional country artist reared in the tradition is willing to make the effort to speak across musical state lines in order to inform, explain, invite a wider audience to take part in a knowledgeable way.

Rodney Crowell is that artist, the consummate country songwriter—"perhaps *the* finest country singer-songwriter of his generation," says one reviewer in the kind of accolade repeated in the music press, which calls him "the Renaissance man of progressive country [with] . . . a poet's reflectiveness. . . . A poet of the vernacular." Says one, "Thank God for Rodney Crowell . . . the best songwriter now punching up country themes."

This "best songwriter" has been on the scene since the 1970s, though much of the listening public first met Crowell in his major breakthrough album, *Diamonds and Dirt* (1988), which broke industry records as an album written, produced, and performed by the same individual from which five songs soared to first place on the charts: "It's Such a Small World" (a duet with country artist and then-wife Rosanne Cash), "I Couldn't Leave You If I Tried," "She's Crazy for Leavin'" (cowritten with Guy Clark), "After All This Time," and "Above and Beyond," a Harlan Howard song and onetime hit for Buck Owens.

But Crowell's song catalog has been brimming with country hitmakers since the 1970s, beginning with the tracks on his inaugural album, *Ain't Living Long Like This* (1978), a gold mine for a wide range of country artists like the Oak Ridge Boys, who recorded "Leavin' Louisiana in the Broad Daylight," and Crystal Gayle and Willie Nelson, each of whom released "Till I Gain Control Again." By the beginning of the 1980s, forty-one of Crowell's songs had been record hits for a wide spectrum of country artists, including "Shame on the Moon" (Bob Seger), "I Ain't Livin' Long Like This" (Waylon Jennings), "An American Dream" (Linda Ronstadt and the Nitty Gritty Dirt Band). Johnny Cash, Jerry Jeff Walker, John Denver all recorded "A Song for the Life." And Emmylou Harris, repeatedly commended for her discerning musical taste, is a virtual album of Crowell songs— "Amarillo," "Till I Gain Control Again," "I Ain't Livin' Long Like This," "Tulsa Queen," "Leavin' Louisiana in the Broad Daylight," "A Song for the Life."

The Crowell discography, meanwhile, grew in the eighties and nineties—*What Will the Neighbors Think* (1980), *Rodney Crowell* (1981), *Street Language* (1986), *Dia-*

*Serious
Songwriting*

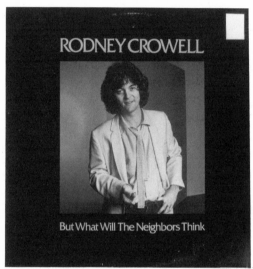

Albums of Rodney Crowell. (Courtesy Warner Brothers, Inc., and Sony Music)

monds and Dirt (1988), *The Rodney Crowell Collection* (1989), *Keys to the Highway* (1989), *Life Is Messy* (1992). One writer accounts for the Crowell phenomenon: "He a writer of unusually sophisticated lyrics."

That sophistication is rooted Crowell's pure country genealogy going back two generations to one grandfather who led a church choir while the other played bluegrass banjo and a grandmother played guitar. (Crowell's parents even met at a Roy Acuff concert.) The senior Crowell, an Arkansas sharecropper's son reared in post-Depression western Kentucky, was lured westward to Houston in the post–World War II years, when he worked construction and played weekends with

his own bar band featuring country standards: Hank Williams and Lefty Frizzell, Roy Acuff, Buck Owens, George Jones—as Crowell says, "All of it."

One day the eleven-year-old Rodney (born 1950) found a drum set in his bedroom, less a gift than an investment from a father seeing in his son a future drummer for his own band. So, at thirteen, Rodney Crowell was playing portside Houston honky-tonks. When the Beatles arrived, Rodney moved from drums to guitar and joined a band trying for "the English sound and the surf beat." In part, Crowell credits the musically eclectic sixties for his wide-ranging tastes. In those years, he recalls, "I would go to the store and buy a Beatles record, a Merle Haggard record, a Buck Owens record, and a Flatt and Scruggs record, all on the same rack. They didn't separate them." And classical music was mixed in that rack too, from "Ravel to the Rolling Stones." (Rodney Crowell describes his continuing eclectic preferences on any given evening—"Peter Gabriel's soundtrack to *The Last Temptation* . . . a fusion of New Age and African rhythms. Then Ravel's *Pavane*. And then I got out Hank Williams's *Forty Greatest Hits*.")

But back in the late sixties, the teenage Crowell was still a ways from Nashville. Finishing high school in Houston, he wrote the graduation song and enrolled in Stephen F. Austin College in Nagadoches, Texas, then dropped out to go to work at the Houston shipyards building ship launchpads before heading to Nashville with friend and fellow music enthusiast (and cosongwriter) Donivan Cowart.

Crowell paid his dues in Music City, washing dishes at the Steak and Ale and, for a time, sleeping in his car. In Nashville, he says, "I got a real cold splash in the face of what serious songwriting is all about." He was "splashed," or maybe baptized, by very talented cohorts: "I think that's the thing that helped me [in 1970s Nashville]. I was in this society of really talented people . . . like [Townes Van Zandt, Guy Clark, David Olney, John Hiatt]. It was a real informative, creative time for me. . . . Everybody was singing their new songs." At that point Crowell began reading serious literature as an aid to songwriting. These days he is apt to compare a country song to a short story by Kurt Vonnegut, Raymond Carver, or Willa Cather, but Crowell emphasizes that his love of reading was not nurtured in school ("I went twelve years of school and two years of college without reading a book. . . . I bluffed my way through and made good grades").

In 1970s Nashville, the ambitious young musician realized that literature and songs were siblings, that knowledge of one could enrich the other. "I started filling my mind with as many symbols and images as I could. I started reading. I got real hungry to have something to contribute."

The contributions started in Emmylou Harris's Hot Band when her producer, Brian Ahern, heard a tape of a Crowell song, "You Can't Keep Me in Tennessee." "Not very memorable," Crowell terms it, but the song led to a stint as Harris's Hot Band guitarist and vocalist (1976–78). Crowell says of that period, "It gave me the opportunity to work with some very fine musicians and get involved in the inner workings of a band. I learned so much about arranging." Crowell later put that knowledge to good use producing the Ramones, the early Blondie, Sissy Spacek, and then Rosanne Cash, notably her acclaimed *King's Record Shop* album.

But what about Crowell the performer? Listening to his voice on albums, you remember the comparisons others have drawn with Elvis and with Roy Orbison. But no list of singers can quite capture the quality of that voice. For a more complete idea of influence, you have to move into the instrumental side of country, in particular to the electric guitar and the ways in which that instrument has been Crowell's vocal model. It seems not at all coincidental that Crowell has performed with the virtuosi of that instrument, including James Burton and Albert Lee—and especially Steuart Smith. Hearing Smith on electric guitar, the listener feels the presence of a musician who mentally hears sounds and tonal shadings that have eluded other players of that instrument, and who has the skill to realize his vision. In Smith's hands, the electric guitar transcends its conventions and traditions. Rodney Crowell has judged Steuart Smith to be the finest electric guitarist with whom he has played, and listening to Crowell sing, it dawns on you that this voice is an analogue to the electric guitar as played by Steuart Smith. This means that the voice creates an entire environment of sound enveloping the listener, that its vibrato, its glide, its amplified resonance make for a total surround. Rodney Crowell's voice—the voice of "Alone but Not Alone," of "Many a Long and Lonesome Highway," of "Things I Wish I'd Said" and every other song he has recorded—surrounds and envelops a listener like a vocal version of the electric guitar played beyond its customary boundaries, from ground-level pulse to the stratospheric ether.

Reflecting on music, Rodney Crowell has many messages: that Nashville is a magnet school for the ambitious and talented in country music, that both country artists and audiences ought to do their homework on the history and tradition of this music, that country cannot flourish in a vacuum, needing the far-flung, invigorating cultural and artistic influences that are the lifeblood of artistic vitality. The bulging *Rodney Crowell* file in the Country Music Foundation Library in Nashville is testimony to this artist's commitment to speak beyond the personal interview gossip mill and to convey instead his ideas on music. The following interview took place on March 6, 1993, at Crowell's contemporary-style home in the Nashville-area hills.

CT: The problem I think country gets itself into is that, in presenting itself as natural, people get the idea that means easy. They think the songs must be easy to write, easy to sing. And in the 1920s when WSM announcer George Hay named the *Grand Ole Opry* in opposition to grand opera, . . . that contrast became a basis for an unfavorable or skeptical view of country music. Grand opera represented high culture and serious training [but] country music represented no training at all—

RC: Slovenliness. . . . Yeah, well, I think country music is responsible for its own poor self-image. . . . I think country music, in a way, sometimes volunteers to be perceived as a music of low self-esteem. . . .

Actually, I think creative, heartfelt, emotional, penetrating insights into humanity happen from a relaxed state a lot more than from a real heavily trained, tradition-bound way. I'm sure you know that you transcend into new places . . . through discipline and tradition.

But I think for the most part creativity comes from being in a relaxed state. To me, that's the good thing about rural, southern folk/country music. . . . I really like to work from that real relaxed place. But I don't want in any way to suggest that I have a poor sense of self-esteem and that I've volunteered to be viewed as a rube or as ignorant or as uneducated, or just uninsightful. Because life as it's been since the sixties, there's a lot of vagaries, a lot of gray areas. If you say, "I'm just one thing"—that's sort of like being the ostrich in the sand.

CT: If I hear you right, you're talking about working in country music but with . . . open boundaries—totally open boundaries—that give you access to resources from everywhere in the culture. I went to the Country Music Foundation library and read the file on you and made a list of the different artists whose names come up in your discussions of music and writers. And it's a long list: Van Gogh, Monet, Rimbaud, Georgia O'Keeffe, poets Galway Kinnell and Stan Rice, short story writer Raymond Carver, Shakespeare, Tolstoy. Now can I ask where you got—

RC: [*laughing*] That could be perceived as pretentious.

CT: Not in the way you're talking about.

RC: Well, for instance, the art: I was living in California and I would go and shop at this place called Gelson's, a designer food store. And they had these—the Great Artists, I think it was. If you bought a certain amount of groceries, you could pick out these giant paperback art history portfolios on the artists. So I started going in and shopping, and I would pick out the one I wanted. I went for the Impressionists. I got 'em all eventually—Monet, Van Gogh, and Renoir and Edgar Degas. I found myself in this world of art and . . . wanted to know everything. I started going to museums wherever I was and really got into Monet, the way he painted the water lilies—painting both sides, looking at the surface of water and trying to paint both sides of it.

And I started experimenting with songwriting that way—like looking at something and squeezing your eyes until you just got the impression of it. That's when I wrote "Stars on the Water" and "Shame on the Moon." I was trying to use Impressionism in songwriting. That's the way it would be practically applicable to what I was doing. . . . It's the most musical—to me, it's the most lyrical, musical art. . . . I think the Beatles' music was Impressionistic . . . especially as they matured. And I know that George Martin, who produced them, was really into [Maurice] Ravel, the first French classical composer . . . who introduced modern music to film scoring. So there was a certain lyrical thing to the way they approached what they did. . . . That's sort of what music like jazz, country, pop, folk music—

CT: But you're talking about country. . . . I mean, I've heard some of those traditional old songs you have called Appalachian dead-baby songs. So you're suggesting that country had to move well out of that old sentimental, old-time formula, that it just wouldn't work for contemporary country music?

RC: Well, that stuff is almost like Edgar Allan Poe. It's like, my thirteen-year-old-daughter, for me to get her to understand a song like "Little Rosewood Casket." . . . [*sings*] "There's a little rosewood casket / Laying on a marble slab." Just real Gothic. Or "Put My Little Shoes Away," which is, "Mama, I'm dyin', just one thing I ask is, put my little shoes away." I mean, you'd have to have a love for literature built in . . . to appreciate those real deep Appalachian songs. Like that song [*sings*] "The eastbound train was crowded, / One cold December day. The conductor shouted, 'tickets!'" Kid comes on and doesn't have a ticket, but his mom has died and his dad's in prison, and he talks to the conductor, and the conductor lets him ride. It's almost like, in a way, like Joseph Conrad's *The Secret Sharer*, where [the protagonist] nurtures this dark scene away from everybody else.

CT: That's interesting, the Gothic. Bluegrass seems to get away with that still. I don't mean *get away with*, I mean, it's part of that genre. And when you enter into the bluegrass world, then it's okay. But not in country as a whole, not rock-age country.

RC: Well, bluegrass is still a little more aligned with that dark, ghost-story aspect. It's a little more aligned with the church, whereas these Appalachian traditional things are . . . aligned with the Irish. Like Irish folktales with their stories of leprechauns and the magical dreams . . . those real deep folksongs that have that fantastic, almost ghost-storyish quality.

CT: [A change of subject, here.] Can I ask you about the relation between your voice and songwriting? . . . Hearing you sing those lines a moment ago reminds me that I've been struck by the fact that writers who write about your music praise your vocal delivery but tend not to describe it or analyze it. I'll first ask, the night you did the University School of Nashville benefit concert [in December 1992], was that Steuart Smith on electric guitar?

RC: Uh huh.

CT: It seems to me that just as he presents the most versatile possible performance on electric guitar, so your voice is most like the electric guitar in that versatility. For instance, your vibrato. And it seems to me that more than any other instrument, the electric guitar creates a total environment. When it's [playing], you're inside that world. Now what I want to ask you is, when you're writing, does your own vocal range of resources enter in any conscious way into your shaping of a song?

RC: Very much so.

CT: Can you talk about that?

RC: Well, sometimes I take ideas—like I was driving down to [Nashville's] Radnor Lake to go for a walk. There was some sort of conflict going on in me, and I said, "Oh, man, just let the picture paint itself." And of course I said, "du-Duh!" So I walked around Radnor Lake, came back and . . . I wrote this song, "Let the Picture Paint Itself." And it was strictly driven from that original idea. And that was a real enjoyable piece of work because I really took a very

Rodney Crowell.
(Courtesy Sony Music)

simplistic approach to it. . . . But then there are times when I'll just sit with a guitar, just strumming cords, and I'll hit the *Record* on my little cassette player, and then I'll just start . . . experimenting with noises, sounds, and I'll sing gibberish. I mean, I've listened to tapes of me with the windows open where I'll be going . . . [*sings gibberish*] . . . you know, just doing nothing, and I'll hear the [*squeaking, squawking*] birds . . . literally turn to the sounds I was making and orchestrate themselves with me. It's like a thing of nature. I mean, it's just sound waves and energy, and they just align themselves with that energy.

So there are times when certain sounds that you make with your voice, maybe three or four words will form themselves to those sounds that you're making. And then I'll have it on tape and I'll listen back to it, and maybe out of a sound I'm hearing, I'll imagine three or four words that I thought might be . . . trying to [take] form from the sounds. And I'll write the phrase down. It's almost like solving a code with yourself. That's the way I wrote "Life Is Messy," which is, like, forty-five minutes of screaming and banging on a piano just, aaargh! And then suddenly out of it comes "Life Is Messy," just as if you were carrying away garbage. And then suddenly "Life Is Messy" jumps out. Then I go back and I listen to all the gibberish and I start to hear, "Shame Falls Down." You know, this is a long-winded way of saying that sometimes it's just sounds that give you the impression to be found in back of what you're trying to say.

CT: What you just said seems really important. I have a friend who interviewed a classical avant-garde composer, and she asked, "How do you work?" and expected some high-minded statement. And what he said was, "It's just like pigs rooting in the mud." I think she was shocked.

But let me ask you to clarify a point. You made a distinction in an interview with country music journalist Alanna Nash between the songs you do as intellectual exercises, and other songs that come from an emotional center to which you gave a higher priority—I think those in the second group are the essential, the *real* songs.

RC: They are. Those are the songs. It's like I've always said—I think I've said it many times—that the enemy of the song is the brain. Besides, my [cerebral] mind has nothing to do with writing the best songs I've written. They're strictly from unplugging my brain and my intellectual judgment.

You know, songwriting is like a window, and the whole thing is to get everything lined up where that window is open. When everything lines up and the window is open, those songs can come through in their totality. And you know, I can tell how many times I get the totality. It's like, sometimes you get the window open and a third of it comes through, and then maybe your brain gets back into the value-judgment process, and maybe you only got a third of it and the rest of it is intellectual creation. And sometimes it's all intellectual. I do have some of those [cerebral] songs and even perform them, but I know the difference. The ones that come through—a song like "Things I Wish I'd Said" was just there waiting until I sat still for a minute. Once I finally sat still, then that experience was *there-it-is*—totality.

CT: Some people hearing what you just said could think that no skill is involved. What I want to suggest is that, in order for that window to be there, you have to be a musician, to have music to the bone, which you do, back to age eleven when you got that drum set. And before that, because your family is all musical, except for your mother. [*pause*] Did she sing?

RC: No. But my mother was the word person. My mother was a limerick mimic in a way. She played with words. She was almost like a word juggler. I think, really, a lot of my fascination with words came from my mother. She was totally an uneducated woman but—

CT: She had an ear for language.

RC: She had an ear for phrases.

CT: Have you ever talked about that? I didn't see that in any of the printed interviews.

RC: I may have. . . . I may have at some point. . . . Some interview said that I got a body full of songs from my father and a head full . . . I forget exactly. Really, my mother and father were most responsible for me being a songwriter.

CT: In that combination. So it's from your mother that you're led to poetry—

RC: Yeah.

CT: And your openness to poetry.

RC: Yes, and from my father I was led to songs.

CT: That explains a lot. I mean, it was a puzzle to me. Where did this word power in your lyrics come from? It's not an add-on, it's not something you can just decide that you're going to borrow later on.

RC: [*nods*] You know, it's funny, I've just had an incredible week of songwriting. I've written about six songs in the last week. And I think I've reached a new level with it. It's the kind of thing that an artist lives for, you know. Last night I went over to see [songwriter and performer] Guy Clark, whose craft I respect. And I played him my new songs. It's like, if I can play a song for Guy, and he can see what the work is—you know, not just be entertained by a song but actually take a look at the craft—

Here's the thing, and why I think that what I've been doing lately is so good for me. You asked the question about the window. What we're really talking about is inspiration. When the window lines up, and it comes from God or wherever it does—that's inspiration.

But it's not a lazy man's gig. Because whenever you do happen to access that window of inspiration, if you don't have your craft finely tuned—*finely*, *finely* tuned—then you don't get those 100 percent intake blocks of songs. You might get . . . three lines. I've heard people play songs where I knew they had a gelling idea, and then they'd get the three lines, then tag on a cliché, short-of-the-mark stuff. And that is strictly from not being dedicated to the craft. Do you know what I'm saying?

CT: Yes I do. I personally know what you're talking about from going so many times to writers' night [at different Nashville music clubs where] you hear somebody that's got a wonderful phrase or even a whole verse. . . . They cobble it together, but it's not a unified work.

RC: Yeah. I'm a good songwriter, I don't mind saying it. But I take my work apart and see where some of them are 5 percent and some capture the thing 50 percent. Some songs I won't do because I can't. When people in the audience call out a song for me that I won't do, it's because I *can't* in all good faith with myself try to pull the sleight-of-hand when I reach the end of the real stuff and get to the tag-on stuff. It embarrasses me, for myself.

I was talking to Guy about it last night, and we were talking about that very thing. Sometimes you succeed with a sleight-of-hand to the point of hiding it from yourself. But usually at some point it comes to you that . . . ahh, *there* . . . I'm trying to pull a sleight-of-hand, there's a weak spot in my bridge. So the thing that I feel real good about right now is, I've just written a block of stuff that came through that window, and I know that I did the job of getting it all. And there's no throwaway here, I know it. And to prove it to myself, I go to somebody who I know is even more keen about that than me and just check on it. [*grins*] Oh, yeah, I'm happening!

CT: There's no feeling like that.

RC: There really isn't. It makes me a lot more of a pleasant human being. [*We laugh.*] And it ain't luck, it's work.

CT: Would you say the craft is in place because way back—since forever—you've been living in music and just constantly honing and fine-tuning? That is, you *know* percussion, you *know* the instruments, you *know* voice. And together with your great gift, all that knowledge enables a week like this. Is that clear?

RC: Well, I would say what enables—that's part of it. Certainly, talent is a big part of it. . . . You know, all the people that we talk about admiring here, this list of [writers and artists], what we're really talking about here is talent.

But talent—we all know talent is God-given, but what you do with it . . . the woods are full of extremely talented people who don't have the—I don't like the word discipline—I think just the ambition to create. You know, to build bridges, to write songs, to build houses, to paint pictures, to take what doesn't exist and bring it through and . . . turn it into something that exists.

But beyond the talent comes the vision and the focus which, to me, is perfecting the craft. Just like, you've seen that poster of Thomas Edison [saying], "I'm never going to give up because before I die I just might get lucky." That's not about getting lucky. He just keeps working at what he does, and then sooner or later the inspiration is going to smile. And then if you've got your window working good, oiled up, when inspiration does smile, then you *get* it. It's a fulfillment. It's not about the money and that other stuff; that stuff will come. But the real reason for doing it is to get that feeling of like—yeah!—I did what I *do*.

[*Pauses*] Maybe I digressed there. I had a thought. The one thing that I think about country music [and for which it must] hold itself accountable is, it has to [undergo] some sort of self-examination. Someone was talking about religion, certain types of religion that are so vulnerable as not to be able to stand . . . self-examination that could reveal the flaws and the inconsistency, the hypocrisy . . . and all of that.

In country music, the songwriting machine that Nashville is, [and maybe on my part] this is high-mindedness, but this is where *I* draw the line. This is *my* set of values about it: there's a lot of craftsmanship that's honed, but gets applied to certain kinds of cliché forms of songwriting that I call Music Row hack songwriting.

I'm not gonna take anybody on individually about it because I respect everybody's right to work in their own way. It's just that, collectively, [those close to us, like] my daughter or your daughter, yourself, and people in the world can feel that [dimension of hack work]. They may not necessarily know what it is on a conscious level, but somewhere inside people can feel the difference in something that settles [profoundly] to the bottom of the heart or something that stops at the [superficial] level. And I think Nashville and the Music Row songwriting machine are very guilty of a lot of stuff that just stops there instead of trying to get to the heart.

CT: Well, this is a longstanding American problem of art in a market-driven capitalist culture. It's a tough balancing act between artistic integrity and sales, and the problem extends back into the last century, for instance in the career of Herman Melville. And not only with *Moby-Dick*. Like so many American artists, Melville played a double game, trying to earn a living and fulfill his private vision too. So there's a burden for the artist to come up with something that will earn you a living. And that's a real problem in this society.

RC: [An important artistic lesson for me along these lines is the example of] Van Gogh. His paintings and drawings are so heartfelt, breathtakingly heartfelt. I went to an exhibition in New York [at the Metropolitan Museum of Art]. It was Van Gogh's Last Hundred and Forty-Four Days, one of the most beautiful exhibitions I've ever seen. The whole exhibition started when Van Gogh arrived at the asylum, when he'd been checked in, flipping out, whatever he did. First there's like, brown pencil drawings . . . almost an infantile, elementary drawing of his room. And then you see that he looked down the hall and he drew the hallway . . . very feeble, uninspired, sort of like just clawing your way, climbing your way out . . . and then it opens up a little bit. Maybe there is a courtyard, and then you turn and go into this deep room. And suddenly it's like he had gone outside and there's these cypress trees, *Big Cyprus, Starry Night*, and all of those olive grove paintings . . . four olive grove paintings he did. . . . It's like suddenly this man had gone outside and the window went up. And there's no intellectual process to this.

[*Crowell describes vividly and in detail Van Gogh's repeated artistic cycle of autobiographic drawing and painting, which he feels expresses a range of Van Gogh's feeling from self-loathing to self-acceptance.*] When I walked out of the museum exhibition, I just wept, he was too much for me—I just stood there and wept—it was just too beautiful, too emotional, but there was nothing [cerebrally] intellectual about it whatsoever.

My point in telling the story—what I'm getting to—is, there is nothing about classic training here, . . . so you could say he's like Hank Williams. You could say he was an alcoholic and drunk. And you could say Van Gogh was a madman, insane. But it's not about those things, which is the point *you've* been trying to get to. It's not about whether these are lazy bums and what they offer up is lazy stuff. It was about real heartfelt stuff, and it had nothing to do with the intellect.

CT: You tell that very powerfully.

RC: The thing that was most powerful about it—and I was talking to Guy [Clark] about this last night—what made me weep was not so much how beautiful . . . his work was, but a combination of the beautiful, otherworldly things he did . . .the ones with those vivid energy lines [combined with] the real human frailties [expressed in] these little brown in-betweeners that weren't inspired. When you looked at it in totality, you saw the human thing about it.

So, I was talking last night about having a little more patience with myself around the dry spells, when what I do write is not truly what I would call inspired. You know, I always want to write something so good that I can go, *Ah!* I've eclipsed, "Till I Gain Control Again" [a landmark Crowell song]. I can't think I'm still stuck back there [in the 1970s]. So when I can write something that I can hold in the light some of certain songs I wrote, I go *yeah!* I'm still on the case.

CT: You know, it might be that without those little drawings, so to speak, you can't get those breakouts. That is, the little brown drawings and sketches are necessary for those ascents. . . . They're like a bridge—or place markers, sustaining and developing artistic expression. They enable those other times—those really inspired times.

RC: Right. They're as much a block in the foundation of opening that window as the day he painted *Starry Night*. The way it applies to me is this: Last fall there was a movie being filmed here in Nashville, and they hired me to write some songs for it [Peter Bogdanovich's *A Thing Called Love*].

CT: Oh, I remember, with River Phoenix?

RC: Yeah, so I was writing five songs for River's character, and I wrote a couple . . . that were pretty intact. Very much craft work. But a couple of songs were actually good. And then I wrote three more that were really hard work for me and really tested my faith in myself. I'd go and sit down every day, five days a week in my little writing place. And sometimes I got three words in that five-day period. Sometimes I got one line. And I said to myself, "Oh god, I used to be a songwriter, I used to be inspired." Then I took off for Christmas and I moved here [to the new house] and started working again and building up to the last ten days, all these songs I've written.

I could actually look back at how hard it was last fall, last November, to write. And I can see, actually, that going through that process is very much a part of what I'm doing right now. If I hadn't gone through that, I don't think I would have been able to do what I've done recently. I can see how they were tied to each other. . . . Even though what I hacked out of granite most often just fell on the floor, it was still part of building that craft.

CT: You've got an interesting pun in that word "hacked" out of granite. I sense anxiety. You'd signed a contract to do this number of songs, and the danger is that it [would] become a sort of hack work.

RC: Yeah. Here's the good news, though. It's about one of the songs which they already have for the film. It's published, and already used in its [original] state. [*grins*] I rewrote it this week.

CT: Really!

RC: Yeah! I rewrote it from the ground up.

CT: I'll bet [the movie people are] not going to like that.

RC: I don't care. [*laughter*] *I* wouldn't have recorded the song, but now I will. I mean, it went [up] from sort of a little self-loathing for having written it [in the first version]. There was a real legitimate seed for a song in there, but what I dressed that seed up with just didn't hang. I couldn't fool myself with that sleight-of-hand. They used it, and they seemed happy, but the rewriting was what made it a song that *I* want to own or enjoy. . . . Your heart is a much better editor than your mind is, and if you can see your work with your heart, then I think it's a lot truer, A to Z.

These three in the evening, harmonica and fiddle and guitar. Playing a reel and tapping out the tune, and the big deep strings of the guitar beating like a heart, and the harmonica's sharp chords and the skirl and squeal of the fiddle. People have to move close. They can't help it.
—*John Steinbeck,*
The Grapes
of Wrath

Ten and a half miles along the road, at the crest of the second hill, you'll be able to see where you're going, a tiny ark in a sea of land.
—*Kathleen Norris,*
Dakota

11

▼ ▼

Last Lick

Over hills and along many roads, country music takes us through American ideals and anxieties persisting in the twentieth century. Rodney Crowell finds cultural crisis especially in the post-sixties era, though country music going much further back shows involvement with the unresolved long-term conflicts of this nation. At first this seems surprising. Concealing its own artistry in a vocabulary based in the natural world, country would seem unlikely to disrupt traditional American values. Yet that is precisely what this music does. As it evolves in sound and in performance styles, its artists and writers continue to highlight the ingrained paradox of a nation representing itself in an ideology of home and of the road, committed to them both in a jam-up of loyalties and yearnings that cannot be reconciled or put to rest even at the turn of the twenty-first century. In lyrics intentionally direct and clear, country shows the fault lines in the red-white-and-blue national ethos known variously as the American Character, Pioneering Spirit, American Way. It does this from the insider's, not outsider's, point of view. This deliberately traditional art form raises consciousness in ways its creators and practitioners probably never intended. Country music thus bears an irony all its own. Pledging allegiance, it shatters domestic tranquility and forever disturbs the peace. This music tells us that this nation is a nomad's land, home a shimmering mirage, the national psyche one of pervasive loneliness.

But country music presents another paradox, this on the positive side, as it speaks the unspoken, validates what is vaguely felt, legitimates the otherwise unvoiced experience of the high, lonesome nation.

Discography

▼ ▼ ▼ ▼ ▼ ▼ ▼ ▼ ▼ ▼ ▼ ▼ ▼ ▼ ▼ ▼ ▼

SONGS

"Alone but Not Alone." Rodney Crowell,
Life Is Messy. Columbia CK 47985.

"Appalachian Memories." Dolly Parton,
Burlap and Satin. RCA AHK1-4691.

"Applejack." Dolly Parton, *Portrait*. RCA
PDK2-1116.

"Ashes by Now." Rodney Crowell, *Rodney
Crowell Collection*. Warner Bros. 9 25965-2.

"Back in the Saddle Again." Gene Autry,
*Gene Autry's Country Music Hall of Fame
Album*. Columbia CS 1035.

"Bad News." Emmylou Harris, *The Ballad of
Sally Rose*. Warner Bros. 25205-2.

"Ballad of the Green Berets, The." Barry
Sadler, *Cruisin': 1966*. Increase 2011.

"Big Wheels in the Moonlight." Dan Seals,
Rage On. Liberty 4-46976.

"Billy the Kid." Billy Dean, *Billy Dean*.
Liberty C4 96728.

"Blue-Blooded Woman." Alan Jackson, *Here
in the Real World*. Arista ARCD-8623.

"Blue-Eyed Kentucky Girl." Loretta Lynn,
Blue-Eyed Kentucky Girl. MCA MCAC-20261.

"Blue Eyes." Barry and Holly Tashian, *Trust
in Me*. Northeastern NR 5001-CD.

"Blue Kentucky Girl." Emmylou Harris,
Blue Kentucky Girl. Warner Bros. 3318-2.

"Blue Moon of Kentucky." Bill Monroe, *Bill
Monroe*. MCA MCAD-10082.

"Blue Rose of Texas." Holly Dunn, *The Blue
Rose of Texas*. Warner Bros. 9 25939-4.

"Boot Scootin' Boogie." Brooks and Dunn,
Hard Workin' Man. Arista 18716-2.

"Bouquet of Roses." Eddy Arnold, *The Best
of Eddy Arnold*. BMG 3675-2-R.

"Brakeman's Blues (Yodeling the Blues
Away), The." Jimmie Rodgers, *Jimmie
Rodgers*. Academy Sound and Vision Ltd.
CD AJA 5042.

"Bramble and the Rose, The." Lynn Morris
Band, *The Bramble and the Rose*. Rounder
CD 0288.

"Bug, The." Mary-Chapin Carpenter, *Come
On, Come On*. Columbia CT 48881.

"Cattle Call." Emmylou Harris and the Nash
Ramblers, *Emmylou Harris and the Nash
Ramblers at the Ryman*. Reprise 9 26664-2.

"Coal Miner's Daughter." Loretta Lynn, *All
My Best*. TeeVee MSC-35011.

"Coat of Many Colors." Dolly Parton, *Best of
Dolly Parton*. RCA AYK1-5146.

"Cold Lonesome Morning." Johnny Cash,
Rockabilly Blues. Columbia JCT 36779.

"Country Club." Travis Tritt, *Country Club*.
Warner Bros. 9 26094-2.

"Cowgirl's Song, The." Laurie Lewis, *Restless,
Rambling Heart*. Flying Fish FF 90406.

"Dear Uncle Sam." Loretta Lynn, *Loretta
Lynn's Greatest Hits*. MCA 37235.

"D-I-V-O-R-C-E." Tammy Wynette, *Tears of
Fire: 1*. Epic EK 53071.

"Dixie Flyer." Travis Tritt, *Country Club*.
Warner Bros. 9 26094-2.

"Don't Fence Me In." Roy Rogers, *Roy Rogers Tribute*. BMG 3024-2-R.

"Drivin' My Life Away." Eddie Rabbitt, *All Time Greatest Hits*. Warner Bros. 9 26467-2.

"Even Cowgirls Get the Blues." Emmylou Harris, *Blue Kentucky Girl*. Warner Bros. 3318-2.

"Foggy Mountain Breakdown." Cody Kilby, *A Tribute to Earl Scruggs*. Mikron 880 91.4.

"Goin' Steady." Faron Young, *Faron Young's Greatest Hits*. Capitol 4XL-9406.

"Got Lonely Too Early." Merle Haggard, *I Think I'll Just Stay Here and Drink*. MCA MCAC-20305.

"Great Speckled Bird, The." Roy Acuff, *The Best of Roy Acuff*. Capitol 4XL-9371.

"Green, Green Grass of Home." Merle Haggard, *Sing Me Back Home*. Capitol 4XL-9028.

"Guitar Town." Emmylou Harris and the Nash Ramblers, *Emmylou Harris and the Nash Ramblers at the Ryman*. Reprise 9 26664-2.

"Guitar Town." Steve Earle, *Guitar Town*. MCA MCAD-31305.

"Happy Trails." Randy Travis, *Heroes and Friends*. Warner Bros. 9 26310-2.

"Hickory Wind." Emmylou Harris, *Blue Kentucky Girl*. Warner Bros. 3318-2.

"Hickory Wind." Gram Parsons, *GP/Grievous Angel*. Reprise 9 26108-2.

"High and Dry." Marty Brown, *High and Dry*. MCA MCAD-10330.

"High Noon." Tex Ritter, *Conversation with a Gun*. Richmond NCD-2148.

"Highway 86." Barry and Holly Tashian, *Ready for Love*. Rounder CD 0302.

"Highway 40 Blues." Ricky Skaggs, *Highways and Heartaches*. Epic PET-37996.

"Hillbilly Highway." Steve Earle, *Guitar Town*. MCA MCAD-31305.

"Hills of Home." Hazel Dickens, *It's Hard to Tell the Singer from the Song*. Rounder 0226.

"Hills of My Home, The." Laurie Lewis, *Love Chooses You*. Flying Fish FF 90487.

"Hobo and the Rose." Webb Pierce, *Sweet Memories*. Decca DL 4739.

"Home." Joe Diffie, *A Thousand Winding Roads*. Epic ET46047.

"Home." Alan Jackson, *Here in the Real World*. Arista ARCD-8623.

"Home." Barry and Holly Tashian, *Trust in Me*. Northeastern NR 5001-CD.

"Home Again." Livewire, *Wired!* Rounder C-0281.

"Homecoming." Tom T. Hall, *Tom T. Hall's Greatest Hits*. Mercury 61369.

"Home on the Range." Gene Autry, *Gene Autry's Country Music Hall of Fame Album*. Columbia CS 1035.

"Hometown Streets." Nanci Griffith, *Late Night Grande Hotel*. MCA MCAC-10306.

"Horse Called Music, A." Willie Nelson, *A Horse Called Music*. Columbia CK 45046.

"If I Had a Boat." Lyle Lovett, *Pontiac*. MCA MCAC-42028.

"If I Needed You." Emmylou Harris, *Duets*. Reprise 9 25791-2.

"I Found You among the Roses." Carter Family, *Clinch Mountain Treasures*. Sony Special Products CCS CD112.

"If You Ain't Lovin'." Faron Young, *Faron Young's Greatest Hits*. Capitol 4XL-9406.

"(I Heard That) Lonesome Whistle." Hank Williams, *Forty Greatest Hits*. Polydor 821 233-2.

"I'll Be Your San Antone Rose." Emmylou Harris, *Luxury Liner*. Warner Bros. 3115-2.

"I'm a Honky-Tonk Girl." Loretta Lynn, *Country Music Hall of Fame Series*. MCA MCAD-10083.

"I'm Lonely and Blue." Jimmie Rodgers, *The Early Years, 1928-29*. Rounder CD 1057.

"I'm Movin' On." Hank Snow, *Hank Snow Collector's Series*. BMG 2279-4-R.

"I'm So Lonesome I Could Cry." Hank Williams, *Forty Greatest Hits*. Polydor 821 233-2.

"I Never Knew Lonely." Vince Gill, *The Best of Vince Gill*. RCA 9814-4-R.

"In the Good Old Days (When Times Were Bad)." Dolly Parton, *Portrait*. RCA PDK2-1116.

"I Still Miss Someone." Johnny Cash, *The Essential Johnny Cash, 1955–1983*. Columbia C3T 47991.

"I Still Miss Someone." Emmylou Harris, *Bluebird*. Reprise 25776-2.

"It's Started Again." Wilma Lee and Stoney Cooper, *Sing*. Decca DL 74484.

"I've Sold My Saddle for an Old Guitar." Roy Rogers, *Country Music Hall of Fame Series*. MCA MCAD-10548.

"I Will Always Love You." Dolly Parton, *Collector's Series*. RCA 6338-4-R.

"Jolene." Dolly Parton, *Best of Dolly Parton*. RCA AYK1-5146.

"Just Call Me Lonesome." Radney Foster, *Del Rio, TX 1959*. Arista 07822-18713-2.

"Kentucky." Osborne Brothers, *The Best of the Osborne Brothers*. MCA 2-4086.

"Leavin' Louisiana in the Broad Daylight." Rodney Crowell, *Rodney Crowell Collection*. Warner Bros. 9 25965-2.

"Leavin' Louisiana in the Broad Daylight." Rodney Crowell, *Ain't Livin' Long Like This*. Warner Bros. BSK3228.

"Leavin' Louisiana in the Broad Daylight." Emmylou Harris, *Quarter Moon in a Ten-Cent Town*. Warner Bros. 3141-2.

"Let Freedom Ring." Rodney Crowell, *Street Language*. Columbia CK 40116.

"Let Me See the Light." Barry and Holly Tashian, *Ready for Love*. Rounder CD 0302.

"Letter, The." Dolly Parton, *Portrait*. RCA PDK2-1116.

"Letter from Home." The McCarters, *The Gift*. Warner Bros. 9 25737-4.

"Life Is Messy." Rodney Crowell, *Life Is Messy*. Columbia CK 47985.

"Little Joe the Wrangler." Roy Rogers, *Roy Rogers Tribute*. BMG 3024-2-R.

"Little Old Cabin in the Lane, The." Fiddlin' John Carson, *The Old Hen Cackled and the Rooster Began to Crow*. Rounder 1003.

"Little Rock 'n' Roller." Steve Earle, *Guitar Town*. MCA MCAD-31305.

"Lodi." Emmylou Harris and the Nash Ramblers, *Emmylou Harris and the Nash Ramblers at the Ryman*. Reprise 9 26664-2.

"Lonely Days (and Nights More Lonely)." Tammy Wynette, *Tammy's Touch*. Columbia LET 10194.

"Lonely Street." Emmylou Harris, *Bluebird*. Reprise 9 25776-2.

"Lonely Street." Kitty Wells, *The Kitty Wells Show*. Decca DL 74831.

"Lonely Street." Tammy Wynette, *Golden Memories*. CSP BT 15915.

"Lonely Violet." Delia Bell and Bill Grant, *A Few Dollars More*. Rounder Rou-0217.

"Long Gone Lonesome Blues." Hank Williams, *Forty Greatest Hits*. Polydor 821 233-2.

"Lost Highway." Hank Williams, *Forty Greatest Hits*. Polydor 821 233-2.

"Lovesick Blues." Hank Williams, *Forty Greatest Hits*. Polydor 821-233-2.

"Luxury Liner." Emmylou Harris, *Luxury Liner*. Warner Bros. 3115-2.

"Mama's Opry." Iris Dement, *Infamous Angel*. Philo CD PH 1138.

"Mammas Don't Let Your Babies Grow Up to Be Cowboys." Waylon Jennings and Willie Nelson, *Waylon and Willie*. RCA 8401-4-R.

"Many a Long and Lonesome Highway." Rodney Crowell, *Keys to the Highway*. Columbia CK 45242.

"Maple's Lament, The." Laurie Lewis, *Restless, Rambling Heart*. Flying Fish FF 90406.

"Me and Billy the Kid." Marty Stuart, *Hillbilly Rock*. MCA MCAD-42312.

"Mississippi River Blues." Jimmie Rodgers, *Riding High, 1929–1930*. Rounder CD 1059.

"Miss the Mississippi and You." Jimmie Rodgers, *No Hard Times, 1932*. Rounder CD 1062.

"Moon and St. Christopher, The." Mary-Chapin Carpenter, *Shooting Straight in the Dark*. Columbia CT 46077.

"Mule Train." Gene Autry, *Gene Autry's Country Music Hall of Fame Album*. Columbia CS 1035.

"My Baby Thinks He's a Train." Rosanne Cash, *Hits, 1979–1989*. Columbia CK 45054.

"My Rose of Old Kentucky." Bill Monroe, *The Essential Bill Monroe and His Blue Grass Boys, 1945–1949*. Columbia C2K 5247K.

"My Tennessee Mountain Home." Dolly Parton, *Best of Dolly Parton*. RCA AYK1-5146.

"Never Knew Lonely." Vince Gill, *When I Call Your Name*. MCA MCAD-42321.

"No Place Like Home." Randy Travis, *Storms of Life*. Warner Bros. 9 25435-4.

"OBG Why Me Blues." Karen Taylor-Good, *3*. KT-Good-3.

"Old Time Corn Shuckin'." Ernest Stoneman Family, *The Bristol Sessions*, vol. 1. Country Music Foundation CMF-011-C.

"Only the Lonely." Roy Orbison, *The Greatest All-Time Hits of Roy Orbison*. CBS PAT44348.

"Orange Blossom Special." Johnny Cash, *The Essential Johnny Cash, 1955–1983*. Columbia C3T 47991.

"Pancho and Lefty." Emmylou Harris, *Luxury Liner*. Warner Bros. 3115-2.

"Peach Pickin' Time Down in Georgia." Jimmie Rodgers, *No Hard Times, 1932*. Rounder CD 1062.

"Picasso's Mandolin." Guy Clark, *Boats to Build*. Asylum 61442-4.

"Precious Memories." Emmylou Harris, *Angel Band*. Warner Bros. 9 25585-2.

"Queen of the Silver Dollar." Emmylou Harris, *Pieces of the Sky*. Reprise 2284-2.

"Ramblin' Fever." Merle Haggard, *Ramblin' Fever*. MCA-2267.

"Ramblin' Man." Hank Williams, *Forty Greatest Hits*. Polydor 821 233-2.

"Ramblin' Rose." Hank Snow, *Hank Snow Collector Series*. BMG 2279-4-R.

"Red, Red Rose." Emmylou Harris, *Brand New Dance*. Reprise 9 26309-2.

"Red River Valley." Gene Autry, *Gene Autry's Country Music Hall of Fame Album*. Columbia CS 1035.

"Reservation Road, The." Bill Miller, *The Red Road*. Warner Western 9 45324-2.

"Restless." Emmylou Harris, *Last Date*. Warner Bros. 92-37404.

"Return of the Grievous Angel." Gram Parsons, *GP/Grievous Angel*. Reprise 9 26108-2.

"River, The." Garth Brooks, *Ropin' the Wind*. Capitol C4 96330.

"River for Him, A." Emmylou Harris, *Bluebird*. Reprise 9 25776-2.

"Road Home, The." Travis Tritt, *Country Club*. Warner Bros. 9 26094-2.

"Rocky Top." Osborne Brothers, *Bluegrass Spectacular*. RCA AHL1-4324.

"Rodeo." Garth Brooks, *Ropin' the Wind*. Capitol 96330-4.

"Rollin' and Ramblin' (The Death of Hank Williams)." Emmylou Harris, *Brand New Dance*. Reprise 9 26309-2.

"Rollin' and Ramblin' (The Death of Hank Williams)." Robin and Linda Williams, *All Broken Hearts Are the Same*. Sugar Hill SH-C-1022.

"Rose Garden." Lynn Anderson, *Rose Garden*. Columbia C 30411.

"Rose of Cimarron." Emmylou Harris, *Cimarron*. Warner Bros. BSK 3603.

"Roses in the Snow." Emmylou Harris, *Roses in the Snow*. Warner Bros. 3422-2.

"San Antonio Rose." Ricky Skaggs, *Comin' Home to Stay*. Epic PET 40623.

"Shame on the Moon." Rodney Crowell, *Rodney Crowell Collection*. Warner Bros. 9 25965-2.

"She's Gone." Marty Brown, *Wild Kentucky Skies*. MCA MCAD-10672.

"Sing Me Back Home." Merle Haggard, *Sing Me Back Home*. Capitol 4XL-9028.

"Six Days on the Road." Dave Dudley, *Dave Dudley Greatest Hits*, vol. 1. Plantation PLC-40.

"Soldier's Last Letter." George Jones, *Twenty Golden Pieces of George Jones*. Bulldog 2009.

"Some Gave All." Billy Ray Cyrus, *Some Gave All*. Mercury 314-510 635-2.

"Sorrow in the Wind." Emmylou Harris, *Pieces of the Sky*. Reprise 2284-2.

"South of the Border." Gene Autry, *Gene Autry's Country Music Hall of Fame Album*. Columbia CS 1035.

"Stand by Your Man." Tammy Wynette, *Tears of Fire: 1*. Epic EK 53071.

"Stars on the Water." Rodney Crowell, *Rodney Crowell Collection*. Warner Bros. 9 25965-2.

"Stones in the Road." Joan Baez, *Play Me Backwards*. Virgin 86458 4.

"Streets of Baltimore." Gram Parsons, *GP/Grievous Angel*. Reprise 9 26108-2.

"Sweetheart of the Rodeo, The." Emmylou Harris, *The Ballad of Sally Rose*. Warner Bros. 25205-2.

"Take Me Home, Country Roads." John Denver, *John Denver's Greatest Hits*. RCA AQL1-0374.

"Tecumseh Valley." Nanci Griffith, *Other Voices, Other Rooms*. Elektra 9 61464-4.

"Tennessee Rose." Emmylou Harris, *Cimarron*. Warner Bros. BSK 3603.

"T for Texas." Northern Lights, *Take You to the Sky*. Flying Fish FF 70533.

"That Silver Haired Daddy of Mine." Gene Autry, *Gene Autry's Country Music Hall of Fame Album*. Columbia CS 1035.

"That's How the West Was Swung." Roy Rogers, *Roy Rogers Tribute*. BMG 3024-2-R.

"They Rage On." Dan Seals, *Rage On*. Liberty 4-46976.

"This Old Road." Barry and Holly Tashian, *Ready for Love*. Rounder CD 0302.

"This Ole House." Statler Brothers, *Oh, Happy Day*. 51 West P-16491.

"'Til I Gain Control Again." Rodney Crowell, *Rodney Crowell Collection*. Warner Bros. 9 25965-2.

"Timberline." Emmylou Harris, *The Ballad of Sally Rose*. Warner Bros. 25205-2.

"Trail of Tears." Peter Rowan and the Nashville Bluegrass Band, *New Moon Rising*. Sugar Hill SH-CD-3762.

"Two Dozen Roses." Shenandoah, *The Road Not Taken*. Columbia CK 44468.

"Wabash Cannonball." Roy Acuff, *The Best of Roy Acuff*. Capitol 4XL-9371.

"Wayfaring Stranger." Emmylou Harris, *Roses in the Snow*. Warner Bros. 3422-2.

"Wayfaring Stranger." Ralph Stanley, *Pray for the Boys*. Rebel C-1687.

"We Shall Be Free." Garth Brooks, *The Chase*. Liberty CDP-98743.

"Wheels." Emmylou Harris, *Elite Hotel*. Reprise 2286-2.

"When I Call Your Name." Vince Gill, *When I Call Your Name*. MCA MCAD-42321.

"When I Get Where I'm Goin'." Nashville Bluegrass Band, *Waitin' for the Hard Times to Go*. Sugar Hill SH-CD-3809.

"Where the Fast Lane Ends." Oak Ridge Boys, *Where the Fast Lane Ends*. MCA MCAC-5945.

"White Line." Emmylou Harris, *The Ballad of Sally Rose*. Warner Bros. 25205-2.

"White Rose, The." Wilma Lee and Stoney Cooper, *Sunny Side of the Mountain*. Columbia HL 11178.

"Wildflowers." Dolly Parton, Linda Ronstadt, Emmylou Harris, *Trio*. Warner Bros. W2-25491.

"Wild Kentucky Skies." Marty Brown, *Wild Kentucky Skies*. MCA MCAD-10672.

"Wreck on the Highway, The." Roy Acuff, *The Best of Roy Acuff*. Capitol 4XL-9371.

"Yellow Roses." Dolly Parton, *White Limozeen*. Columbia CK 44384.

"Yodeling Cowboy." Jimmie Rodgers, *On the Way Up, 1929*. Rounder CD 1058.

"You Are My Flower." Carter Family, *The Carter Family*. MCA MCAC-10088.

"Your Cheatin' Heart." Hank Williams, *Forty Greatest Hits*. Polydor 821-233-2.

ADDITIONAL ALBUMS

Alabama. *Greatest Hits*. RCA PCD1-7170.

All American Cowboys. Various artists. Kat Family FZT 38126.

Anderson, John. *Seminole Wind*. BNA 07863-61029-4.

———. *Too Tough to Tame*. Capitol UVLC 76008.

Anderson, Lynn. *Cowboy's Sweetheart*. LaserLight 12-128.

———. *Outlaw Is Just a State of Mind*. CBS KC 35776.

———. *What She Does Best*. Mercury/ PolyGram 8346251.

Arnold, Eddy. *My World*. RCA LSP-3466.

Asleep at the Wheel. *Greatest Hits, Live and Kickin'*. Arista 18698-2.

Atkins, Chet. *Chet Atkins: The RCA Years*. RCA 61095-2.

———. *Chet Atkins' Workshop*. RCA LPM 2232.

———. *Christmas with Chet Atkins*. RCA LSP2423.

———. *Music for Nashville: My Home Town*. RCA Camden CAS-981.

Auldridge, Mike. *Eight-String Swing*. Sugar Hill SH-CD-3725.

Autry, Gene. *Gene Autry*. Columbia PCT 37465.

———. *Gene Autry's Country Music Hall of Fame Album*. Columbia CS 1035.

Belew, Carl. *Another Lonely Night*. Hilltop JM-6013.

Bell, Delia. *Delia Bell*. Warner Bros. 9 23838-4.

Bell, Delia, and Bill Grant. *The Cheer of the Home Fires*. Rounder ROU-1087.

———. *Following a Feeling*. Rounder C-0257.

Best of Cajun Country, The. Various artists. Era 339-4.

Black, Clint. *The Hard Way*. BMG 66003-2.

Bluegrass: The World's Greatest Show. Various artists. Sugar Hill SH-CD-2201.

Boatwright, Ginger. *Fertile Ground*. Flying Fish FF 70550.

Bristol Sessions, The. Various artists. 2 vols. Country Music Foundation CMF-011-C.

Brooks, Garth. *No Fences*. Liberty C4 93866.

Brother Boys. *The Brother Boys*. New Hillbilly Records NHD-1101.

———. *Plow*. Sugar Hill SH-CD-3805.

Byrds. *Sweetheart of the Rodeo*. Columbia CK 9670.

California. *Traveler*. Sugar Hill SH-CD-3803.

Campbell, Glen. *By the Time I Get to Phoenix*. Capitol ST 2851.

———. *Galveston*. Capitol ST-210.

Carpenter, Mary-Chapin. *Hometown Girl*. Columbia CK 40758.

Carter Family. *The Carter Family*. MCA MCAC-10088.

———. *The Carter Family*, vol. 4. Old Homestead OHCS 117.

Cash, Johnny. *Country Classics*. CSP BT 16915.

———. *The Essential Johnny Cash, 1955–1983*. Columbia C3T 47991.

———. *Johnny Cash at Folsom Prison and San Quentin*. Columbia CG 33639.

Cash, Rosanne. *Interiors*. Columbia CK 46079.

———. *King's Record Shop*. Columbia FCT 40777.

Charles, Ray. *Greatest Country and Western Hits*. DCC Compact Classics DZS040.

Chiavola, Kathy. *Labor of Love*. My Label KCP 1001.

Cline, Patsy. *The Patsy Cline Commemorative Collection*. MCA MCAD2-8925.

———. *The Patsy Cline Story*. MCA MCA2-4038.

Coe, David Allan. *David Allan Coe Rides Again*. CBS X598.

Conley, John. *Busted*. MCA 5310.

Copland, Aaron. *"Billy the Kid" and "Appalachian Spring"*. William Steinberg and the Pittsburgh Symphony Orchestra. Command CC 11038 SD.

Crowell, Rodney. *But What Will the Neighbors Think?* Warner Bros. BSK 3407.

———. *Diamonds and Dirt*. Columbia CK 44076.

———. *Rodney Crowell*. Warner Bros. 23587.

Dalton, Lacy J. *Blue-Eyed Blues*. Columbia FCT 40780.

———. *Highway Diner*. Columbia FCT 40393.

———. *Lacy J*. Capitol C4-93912.

Delmore Brothers. *Sand Mountain Blues*. County C-110.

Desert Rose Band. *Running*. MCA MCAC-42169.

Diffie, Joe. *A Thousand Winding Roads*. Epic ET46047.

Doug Dillard Band. *Heartbreak Hotel*. Flying Fish FF 90477.

Douglas, Jerry. *Changing Channels*. MCA
    MCAD-5965.
————. *Slide Rule*. Sugar Hill SH-CD-3797.
Duncan, Stuart. *Stuart Duncan*. Rounder
    CD 0263.

Earle, Steve. *The Hard Way*. MCA
    MCAD-6430.
Everly Brothers. *The Everly Brothers' All-Time
    Greatest Hits*. Such a Deal R4 70339.

Foster, Radney. *Del Rio, TX 1959*. Arista
    07822-18713-2.
Fricke, Janie. *The Very Best of Janie Fricke*.
    Columbia PCT 40165.
Frizzell, Lefty. *Lefty Frizzell Sings the Songs of
    Jimmie Rodgers*. Columbia C 32249.
————. *Lefty's Twenty Golden Hits*. TeeVee
    TVCD 6007.
Front Porch String Band. *Lines and Traces*.
    Rebel C-1689.

Gatlin Brothers. *A Gatlin Family Christmas*.
    Columbia 38183.
Gill, Vince. *Pocket Full of Gold*. MCA
    MCAC-10140.
Gilmore, Jimmie Dale. *After Awhile*. Electra
    9 61148-4.
————. *Fair and Square*. Hightone 8011.
————. *Jimmie Dale Gilmore*. Hightone
    Records HCD 8018.
Gosdin, Vern. *If Jesus Comes Tomorrow (What
    Then)*. Compleat 671011-4.
————. *Ten Years of Greatest Hits—Newly
    Recorded*. Columbia CT 45409.
Greene, Jack. *Twenty Greatest Hits*. Deluxe
    Records TVC 1023.
Griffith, Nanci. *Lone Star State of Mind*. MCA
    MCAC-5927.
————. *One Fair Summer Evening*. MCA
    MCAC-42255.

————. *Other Voices, Other Rooms*. Elektra
    9 61464-4.
————. *Poet in My Window*. Philo C-PH-1098.
————. *Storms*. MCA MCAC-6319.

Haggard, Merle. *Best of the Early Years*. Curb
    DH-77438.
————. *The Epic Collection*. Epic PET 39159.
————. *A Friend in California*. Epic
    PET 40286.
————. *Kern River*. Epic PET 39602.
————. *Rainbow Stew*. MCA MCAC-1464.
————. *Songwriter*. MCA MCAC-5698.
Hall, Tom T. *Tom T. Hall's Greatest Hits*.
    Mercury SR 61369.
Hancock, Butch, and Jimmie Dale Gilmore.
    Two Roads—Live in Australia. Virgin
    VOZCD 2036.
Harris, Emmylou. *Angel Band*. Warner Bros.
    9 25585-2.
————. *The Ballad of Sally Rose*. Warner Bros.
    25205-2.
————. *Bluebird*. Reprise 9 25776-2.
————. *Brand New Dance*. Reprise
    9 26309-2.
————. *Cowgirl's Prayer*. Asylum 9 61541-2.
————. *Pieces of the Sky*. Reprise 2284-2.
Hartford, John. *Catalogue*. Flying Fish FF 259.
Hiatt, John. *Bring the Family*. A&M c8 5158.
Highway 101. *Highway 101*. Warner Bros.
    9 25742-2.
Hobbs, Becky. *All Keyed Up*. MTM D1-71067.
Homer and Jethro. *Homer and Jethro at the
    Country Club*. RCA LPM 2181.
Horton, Johnny. *The World of Johnny Horton*.
    Columbia CG 30884.
Husky, Ferlin. *Ferlin Husky*. First Generation
    FGC-11.
————. *Ferlin Husky Sings the Songs of Music
    City, U.S.A.* Capitol ST 2439.

Jackson, Carl. *Song of the South*. Sugar Hill
SH-C-3728.

Jackson, Carl, and John Starling. *Spring
Training*. Sugar Hill SH-CD-3789.

Jennings, Waylon. *Collector's Series*.
RCA 8400-4-R.

———. *A Man Called Hoss*. MCA
MCAC-42038.

———. *Too Dumb for New York City, Too Ugly
for L.A.* Epic EK 48982.

Jennings, Waylon, and Willie Nelson. *WWII*.
RCA AHK1-4455.

Jennings, Waylon, Willie Nelson, Jessi Colter,
and Tompall Glaser. *Wanted: The Outlaws*.
RCA APL1-1321.

Johnson Mountain Boys. *Walls of Time*.
Rounder 0160.

Jones, George. *He Stopped Loving Her Today*.
Highland HT-380.

———. *Super Hits*. Epic PET 40776.

———. *Tender Years*. LaserLight 15 488.

———. *Twenty-four Gospel Hits*. Highland
DLX-7791.

———. *Who's Gonna Fill Their Shoes*. Epic
PET-39598.

Jones, George, and Melba Montgomery.
Bluegrass Hootenanny. United Artists
UAS 6352.

Jones, George, and Tammy Wynette. *Greatest
Hits*, vol. 2. Epic EK 48839.

———. *The President and First Lady*.
CSP BT 15769.

Judds. *Collector's Series*. BMG 2278-4-R.

———. *Heartland*. RCA 5916-4-R.

———. *Why Not Me*. RCA AHK1-5319.

Judd, Wynonna. *Wynonna Judd*. Curb/MCA
MCAC-10529.

Ketchum, Hal. *Sure Love*. Curb D2-77581.

Kilby, Cody. *Cowan Jubilee*. Mikron 494 92.3.

lang, k. d. *Angel with a Lariat*. Warner Bros.
4-25441.

Lewis, Laurie. *True Stories*. Rounder CD0300.

Lewis, Laurie, and Kathy Kallick. *Together*.
Kaleidoscope Records K-44.

Lewis, Laurie, and Grant Street. *Singin' My
Troubles Away*. Flying Fish FF 70515.

Lonesome River Band. *Carrying the Tradition*.
Rebel REB-CD 1690.

Lost and Found. *January Rain*. Rebel C-1702.

Louvin Brothers. *The Best of the Early Louvin
Brothers*. Rebel REBC 852.

———. *Greatest Hits*. Capitol 4XL 57222.

———. *The Louvin Brothers*. Rounder
C-55-07.

———. *New River Ranch*. Copper Creek
C-0105.

———. *Radio Favorites, '51–'57*. Country
Music Foundation CMF 009.

———. *Tragic Songs of Life*. Stetson
HATC 3043.

Lovett, Lyle. *Lyle Lovett and His Large Band*.
Curb MCAC-42263.

Lynn, Loretta. *The Best of Loretta Lynn*. MCA
HANC 20224.

———. *I Lie*. MCA MCAC-5293.

———. *Loretta Lynn*. MCA Coral
CRC-20163.

———. *Loretta Lynn Country Music Hall of
Fame Series*. MCA MCAD-10083.

McCarter, Jennifer, and the McCarters.
Better Be Home Soon. Warner Bros.
9 25896-4.

McCarters. *The Gift*. Warner Bros. 9 25737-1.

McClinton, Delbert. *Never Been Rocked
Enough*. Curb D4-77521.

McCoury, Del. *Blue Side of Town*. Rounder
CD 0292.

———. *Don't Stop the Music*. Rounder
CD 0245.

McEntire, Reba. *Reba McEntire Live*. MCA MCAD-8034.

Martin, Jimmy. *The Best of Bluegrass*. Starday N5-2192.

————. *King of Bluegrass*. Stanley King SK5-739.

Miller, Bill. *The Red Road*. Warner Western 9 45324-2.

Monroe, Bill. *Bill Monroe's Country Music Hall of Fame Album*. MCA MCAC-140.

————. *The Essential Bill Monroe and His Blue Grass Boys*. Columbia C2K 52478.

Montgomery, Melba. *Down Home*. United Artists UAS 8369.

————. *Miss Country Music*. Hilltop JS-6031.

Morgan, Lorrie. *Put Yourself in My Shoes*. BMG 2372-2-R.

Murphy, Michael Martin. *Land of Enchantment*. Warner Bros. 9 25894-1.

Nashville Bluegrass Band. *Home of the Blues*. Sugar Hill SH-C-3793.

Nelson, Willie. *Born for Trouble*. Columbia CK 45492.

————. *Red-Headed Stranger*. Columbia CK 33482.

New Grass Revival. *Live*. Sugar Hill SH-C 3771.

————. *On the Boulevard*. Sugar Hill SH-C-3745.

New Tradition Band. *Sweet Memories*. Suite 2000 NDQ 4805.

Nitty Gritty Dirt Band. *Will the Circle Be Unbroken?* 2 cassettes. EMI E4-46589.

Northern Lights. *Take You to the Sky*. Flying Fish FF 70533.

O'Day, Molly. *Molly O'Day and the Cumberland Mountain Folks*. Bear Family BCD 15565.

O'Kanes. *Imagine That*. Columbia CK 45131.

————. *The O'Kanes*. Columbia B6T 40459.

Old Time Camp Meeting. Various artists. Hollywood HCD 358.

Osborne Brothers. *Bobby and His Mandolin*. CMH CMH-C-6256.

————. *Hillbilly Fever*. CMH CMH-C-6269.

Oslin, K. T. *8os Ladies*. RCA 5924-4-R.

Owens, Buck. *The Best of Buck Owens*. Capitol ST 2135.

————. *I Wouldn't Live in New York City*. Capitol ST-628.

Parsons, Gram. *The Early Years*, vol. 1. Sierra Records SEC-4215.

Parton, Dolly. *Burlap and Satin*. RCA AHK1-4691.

————. *Dolly Parton: The RCA Years*. RCA 66127-2.

————. *Golden Streets of Glory*. BMG 54398-2.

————. *Just the Way I Am*. RCA CAS-2583.

————. *Slow Dancing with the Moon*. Columbia CT 53199.

————. *White Limozeen*. Columbia CK 44384.

————. *The World of Dolly Parton*, vol. 2. CBS AK 44362.

Price, Ray. *San Antonio Rose*. Columbia CS 8556.

————. *Sometimes a Rose*. Columbia CK 48980.

————. *Town and Country*. Dimension DL 5003.

Reeves, Jim. *Missing You*. RCA LSP-4749.

————. *Moonlight and Roses*. RCA LSP-2854.

————. *A Touch of Velvet*. RCA LSP-2487.

Reno, Jack. *Hitchin' a Ride*. Target Records Stereo T13-1313.

Riders in the Sky. *Harmony Ranch*. Columbia CK 48589.

————. *New Trails*. Rounder CD 0220.

Ritter, Tex. *Collectors Series*. Capitol CDP 7 95036 2.

————. *Greatest Hits*. Curb D2-77297.

————. *Green, Green Valley*. Capitol ST-467.

Robbins, Marty. *Everything I've Always Wanted*. Columbia JCT 36860.

Rodgers, Jimmie. *Train Whistle Songs: The Legendary Jimmie Rodgers*. RCA LPM 1640.

Rowan, Peter. *All on a Rising Day*. Sugar Hill SH-CD 3791.

————. *Dust Bowl Children*. Sugar Hill SH-CD-3761.

Royal, Billy Joe. *Looking Ahead*. Atlantic America 7 90508-4.

————. *Tell It Like It Is*. Atlantic America 7 91064-4.

Sawyer Brown, *The Dirt Road*. Curb C4-95624.

Schnaufer, David. *Dulcimer Player Deluxe*. Sounds from Lomax SFL #3.

Scruggs, Earl, and Tom T. Hall. *The Storyteller and the Banjo Man*. Columbia PCT 37953.

Seldom Scene. *A Change of Scenery*. Sugar Hill SH-CD-3763.

————. *Fifteenth Anniversary Celebration, Live at the Kennedy Center*. Sugar Hill SH-CD-2202.

Sixty Years of Grand Ole Opry. Various artists. RCA CPK 2-9507 P1; CPK 2-9507 P2 (double cassette).

Skaggs, Ricky. *Comin' Home to Stay*. Epic PET 40623.

————. *Favorite Country Songs*. Epic PET 39409.

————. *Kentucky Thunder*. Epic PET 45027.

Skillet Lickers. *Old Time Fiddle Tunes and Songs from North Georgia*. County Records 526.

Smith, Connie. *The Best of Connie Smith*. Dominion 574-4.

Snow, Hank. *Hank Snow Collectors' Series*. RCA 2279-4-R.

Sonnier, Jo-El. *Have a Little Faith*. RCA 9718-4-R.

Sons of the Pioneers. *Sons of the Pioneers*. Columbia PCT 37439.

Southern Pacific. *Greatest Hits*. Warner Bros. 9 26582-2.

Stanley, Ralph. *I Can Tell You the Time*. Rebel C-1637.

————. *Pray for the Boys*. Rebel C-1687.

————. *Saturday Night and Sunday Morning*. CRFRC TC-9001.

Stanley Brothers and the Clinch Mountain Boys. *Mountain Song Favorites*. Nashville NLP-2014.

Strait, George. *Beyond the Blue Neon*. MCA MCAD-42266.

————. *Holding My Own*. MCA MCAD-10532.

Strength in Numbers, *The Telluride Sessions*. MCA MCAD-6293.

Stuart, Marty. *Tempted*. MCA MCAC-10106.

————. *This One's Gonna Hurt You*. MCA MCAD-10596.

Sweethearts of the Rodeo. *Sisters*. Columbia CT 47358.

Tashian, Barry, and Holly Tashian. *Live in Holland*. Strictly Country Records SCR-27.

Thompson, Hank. *Hank Thompson*. MCA MCAD-10545.

Tillis, Pam. *Above and Beyond the Doll of Cutey*. Warner Bros. 23871-4.

Travis, Randy. *Heroes and Friends*. Warner Bros. 9 26310-2.

Tubb, Ernest. *Ernest Tubb's Greatest Hits*. MCA MCAC-16.

————. *Honky Tonk Classics*. Rounder C-SS-14.

————. *The Importance of Being Ernest Tubb*. Longhorn HATC 3006.

Twain, Shania. *Shania Twain*. Mercury 314-514 433-4.

Twenty Bluegrass Originals. Various artists. Highland DLX-7909.

Twitty, Conway. *House on an Old Lonesome Road.* MCA 42297.

Van Shelton, Ricky. *Backroads.* Columbia CK 46855.
———. *Don't Overlook Salvation.* Columbia CK 46854.

Van Zandt, Townes. *At My Window.* Sugar Hill SH 1020.
———. *Delta Momma Blues.* Tomato 2696292.

Wagoner, Porter, and Dolly Parton. *Just Between You and Me.* RCA LSP-3926.
———. *Porter Wayne and Dolly Rebecca.* RCA LSP-4305.
———. *Sweet Harmony.* RCA PDK2-1013.

Wells, Kitty. *Kitty Wells.* MCA MCAC-10081.
———. *Lonesome, Sad, and Blue.* Decca DL 4658.

Whites. *Forever You.* Curb MCAC-5490.

Williams, Don. *Country Boy.* Dot DO2088.

Williams, Hank. *Hank Williams: The Original Singles Collection . . . Plus.* Polydor 847 194-2.

Williams, Robin, and Linda Williams. *Close as We Can Get/Nine 'til Midnight.* Flying Fish FF 70359.
———. *Live in Holland.* Strictly Country Records SCR-31.

———. *The Rhythm of Love.* Sugar Hill SH-CD-1027.
———. *Turn toward Tomorrow.* Sugar Hill SH-CD-1040.

Willis, Kelly. *Bang, Bang.* MCA MCAD-10141.

Wills, Bob. *The Best of Bob Wills.* Special Music CBK 3023.

Wiseman, Mac. *Mac Wiseman.* MCA MCAC-39086.

Wynette, Tammy. *Best-Loved Hits.* Epic ET48588.
———. *It's Just a Matter of Time.* CSP BT 13260.
———. *Tammy's Touch.* Columbia LET 10194.
———. *Tears of Fire: The Twenty-Fifth Anniversary Collection.* 3-CD set. Epic E3K 52741.

Yoakam, Dwight. *Guitars, Cadillacs, Etc., Etc.* Reprise 9 25372-4.
———. *Hillbilly DeLuxe.* Reprise 9 25567-4.
———. *This Time.* Reprise 4-45241.

Young, Faron. *Faron Young's Greatest Hits.* Capitol 4XL-9406.
———. *Greatest Hits,* vol. 1. Step One Records SOR-0043.

Zonn, Andrea. *Goodbye to the Rose.* Zondrea 0001.

Sources

▼ ▼ ▼ ▼ ▼ ▼ ▼ ▼ ▼ ▼ ▼ ▼ ▼ ▼ ▼ ▼ ▼ ▼

The listings below give the sources that are quoted or used as references in the text, for the most part in the order in which they occur in each chapter. To avoid repetition of the same sources, page numbers relevant to an entire chapter are listed with the first citation of each source. Songs and albums mentioned or quoted in the text can be found in the discography preceding this section.

PREFACE

Williams, "Nashville Numbering System," 41, 43.

1. PATHOS, MISERIES, HAPPINESS, LIFE ITSELF

Malone, *Country Music U.S.A.*, 1; Lomax, "Bluegrass Background"; Kerouac, *On the Road*; Walt Whitman, "Song of Myself" and "Song of the Open Road," in *Leaves of Grass*, 65, 83, 149–59; Twain, *Huckleberry Finn*, 68, 94, 96, 171, 35–36, 8; Rodgers, *Country Music Message, Revisited*; Cantwell, *Bluegrass Breakdown*; Roger M. Williams, *Sing a Sad Song*; Nash, *Behind Closed Doors*, 38–39, 49, 65, 68, 100, 117, 119, 127, 163, 189, 191, 196, 383, 466, 384, 329, 351, 544, 466; Lee Smith, *Devil's Dream*; Carr et al., *Illustrated History of Country Music*, 272; Flippo, *Your Cheatin' Heart*, 233; Herbert,

"Laurie Lewis"; Nash, *Dolly*, 107, 131; "In the Hank Williams Tradition" (includes comments by Randy Travis and Emmylou Harris on Hank Williams's music as poetry; Travis on country music as stories; and Chet Atkins on Hank Williams's vocal registers and superb yodelling); Scoby, liner notes for *Delta Momma Blues*; Clark, Harris, and Cash, liner notes for *Diamonds and Dirt*; Holly Tashian interview; Painton, "Country Rocks the Boomers"; Ferris, *Blues from the Delta* and discussion with author, April–May 1993; Richard Bennett interview; Sandmel, liner notes for *After Awhile*; Farlekas, "Harris Returns to Mid-Hudson"; Ardoin, *Callas Legacy*, 109, 110, 205; Robinson, *Opera and Ideas*, 48; Scott, *Great Caruso*, 59–60.

2. HOME

Wolfe, liner notes for *The Bristol Sessions*, vol. 2; Malone, *Country Music U.S.A.*, 64–65; Silber, *Songs of the Civil War*, 120–21, 143–44. Crèvecoeur, *Letters from an American Farmer*, 1–91; Ralph Waldo Emerson, "The American Scholar," in *Selections from Ralph Waldo Emerson*, 63–80; Emerson, "Considerations by the Way," in *Conduct of Life*, 274; Emerson, "Domestic Life," "Farming," and "Notes," in *Society and Solitude*, 103–33, 135–54, 380; Emerson, "Self-Reliance," in *Selections from Ralph*

Waldo Emerson, 147–68; Garland, *Main-Travelled Roads*; Cook, *From Tobacco Road to Route 66*; Caldwell, *Tobacco Road*; Wallace Stevens, "Anecdote of the Jar," in *Collected Poems*, 76; Stowe, *Uncle Tom's Cabin*, 214–25; Beecher and Stowe, *American Woman's Home*, 18, 19, 158, 199; Clark, *American Family Home*; Chapman, *Homeplace*, 1–4; Rybczynski, *Home*, 38–56; Wilder, *Farmer Boy*, 188–89; Wilder, *Little House in the Big Woods*, 22–23, 37–38, 73, 97, 99–101; Wilder, *Little House on the Prairie*, 40, 50–51, 66–70, 165–66; White and White, *Intellectual versus the City*, 14, 19, 38, 39, 45, 24, 27, 162, 173, 195; James, *American Scene*, 75; Thomas Wolfe, *You Can't Go Home Again*; Hemingway, *In Our Time*; Anderson, *Winesburg, Ohio*; O'Connor, *Collected Stories*; Edwin Arlington Robinson, *Collected Poems*; Nash, *Dolly*, 10, 30, 88; Wilder, *The Long Winter*, 94–95, 120; Wilder, *By the Shores of Silver Lake*, 264, 290–91.

3 . ROAD

Nash, *Behind Closed Doors*, 11–12, 112, 142, 139; Rodgers, *Country Music Message, Revisited*, 209, 227; Altschiller, *Transportation in America*, 6–7; Dunbar, *History of Travel in America*, 1326, 142, 145; Stilgoe, *Common Landscape of America*, 21–23; Limerick, *Legacy of Conquest*, 194; Jefferson, *Notes on the State of Virginia*, 142–43; Jehlen, *American Incarnation*, 30–75; Kerouac, *On the Road*, 105; Walt Whitman, "On Journeys through the States," "Song of Myself" (no. 46), "Song of the Open Road," and "Pioneers! O Pioneers!," in *Leaves of Grass*, 229–32, 149–59, 83, 311, 325; Nash, *Dolly*, 111; Melville, *Moby-Dick*, 202–3; Roger M.

Williams, "Hank Williams"; Williams, *Sing a Sad Song*; Flippo, *Your Cheatin' Heart*; Kuralt, *A Life on the Road*; Tucker, "9 to 5"; Hauslohner, "Emmylou Harris," 20; Rockwell, "European Tour Buoys New York Orchestra"; Steinbeck, *Grapes of Wrath*, 253, 151–56; Garland, *Main-Travelled Roads*, 54, 141; Twain, *Huckleberry Finn*; Douglass, *Narrative of the Life of Frederick Douglass*, 160; Tocqueville, *Democracy in America*, 2:136–39; Du Bois, *Souls of Black Folk*, 186; Ezra Pound, "Patria Mia," in *Selected Prose*, 99–141; Fuller, *Summer on the Lakes*, 26; Clinton, "Inaugural Address"; Horstman, *Sing Your Heart Out*, 344, 345–46.

4 . HIGH LONESOME

Wilder, *Little House on the Prairie*, 13, 40, 166, 208, 311, 325; Slater, *Pursuit of Loneliness*; Walt Whitman, "Song of Myself," in *Leaves of Grass*, 38–39; William Carlos Williams, "Danse Russe," in *Selected Poems*, 8; Anderson, *Winesburg, Ohio*, 167–78, 115–20; Edwin Arlington Robinson, *Collected Poems*; Mather, *Theopolis Americana*, 8; Winthrop, "A Modell of Christian Charity," 278; Edward Johnson, *Wonder-Working Providence*, 51–53; Douglass, *Narrative of the Life of Frederick Douglass*, 142; Cressy, *Coming Over*, 191–212; Jeffrey, *Frontier Women*, 37, 21, 31; Breitwieser, *American Puritanism*, 26–40, 71–129; Delbanco, *Puritan Ordeal*, 1–97; Riley, *Female Frontier*, 48; Irving, *Tour on the Prairies*, xx; Fuller, *Summer on the Lakes*, 38, 47; Gillespie and Rockland, *Looking for America*, 16; Bellah et al., *Habits of the Heart*, 3–55; Kincaid, *A Small Place*, 80; William Carlos Williams, *In the Ameri-*

can Grain, 27, 65, 66, 128, 111, 131–32, 135, 136–37; Cahan, *Rise of David Levinsky*, 100; Yezierska, *Children of Loneliness*; Kerouac, *On the Road*, 179–80, 240; Tichi, *New World, New Earth*, 147–48; Thoreau, "Walking," 224; Twain, *Life on the Mississippi*, 234, 228, 293, 201–2; Twain, *Huckleberry Finn*, 68, 94, 96, 171, 35–36, 8; Lomax, "Bluegrass Background."

5. WILD WILD WEST

Hank Williams, *Hank Williams*, 14; Roger M. Williams, *Sing a Sad Song*, 96; Frank, "Waylon Jennings"; Porterfield, "Hey, Hey, Tell 'Em 'Bout Us," 13, 115, 142; Collins, Green, and LaBour, *Riders in the Sky*, 10, 16; Donald McQuade, "The Literature of the New Republic," in McQuade et al., *Harper American Literature*, 1:504–5; Crèvecoeur, *Letters from an American Farmer*, 48–91; Ralph Waldo Emerson, "Self-Reliance," in *Selections from Ralph Waldo Emerson*, 148, 149, 151, 153, 165; Emerson, "Society and Solitude," in *Complete Works of Ralph Waldo Emerson*, 7:1–17; Emerson, "The Young American," in *Nature, Addresses, and Lectures*, 222–44; Thoreau, "Walking," 205–48, 217–24, 221–22; Walt Whitman, "Pioneers! O Pioneers!," in *Leaves of Grass*, 229–32; Cooper, *The Deerslayer*; Cooper, *Last of the Mohicans*; Cooper, *The Pathfinder*; Cooper, *The Prairie*, 450; Cooper, *The Pioneers*; Tompkins, *West of Everything*, 4, 31, 12, 25, 47–55, 71, 104–5; Dary, *Cowboy Culture*, 145–56, 254–307; Horstman, *Sing Your Heart Out, Country Boy*, 320, 312; Green, "Singing Cowboy"; Fife and Fife, *Heaven on Horseback*; Fussell, *Frontier*; Lamar, "Overview of Westward Expansion"; Limerick, *Legacy of Conquest*, 22; Allmendinger, *The Cowboy*; Trachtenberg, *Incorporation of America*; Tocqueville, *Democracy in America*, 2:98–99; Bellah et al., *Habits of the Heart*, 6, 16, 37–39; Franklin, *Autobiography*, 26, 36–38, 42–43; Cody, *Life of Hon. William F. Cody*, 70; Wister, *The Virginian*, 13, 136; Grey, *Riders of the Purple Sage*, 14, 72, 20, 136; Schaefer, *Shane*, 36, 105, 100, 88, 57, 53; L'Amour, *Flint*, 8, 75, 35, 47; Davis, *Honey in the Horn*; London, "All Gold Canyon."

6. RED RED ROSE

Malone and McCulloh, *Stars of Country Music*, 322, 338; Wheeler, *Content in a Garden*, 33; Hawthorne, *The Scarlet Letter*, 75–76; Cash, *Mind of the South*, 50; Wharton, *Summer*, 63, 65, 242–57; Willingham, *Rambling Rose*; Dickey, *Deliverance*; Nash, *Dolly*, 262; Seward, *Symbolic Rose*; Shepherd, *History of the Rose*; Fuller, *Summer on the Lakes*, 24, 25, 69; Levine, *Highbrow/Lowbrow*, 85–168; Banner, *American Beauty*, 242; Doyle, *New Men, New Cities, New South*, 189–259; Hooper, *Lady's Book of Flowers and Poetry*, n.p.; Atkins, "Carter Family"; Charles K. Wolfe, *Tennessee Strings*; Roger M. Williams, *Sing a Sad Song*, 87; Hurst, *Nashville's Grand Ole Opry*, 191; Bacon and Day, *Ultimate Guitar Book*; Cantwell, *Bluegrass Breakdown*, 215; Stein, *The Yale Gertrude Stein*.

7. PILGRIMS ON THE WAY

Robert Frost, "The Road Not Taken," in *Poems of Robert Frost*, 117; Du Bois, *Souls of Black Folk*, 189, 182, 184–85, 11–12;

Sundquist, *To Wake the Nations*, 457–539; Fisher, *Albion's Seed*, 705–8; Malone, *Country Music U.S.A.*, 10–13; Malone, *Southern Music/American Music*, 67–69; Bradford, *Of Plymouth Plantation*, 61–63; Bunyan, *Pilgrim's Progress*, 42; Sadler, *John Bunyan*, 54–63; Smith, *John Bunyan in America*, 10–11, 95–96; Starr, *Defoe and Spiritual Autobiography*, 5; Tichi, "Spiritual Biography and the 'Lords Remembrancers'"; Steinbeck, *Grapes of Wrath*, 156; Walt Whitman, "Song of the Open Road," in *Leaves of Grass*, 153; Dickinson, "I cross till I am weary"; Hall Johnson, *Thirty Spirituals*, 74; James Weldon Johnson, *Book of American Negro Spirituals*, 59, 62, 70, 100–103, 134–35, 64, 68–69, 98–99, 134–35, 184–85, 184, 180–81; Logan, *Road to Heaven*, 19; Thoreau, "Walking," 205–48; Lindsay, *Prose of Vachel Lindsay*, 7, 1, 71–72, 101, 106; Albanese, *Nature Religion in America*, 20–21; Bryant, "A Forest Hymn"; Cather, *O Pioneers!*, 76–77; Norris, *The Octopus*, 274; Bane, "Twenty Questions with Dolly Parton"; Stambler and Landon, *Encyclopedia of Folk, Country, and Western Music*, 550; Ralph Waldo Emerson, "Fate," in *Conduct of Life*, 6–8, 17; Schlissel, "Frontier Family," 85; Wharton, *Custom of the Country*, 123; Garland, *Main-Travelled Roads*, 141–55; Sinclair, *The Jungle*, 83–86. Thoreau, *Cape Cod*, 9–10; Melville, *Moby-Dick*, 203; Goldberg, *Long Quiet Highway*; Peck, *Road Less Traveled*; May, *Cry for Myth*, 26; Dillard, *Pilgrim at Tinker Creek*; Hilts, "Minister's Ties to Church Are Sundered by AIDS"; Rothstein, "Freshman Orientation at Columbia."

8. NATURE'S MUSIC

See "Emmylou Harris" file at the Country Music Foundation Library, Nashville, Tennessee. The file includes newspaper and magazine reviews and articles in addition to press releases and publicity flyers. Horstman, *Sing Your Heart Out, Country Boy*, 209, 180–81, 240, 224, 220, 207, 184; Thoreau, "Homer, Ossian, Chaucer," 290–91; Nash, *Dolly*, 90; "An Evening with Rodney Crowell"; Flippo, liner notes for *Rodney Crowell Collection*; Morthland, "Jimmie Dale Gilmore"; Hirshberg, "Ballad of A. P. Carter," 104; Ralph Waldo Emerson, "The Uses of Great Men," in *Representative Men*, 3; Muir, *Our National Parks*, 135; Roger M. Williams, *Sing a Sad Song*, 121–31; Flippo, *Your Cheatin' Heart*, 166; Morthland, *Best of Country Music*, 199; *Country Musicians*, 56; Cantwell, *Bluegrass Breakdown*, 9; "Duet Climbing"; Rodney Crowell interview; Patsy Montana interview; Bacon and Day, *Ultimate Guitar Book*, 48–55; Stambler and Landon, *Encyclopedia of Folk, Country, and Western Music*, 521, 100; Roy Acuff, introduction to Hurst, *Nashville's Grand Ole Opry*; Holland, "Barenboim's Evening with Schubert."

9. ARTISTS' ART

On Barry and Holly Tashian: *Musik Enzyklopadie, Band 6: Barry Tashian* (Star Cluster: Verlag U. Zimmermann, Germany, 1992), 1–29; Don McLeese, "Country and Western," *Rolling Stone*, May 13, 1993; Chris Flisher, "Tashians Keep Vocal Duets Alive," *Minuteman Chronicle*, March 27, 1993; Chris Morris, "Tashian Touted,"

Billboard, April 17, 1993; Don McLeese, "Beauty and the Blast: Tashians, Dinosaur Jr. Both Ideal," *Austin American-Statesman*, April 20, 1993; Peter North, "Powerful Producer," *Edmonton Journal*, April 24, 1993; Don Heckman, "Tashians: Gently into the Night," *Los Angeles Times*, March 27, 1993, Orange County edition.

On Mike Lawler: Doerschuk, "Country Keyboards."

On Andrea Zonn: Eichenlaub and Eichenlaub, "Patricia's Thoughts on Women in the Country Music Business."

On Kathy Chiavola: Dan Mazur, "Kathy Chiavola," *Bluegrass Unlimited* 20, no. 1 (July 1993): 55–61; "Kathy Chiavola— *Labor of Love*," *Billboard*, February 13, 1993; Dan Mazur, "Mozart to Monroe: Kathy Chiavola's Strange Trip," *Riff*, February 1993, 10–11; Greg Drust, "*Labor of Love*: Kathy Chiavola," *Live Wire*, Spring 1991; Tony May, "Kathy Chiavola—*Labor of Love*," *Folk Roots Magazine*, January/February 1993; Jon Philbert, "Spotlight Album: Kathy Chiavola—*Labor of Love*," *Country Music People*, February 1993; Brian Clough, "Northern Echo," *Country*, May 1993; Brian Ahern, "Kathy Chiavola— Lots of Love—Ragged but Right," *International Country Music News and Routes*, June 1993; Maureen Miller, "Album Review: Kathy Chiavola, *Labor of Love*," *Country Song Roundup*, April 1993; Maurice Hope, "Maurice Hope's Reviews," *Express*, May 1993.

On Laurie Lewis: Alan Senauke, "Laurie Lewis: Far from the Hills of Home," *Sing Out!*, February/March 1993, 11–15; Derk Richardson, "Love Chooses Laurie Lewis," *Express*, June 16, 1989, 24; Larry Kelp, "Singer Laurie Lewis Sounds a Soulful Country Chord," *Oakland Tribune*, June 13, 1989; Herbert, "Laurie Lewis— with Fiddle and Song"; Ronni Lundy, "Spotlight On: Three Leaders in the Bluegrass Women's Movement," *Louisville Courier-Journal*, March 19, 1989; Ira Gitlin, "Laurie Lewis: I'm Gonna Be the Wind," *Bluegrass Unlimited*, April 1990, 24–31.

10. "WHAT SERIOUS SONGWRITING IS ALL ABOUT"

Arnett, "Rodney Crowell Steps on a Landmine"; Bernhardt, "Paying Dues to Get His Due"; Claypool, "Rodney Crowell Basks in His Well-Earned Success"; Claypool, "Hometown Boy Increasing His Country-Music Stature"; Crawford, "Country Cool"; Dunham, "Cult Hero Strikes Back"; Flippo, liner notes for *Rodney Crowell Collection*; Kennedy, "Rodney Crowell"; Marymount, "Crowell Glad to Be Country"; Mason, "Why Rodney Shuns the Cash Flow"; Nager, "Rodney Crowell"; Perry, "All Roads Lead Back to Nashville"; Petty, "Crowell Spearheads Country's New Wave"; "Rodney Crowell Gets to the Heart of Country"; "Rodney Crowell Hams It Up for the Reporter's Camera"; Sandmel, "Rodney Crowell Finds the Right 'Keys'"; Trujillo, "Crowell's Country Clan"; Tucker, "But What Will the Neighbors Think?"; Zito, "Rodney Crowell."

Bibliography

Aaron, Daniel. *The Unwritten War: American Writers and the Civil War.* 1973. Reprint. Madison: University of Wisconsin Press, 1987.

Adams, Henry. *The Education of Henry Adams.* 1918. Reprint. Boston: Houghton Mifflin, 1973.

Albanese, Catherine L. *Nature Religion in America: From the Algonkian Indians to the New Age.* Chicago: University of Chicago Press, 1990.

Allmendinger, Blake. *The Cowboy: Representations of Labor in an American Work Culture.* New York: Oxford University Press, 1992.

Altschiller, Donald, ed. *Transportation in America.* New York: H. W. Wilson, 1982.

Anderson, John. "Nashville Hip." *Newsday,* February 4, 1990, Entertainment section.

Anderson, Sherwood. *Winesburg, Ohio.* 1919. Reprint. New York: Viking, 1960.

Ardoin, John. *The Callas Legacy: The Complete Guide to Her Recordings.* New York: Scribners, 1991.

Arnett, Matthew. "Rodney Crowell Steps on a Landmine." *Monterey Peninsula-Herald,* June 11, 1989.

Atkins, John. "The Carter Family." In *Stars of Country Music,* edited by Bill C. Malone and Judith McCulloh, 95–120. 1975. Reprint. New York: Da Capo, 1991.

Bacon, Tony, and Paul Day. *The Ultimate Guitar Book.* New York: Knopf, 1991.

Bane, Michael. "Twenty Questions with Dolly Parton." *Country Music,* May/June 1993, 48–49.

Banner, Lois. *American Beauty.* Chicago: University of Chicago Press, 1983.

Beecher, Catharine E., and Harriet Beecher Stowe. *The American Woman's Home: Or, Principles of Domestic Science; Being a Guide to the Formation and Maintenance of Economical, Healthful, Beautiful, and Christian Homes.* New York: J. B. Ford, 1869.

Bellah, Robert N., William M. Sullivan, Ann Swidler, and Steven M. Tipton. *Habits of the Heart: Individualism and Commitment in American Life.* Berkeley: University of California Press, 1986.

Bennett, Richard. Interview with author. Nashville, Tenn., April 1993.

Bernhardt, Jack. "Paying Dues to Get His Due." *Raleigh News and Observer,* August 26, 1988.

Bradford, William. *Of Plymouth Plantation, 1620–1647.* Edited by Samuel Eliot Morison. New York: Knopf, 1966.

Breitwieser, Mitchell Robert. *American Puritanism and the Defense of Mourning: Religion, Grief, and Ethnology in Mary Rowlandson's Captivity Narrative.* Madison: University of Wisconsin Press, 1990.

Bryant, William Cullen. "A Forest Hymn." In *The American Landscape: A Critical Anthology of Prose and Poetry,* edited by John Conron, 292–95. New York: Oxford University Press, 1973.

Bufwack, Mary A., and Robert K. Oermann.

Finding Her Voice: The Saga of Women in Country Music. New York: Crown, 1993.

Bunyan, John. *The Pilgrim's Progress from This World to That Which Is to Come.* 1678. Reprint. Edited by James Blanton Wharey; revised by Roger Sharrock. Oxford: Oxford University Press, 1960.

Cahan, Abraham. *The Rise of David Levinsky.* 1917. Reprint. New York: Harper and Row, 1966.

Caldwell, Erskine. *Tobacco Road.* New York: Duell, Sloan and Pearce, 1932.

Cantwell, Robert. *Bluegrass Breakdown: The Making of the Old Southern Sound.* Urbana: University of Illinois Press, 1984.

Carr, Patrick, ed. *The Illustrated History of Country Music.* Garden City, N.Y.: Doubleday, 1980.

Cash, W. J. *The Mind of the South.* 1941. Reprint. New York: Vintage, 1991.

Cather, Willa. *O Pioneers!* 1913. Reprint. New York: Viking Penguin, 1989.

———. *The Song of the Lark.* 1915. Reprint. New York: New American Library, 1991.

Chapman, Mariston. *Homeplace.* New York: Viking, 1929.

Clark, Clifford Edward, Jr. *The American Family Home, 1800–1960.* Chapel Hill: University of North Carolina Press, 1986.

Clark, Susanna, Emmylou Harris, and Rosanne Cash. Liner notes for Rodney Crowell, *Diamonds and Dirt.* 1988. Columbia Records FCT 44076.

"Classical Connection, A." *The Tennessean,* April 30, 1992, sec. A.

Claypool, Bob. "Hometown Boy Increasing His Country-Music Stature." *Houston Post,* February 17, 1989.

———. "Rodney Crowell Basks in His Well-Earned Success." *Houston Chronicle Zest,* February 12, 1989.

Clemens, Samuel Langhorne. *See* Mark Twain.

Clinton, William Jefferson. "Inaugural Address," January 20, 1993.

Cody, William F. *The Life of Hon. William F. Cody, Known as Buffalo Bill.* 1878. Reprint. Lincoln: University of Nebraska Press, 1978.

Collins, William, Douglas P. Green, and Frederick LaBour. *Riders in the Sky.* Salt Lake City, Utah: Gibbs Smith, 1992.

Cook, Sylvia Jenkins. *From Tobacco Road to Route 66: The Southern Poor White in Fiction.* Chapel Hill: University of North Carolina Press, 1976.

Cooper, James Fenimore. *The Deerslayer: Or, the First War-Path.* 1841. Reprinted as vol. 2 of *Leatherstocking Tales.* New York: Library of America, 1985.

———. *The Last of the Mohicans.* 1826. Reprint. Boston: Houghton Mifflin, 1958.

———. *The Pathfinder: Or, the Inland Sea.* 1840. Reprint. Albany: State University of New York Press, 1981.

———. *The Pioneers: Or, Sources of the Susquehanna.* 1823. Reprint. Albany: State University of New York Press, 1980.

———. *The Prairie: A Tale.* 1827. Reprint. New York: Holt, Rinehart and Winston, 1950.

Country Musicians. By the editors of *Guitar Player, Keyboard,* and *Frets* magazines. New York: Grove, 1987.

Crawford, Sherry. "Country Cool." *Evansville Courier,* April 23, 1989.

Cressy, David. *Coming Over: Migration and Communication between England and New England in the Seventeenth Century.* Cambridge: Cambridge University Press, 1987.

Crèvecoeur, J. Hector St. John de. *Letters from*

an *American Farmer.* 1782. Reprint. New York: Fox, Duffield, 1904.

Crowell, Rodney. Interview with author. Nashville, Tenn., March 1993.

Dary, David. *Cowboy Culture: A Saga of Five Centuries.* Lawrence: University Press of Kansas, 1981.

Davis, H. P. *Honey in the Horn.* Excerpted in *The Frontier in American Literature*, edited by Philip Durham and Everett L. Jones, 224–30. New York: Odyssey, 1969.

Davis, John T. "No Rhinestones." *The American Way*, January 1, 1989, 61.

Delbanco, Andrew. *The Puritan Ordeal.* Cambridge, Mass.: Harvard University Press, 1989.

Dickey, James. *Deliverance.* Boston: Houghton Mifflin, 1970.

Dickinson, Emily. "I cross till I am weary." In *The American Landscape: A Critical Anthology of Prose and Poetry*, edited by John Conron, 299. New York: Oxford University Press, 1973.

Dillard, Annie. *Pilgrim at Tinker Creek.* New York: Harper and Row, 1974.

Doerschuk, Robert L. "Country Keyboards: New Sounds, New Players." *Keyboard* 18, no. 11 (November 1992): 60–81.

Douglass, Frederick. *Narrative of the Life of Frederick Douglass.* Edited by Benjamin Quarles. Cambridge, Mass.: Harvard University Press, 1960.

Doyle, Don. *New Men, New Cities, New South: Atlanta, Nashville, Charleston, Mobile, 1860–1910.* Chapel Hill: University of North Carolina Press, 1990.

Dreiser, Theodore. *Sister Carrie.* 1900. Reprint. Boston: Houghton Mifflin, 1959.

Du Bois, W. E. B. *The Souls of Black Folk.* 1903. Reprint. New York: Vintage/ Library of America, 1990.

"Duet Climbing." *Lancaster News*, July 4, 1988.

Dunbar, Seymour. *A History of Travel in America.* New York: Tudor, 1937.

Dunham, Elizabeth. "Cult Hero Strikes Back." *News-Times*, October 13, 1989.

Eichenlaub, Frank, and Patricia Eichenlaub. "Patricia's Thoughts on Women in the Country Music Business." In *All American Guide to Country Music*, 109–13. Castine, Maine: Country Roads Press, 1992.

Emerson, Ralph Waldo. *The Complete Works of Ralph Waldo Emerson.* 12 vols. Boston: Houghton Mifflin, 1912.

———. *The Conduct of Life.* Boston: Houghton Mifflin, 1904. Reprint. New York: AMS, 1968.

———. *Nature, Addresses, and Lectures.* Vol. 1 of *Collected Works of Ralph Waldo Emerson.* Cambridge, Mass.: Harvard University Press, 1971.

———. *The Portable Emerson.* Edited by Mark Van Doren. New York: Viking, 1946.

———. *Representative Men.* Boston: Houghton Mifflin, 1903.

———. *Selections from Ralph Waldo Emerson.* Edited by Stephen E. Whicher. Boston: Houghton Mifflin, 1957.

———. *Society and Solitude.* Boston: Houghton Mifflin, 1904.

"Evening with Rodney Crowell, An." Nashville: The Nashville Network, 1993. Television broadcast, aired February 22, 1993.

Farlekas, Chris. "Harris Returns to Mid-Hudson." *Middletown Times Herald Record*, July 27, 1990.

Ferris, William. *Blues from the Delta.* 1978. Reprint. New York: Da Capo, 1984.

Fife, Austin, and Alta Fife. *Heaven on Horseback: Revivalist Songs and Verse in the Cowboy*

Idiom. Logan: Utah State University Press, 1989.

Fisher, David Hackett. *Albion's Seed: Four British Folkways in America.* New York: Oxford University Press, 1989.

Flippo, Chet. Liner notes for *Rodney Crowell Collection.* 1989. Warner Bros. 9 25965–2.

———. *Your Cheatin' Heart: A Biography of Hank Williams.* 1981. Reprint. New York: St. Martin's, 1989.

Frank, Joseph. "Waylon Jennings." In *Country Musicians,* by the editors of *Guitar Player, Keyboard,* and *Frets* magazines, 52–55. New York: Grove, 1987.

Franklin, Benjamin. *Autobiography, Representative Selections.* Edited by Chester E. Jorganson and Frank Luther Mott. New York: Hill and Wang, 1962.

Frost, Robert. *The Poems of Robert Frost.* New York: Modern Library, 1946.

Fuller, Margaret. *Summer on the Lakes, in 1843.* 1844. Reprint. Urbana: University of Illinois Press, 1991.

Fussell, Edwin. *Frontier: American Literature and the American West.* Princeton, N.J.: Princeton University Press, 1965.

Garland, Hamlin. *Main-Travelled Roads.* 1891. Reprint. New York: New American Library, 1962.

Gillespie, Angus Kress, and Michael Aaron Rockland. *Looking for America on the New Jersey Turnpike.* New Brunswick, N.J.: Rutgers University Press, 1989.

Goldberg, Natalie. *Long Quiet Highway: Waking Up in America.* New York: Bantam, 1993.

Green, Douglas P. "The Singing Cowboy: An American Dream." *Journal of Country Music* 7, no. 2 (May 1978): 4–61.

Grey, Zane. *Riders of the Purple Sage.* 1912. Reprint. New York: Bantam, 1990.

Hauslohner, Amy Worthington. "Emmylou Harris: Goin' Back to Bluegrass School." *Bluegrass Unlimited,* September 1992, 18–21.

Hawthorne, Nathaniel. *The Scarlet Letter.* 1851. Reprint. New York: Penguin, 1983.

Hemingway, Ernest. *In Our Time.* 1925. Reprint. New York: Scribners, 1970.

Herbert, Susan. "Laurie Lewis—with Fiddle and Song." *San Francisco Independent,* July 17, 1990.

Hilts, Philip J. "Minister's Ties to Church Are Sundered by Aids." *New York Times,* September 8, 1992, National edition, sec. A.

Hirshberg, Charles. "The Ballad of A. P. Carter." *Life,* December 1991, 103–10.

Holland, Bernard. "Barenboim's Evening with Schubert." *New York Times,* January 6, 1993, National edition, sec. B.

Hooper, Lucy, ed. *The Lady's Book of Flowers and Poetry.* New York: J. C. Riker, 1852.

Horstman, Dorothy. *Sing Your Heart Out, Country Boy: Classic Country Songs and Their Inside Stories, by the Writers Who Wrote Them.* Rev. ed. Nashville, Tenn.: The Country Music Foundation, 1986.

Hurst, Jack. *Nashville's Grand Ole Opry.* New York: Abrams, 1975.

"In the Hank Williams Tradition." Written by Bill Ivey. Nashville, Tenn.: The Country Music Foundation, 1989. Video production.

Irving, Washington. *A Tour on the Prairies.* 1835. Reprint. Norman: University of Oklahoma Press, 1956.

James, Henry. *The American Scene.* 1904. Reprint. Bloomington: Indiana University Press, 1968.

Jefferson, Thomas. *Notes on the State of Vir-*

ginia. In Jefferson, *Writings*, 123–326. New York: Library of America, 1984.

Jeffrey, Julie Ray. *Frontier Women: The Trans-Mississippi West*. New York: Hill and Wang, 1979.

Jehlen, Myra. *American Incarnation: The Individual, the Nation, and the Continent*. Cambridge, Mass.: Harvard University Press, 1986.

Johnson, Edward. *The Wonder-Working Providence of Sions Saviour in New England*. 1655. Reprint. New York: Barnes and Noble, 1910.

Johnson, Hall, ed. and arr. *Thirty Spirituals*. New York: G. Schirmer, 1949.

Johnson, James Weldon, ed. *The Book of American Negro Spirituals*. Musical arrangements by J. Rosamond Johnson. New York: Viking, 1931.

Kakutani, Michiko. "Winning the West, and Then Reinventing It." *New York Times*, December 19, 1992, National edition, sec. B.

Kennedy, Joe. "Rodney Crowell." *Roanoke Times and World News*, February 12, 1989.

Kerouac, Jack. *On the Road*. 1955. Reprint. New York: Penguin, 1991.

Kincaid, Jamaica. *A Small Place*. New York: Plume, 1978.

Kuralt, Charles. *A Life on the Road*. 1990. Reprint. New York: Ivy, 1991.

Lamar, Howard R. "An Overview of Westward Expansion." In *The West as America: Reinterpreting Images of the Frontier*, edited by William H. Truettner, 1–26. Washington, D.C.: Smithsonian Institution Press, 1991.

L'Amour, Louis. *Flint*. New York: Bantam, 1960.

———. *High Lonesome*. New York: Bantam, 1962.

———. *The Lonely Men*. New York: Bantam, 1969.

Levine, Lawrence W. *Highbrow/Lowbrow: The Emergence of Cultural Hierarchy in America*. Cambridge, Mass.: Harvard University Press, 1988.

Limerick, Patricia Nelson. *The Legacy of Conquest: The Unbroken Past of the American West*. New York: Norton, 1987.

Lindsay, Vachel. *The Prose of Vachel Lindsay, Complete and with Lindsay's Drawings*. Edited by Dennis Camp. Peoria, Ill.: Spoon River Poetry Press, 1989.

Logan, William A., ed. *Road to Heaven: Twenty-Eight Negro Spirituals*. Collected by William A Logan; edited by Allen M. Garrett. University: University of Alabama Press, 1955.

Lomax, Alan. "Bluegrass Background: Folk Music in Overdrive." *Esquire*, October 1959, 108–9.

———. *The Folk Songs of North America*. Garden City, N.Y.: Doubleday, 1960.

London, Jack. "All Gold Canyon." Excerpted in *The Frontier in American Literature*, edited by Philip Durham and Everett L. Jones, 192–208. New York: Odyssey, 1969.

McQuade, Donald, Robert Atwan, Martha Banta, Justin Kaplan, David Minter, Cecelia Tichi, and Helen Vendler, eds. *The Harper American Literature*. 2 vols. New York: Harper and Row, 1986.

Malone, Bill C. *Country Music U.S.A.* Rev. ed. Austin: University of Texas Press, 1985.

———. *Southern Music/American Music*. Lexington: University Press of Kentucky, 1979.

Malone, Bill C., and Judith McCulloh. *Stars of Country Music: Uncle Dave Macon to Johnny Rodriquez*. 1975. Reprint. New York: Da Capo, 1991.

Marcus, Greil. *Mystery Train: Images of America in Rock 'n' Roll Music.* 3d rev. ed. New York: Plume, 1990.

Marymount, Mark. "Crowell Glad to Be Country." *Little Rock Gazette*, September 12, 1988.

Mason, Rick. "Why Rodney Shuns the Cash Flow." *St. Paul Evening Pioneer Press Dispatch*, November 10, 1988.

Mather, Cotton. *Theopolis Americana.* Boston: n.p., 1710.

Matthiessen, F. O. *American Renaissance: Art and Expression in the Age of Emerson and Whitman.* New York: Oxford University Press, 1941.

May, Rollo. *The Cry for Myth.* 1991. Reprint. New York: Delta, 1992.

Media Information. Burbank, Calif.: Reprise Records, 1990.

Melville, Herman. *Moby-Dick.* 1851. Reprint. New York: Penguin, 1986.

Patsy Montana. Interview with author. International Country Music Conference, Meridian, Miss., May 1993.

Morthland, John. *The Best of Country Music.* Garden City, N.Y.: Doubleday, 1984.

———. "Jimmie Dale Gilmore: And the Beat Goes On." *Country Music*, November/December 1992, 54, 56, 58.

Muir, John. *Our National Parks.* 1901. Reprint. Madison: University of Wisconsin Press, 1981.

Nager, Larry. "Rodney Crowell." *Poughkeepsie Journal*, March 24, 1989.

Nash, Alanna. *Behind Closed Doors: Talking with the Legends of Country Music.* New York: Knopf, 1988.

———. *Dolly.* Los Angeles, Calif.: Reed, 1978.

Norris, Frank. *The Octopus.* 1901. Reprint. New York: New American Library, 1964.

Norris, Kathleen. *Dakota: A Spiritual Geography.* New York: Tichnor and Fields, 1993.

O'Connor, Flannery. *The Collected Stories.* New York: Farrar, Straus and Giroux, 1992.

Painton, Priscilla. "Country Rocks the Boomers." *Time*, March 30, 1992, 62–66.

Pareles, Jon. "It's Noisy! It's New! It's 90's!" *New York Times*, January 3, 1993, sec. 2.

———. "Travis Tritt, Emissary from Another Country." *New York Times*, May 24, 1993, sec. B.

Peck, M. Scott. *The Road Less Traveled: A New Psychology of Love, Traditional Values, and Spiritual Growth.* New York: Simon and Schuster, 1978.

Perry, Claudia. "All Roads Lead Back to Nashville." *Houston Post*, February 17, 1989.

Petty, Milt. "Crowell Spearheads Country's New Wave." *Van Nuys Valley News*, June 8, 1980.

Porterfield, Nolan. "Hey, Hey, Tell 'Em 'Bout Us: Jimmie Rodgers Visits the Carter Family." In *Pickers, Slickers, Cheatin' Hearts, and Superstars: Country Music and the Musicians*, edited by Paul Kingsbury and Alan Axelrod. New York: The Country Music Foundation and Abbeville Press, 1988.

———. *Jimmie Rodgers: The Life and Times of America's Blue Yodeler.* 1979. Reprint. Urbana: University of Illinois Press, 1992.

Pound, Ezra. *Selected Prose, 1909–1965.* New York: New Directions, 1973.

Price, Robert. *Johnny Appleseed: Man and Myth.* Bloomington: Indiana University Press, 1954.

Riley, Glenda. *The Female Frontier: A Comparative View of Women on the Prairie and the*

Plains. Lawrence: University Press of Kansas, 1988.

Robinson, Edwin Arlington. *Collected Poems.* New York: Macmillan, 1937.

Robinson, Paul. *Opera and Ideas: From Mozart to Strauss.* 1985. Reprint. Ithaca, N.Y.: Cornell University Press, 1986.

Rockwell, John. "European Tour Buoys New York Orchestra." *New York Times,* April 5, 1993, National edition, sec. B.

"Rodney Crowell Gets to the Heart of Country." *Boston Globe,* March 29, 1989, sec. C.

"Rodney Crowell Hams It Up for the Reporter's Camera." *Ogden Reporter,* August 2, 1989.

Rodgers, Jimmie N. *The Country Music Message: All about Lovin' and Livin'.* Englewood Cliffs, N.J.: Prentice-Hall, 1983.

———. *The Country Music Message, Revisited.* Fayetteville: University of Arkansas Press, 1989.

Rothstein, Mervyn. "Freshman Orientation at Columbia Is More than Just Picnics." *New York Times,* September 8, 1992, National edition, sec. A.

Rybczynski, Witold. *Home: A Short History of an Idea.* New York: Viking Penguin, 1986.

Sadler, Lynn Veach. *John Bunyan.* Boston: G. K. Hall, 1979.

Sandmel, Ben. Liner notes for Jimmie Dale Gilmore, *After Awhile.* Electra 9 61148–4.

———. "Rodney Crowell Finds the Right 'Keys.'" *Chicago Sun-Times,* November 12, 1989.

Schaefer, Jack. *Shane.* 1949. Reprint. New York: Bantam, 1960.

Schlissel, Lillian. "The Frontier Family: Dislocation and the American Experience." In *Making America: The Society and Culture of the United States,* edited by Luther S.

Luedtke, 83–94. Chapel Hill: University of North Carolina Press, 1992.

Scoby, Lola. Liner notes for Townes Van Zandt, *Delta Momma Blues.* 1989. Tomato Records 2696292.

Scott, Michael. *The Great Caruso.* Boston: Northeastern University Press, 1989.

Seward, Barbara. *The Symbolic Rose.* New York: Columbia University Press, 1960.

Shepherd, Roy E. *History of the Rose.* New York: Macmillan, 1954.

Silber, Irwin, ed. *Songs of the Civil War.* New York: Columbia University Press, 1960.

Sinclair, Upton. *The Jungle.* 1906. Reprint. New York: New American Library, 1980.

Slater, Philip. *The Pursuit of Loneliness: American Culture at the Breaking Point.* Rev. ed. Boston: Beacon Press, 1976.

Smith, David E. *John Bunyan in America.* Bloomington: Indiana University Press, 1966.

Smith, Lee. *The Devil's Dream.* New York: Putnam, 1992.

Stambler, Irwin, and Grelun Landon. *The Encyclopedia of Folk, Country, and Western Music.* 2d ed. New York: St. Martin's, 1984.

Starr, G[eorge] A. *Defoe and Spiritual Autobiography.* Princeton, N.J.: Princeton University Press, 1965.

Stein, Gertrude. *The Yale Gertrude Stein: Selections.* Edited by Richard Kostelanetz. New Haven, Conn.: Yale University Press, 1980.

Steinbeck, John. *The Grapes of Wrath.* 1939. Reprint. New York: Penguin, 1976.

———. *Travels with Charley: In Search of America.* 1962. Reprint. New York: Penguin, 1980.

Stevens, Wallace. *Collected Poems.* New York: Knopf, 1991.

Stilgoe, John. *Common Landscape of America, 1580 to 1845.* New Haven, Conn.: Yale University Press, 1982.

Stowe, Harriet Beecher. *Uncle Tom's Cabin: Or, Life among the Lowly.* 1852. Reprint. New York: Penguin, 1981.

Sullivan, Elizabeth. "Emmylou Harris Gets Back to Basics." *Cleveland Plain Dealer*, July 27, 1990.

Sundquist, Eric J. *To Wake the Nations: Race in the Making of American Literature.* Cambridge, Mass.: Harvard University Press, 1993.

Tashian, Holly. Interview with author. Nashville, Tenn., May 1992.

Thoreau, Henry David. *Cape Cod.* Edited by Joseph J. Moldenhauer. Princeton, N.J.: Princeton University Press, 1988.

———. "Homer, Ossian, Chaucer." *Dial* 4 (April 1844): 290–305.

———. "Walking." In *Excursions and Poems*, 205–48. Vol. 5 of *The Writings of Henry David Thoreau.* 1906. Reprint. New York: AMS, 1968.

Tichi, Cecelia. *New World, New Earth: Environmental Reform in American Literature from the Puritans through Whitman.* New Haven, Conn.: Yale University Press, 1979.

———. "Spiritual Biography and the 'Lords Remembrancers.'" *William and Mary Quarterly*, 3d ser., vol. 28, no. 1 (January 1971): 64–85.

Tocqueville, Alexis de. *Democracy in America.* 2 vols. 1840. Reprint. New York: Vintage, 1990.

Tompkins, Jane. *West of Everything: The Inner Life of Westerns.* New York: Oxford University Press, 1992.

Trachtenberg, Alan. *The Incorporation of America: Culture and Society in the Gilded Age.* New York: Hill and Wang, 1982.

Trujillo, Ron. "Crowell's Country Clan." *Visalia Times-Delta*, October 6, 1990.

Tucker, Ken. "But What Will the Neighbors Think?" *Rolling Stone*, June 12, 1980.

———. "9 to 5: How Willie Nelson and Dolly Parton Qualified for 'Lifestyles of the Rich and Famous.'" In *Pickers, Slickers, Cheatin' Hearts, and Superstars: Country, the Music and the Musicians*, 375–405. New York: The Country Music Foundation and Abbeville Press, 1988.

Twain, Mark. *The Adventures of Huckleberry Finn.* Edited by Sculley Bradley, Richard Croom Beatty, and E. Hudson Long. New York: Norton, 1961.

———. *Life on the Mississippi.* 1883. Reprint. New York: Penguin, 1984.

Von Flotow, Friedrich. *Martha: Grand Opera in Five Acts.* New York: F. Rullman, n.d.

Wharton, Edith. *The Custom of the Country.* New York: Scribners, 1913.

———. *Summer.* 1917. Reprint. New York: Harper and Row, 1980.

Wheeler, Candace. *Content in a Garden.* Boston: Houghton Mifflin, 1902.

White, Morton, and Lucia White. *The Intellectual versus the City.* Cambridge, Mass.: Harvard University Press and M.I.T. Press, 1962.

Whitman, Walt. *Leaves of Grass.* Edited by Sculley Bradley and Harold W. Blodgett. New York: Norton, 1973.

Wilder, Laura Ingalls. *By the Shores of Silver Lake.* 1939. Reprint. New York: Harper and Row, 1971.

———. *Farmer Boy.* 1933. Reprint. New York: Harper and Row, 1971.

———. *Little House in the Big Woods.* 1932. Reprint. New York: Harper and Row, 1971.

———. *Little House on the Prairie.* 1935. Reprint. New York: Harper and Row, 1971.

———. *The Long Winter.* 1940. Reprint. New York: Harper and Row, 1971.

Williams, Chas. "The Nashville Numbering System." In *The Songwriter's and Musician's Guide to Nashville,* edited by Sherry Bond. Cincinnati, Ohio: Writer's Digest Books, 1991.

Williams, Hank. *Hank Williams: The Complete Lyrics.* Edited by Don Cusic. New York: St. Martin's, 1993.

Williams, Roger M. "Hank Williams." In *Stars of Country Music: Uncle Dave Macon to Johnny Rodriquez,* edited by Bill C. Malone and Judith McCulloh, 237–54. 1975. Reprint: New York: Da Capo, 1991.

———. *Sing a Sad Song: The Life of Hank Williams.* 2d ed. Urbana: University of Illinois Press, 1981.

Williams, William Carlos. *In the American Grain: Essays by William Carlos Williams.* 1933. Reprint. New York: New Directions, 1956.

———. *Selected Poems.* New York: New Directions, 1963.

Willingham, Calder. *Rambling Rose.* 1972. Reprint. New York: Avon, 1991.

Winthrop, John. "A Model of Christian Charity." In *The Winthrop Papers,* 2:282–95. Boston: Massachusetts Historical Society, 1931.

Wister, Owen. *The Virginian.* 1902. Reprint. Edited by Philip Durham. Boston: Houghton Mifflin, 1968.

Wolfe, Charles K. Liner notes for *The Bristol Sessions,* vol. 2. 1987. Country Music Foundation CMF-011-C.

———. *Tennessee Strings: The Story of Country Music in Tennessee.* Knoxville: University of Tennessee Press for the Tennessee Historical Commission, 1977.

Wolfe, Thomas. *You Can't Go Home Again.* New York: Scribners, 1940.

Yezierska, Anzia. *Children of Loneliness.* New York: n.p., 1923.

Zito, Tom. "Rodney Crowell: The Music and the Method." *Washington Post,* May 21, 1980, sec. B.

Music Permissions

▼ ▼

"High Noon," written by Ned Washington/ Dimitri Tiomkin. Copyright © 1952 Leo Peist, Inc. Copyright renewed 1980 by Volta Music Corp./Catherine Hinen/Mrs. Ned Washington. All rights reserved. Used by permission.

"Highway 86," written by Barry Tashian/ Holly Tashian. Copyright © 1993 Foreshadow Songs, Inc. (BMI)/Forerunner Music, Inc. (ASCAP). All rights reserved. Used by permission.

"Home," written by Andy Spooner/Fred Lehner. Copyright © 1990 Texas Wedge Music. All rights reserved. Used by permission.

"Home," written by Holly Tashian. Copyright © 1987 Forerunner Music, Inc. (ASCAP). All rights reserved. Used by permission.

"Home Again," written by Robert Hale. Copyright © Happy Valley Music. All rights reserved. Used by permission.

"Hometown Streets," written by Nanci Griffith/James Hooker. Copyright © 1991 Irving Music, Inc./Ponder Heart Music (BMI); copyright © 1992 James Hooker/ Rick Hall Music, Inc. (ASCAP). International copyright secured. All rights reserved. Used by permission.

"Horse Called Music, A," written by Wayne Carson. Copyright © Wayne Carson. All rights reserved. Used by permission.

"I'm So Lonesome I Could Cry," written by Hank Williams, Sr.. Copyright © 1949 Hiriam Music/Acuff-Rose Music, Inc. Copyright renewed 1976 Acuff-Rose Music, Inc., 65 Music Square West, Nashville, Tenn. 37203/Warner-Chappell Music on behalf of

Hiriam Music. All rights on behalf of Hiriam Music administered by Rightsong Music, Inc. International rights secured. All rights reserved. Used by permission.

"I Want to Be a Cowboy's Sweetheart," written by Patsy Montana. Copyright © 1935 Leeds Music Corp. Copyright renewed. All rights controlled and administered by MCA Music Publishing, a division of MCA, Inc., New York, N.Y. 10019. All rights reserved. Used by permission.

"Leavin' Louisiana in the Broad Daylight," written by Donivan Cowart/Rodney Crowell. Copyright © 1978 Visa Music/Drunk Monkey Music (ASCAP). Rights administered on behalf of Visa Music by Copyright Managment, Inc.; rights administered on behalf of Drunk Monkey Music by Bug Music/Jolly Cheeks Music. All rights reserved. Used by permission.

"Let Freedom Ring," written by Rodney Crowell/Keith Sykes. Copyright © 1985 Coolwell Music/Granite Music Corp./Keith Sykes Music. All rights reserved. Used by permission.

"Let Me See the Light," written by Barry Tashian/Holly Tashian. Copyright © 1993 Foreshadow Songs, Inc. (BMI)/Forerunner Music, Inc. (ASCAP). All rights reserved. Used by permission.

"Mama's Opry," written by Iris DeMent. Copyright © 1992 Songs of Iris/Forerunner Music, Inc. (ASCAP). All rights reserved. Used by permission.

"Mammas Don't Let Your Babies Grow Up to Be Cowboys," written by Ed Bruce/Patsy Bruce. Copyright © 1975 Tree Publishing Co., Inc. All rights administered by Sony

Music Publishing, 8 Music Square West, Nashville, Tenn. 37203. Used by permission.

"Many a Long and Lonesome Highway," written by Rodney Crowell/Will Jennings. Copyright © 1990, 1993 Sony Tunes, Inc./ Coolwell Music/Willin' David/Blue Sky Rider Songs/Granite Music Corp. All rights on behalf of Sony Tunes and Coolwell Music administered by Sony Music Publishing, 8 Music Square West, Nashville, Tenn. 37203. All rights on behalf of Blue Sky Rider Songs administered by Rondor Music (London) Ltd.; Irving Music, Inc. (BMI) administers in the U.S. and Canada. International copyright secured. Used by permission.

"Maple's Lament, The," written by Laurie Lewis. Copyright © 1986 Spruce and Maple Music, Berkeley, Calif. All rights reserved. Used by permission.

"Maybe It Was Memphis," written by Michael Anderson. Copyright © 1984 Atlantic Music Corp./First Release Music/ Cadillac Pink Music; administered by Atlantic Music Corp. International copyright secured. All rights reserved. Used by permission.

"Mississippi Delta Land," written by Harlan Howard. Copyright © 1970 Tree Publishing Co., Inc. All rights administered by Sony Music Publishing, 8 Music Square West, Nashville, Tenn. 37203. Used by permission.

"Miss the Mississippi and You," written by Bill Halley. Copyright © 1932 Southern Music Publishing Co., Inc. Copyright renewed. International copyright secured. All rights reserved. Used by permission.

"My Tennessee Mountain Home," written by Dolly Parton. Copyright © Velvet Apple

Music, Nashville, Tenn. All rights reserved. Used by permission.

"No Place Like Home," written by Paul Overstreet. Copyright © Cherry Lane Music. All rights reserved. Used by permission.

"Ramblin' Fever," written by Merle Haggard. Copyright © 1977 Shade Tree Music, Inc. Administered by Music of the World. International copyright secured. All rights reserved. Used by permission.

"Ramblin' Man," written by Hank Williams, Sr. Copyright © 1949, 1951 Hiriam Music/ Acuff-Rose Music, Inc. Copyright renewed 1979 by Acuff-Rose Music, Inc., 65 Music Square West, Nashville, Tenn. 37203/ Warner-Chappell Music on behalf of Hiriam Music. International rights secured. All rights reserved. Used by permission.

"Red Red Rose," written by David B. Mallett. Copyright © 1990 TEMI Combine, Inc. All rights controlled by Music City Music, Inc., and administered by EMI April Music, Inc. International copyright secured. All rights reserved. Used by permission.

"River for Him, A," written by Emmylou Harris. Copyright © 1989 Sorghum Music; administered by Copyright Management, Inc. All rights reserved. Used by permission.

"Road Home, The," written by Jim McBride and Stewart Harris. Copyright © 1990 EMI April Music, Inc./EMI Blackwood Music, Inc. International copyright secured. All rights reserved. Used by permission.

"Rollin' and Ramblin' (The Death of Hank Williams)," written by Robin Williams/ Linda Williams/Jerome Clark. Copyright © 1986, 1989 Songs of PolyGram Interna-

Index

▼ ▼

Page numbers in italics refer to illustrations.